The rough PARIS

=The=
rough
guides

Other available rough guides
**FRANCE, SPAIN, PORTUGAL, GREECE, YUGOSLAVIA
AMSTERDAM & HOLLAND, NEW YORK, MOROCCO,
TUNISIA, MEXICO, PERU, KENYA** and **CHINA**

Forthcoming
**BRITTANY & NORMANDY, CRETE,
SCANDINAVIA, EASTERN EUROPE**

Series Editor
MARK ELLINGHAM

Thanks for help, information and encouragement to Peter Polish, Jo, Ali Ertan, Rosi Braidotti, Oristelle Bonis, S.D.Saint-Leger, Fergus Fergusson, Christiane Rousseau, Stéphane Rousseau, Jean Llasera, Nicos Papadimitriou, Bianca Glavanis, David Kelly and Florica Kyriacopoulos.

First published in 1987 by
Routledge & Kegan Paul Ltd
11 New Fetter Lane, London EC4P 4EE

Published in the USA by
Routledge & Kegan Paul Inc.
in association with Methuen Inc.
29 West 35th Street, New York, NY 10001

Phototypeset in Linotron Helvetica and Sabon
by Input Typesetting Ltd, London SW19 8DR
and printed in Great Britain
by Cox & Wyman Ltd, Reading

Library of Congress Cataloging in Publication Data

Baillie, Kate.
  The rough guide to Paris.

  (The Rough guides)
  Includes index.
  1. Paris (France)—Description—1975— ——
Guide–books. I. Salmon, Tim. II. Title. .III. Series.
DC708.B26 1987 914.4'3604837 86–26181

British Library CIP Data also available
ISBN 0–7102–0712–3

The rough guide to

PARIS

Written and researched by
KATE BAILLIE AND TIM SALMON

Routledge & Kegan Paul London and New York

CONTENTS

Part three CONTEXTS

PARIS

River Seine

LA DEFENSE

Ile de la Jatte

NEUILLY

RUE VICTOR HUGO

BOULEVARD PERIF

BOULEVARD J.JAURES

AVENUE DE CLICHY

AVENUE DE ST.OUEN

BOULEVARD BINEAU

PONT DE NEUILLY

AVENUE CHARLES DE GAULLE

AV. DE VILLIERS

AVENUE DE WAGRAM

BD. DE COURCELLES

BD. DES BATIGNOLLES

BOULEVARD MALESHERBES

Ile de Puteaux

BOULEVARD DE L'EST. CHARCOT

AV. DE LA GRANDE-ARMEE

Parc Monceau

BOUL

ALLEE DE LONGCHAMPS

BOULEVARD PERIPHERIQUE

Arc de Triomphe

PLACE CHARLES DE GAULLE

AVENUE DES CHAMPS ELYSEES

AVENUE FOCH

La Madeleine

BOULEVARD LANNES

AVENUE VICTOR HUGO

AVENUE ALBERT

AVENUE KLEBER

Grand Palais

Petit Palais

PL. DE LA CONCORDE

Bois de Boulogne

AVENUE VICTOR HUGO

ALBERT 1ER CRS. LA REINE

ROUTE DE L'HIPPODROME

AVENUE P. DOUMER

Palais de Chaillot

Tour Eiffel

AVENUE BOSQUET

Hôtel des Invalides

ALLEE DE LA REINE MARGUERITE

AVENUE DE ST.CLOUD

BOULEVARD SUCHET

AVENUE MOZART

AVENUE DE NEW YORK

AVENUE DE LOWENDAL

AVENUE EMILE ZOLA

AVE. DE VERSAILLES

River Seine

RUE DE LA CONVENTION

MONTPARNASSE

Tour Montparnasse

RUE DE

BOULEVARD

BOULEVARD MURAT

Gare Montparnasse

DE LA REINE

PTE. DE ST-CLOUD

Montparnasse Cemetery

RUE DE VAUGIRARD

AVENUE DU MAINE

RUE D'ALESIA

BOULEVARD VICTOR

Palais des Sports

AVENUE E. VAILLANT

AVENUE P. GRENIER

BOULOGNE-BILLANCOURT

BOULEVARD PERIPHERIQUE

BOULEVARD LEFEBVRE

BOULEVARD BRUNE

ISSY-LES-MOULINEAUX

AVENUE DE VERDUN

AVE. P. BROSSOLETTE

Part one
BASICS

ARRONDISSEMENTS

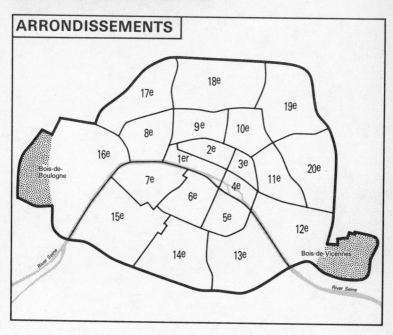

PARIS: WHY TO GO AND WHEN

Pre-eminent as the centre of French cultural, political, intellectual and commercial life, **Paris** is a self-conscious and assertive city. You see it in the grandiose architecture of both past and present – in the Beaubourg Centre or La Villette, as much as in the Eiffel Tower, Napoleon's Arc de Triomphe, or Notre Dame. And you sense it, above all, in the people. Often arrogant and impatient with outsiders, but entertaining too, the Parisians with their attachment to style and the figure they cut in the street, reflect the pride of the city where so much of life is carried on in public. The animation and variety of **streetlife** makes just strolling along, browsing visually at the café-patisserie level of existence, one of the greatest Paris pleasures.

For big city dwellers, the **compactness** of Paris is a novelty. Strictly confined within the 78 square km limits of the Boulevard Périphérique, the character and contrasts of the different **quartiers** are sharper and more intensely experienced than in the giant sprawls of a London or Chicago. You can move easily, even on foot, from the calm, village-like atmosphere of Montmartre and parts of the Latin Quarter to the busy commercial centre of the Bourse and Opéra or to the aristocratic mansions of the Marais; cars can cross the city in minutes along the right bank expressway, while below, on the *quais*, the classic panoramas of the Louvre and Cité fall within a single glance; at Les Halles shopping is in an ultra-modern mall, in Belleville in markets that resemble a North African souk.

Ethnic diversity is an important, if contentious, element in the weft of the city's life. Long a haven and magnet for foreign refugees and artists, Paris in this century has sheltered Lenin and Ho Chi Minh, White Russians and Iranians (the Ayatollah as well as the Shah's son), dissidents from Eastern Europe, disillusioned writers from America, and a host of assorted expatriates. The newest settlers are immigrants from the ex-French colonies of South-East Asia, West and North Africa. Well entrenched, if not assimilated, they have their own *quartier*s, shops, cafés and culture.

In terms of concrete and immediate **pleasures**, few cities can compete with the thousand and one **cafés, bars and restaurants** – modern and trendy, local and traditional, and for every pocket – that line each Paris street and boulevard. Most are French but choice is enlarged by the tempting range of ethnic and foreign cuisines.

Where **entertainment** is concerned, the city's strongpoints are movies and music. Paris is a real **cinema** capital, and the **music**, whilst French rock is notoriously dire, encompasses excellent jazz, avant-garde experiment, and, again, an important foreign component. If you want to hear good salsa or some of the West African rock more or less absent elsewhere in Europe, Parisian clubs are exciting ground to discover.

Of more formal cultural pursuits, Paris is a city of great art but few exceptional buildings. The general backdrop of the streets is part of the city's glamour, the style predominantly neo-classical thanks to 19C restructuring. Responses to individual structures are only really demanded by the more recent architectural experiments – like Beaubourg or the new arts and science complex at La Villette. The **museums and galleries**, however, are probably the finest in Western Europe, and, with the tradition of state cultural endowment very much alive, certainly the best displayed. The superb Impressionist collection of the Jeu de Paume is now brilliantly installed in the old Gare d'Orsay railway station; the Picasso museum opened in 1985 to reveal the largest collection of the artist's works under one roof; Beaubourg fills in much of the rest of the 20C, including the most contemporary; and there is of course the Louvre, currently undergoing dramatic modernisation.

When to visit is largely a question of personal taste and time. The city has a more reliable **climate** than London, with uninterrupted stretches of sun (and rain) all year round. It maintains a vaguely southern feel for anyone crossing the Channel, but Mediterranean it is not. Winter temperatures drop below freezing and the winds can be biting. If you're lucky, spring and autumn will be mild and sunny – in summer it can reach the high 20sC (80sF).

What is perhaps more important is

when not to go. If you visit during the French summer holidays, from 15 July to the end of August, you will find large numbers of Parisians have fled the city, a lot of shops and restaurants will be closed, and the people that remain can be more ill-humoured than usual. There is too the commercial calendar to consider – fashion shows, trade fairs, etc. Paris hoteliers warn against September and October, and finding a room even at the best of times can be problematic. Given the choice, early spring, autumn if you book ahead, or even the midwinter months, are most rewarding.

Average daily temperatures		
	°C	°F
January	7.5	45.5
February	7.1	44.8
March	10.2	50.4
April	15.7	60.3
May	16.6	61.9
June	23.4	74.1
July	25.1	77.2
August	25.6	78.1
September	20.9	69.6
October	16.5	61.7
November	11.7	53.1
December	7.8	46.0

GETTING THERE

● FROM BRITAIN
Flights

Deals on flights to Paris change all the time. To find the best you should always shop around – ideally a month or so before you plan to leave. Good sources for checking the options are the classified travel sections in the Sunday newspapers (*The Observer*, especially) and, if you live in London, *Time Out* and the giveaway magazine *LAM*.

That said, a number of bargain flight options do seem more or less permanent – and are detailed below.

GENERAL DEALS FROM LONDON

The choice is between a charter (Orion, Air UK and British Island Airways are among regular operators), an APEX fare scheduled ticket (on British Airways or Air France) or, often cheapest, a flight with an airline that makes Paris a short-haul stop en route to more distant destinations (as Malaysian Air, Pakistan Air lines or Kuwait Air).

Charters are officially sold in conjunction with accommodation (see *Packages*, p.7) and if you're after just a flight it's generally a matter of luck, filling whatever seats remain – often at the last minute. The British Island Airways flights, however, are sold as regular flight-only deals by *Nouvelles Frontières* (see address below). Departures are from London-Gatwick to Paris-Orly, Fridays and Sundays only; current prices from £49 rtn.

British Airways and Air France return **APEX tickets** must be booked two

weeks in advance and your stay (maximum one month) must include one Saturday night. Your return date must be fixed at the time of booking and you cannot subsequently make any changes. Current price, £65 rtn.

Bargains with **long-haul airlines** are harder to predict. Like charters, availability can be chancy but a good travel agent (STA – see below – are specialists) should usually find you something. One of the best deals currently available is on Malaysian Air: £45 single, £65 rtn. The drawback – on this and similar flights – is only one flight a week and that on variable days, though there's no maximum stay and you've a chance of making changes if needs be.

Recommended **agents** for any of the above include:
STA Travel, 74 Old Brompton Rd, SW7 (01–581 1022).
Worldwide, 39 Store St, WC1 (01–580 7733).
Nouvelles Frontières, 1–2 Hanover St, W1 (01–629 7772).
Air Travel Advisory Bureau (01–636 5000); see below.

GENERAL DEALS OUTSIDE LONDON

As often as not, whether you live in Birmingham or Newcastle, Manchester or Aberdeen, you will find it pays to go first **to London** and then fly on to Paris from there. Scheduled **direct flights** from British regional airports are very expensive. **Charters** do exist, though availability is a big problem and prices often unfavourable in relation to London flights – even with added rail/coach travel. What *is* worth considering, however, is a **package deal** (see p.7) which often offers exceptional bargain rates on the part of your journey to the airport.

If you want to go it your own way, perhaps the best initial phone call is to the *Air Travel Advisory Bureau*. ATAB are not themselves an agent but act as a telephone information service for numerous budget travel agents and operators, supplying details of current best buys. Their two offices – in Manchester and London – can give out information on flights from any British (or Irish) destination. Addresses/Numbers are:
MANCHESTER: 59 Royal Exchange (061–832 2000)
LONDON: 320 Regent St, W1 (01–636 5000)

STUDENT/YOUTH FLIGHTS

The cheaper flights are again predominantly from London. The cheapest, at the time of writing, are USIT's twice-weekly **student charter to Beauvais**. Departures are from Gatwick every Friday and Saturday at 6.30pm throughout the year, except for a period of 3 weeks prior to Christmas. Elegibility is for anyone under 26 and all students under 32. The only drawback is the arrival at Beauvais, 70km (and a 1¼hr coach ride) from Paris. The coachride is included in the ticket price but it makes the journey rather long (flight time is 50mins) and delivers you in Paris, place de Stalingrad, around 11pm – not the best time for accommodation-hunting. Return flights leave Beauvais on Friday and Saturday evenings at 9, but you have to be in time for the coach from place de Stalingrad – something a lot of people find difficult, according to the travel agents.

The USIT charter can be booked at any of their offices in Britain and Ireland, at STA offices and through most other college/university travel offices. A phonecall to STA or one of the other agents below to find out if there are any other **cheaper deals** – not necessarily specifically for students – is also advisable. **Packages**, too, can be worth considering (see p.7); many offer flights plus basic (£8–9 a person) accommodation.

Recommended **student travel firms** include:
STA Travel, 74 Old Brompton Rd, London SW7 (01–581 1022). Also at various London universities and in Bristol 25 Queens Rd, BS8; 0272–294399
USIT, 52 Grosvenor Gdns, London SW1 (01–730 8111). Also numerous other branches throughout Britain.
Worldwide/Travel Young, 38/39 Store St, London WC1 (01–580 7733/01–580 6762).
Nouvelles Frontières, 1–2 Hanover St, London W1 (01–629 7772).

Train

The choice is between train and hovercraft (London to Paris in 5½hrs) or train and ordinary ferry (around 8hrs). Fare options include special student/youth deals on Transalpino/Eurotrain and Senior Citizen reductions for the over 65s. If you plan to take in Paris as part of a longer trip round France – or Europe – you might also consider the InterRail or EurRail pass, again limited to those under 26 or over 65.

The **Hovercraft** crossing is from Dover to Boulogne. Services are very frequent (up to 27 a day in peak season) and tie in well with the trains. Regular adult fares, inclusive of rail travel from London-Victoria, are £38 single, £76 return; £48.50 return for short stays with the 5-day Excursion Fare. Tickets are available from any British Rail (or French Railways) travel centre and there are reductions for over 65s (£23/£46, with the Rail Europe Senior Card) and under 11s (£19/£38). Students and anyone under 26 can buy heavily discounted *BIGE* tickets (£27.58/£54.90) from Transalpino or Eurotrain (see addresses below) and most of the student travel agents detailed above.

By **train and ordinary ferry**, crossing at Dover/Folkestone to Calais/Boulogne (or sometimes Dieppe), the *BIGE* tickets cost £19.50/£37.90 from London, as against regular adult InterCity fares of £33.70/£67.40. British Rail also offer a 5-day Excursion on this route (£42 return; you can stay for five full days or less) and a reduction on the night train (£20/£40). The night train leaves London-Victoria at 8.40pm and arrives in Paris at 7.02am.

All standard rail tickets, including the BIGE fares, are valid for two months.

The **InterRail pass**, available from British Rail or any sizeable travel agent, is currently £120.00. For this you get a month's unlimited travel on all European railways, plus half-price discounts in Britain and on the Channel ferries. The only restriction, other than age, is that you need to have been resident in Europe for at least six months in order to be eligible. In theory this excludes most North Americans, though you'll find some travel firms don't stick too finely to the small print. The **EurRail pass**, the official American alternative, is more expensive and does not cover travel in Britain or the Channel ferries. Although it is supposed to be bought outside Europe, you can get it in France at Paris airports and at the St-Lazare railway station.

Useful **agency/travel centre addresses**, for further details, are:

Transalpino, 71–75 Buckingham Palace Rd, London SW1 or at STA Travel, 117 Euston Rd, London SW7 (01–388 2261). Also addresses all over Britain. *BIGE* tickets.
Eurotrain/London Student Travel, 52 Grosvenor Gdns, London SW1 (01–730 8111). *BIGE* tickets.
Victoria Station (European Rail Enquiries), London SW1 (01–834 2345).

Coach
Again there is the choice between coach and hovercraft (7hrs London to Paris) and coach and ordinary ferry (8hrs). Ticket prices are very much lower than by train, especially for the hovercraft.

The **Hoverspeed City Sprint service**, again crossing at Dover to Calais/Boulogne, leaves like the rest of the coaches from London's Victoria Coach Station. Regular adult fares are £21 single, £37 return; for under 18s, or under 26s in full-time education, £20 and £36; for under 14s, £16.50 and £32; children under 4, free. Tickets can be booked through any local agent, or for details call Hoverspeed direct on 01–554 7061.

Of the **coach and regular ferry** options, you've a choice between **Supabus** (bookable through any National Express agent, details 01–709 6481) or **Euroways** (Grosvenor Gdns, London SW1, 01–730 8235). Prices and services – at least daily (often with a day/night choice) – are pretty standard

between the two, indeed sometimes they seem to share the same coach. Regular adult fare – London-Paris – is currently £19 single, £35 return. Student/youth rates, £14.25, £26.50.

By car/hitching: the ferries
The best cross-channel options for most drivers and hitchers will be the **standard ferry/hovercraft links** between Dover and Calais or Boulogne, Folkestone and Boulogne, or Ramsgate to Dunkerque. Driving time to Paris from any of these ports is around 3 hrs by the Autoroute A1 or 4hrs on the toll-free N1.

DOVER-CALAIS/BOULOGNE. 35mins/40mins on *Hoverspeed* who do 5-day minibreaks from £61, student rates from £34 one way (both prices for car plus driver). Otherwise, *Sealink* or *Townsend Thoresen* ferries run to Calais in 1hr15, Boulogne in 1hr40.
FOLKESTONE-BOULOGNE. 1hr50 on *Sealink*.
RAMSGATE-DUNKERQUE. 2hrs30 on *Sally Line*.

Longer crossings, which may save time or money, depending on where you live, include:

NEWHAVEN-DIEPPE. 4hrs15 on *Sealink*.
WEYMOUTH-CHERBOURG. 3hrs55 on *Sealink*.
PORTSMOUTH-CAEN. 5hrs45 on *Brittany Ferries*.
PORTSMOUTH-LE HAVRE. 5hrs30 on *Townsend Thoresen*.
POOLE-CHERBOURG. 4hrs on *Brittany Ferries*.
PLYMOUTH-ROSCOFF. 6hrs on *Brittany Ferries*.
FELIXSTOWE-ZEEBRUGGE. 2hrs55 on *Townsend Thoresen*.

And if you plan to **take time** approaching Paris:

PORTSMOUTH-ST MALO. 9hrs on *Brittany Ferries*.
PORTSMOUTH-CHERBOURG. 4hrs45 on *Sealink/Townsend Thoresen*.

Frequency of crossings varies enormously, according to season, on all these routes, as do **ticket prices**, which are calculated by length of car and number of passengers. The cheapest deal is currently *Sally Line's* Ramsgate-Dunkerque: single adult fare £11, child

£6, 4m car plus two people £38–62. *Hoverspeed* do economical 5-day Excursions: adult £17.50, child £9, 4m car £33–92 (return prices). *Townsend Thoresen* offer a 10% discount for students, bookable through any Transalpino office, on passenger transport. *Hoverspeed* also do attractive student offers, at the time of writing £34 one way for a car and driver.

Any travel agent – in Britain or in France – will be able to provide up-to-date schedules and book you up in advance (which in season, if you're driving, is essential). Or you can contact the **ferry companies** direct:

Brittany Ferries (Portsmouth: 0705-827701; Plymouth 0752-21321).
Sally Lines (01-409 2240; Ramsgate: 0843-595522).
Sealink (Dover: 0304-210755; Folkstone: 0303-42954; Portsmouth 0705-833333; Weymouth: 0305-770308).
Townsend Thoresen (01-734 4431; Dover: 0304-203388; Portsmouth 0705-827677; Felixstowe: 0394-604802).
Hoverspeed (01-554 7061; Dover: 0304-214514).

If you're **hitching**, consider taking the quicker – and only slightly more expensive – and Hoverspeed crossings. The gain in journey time gives you a head start on the other side, though, it has to be said, hitching to Paris in high season these days is a lot more pain than pleasure. If you can possibly afford one of the cheaper coach fares, then give it a miss. If not, go all out to talk to people on the ferry over and to push one of them into the promise of a lift.

Hitching back, out of Paris, things are even worse – it is possible to stand a full day on the motorway slip road without getting a ride. Taking a local bus or train out to Montmorency makes matters a lot easier. Or you could, as many French students do, contact the hitchers' organisation *Allostop* (84 passage Brady, 10e; 42.46.00.66; Mon-Fri 9–7.30, Sat 9–1 & 2–6). The organisation matches hitchers with drivers for an introduction charge of 40F for one journey or 150F annual subscription, plus shared expenses up to a maximum charge of 16 centimes per kilometre.

Packages

There's a lot to be said for taking an all-in, **travel–plus–accommodation**, pack-

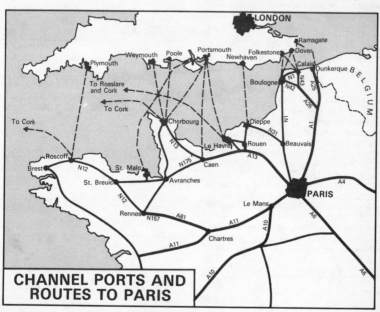

CHANNEL PORTS AND ROUTES TO PARIS

age to Paris, especially if you live some way from London. Many companies offer travel over (on flights, train, coach or ferry) at rates as competitive as you could find on your own and offer a range of hotels from as little as £8 per person upwards. The big savings, however, can come in the special discounts available for travel from where you live to the 'start of your journey' at London, or on very high discounts on regional charter flights from Manchester, Birmingham, Glasgow and elsewhere.

Any travel agent should have a selection of package deals on offer – and most of these will include 'independent' packages, i.e. flight/travel plus a room (no inclusive meals or sightseeing). Among **companies** worth enquiring about are:

Paris Travel Service (Bridge House, Ware, Herts; 0920–3922). Very wide range of packages, from £79 (Feb-Nov) for a flight and 3 nights' basic accommodation. Good for regional flights (Aberdeen, Birmingham, East Midlands, Edinburgh, Glasgow, Leeds/Bradford, Manchester), they also offer all ex-London deals with a £7 supplement (£15 from Scotland) for rail travel from anywhere in Britain.

Travelscene (22a Cheapside, Bradford, 0274–392911; and 94 Baker St, London W1, 01–935 1025). Again a good range of regional flights on offer – and very flexible (any hotel – any amount of time) packages.

USIT (52 Grosvenor Gdns, London SW1; 01–730 3402). Youth/Student orientated packages in 1, 2 and 3 star hotels. 7 nights and a flight from £120 up.

Travel Young (38 Store St, London WC1; 01–580 6762). Similar deals to the above, at similar prices.

● **FROM EIRE**

Dublin-Paris **flights** are on the pricey side – you'd be lucky to find a return for much less than IR£160. Dublin-London flights (or other transport) aren't cheap either, however, and with the added time involved alternatives via Britain are not likely to be very attractive. For up-to-date details on the situation, try phoning the Manchester office of the **Air Travel Advisory Bureau** (061–832 2000). And in Dublin contact **USIT** (7 Anglesea St, Dublin 2; 778117), specialists in independent and student/youth travel. At the

time of writing they have special charter flights available at £99 return.

There are four Ireland-France **ferry links**: *Irish Continental Lines* from Cork to Cherbourg (20¾hrs) and Cork to Le Havre (21½ hrs) and Rosslare to Le Havre (17hrs); *Brittany Ferries* also operate from Cork to Roscoff (13½–17hrs). These are long crossings – and Paris is a further 2hrs drive/1½hrs train from Le Havre, 4hrs/3¼hrs from Cherbourg – or a highly circuitous 7hrs/6hrs from Roscoff. The routes to Le Havre and Cherbourg, however, are again likely to prove more convenient as well as more economical than going via Britain, especially out of season when 10-day excursion fares are available. Frequencies and sample prices (high season, one way):

CORK-LE HAVRE. Weekly. Adult £65, child £43, car and two adults £211.
ROSSLARE-LE HAVRE. 4 weekly. Similar fares.
CORK-CHERBOURG. 2 weekly. Similar fares.
CORK-ROSCOFF. Weekly. Adult £43, child £23, car and two adults £185.

Further details/bookings from any Irish travel agent or from:
Irish Continental Lines (19–21, Aston Quay, Dublin 2; 774–331).
Brittany Ferries (42 Grand Parade, Cork; 215–07666).

● **FROM THE USA**

Unless Paris is your sole European destination – and you're very pushed for time – you will almost always do better to fly to London, Amsterdam, Brussels or Luxembourg and make your own way on from there. **Direct flights to Paris** from the US are very overpriced. Even the French discount travel firm, *Nouvelles Frontières* (see below) quote prices of around $325–500 from New York, $675–800 from San Francisco or Los Angeles.

Flights **elsewhere in Europe** are a very different matter, with a whole host of US and foreign charter companies and national airlines right in the marketplace. It will always pay to shop around, phoning as wide a range of travel companies as you have time and patience for. Among options you should be considering are the *Virgin Airways* services to London from New York and

Miami, *Iceland Air* or *Orlando* to Luxembourg, *KLM* to Amsterdam, *British Caledonian* to London, *Sabena* to Brussels or flights on *Capital* or *International* or with charter companies like *Travac* or *DER Tours*. Aside from the regular *Virgin* fares, what you're looking for are special offers or standbys. Among the more switched on and reliable **travel firms**, who can guide you through this process, are:

NEW YORK
CIEE (Council for International Education Exchange), NY Student Centre, Sloan House YMCA, 356 West 34th St, NY10001 (212–695 0291). CIEE also have offices in Berkeley, Boston, Los Angeles, Miami, San Diego and Seattle: phone their NY office for details.
Nouvelles Frontières, 19 West 44th St, NY10036 (212–764 6494).
Travac, 989 6th Av, NY10018 (212–563 3303).

SAN FRANCISCO
STA/STN, Suite 701, 166 Geary St, CA94108 (415–391 8407).
Nouvelles Frontières, 209 Post St, CA 94108 (415–781 4480).

LOS ANGELES
STA/STN: Suite 507, 2500 Wiltshire Blvd (213–380 2184).

HAWAII
STA/STN, Suite 202, 1831 South King St, Honolulu, HA96826 (808–942 7755).

● **FROM CANADA**
Flights from **Canada to France** are if anything more expensive than from the US. *Nouvelles Frontières*, who maintain offices in Montreal and Quebec, quote return fares to Paris of around CA$250–360 from Montreal, CA$580 from Vancouver, and – these last two summer-only – CA$280–360 from Quebec or Toronto. Once again, it may prove very much cheaper to fly **elsewhere in Europe** – or/and to fly **from the US**.

Recommended **agents** to help you out, especially on student and youth flights are:

Travel Cuts, 44 St George St, Toronto M5S 2E4 (416–979 2406). This is the Canadian student travel service – a really reliable and excellent operation.

Call their Toronto office for details of their offices elsewhere in the country.
Nouvelles Frontières: 1130 ouest, bd de Maisonneuve, Montreal H3A 1M8 (514–842 1450); and 176 Grande Allée Ouest, Quebec G1R2G9 (418–525 5255).

● **FROM AUSTRALIA AND NEW ZEALAND**
Consensus, once again, is that Paris is not the most logical or economic flight destination from Australia or New Zealand. If you did want to go **direct**, you'd be paying upwards of AUS £810–860 from Melbourne or Sydney, considerably more from Brisbane or from Auckland. More promising alternatives are the plethora of flight deals that end up in **London or Amsterdam**.

The most useful **agents** in Australia and New Zealand are the long established STA/STS. Addresses include:

AUSTRALIA
ADELAIDE: **STA Travel**, Union House, Adelaide University, Adelaide 5000 (08–223 6620).
BRISBANE: **STA Travel**, Shop 2, Société Générale House, 40 Creek St (04–221 9629).
CANBERRA: **STA Travel**, Concessions Building, ANU, ACT 2600 (062–470800).
MELBOURNE: **STA Travel**, 220 Faraday St, Carlton, Victoria 3053 (03–347 6911).
PERTH: **STA Travel**, Hackett Hall, Univ of W.A., Crawley 6009 (09–380 2302).
SYDNEY: **STA Travel**, 1A Lee St, Sydney 2000 (02–212 1255).

NEW ZEALAND
AUCKLAND: **STS NZ**, 10 O'Connel St (399 191).
WELLINGTON: **STS NZ**, Courtenay Chambers, 15 Courtenay Place (850 561).

● **POINTS OF ARRIVAL**

By Air
Unless you are taking a charter to Beauvais (which will include a coach ride into the centre of Paris – place Stalingrad, see *By Coach* below–you will arrive at either of **two Paris airports**: *Roissy-Charles de Gaulle* or *Orly Sud/Orly Ouest*. There is a third airport, *Le*

Bourget, but this handles internal flights only.

Roissy, to the north-east of the city, is connected with the centre by: *Roissy-Rail*, a combination of airport bus and RER Ligne B train to the Gare du Nord (every 15min from 5am to 11.15pm), where you can transfer to the ordinary métro; *Air France bus* to Porte Maillot (métro) on the north-west edge of the city beyond the Arc de Triomphe (every 15min from 5.45am to 11pm); *buses 350* to Gare du Nord and Gare de l'Est, and *351* to place de la Nation. *Roissy-Rail* is cheapest and quickest (about 35mins).

Orly, to the south, also has a bus-rail link, *Orly Rail*. RER Ligne C trains leave every 15mins from 5.30am to 11.30pm for the Gare d'Austerlitz and other Left Bank stops which connect with the métro. Alternatively, there are *Air France coaches* to the Gare des Invalides in the 7ᵉ or *Orlybus* to Denfert-Rochereau métro in the 14ᵉ. Both leave every 10–15mins from 6am to 11pm. Journey time is about 35mins.

Roissy and Orly both have *bureaux de change* open every day from 7–11.

By Rail
Paris has **six mainline stations**, all equipped with cafés, restaurants, *tabacs*, banks, *bureaux de change* (long waits in season) and connected with the **métro** system.

Coming from Britain off the main ferry routes, you will arrive either at the **Gare du Nord**, in the north-east of the city, or **Gare St-Lazare**, a little to the west. The former serves Boulogne, Calais, Belgium, Holland and Scandinavia; the latter, Dieppe and the Normandy coast. If you have made your way over to Paris from one of the Brittany ports, you will come in at the **Gare Montparnasse**, across the city on the Left Bank. This station also serves Versailles, Chartres and the Atlantic coast. Information/Reservation numbers are: *Nord* (42.80.03.03/48.78.87.54), *St-Lazare* (45.38.52.29/42.06.49.38), *Montparnasse* (45.38.52.29).

Other Paris stations, for moving on and out, are:
Gare de l'Est. Eastern France, Germany, Switzerland, Austria. Information – 42.08.49.90, Reservations – 42.08.49.38.
Gare de Lyon. Alps, Southern France, Italy, Greece. Information – 43.45.92.22, Reservations – 43.45.93.33.
Gare d'Austerlitz. South-west France, Spain, Portugal. Information – 45.84.16.16, Reservations – 45.84.15.20.

By coach
Almost all **coaches** – whether **international** or **domestic** – use the main *gare routière* in **place Stalingrad**. Métro Stalingrad, on the square, will take you from here into the centre. It is just possible, with some operators, that you'll be dropped on **place de la Madeleine**, right in the centre of Paris at the bottom end of the Champs-Elysées.

For information on coach departures ring VIA International – 42.05.12.10.

By car
Driving into Paris, don't try to cross the city to your destination. Take the ring road – the **boulevard périphérique** – to the *porte* closest to it. Except at rush hour this will be much quicker, and it's a lot easier to find your way.

RED TAPE AND VISAS

Everyone apart from EEC nationals – even the Swiss and Swedes – now must have **visas** to enter France. This security measure was introduced, for a year provisionally, following the bomb attacks in Autumn 1986. Since previously **Americans, Australians, Canadians** and **New Zealanders** could visit France with just a passport, the queues at ill-equipped French consulates and embassies abroad have been very long. However, waiting aside, there should be little problem in getting the requisite stamp in your passport.

For **British, Irish** and other **EEC** nationals, entry on a standard **passport** continues to allow 90 days stay. The temporary *British Visitor's Passport* and the new *Excursion Pass* (both available over the counter at post offices) remain valid.

If you want to stay longer than three months you are supposed to apply for a **Carte de Séjour**. Unless you're enrolled as a student (see p.35), you will have to show an income at least equal to the current minimum wage. However, if you are an EEC national, your passport is most unlikely to be stamped anyway, so there is no evidence of how long you've been in the country. It is perfectly legal for EEC nationals to look for work (see p.34), and if you do find a steady job you should have no difficulty getting a Carte de Séjour. Non-EEC nationals need a work permit and these are hard to get.

French embassies and consulates abroad, for visas/enquiries, include:
AUSTRALIA *Embassy:* 6 Perth Avenue, Yarralumla, Canberra 2600 (951 0000). *Consulates:* 492 St Kilda Road, Melbourne, Victoria 3004 (266 2591); St Martin Tower, 31 Manet Street, Sydney, NSW 2000 (328 1250).
BRITAIN *Embassy:* 58 Knightsbridge, London SW1 (235 8080). *Consulates:* 24 Rutland Gate, London SW7 (581 5292); 11 Randolph Crescent, Edinburgh EH3 (031 225 7954); Cunard Building, Pierhead, Water St, Liverpool L3 (061 236

7949).
CANADA *Embassy:* 42 Promenade Sussex, Ottawa, Ontario KIM 2C9 (512 1715). *Consulates:* Guardian Building, Suite 300, 124th Street, Edmonton, Alberta T59 3 W6 (428 0232); 1110 Avenue des Laurentides, Quebec 6PQ (688 0430); 40 University Avenue, Suite 620, Toronto, Ontario M5J (977 3131).
EIRE *Embassy:* 36 Ailesbury Road, Balls Bridge, Dublin 4 (69 4777).
NETHERLANDS *Embassy:* 1 Smidsplein, BP 683, Den Haag (46 94 53).
NEW ZEALAND *Embassy:* 1 Williston Street, DBP 1695, Wellington (720 200).
SWEDEN *Embassy:* Narvag 28, Stockholm 11523 (63 02 70).
USA *Embassy:* 4101 Reservoir Rd NW, Washington DC, 20007; 94 46000. *Consulates:* 3 Commonwealth Avenue, Boston, Mass 02116 (266 168480); 444 North Michigan Avenue, Suite 3140, Chicago 111 61611 (78 75359); 1 Biscayne Tower, Miami, Florida 33131 (37 29798); 934 5th Avenue, New York 10021 (535 0100); 540 Bush Street, San Francisco, CA 94108 (39 74330).

COSTS, MONEY AND BANKS

Because of the **relatively low cost of accommodation and eating out**, at least by capital city standards, Paris is not an outrageously expensive place to visit. For a reasonably comfortable existence, including hotel room, restaurant and café stops, you need to allow about 300F a day per head (1£=10.51F; 1$US=6.93F). But by watching the pennies, staying at the Youth Hostel (53F bed and breakfast) and being strong-willed about cups of coffee and culture, you could manage on 150F, including a cheap restaurant meal, considerably less if you limit eating to street snacks or market food.

For two or more people **hotel accommodation** can be almost as cheap as the hostels, though a sensible average estimate for a double room would be around 150F. As for food, you can spend as much or as little as you want. There are large numbers of good **restaurants** with 3- or 4-course menus around 45F. **Picnic fare**, obviously, is much cheaper, especially when you buy in the markets and cheap supermarket chains. More sophisticated meals – **takeaway** salads and ready-to-heat dishes – can be put

together for reasonable prices if you shop at *charcuteries* and the equivalent counters of many supermarkets.

Transport within the city is inexpensive. The 43F Carte Orange *hebdomadaire* gives you a week's unlimited travel on buses and métro. **Museums** are likely to prove one of the biggest invisible eroders of the budget. If you're entitled to one, be sure to carry an **ISIC student card**. It will get you into most places at half-price. But, above all, budget-watchers need to be wary of **night-life** activities and **snacks**.

Standard **banking hours** are Mon-Fri 8.30–5. Branches open on Sats include *Crédit Commercial de France*, 115 av des Champs-Élysées, 8ᵉ – all day; *BNP* 49 av des Champs-Élysées/2 place de l'Opéra (2ᵉ) – mornings; and *UBP* at 125 av de Champs-Élysées – open Sat and Sun 10.30–1 & 2–6. The *bureaux de change* at the railway stations are open all day until 9 or 10 at night: at Gare de Lyon and Gare du Nord every day; St-Lazare and Austerlitz every day except Sunday. **Rates of exchange** and **commission** vary from bank to bank. *BNP* (*Banque Nationale de Paris*) offers the best exchange and takes the lowest commission.

Travellers' Cheques are one of the safest ways of carrying your money, available at any British bank, or Thomas Cook for a small commission. Alternatives for Europeans are the special **Eurocheques**, backed up with a card, which can be used for paying shop and restaurant bills in the same way as your ordinary chequebook at home. A further possibility are post office **International Giro cheques**. Available at any large British post office, these work in a similar way to ordinary bank cheques, except that you can cash them through post offices, without paying a commission.

Credit cards are widely accepted. Just look out for the signs. *Visa* – known as the *Carte Bleue* in France – is almost universal. Access (*Mastercard/Eurocard* in France) comes a very poor second. For Access cash advances, *Crédit Agricole* have branches at 166bis bd Sébastopol, 4e; 31 rue de Constantine, 7e; 14 rue de la Boétie, 8e; and 91/93 bd Pasteur, 15e. **International banks** include *American Express*, 11 rue Scribe, 9e; *Bank of America*, 28 place Vendôme, 1er; *Barclays* at 157 bd St-Germain, 6e; *Lloyds*, 43 bd des Capucines, 2e; *Midland*, 6 rue Piccini, 16e; *National Westminster*, 18 place Vendôme, 1er; *Royal Bank of Canada*, 3 rue Scribe, 9e.

There are **bureaux de change** at all points of arrival (see p.10). However, it is always a sensible precaution to **buy some French francs before leaving**.

HEALTH AND INSURANCE

Citizens of all **EEC countries** are entitled to take advantage of each other's **health services** under the same terms as residents of the country, if they have the correct documentation. So British citizens in France may expect to receive medical attention on the same terms as a French citizen, if they have with them Form E111. In theory you should apply for this on Form SA30 by post, one month in advance, to any DHSS office. In practice you can go along to any office with a Contributions counter – not a Supplementary Benefits counter – and have the counter clerk fill out a form for you on the spot.

Under the French Social Security System, every **hospital visit, doctor's consultation** and **prescribed medicine** is charged (though in emergency not upfront). Although you will be entitled to a refund of 75–80 per cent of your medical expenses, this can still leave a hefty shortfall, especially after a stay in hospital. And getting your refund requires a complicated bureaucratic procedure.

According to DHSS explanatory leaflet SA36, you should post all receipts plus your E111 to a local office of the *Caisse Primaire d'Assurance-Maladie* (sickness-insurance office). Be sure to keep a copy of everything since it's not unusual for the Caisse Primaire to 'lose' the papers of foreign applicants. A visit in person has no advantages. There are no on-the-spot payments – it can take a couple of months. There is a catch: parting with your E111 makes it impossible to visit a doctor again under the insurance scheme. The best thing is to make a note of the *Caisse Primaire's* address, then hang on to the documents until the end of your visit.

A better idea is to take out ordinary **travel insurance**, which generally allows 100 per cent reimbursement, minus the first £5 or so of any claim. This is much more useful in the event of a serious accident. In France, accident victims have to pay even for the ambulance that takes them to hospital. North Americans and others will be well used to this and should ensure they have an insurance policy which covers health care abroad. Travel insurance also covers loss or theft of luggage, tickets, money, etc., but remember that claims can only be dealt with if a report is made to local police within 24 hours and a copy of the report sent with the claim. Insurance **policies** can be taken out, on the spot, at just about any British bank or travel agent. *ISIS*, originally designed for students but now available to all, is a particularly good one – obtainable at any of the student-youth companies detailed under *Flights* (p.5).

A **visit to a doctor** costs around 70F, if it is straightforward, and you will be given a *Feuille de Soins* (a signed statement of treatment). You should take any prescription to the *pharmacie*, where the medicines you buy will have little stickers (*vignettes*) attached to them, which you must remove and stick to your *Feuille de Soins*, together with the prescription itself.

Emergencies

For **immediate assistance**:
dial 17 for Police/Rescue service
dial 18 for SAMU (public ambulances)
For **doctors**:
SOS *Médecins* (24hrs; 43.37.77.77)
SOS 92 (24hrs; 46.03.77.44)
Association pour les Urgences Médicales de Paris (24hrs; 48.28.40.04)
For **specific injuries**:
Hands:
Hôpital Boucicaut, 78 rue Convention, 15e (8–1, 2–4; cl.Sat, Sun & hols; 45.54.92.92);
Eyes:
Hôtel-Dieu, 1 place du Parvis-Notre-Dame, 4e (24hrs; Mon-Sat; 43.29.12.79)
Hôpital des Quinze-Vingts, 28 rue de Charenton, 12e (24hrs every day; 43.46.15.20).
Burns/adults:
Hôpital Saint-Antoine, 184 rue du Fbg-St-Antoine, 12e (43.44.33.33).
Hôpital Cochin, 27 rue du Fbg-St-Jacques, 14e (42.34.12.12)
Hôpital Foch, 40 rue Worth, Suresnes (47.72.91.91)
Burns/children:
Hôpital Trousseau, av du Dr-Arnold-Netter, 12e (43.46.13.90)

Drugs:
Hôpital Marmottan, 19 rue d'Armaillé, 17e (45.74.00.04)
Poisoning:
Hôpital Fernand-Widal, 200 rue du Fbg-St-Denis, 10e (42.05.63.29)
Dog bites:
Institut Pasteur, 213 rue de Vaugirard, 15e (45.67.35.09)
For urgent **dental treatment**:
Ring SOS *Dentistes* on 43.37.51.00.
For emergency **nursing**:
Ring SOS *Infirmiers* on 48.87.77.77.
For **VD** (syphilis and gonorrhea are treated free by law):
Croix Rouge, 43 rue de Valois, 1er (42.61.30.04) and 35 rue Claude-Terrasse, 16e (42.88.33.42)
Dispensaire A-Tournier, 2 rue Dareau, 14e (43.37.95.40)
Institut Prophylactique, 36 rue d'Assas, 6e (45.44.38.94).

To trace someone who has been hospitalised, the number to ring is 42.77.11.22, between 8.30–5.30. The **American Hospital** is at 63 bd Victor-Hugo, Neuilly (47.47.53.00; Mo Porte-Maillot, bus 82 to end of line).

All **pharmacies** are also equipped, and obliged, to give first aid on request – though they will make a charge. *Pharmacie Les Champs*, 84 av des Champs-Elysées, 8e, and 61 rue de Panthieu, 8e, are **open 24 hours**.

INFORMATION AND MAPS

The **French Government Tourist Office** give away large quantities of glossily produced brochures for every region of France. **For Paris** these include some useful fold-out leaflets detailing sights to see, markets, shops, museums, ideas for excursions, useful phone numbers and opening hours, as well as maps and more esoteric information like lists of Paris gardens and squares.

Principal **FGTO offices abroad** include:

AUSTRALIA BWP House, 12 Castlereigh St, Sydney, NSW 2000 (612–2315244)
BRITAIN 178 Piccadilly, London W1 (01–491 7622)
CANADA 1840 Ouest rue Sherbrooke, Montreal, Quebec H3H 1E4 (514–931 3855). 1 Dundas St W, Suite 2405, (Box 8), Toronto, Ontario M5G 1Z3 (416–593 4717).
EIRE c/o CIE Tours International, 35 Lower Abbey Street, Dublin 1 (35–07–77).
NETHERLANDS Prinsengracht 670, 1017 KX Amsterdam (20–24 75 34).
SWEDEN Nerrmaimstorg 1–511146, Stockholm (8–24 39–75).
USA 610 Fifth Avenue, New York, NY 10020 (212–757 1125); 646 N Michigan Avenue, Suite 630, Chicago, IL 60611 (312–337 6301); 9401 Wilshire Bvd, Beverley Hills, CA 90212 (213–272 2661); 360 Post St, San Francisco, CA 94108 (415–986461);

THE METRO

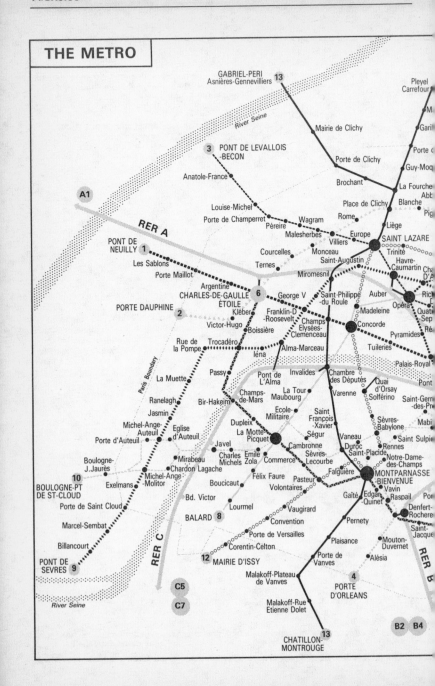

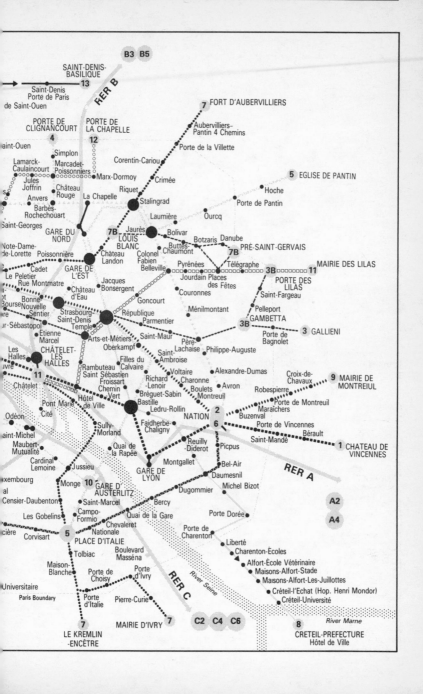

World Trade Center no 103, 2050 Stemmons Freeway, (Box 58610) Dallas, TX 75258 (214–742 7011).

In Paris the **main tourist office** is at 127 av des Champs-Elysées, 8e (47.23.61.72; open 9–8/10, Sun 9–6/8), where the efficient but overworked staff will answer questions from the predictable to the bizarre. There are branch offices at the four main railway stations: Austerlitz, Est, Lyon and Nord. For tourist **info in English** phone 47.20.88.98. **Alternative sources** of information are the **Hôtel de Ville** cultural service (42.74.22.20 and 42.76.40.40; 9–6.30; cl. Sun) and electronic billboards in the streets.

For the clearest picture of the layout of the city, the best map you can get is *Michelin no 10*. the 1:10,000 *Plan de Paris*. More convenient is the pocket-sized *Falkplan*, which folds out only as much as you want it to, or, if you're staying any length of time, *Paris-Eclair:* an **A-Z**, with street index, bus route diagrams, useful addresses, car parks and one-way streets – all a great deal more detailed than the tourist office free handouts. *Paris-Eclair* also includes a pull-out **environs of Paris** map, though you will get more detail as well as a larger area from *Michelin No 196, Environs de Paris*.

The number after Paris addresses – 3e, 11e, etc. – indicates the postal district or *arrondissement*. There are twenty of them altogether, the first (written 1er) centred on the Louvre with the rest unfurling in a clockwise spiral from there. Their boundaries are clearly marked on all maps, and are an important aid to locating places.

GETTING AROUND THE CITY

Finding your way around is remarkably easy, for Paris proper, without its suburbs, is compact and relatively small, with a public transport system that is cheap, fast and meticulously signposted.

To help you get your bearings above ground, think of the **Louvre** as the centre. The Seine flows east to west, cutting the city in two. The **Eiffel Tower** is west, the white pimples of the **Sacré-Coeur** on top of the hill of Montmartre north. These are the landmarks you most often catch glimpses of as you move about. The area north of the river is known as the **Right Bank** or *rive droite*, to the south is the **Left Bank** or *rive gauche*. Roughly speaking, west is smart and east is scruffy.

The **métro** is the simplest way of moving around. Trains run from 5.30am to 12.30am. Stations (abbreviated: Mo Concorde, etc.) are far more frequent than on the London Underground. **Free maps** are available at most stations. In addition, every station has a big plan of the network outside the entrance and several inside. The lines are colour-coded and numbered, although they are signposted within the system with the names of the stations at the ends of the lines. For instance, if you're travelling from Gare du Nord to Odéon, you follow the sign *Direction Porte d'Orléans;* from Gare d'Austerlitz to Grenelle you follow *Direction Pont de St-Cloud*. The numerous junctions (*correspondances*) make it possible to travel all over the city in a more or less straight line. For the latest in subway technology, use the express stations' computerised route-finders – at a touch of the button they'll give you four alternative routes to your selected destination, on foot or by public transport.

Don't however use the métro to the exclusion of the **buses**. They are not difficult and of course you see much more. There are **free route maps** available at métro stations, bus terminals and the tourist office. Every bus stop displays the numbers of the buses which stop there, a map showing all the stops on the route and the times of the first and last buses. If that is not enough, each bus has a map of its own route inside. Generally speaking, they start around 6.30am and begin their last run around 9pm. **Night buses** run every hour from place du Châtelet near the Hôtel de Ville. There is a reduced service on Sundays. Further information from the transport board, *RATP* (43.46.14.14), which incidentally runs numerous excursions, including some to quite far-flung places, much cheaper than the commercial operators; their brochure is available at all railway and some métro stations.

The **same tickets** are valid for bus, métro and, within the city limits, the **RER express rail lines**, which also extend far out into the suburbs. Long bus journeys can cost two tickets; ask the driver, if in doubt.

The most economical **ticket**, if you are staying more than a day or two, is the **Carte Orange**, obtainable at all métro stations (you need a passport photo), with a weekly (*hebdomadaire;* valid Mon am – Sun pm) or monthly (*mensuel*) coupon. It entitles you to unlimited travel on bus or métro. On the métro you put the coupon through the turnstile slot, but make sure to return it to its plastic folder; it is re-usable throughout the period of its validity. On a bus you show the whole *Carte* to the driver as you board – don't put it into the punching machine. There is a tourist ticket, *billet de tourisme*, but it is overpriced. For a short stay in the city **single tickets** can be bought at reduced rate in *carnets* of ten (from any station). Don't buy from the touts who

hang round the main stations; you'll pay well over the odds. All tickets are available as first or second class (though class distinctions are only in force between 9am and 5pm) and there's a **flat rate** across the city – one ticket per journey. Be sure to keep your ticket until the end of the journey; you'll be fined on the spot if you can't produce one.

If it's late at night or you feel like treating yourself, don't hesitate to use the **taxis**. Their charges are very reasonable. Three small lights on the roof indicate which fare rate the metre is switched to: A (passenger side) is daytime, B is night rate, and C (driver's side) is for out of town. Some **numbers to call** are: 42.03.99.99; 42.70.44.22; 47.30.23.23; 42.00.67.89.

In the daytime, at least, travelling around **by car** is hardly worth it because of the difficulty of finding parking space. Should you be towed away, you'll find your car in the pound belonging to that particular *arrondissement*. You'll have to

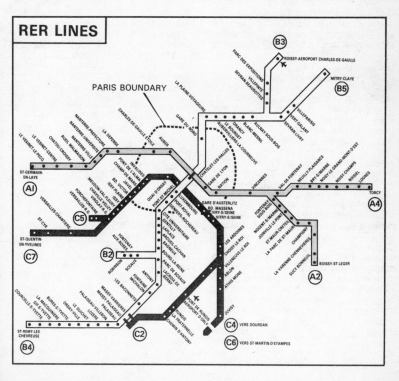

RER LINES

phone the local town hall or *mairie* to get the address. In the event of a **breakdown** you can call 42.57.33.44, but only between 7am–10pm.

For **car hire**, some good French firms are: *Mattei*, 205 rue de Bercy, 12e (43.46.11.50), 102 rue Ordener, 18e (42.64.32.90) and *Autorent*, 11 rue Casimir-Perier, 11e (45.55.53.49), 98 rue de la Convention, 15e (45.54.22.45) and 196 rue St-Jacques, 5e (43.25.88.10). In addition there's Avis, Hertz and the rest–

the tourist office will have all the bumf.

If you are reckless enough to want to **cycle** and don't have your own machine, you can hire from: *Autothèque*, 16 rue Berger, 1er (42.36.39.36) and 80 rue Montmartre, 2e (42.36.50.93) – the latter has Solex and motorbikes as well; *Paris-Vélo*. 2 rue de Fer-à-Moulin, 5e (43.37.59.22); and *Locacycles*, 3 rue de Vieux-Colombier, 6e. Take care!

FINDING A PLACE TO STAY

Paris **hotels and youth hostels** are often heavily booked,* so it's wise to **reserve** a place well ahead of time, if you can. If not, there are two **agencies** you can turn to for help: the tourist board's *bureaux d'accueil* and the youth-oriented *Accueil des Jeunes en France* (AJF). The former charge a small commission – their function is to bale you out of last-minute difficulty rather than find the most economical deal. The AJF, however, actually guarantee 'decent and low-cost lodging' (currently in the 56–75F range for B and B).

Addresses:
Bureaux d'accueil:
Office du Tourisme, 127 av des
   Champs-Elysées, 8e (daily 9–10/8).
Gare d'Austerlitz (Mon-Sat 9–10/8).
Gare de l'Est (Mon-Sat 8–1,5–10/8).
Gare de Lyon (Mon-Sat 8–1,5–10/8).
Gare du Nord (Mon-Sat 8–1,5–10/8).

Accueil des Jeunes en France:
Gare du Nord arrival hall (Mon-Fri
   9.15–6.15; June 1–Sept 30, daily
   8–10; cl.Nov-Feb; 42.85.86.19).
119 rue St-Martin, 4e opposite Centre
   Beaubourg (Mo Chatelet-Les Halles;
   Mon-Sat 9.30–7; 42.77.87.80).
16 rue du Pont-Louis-Philippe, 4e (Mo
   Hôtel-de-Ville; Mon-Fri – Sats as well
   in July – 9.30–6.30; cl.Nov-Feb;
   42.78.04.82).
139 bd St-Michel, 5e (Mo Port-Royal;
   Mon-Sat 9.30–7; 43.54.95.86).
*The Paris hoteliers' organisation publishes an annual list of the most heavily booked periods, based on the dates of the *salons* or trade fairs (obtainable from FGTO offices). September is invariably the worst month. Otherwise dates vary slightly from year to year. It is worth checking them out when planning a trip.

Youth hostels, *foyers*, and campsites
The cheapest **youth accommodation** are the hostels organised by the French **Youth Hostel Association** and the **AJF**. For the former you need International YHA membership, for which there is no age limit. Current costs are 53F a night, including breakfast. The AJF hostels, known as *foyers*, are marginally more expensive at 62F and, nominally at least, restricted to 18–30-year-olds, though this rule can be waived.

There are only two **Youth Hostels** in Paris proper and it's advisable to book ahead in summer (send a cheque or postal order for 50F):

Jules Ferry, 8 bd Jules Ferry, 11e (Mo
   République; 43.57.55.60) – in a
   colourful Arab-African neighbourhood
   near the Canal St-Martin
D'Artagnan, 80 rue Vitruve, 20e (Mo Porte
   de Bagnolet; 43.61.08.75)

Suburban hostels – all rather inconveniently located – are at:

3 voie du Loup-Pendu, Châtenay-
Malabry (46.32.17.43; RER *ligne* B2 to
Robinson, then bus 198A to Cyrano-
Bergerac)
3 rue Marcel-Duhamel, Arpajon
(44.90.28.85).
125 av Villeneuve-Saint-Georges,
Choisy-le-Roi (48.90.92.30); RER *ligne*
C from St-Michel to Choisy-le-Roi,
where you cross the Seine, turn right
and follow the signs – 20 mins.
4 rue des Marguerites, Rueil-
Malmaison (47.49.43.97; 15 mins by
train from Gare St-Lazare to Suresnes,
plus 15 mins walk).

The **AJF's *foyers***, which cannot be booked in advance, are:

Résidence Bastille, 151 av Ledru-Rollin, 11e (Mo Ledru-Rollin, Bastille, Voltaire; 43.79.53.86)

Le Fourcy, 6 rue de Fourcy, 4e (42.74.23.45)

Le Fauconnier, 11 rue du Fauconnier, 4e (42.74.23.45)

Maubuisson, 12 rue des Barres, 4e (42.72.72.09)

François Miron, 6 rue François Miron, 4e (42.72.72.09)

The last four are all accessible from métro stops St-Paul, Pont-Marie, Hôtel-de-Ville, and sited in renovated historic buildings in the Marais, with a communal restaurant serving meals at 39F.

In addition, from July to September, the AJF has the use of three **student halls of residence**:

Résidence Luxembourg, 270 rue St-Jacques, 5e (Mo Luxembourg, Port-Royal; 43.25.06.20)

Résidence Coubertin, 53 rue Lhomond, 5e (Mo Censier-Daubenton; 43.36.18.12)

Résidence Tocqueville, 49 rue de Tocqueville, 17e (Mo Villiers; 47.66.51.34).

Further possibilities are the *Centre International de Séjour de Paris* at 17 bd Kellerman, 13e (Mo Porte d'Italie; 45.80.70.76) and 6 av Maurice-Ravel, 12e (Mo Porte de Vincennes; 43.43.19.01), open to all ages at prices ranging from 45F–85F depending on whether you share or have your own room. Similar accommodation is available at the *Foyer International d'Accueil de Paris* at La Défense (19 rue Salvador-Allende, Nanterre; 47.25.91.34) – cheap restaurant, too. In July and August this *foyer* has some special arrangements for **families**, including meals, baby-sitting etc, provided you stay at least a week; it could be worth investigating if you have young children.

There is a **campsite** – usually booked out in summer and in theory reserved for French camping club members – by the Seine in the Bois de Boulogne (allée du Bord-de-l'Eau, 16e; Mo Porte-Maillot; 45.06.14.98). Three more are further out to the east of the city:

Camping du Tremblay, quai de Polangis, Champigny-sur-Marne (RER: Champigny; 42.83.38.24)

Camping du Camp des Cicognes, bord-de-Marne, Créteil (RER: Créteil-l'Echat; 42.07.06.75)

Camping de Paris-Est, bd des Alliés, Champigny-sur-Marne (Mo Joinville-le-Pont; 42.83.38.24).

Another is out to the west at Versailles:

Camping Municipal de Versailles, 31 rue Berthelot (RER: Porchefontaine; 49.51.23.61).

The additional cost of transport in getting to and from these suburban sites is likely to bring costs well up to the hostel level.

Hotels

For independence and choice of location there's obviously more scope in **booking a hotel yourself**. There are a great many in all price categories and Paris scores heavily, especially in relation to London, in the large number of small family-run hotels with rooms under £20 for two, indeed even under £10.

The **hotels listed below** have been divided into **Central** (*arrondissements* 1–8) and **Outer** (*arrondissements* 9–20) and arranged in three broad **price categories**: under 150F, between 150–250F, and over 250F. Many hotels in the higher categories have some very much cheaper rooms, though they are not easy to get at short notice because they tend to be taken by long-term residents.*

Most of the hotels in the first two categories are perfectly adequate. That means the sheets are clean, you can wash decently and there isn't a brothel on the floor below. There won't be much luxury, however. Most small Paris hotels are in converted old buildings, so the stairs are often dark, and the rooms cramped, with a view onto an internal courtyard, and the decor hardly spanking new. We've assumed that most visitors come to Paris to see the city and will treat their hotel simply as a convenient and inexpensive place to spend a few of the night hours. Where we think conditions are at the limit of

*If you're seriously interested in a **long stay on a low budget**, then it would be worth checking out the numerous basic and star-less hotels you'll see as you go about the streets, especially in less central districts. Many only let rooms by the month, with prices as low as 30 or 40F a day.

what most people will accept, we say basic.

All hotel **room prices** have to be displayed somewhere prominent, in the entrance or by the reception desk usually. Certain **standard terms** recur. *Eau courante* (EC) means a room with washbasin only. *Cabinet de toilette* (CT) means basin and bidet. In both cases there will be communal toilets on the landing and probably a shower as well. *Douche/WC* and *Bain/WC* mean that you have shower or bath as well as toilet in the room. A room with *grand lit*/double bed is invariably cheaper than one with *deux lits*/two separate beds.

Breakfast (*petit dejeuner* or PD) is sometimes included (*compris*) in the room price, sometimes extra (*en sus*). The amount varies between about 15F and 24F per person. It isn't supposed to be obligatory, though some hotels make a sour face when you decline it. Always make it clear whether you want breakfast or not when you take the room. It's usually a fairly indifferent continental breakfast, and you'll get a fresher, cheaper one at the local café.

Don't get the idea that you'll be out in the sticks if you choose hotels detailed in **outer sections** below. We've listed several good bargains in the 10e, for instance, which is not at all far from the centre of things.

Within each section the hotels are arranged alphabetically by *arrondissement*. **Prices** are for an average double room.

● *UNDER 150F/CENTRAL*
Hôtel Henri IV, 25 place Dauphine, 1er. Mo Pont-Neuf, Cité (43.54.44.53). An ancient and well-known cheapie in the beautiful place Dauphine at the sharp end of the Ile de la Cité. Nothing more luxurious than *cabinet de toilette*. Need to book.

Hôtel Lion d'Or, 5 rue de la Sourdière, 1er. Mo Tuileries (42.60.79.04). Spartan, but clean, friendly and very central.
Hôtel de l'Ouest, 144 rue St-Honoré, 1er. Mo Louvre, Palais-Royal (42.60.29.89). Rooms rather small and dilapidated. Very close to Louvre and consequently popular. Book 2 weeks ahead. Around 100F for two.
Hôtel de la Place du Louvre, 21 rue des Prêtres-St-Germain-l'Auxerrois, 1er. Mo Louvre (42.33.77.68). Bit touristy and fills up quickly. CTs from 77F; showers between 95–150F.

Hôtel St-Honoré, 85 rue St-Honoré, 1er. Mo Châtelet-les-Halles, Louvre. (42.36.20.38). Around 120F for two.
Hôtel de Bayonne, 41 rue d'Aboukir, 2e. Mo Sentier (45.08.40.09). 65–120F. Basic.
Hôtel de Cambrai, 30 rue de Turenne, 3e. Mo Bastille, St-Paul (42.72.73.47). Ugly rooms, but clean and adequate. 80–150F for two, with shower.
Castex Hôtel, 5 rue Castex, 4e. Mo Bastille, Sully-Morland (42.72.31.52). Awful wallpaper, but very clean, and a sweet *patron*. CT for 90F, bath for 150F.
Hôtel Moderne, 3 rue Caron, 4e. Mo St-Paul (48.87.97.05). Several rooms at 70F, bath at 160F. Much better than first impression of staircase would suggest.
Hôtel Pratic, 9 rue d'Ormesson, 4e. Mo St-Paul, Bastille (48.87.80.47). Up to 120F, but plenty of rooms at 60 and 65F.
Hôtel Stella, 14 rue Neuve-St-Pierre, 4e. Mo St-Paul (42.72.23.66). Cheap and basic.
Sully Hotel, 48 rue St-Antoine, 4e. Mo St-Paul, Bastille (42.78.49.32). Cheap and basic.
Hôtel des Alliés, 20 rue Berthollet, 5e. Mo Censier-Daubenton (43.31.47.52). Simple and clean. CTs up to 120F, bath 165F for two.
Hôtel Gay-Lussac, 29 rue Gay-Lussac, 5e. Mo Luxembourg (43.54.23.96). CTs under 100F, showers just over, but need to book at least a week in advance.
Hôtel Alsace-Lorraine, 14 rue des Canettes, 6e. Mo St-Germain, St-Sulpice (43.25.10.14). An old and dingy building in a picturesque lane off place St-Sulpice, in the heart of St-Germain. Rooms clean and okay; range from 93–163F for two.
Le Petit Trianon, 2 rue de l'Ancienne-Comédie, 6e. Mo Odéon (43.54.94.64). Cheap, basic and right in the heart of things. Disagreeable people.
Hôtel St-Michel, 17 rue Gît-le-Coeur, 6e. Mo St-Michel (43.26.98.70). Simple and okay – right near place St-Michel and Notre-Dame.
Hôtel St-Placide, 6 rue St-Placide, 6e. Mo Rennes, St-Placide (45.48.80.08). Very cheap and very basic – well under 100F for two.
Grand Hôtel Lévèque, 29 rue Cler, 7e. Mo Ecole-Militaire, Latour-Maubourg (47.05.49.15). Clean and decent; nice people. Good location smack in the middle of the rue Cler market. Redecorating, so prices will rise. Book one month ahead.

Hôtel Malar, 29 rue Malar, 7ᵉ. Mᵒ Alma, Latour-Maubourg (45.51.38.46). Small, with slightly poky rooms, but in a very attractive street close to the river.
Royal Phare Hôtel, 40 av de la Motte-Picquet, 7ᵉ. Mᵒ Ecole-Militaire (47.05.57.30). A bit scruffy and impersonal, but very convenient and has some good views. Also close to rue Cler.

● *UNDER 150F/OUTER*

Grand Hôtel d'Amérique, 53 rue de Provence, 9ᵉ. Mᵒ Trinité, Chaussée-d'Antin (45.26.44.43). Immaculately clean and very old fashioned: canaries, pot plants and wall-papered ceilings. Several rooms under 100F. Lively, interesting street.
Hôtel Beauséjour, 71 av Parmentier, 10ᵉ. Very cheap and very basic.
Hôtel du Centre Est, 4 rue Sibour, 10ᵉ. Mᵒ Gare de l'Est (46.07.20.74). An excellent value cheapie, but you'll generally need to book.
Hôtel des Familles, 216 rue du Faubourg-St-Denis, 10ᵉ. Mᵒ Gare du Nord, Chapelle (46.07.76.56). Large, gloomy, cheap, and near the station . . . would do for a stop-gap.
Hôtel du Jura, 6 rue de Jarry, 10ᵉ. Mᵒ Gare de l'Est, Château-d'Eau (47.70.06.66). Primitive, but friendly and decent.
Hôtel Pierre Dupont, 1 rue Pierre-Dupont, 10ᵉ. Mᵒ Château-d'Eau, Gare de l'Est (42.06.93.66). Primitive but okay, in a quiet working-class street by the canal.
Hôtel Savoy, 9 rue Jarry, 10ᵉ. Mᵒ Gare de l'Est, Château-d'Eau, (47.70.03.72). Poky and basic.
Hôtel de Spa, 52bis rue des Vinaigriers, 10ᵉ. Mᵒ Bonsergent, Gare de l'Est (46.07.93.16). Bottom-line, though close to the canal.
Hôtel de Verdun, 5 rue St-Laurent, 10ᵉ. Mᵒ Gare de l'Est (46.07.70.93). A dingy building in a dingy street, though fairly cheap, friendly and very close to the Gare de l'Est and Gare du Nord. The rooms are clean, and if you can get a top floor one, there's a superb view of the Sacré Coeur across grey pigeon-shitted mansard roofs.
Hôtel de l'Europe, 74 rue Sedaine, 11ᵉ. Mᵒ Voltaire (47.00.54.38). Basic.
Hôtel de la Fontaine Beauséjour, 1 rue de la Fontaine-au-Roi, 11ᵉ. Mᵒ République, Goncourt. Bottom line.
Luna Park Hôtel, 1 rue Jacquard, 11ᵉ. Mᵒ Parmentier (48.05.65.50). 5 rooms at

75F; most expensive is 190F – including the price of breakfast.
Hôtel de la Poste, 66 rue de Malte, 11ᵉ. Mᵒ République. Cheap, gloomy and basic.
Hôtel Résidence Alhambra, 11–13 rue de Malte, 11ᵉ. Mᵒ Oberkampf (47.00.35.52). 50F B and B in multi-bed room.
Mistral Hôtel, 3 rue Chaligny, 12ᵉ. Mᵒ Faidherbe-Chaligny. Communal showers, but not bad.
Hôtel de la Poste-Ouest, 80 rue de l'Ouest, 14ᵉ. Mᵒ Pernety (43.22.20.59). Less than 60F. Very Spartan: in an interesting district, caught between demolition and renovation. Looks like a slum outside, but is immaculately clean. Run by a friendly and dignified old Chinese.
Mondial Hôtel, 136 bd de Grenelle, 15ᵉ. Mᵒ La Motte-Picquet (45.79.73.57). Simple lodgings for workers and commercial travellers. Friendly and decent. Right under the raised métro.
Hôtel du Ranelagh, 56 rue de l'Assomption, 16ᵉ. Mᵒ Ranelagh (42.88.31.63). A posh neighbourhood cheapie. Its growing popularity makes advance booking essential.
Idéal Hôtel, 3 rue des Trois-Frères, 18ᵉ. Mᵒ Abbesses (46.06.63.63). Under 100F for two. Absolutely no frills, though the location on the slopes of Montmartre is marvellous. No reservations: you have to call round before 11am.
Hôtel Tholozé, 24 rue Tholozé, 18ᵉ. Mᵒ Blanche, Abbesses (46.06.74.83). Dirt cheap, but very basic.

● *150–250F/CENTRAL*

Lux Hôtel, 12 rue du Roule, 1ᵉʳ. Mᵒ Louvre, Châtelet, Pont-Neuf (42.33.00.71). Bottom end of the range. Quiet; efficient management; well appointed.
Hôtel Richelieu-Mazarin, 51 rue de Richelieu, 1ᵉʳ. Mᵒ Palais-Royal (42.97.46.20). Very good for the price – with a laundry.
Grand Hôtel du Roule, 14 rue du Roule, 1ᵉʳ. Mᵒ Louvre Châtelet. Three rooms at 100F; rest around 200F.
Hôtel Ile de France, 26 rue St-Augustin, 2ᵉ. Mᵒ Septembre (47.42.40.61). Three rooms with shower for 107F; rest 200F and over.
Grand Hôtel Jeanne d'Arc, 3 rue de Jarente, 4ᵉ. Mᵒ St-Paul (48.87.62.11). Clean and attractive, though the Marais location means it's beginning to be

touristy. Some EC singles for as little as 65F.

Royal Cardinal Hôtel, 1 rue des Ecoles, 5e. Mo Jussieu, Cardinal-Lemoine (46.33.93.62). A comfortable and unexciting two-star, used to foreigners.

Hôtel California, 32 rue des Ecoles, 5e. Mo Jussieu, Cardinal-Lemoine (46.34.12.90). Another comfortable Latin Quarter tourist hotel.

Hôtel des Carmes, 5 rue des Carmes, 5e. Mo Maubert-Mutualité (43.29.78.40). A cheaper version of the above, with some CTs at just over 100F.

Hôtel Esmeralda, 4 rue St-Julien-le-Pauvre, 5e. Mo St-Michel, Maubert-Mutualité (43.54.19.20). A narrow old house on square Viviani with a superb view of Notre-Dame, which will cost you 280F. Other rooms with showers for 170F, plus some very much cheaper.

Grandes Ecoles, 75 rue du Cardinal Lemoine, 5e. Mo Cardinal-Lemoine (43.26.79.23). CTs at 140F, with communal showers on the landing. With bath, up to 220F – plus a view over the garden.

Le Latania, 22 rue de la Parcheminerie, 5e. Mo St-Michel, Maubert-Mutalité (43.54.32.17). Unprepossessing from outside, but reasonable rooms.

Hôtel Marignan, 13 rue du Sommerard, 5e, Mo Maubert-Mutualité (43.54.63.81). Must be the best bargain in town – and totally sympathetic to the needs of rucksack-toting foreigners, especially from AUS and NZ. Laundry and ironing facilities provided free, plus a room to eat your own food in – plates provided. Even the maid speaks English and the communal showers are free. Summer prices range from 160F for a double bed to 300F for one double and two singles. Need to book a month ahead in summer, five days in winter, when the prices are lower – though they do hold a few rooms back for people who turn up on spec.

Hôtel Mont-Blanc, 28 rue de la Huchette, 5e. Mo St-Michel (43.54.49.44). Simple but decent. The highest rooms are lightest.

Grand Hôtel Oriental, 2 rue d'Arras, 5e. Mo Jussieu, Cardinal-Lemoine, Maubert-Mutualité (43.54.38.12). Dark and a bit dilapidated, but pretty good bargain for this locality – and nice people. Nothing over 220F, and some singles under 150F.

Hôtel du Dragon, 36 rue du Dragon, 6e. Mo St-Germain-des-Prés, Sèvres-Baby-lone (45.48.51.05). Great location and nice people make up for slightly primitive conditions.

Hôtel Michelet Odéon, 6 place de l'Odéon, 6e. Mo Odéon, Luxembourg (46.34.27.80). Another fantastic location. The hotel has been modernised, but still has 2 double rooms for 98F if you can get them. Otherwise it'll be well over 200F.

Hôtel Le Montana, 28 rue St-Benoît, 6e. Mo St-Germain-des-Prés. (45.48.62.15). A good, well-placed hotel at the top of the range.

Hôtel Récamier, 3bis place St-Sulpice, 6e. Mo St-Sulpice, St-Germain (43.26.04.89). Comfortable, superbly sited.

Hôtel St-André-des-Arts, 66 rue St-André-des-Arts, 6e. Mo Odéon (43.26.96.16). Reasonable and very central. Some cheaper rooms under 150F, but no reservations on these.

Ste-Eugénie Hôtel, 31 rue St-André-des-Arts, 6e. Mo Odéon, St-Michel (43.26.29.03). Rooms are fine, though nothing to write home about. Several under 150F.

Hôtel St-Pierre, 4 rue de l'Ecole de Médecine, 6e. Mo Odéon, St-Michel (46.34.78.80). Comfortable and adequate – up to 223F.

Hôtel du Centre, 24bis rue Cler, 7e. Mo Ecole-Militaire (47.05.52.53). An old-fashioned, no frills establishment in a posh and attractive neighbourhood. Around 190F for two; cheaper rooms tend to have long-term occupants.

Hôtel du Champs-de-Mars, 7 rue du Champs-de-Mars, 7e. Mo Ecole-Militaire (45.51.52.30). Prices towards the top end of the range. Cleaner and better fittings than the adjacent Résidence.

La Résidence du Champs-de-Mars, 7e. Mo Ecole-Militaire (47.05.25.45). Dark and a bit scruffy and worn. Some rooms at under 120F (one even at 56F), but they're hard to get, as usual.

Hôtel du Palais Bourbon, 49 rue de Bourgogne, 7e. Mo Varenne (45.51.63.32). A handsome old building in a sunny street by the Musée Rodin. Rooms are spacious and light, and mostly under 200F.

Le Pavillon, 54 rue St-Dominique, 7e. Mo Invalides, Latour-Maubourg (45.51.42.87). A tiny former convent set back from the tempting shops of the rue St-Dominique in a leafy courtyard. Small rooms but nice: around 240F for two.

Splendid Hôtel, 29 av de Tourville, 7e. Mo Ecole-Militaire (45.51.24.77). Singles under 100F, CTs for two under 135F. A little noisy, but a great area with views, from the top floor, of the Eiffel Tower and Invalides.

Hôtel de la Tulipe, 33 rue Malar, 7e. Mo Latour-Maubourg (45.51.67.21). Patio for summer breakfast and drinks. Newly renovated: beamy and cottagey. Out of the range at the top end.

Hôtel de Turenne, 20 av de Tourville, 7e. Mo Ecole-Militaire (47.05.99.92). Very adequate; great area.

Hôtel Madeleine Elysées, 22 rue Tronchat, 8e. Down-market for the area.

● **150–250F/OUTER**

Hôtel de Beauharnais, 51 rue de la Victoire, 9e. Mo Le Peletier, Havre-Caumartin (48.74.71.13). Louis Quinze, First Empire . . . every room decorated in a different period style.

Hôtel Campaville (Paris-Montholon), 11 rue Pierre Semard, 9e. Mo Poissonière (47.57.11.11). Okay: rooms a little small and dark. Part of a chain, the other three Parisian links being: 21 bd de Clichy, 9e; 26 rue de l'Aqueduc, 10e; 30 rue St-Charles, 16e.

Hôtel de la Cité Bergère, 4–6 Cité Bergère, 9e. Mo Montmartre (47.70.52.98). Well-used tourist hotel, close to Folies Bergère etc.

Hôtel Chopin, 46 passage Jouffroy, 9e. Mo Montmartre (47.70.58.10). Entrance on bd Montmartre, near corner with rue du Faubourg-Montmartre – right in the old *passage*.

Hôtel Comprador, 2 Cité Rougemont, 9e. Mo Montmartre (47.70.44.42). Entrance by 19 rue Bergère. One of the cheaper hotels hereabouts.

Hôtel Haussmann, 89 rue de Provence, 9e. Mo Chaussée d'Antin, Havre-Caumartin (48.74.24.57).

Hôtel de Madrid, 1 rue Geoffroy-Marie, 9e. Mo Le Péletier, Cadet (47.70.85.87). A little worn and dark, but the rooms have character, with marble fireplaces and big, framed mirrors.

Mondial Hôtel, 21 rue Notre-Dame-de-Lorette, 9e. Mo St-Georges (48.78.60.47). Acceptable, if uninspired; has some cheaper rooms.

Hôtel Monte-Carlo, 44 rue du Faubourg-Montmartre, 9e. Mo Le Péletier, Montmartre (47.70.36.75). Doubles around 200F, but with some below 100F.

Victoria Hôtel, 2bis Cité Bergère, 9e. Mo Montmartre (47.70.18.83). Situated in quiet, pleasant courtyard opposite Chartier's restaurant, along with several other slightly overpriced touristy hotels.

Adix Hôtel, 30 rue Lucien Sampaix, 10e. Mo Bonsergent (42.08.19.74). In a pleasant street close to the St-Martin canal, and surprisingly smart for the area, with prices at the top of the range.

Grand Hôtel de Famille, 46 rue Lucien Sampaix, 10e. Mo Gare de l'Est (46.07.23.87). A rather gloomy old-fashioned barrack, but great value – most doubles 166–210F, with shower and WC – and location on the canal bank in a very interesting old-time working-class neighbourhood on the up and up.

National Hôtel, 224 rue du Faubourg-St-Denis, 10e. Mo Gare du Nord, La Chapelle (42.06.99.56). Bloody-minded but convenient shelter near the **Nord** and **Est** stations and the international bus depot at place Stalingrad.

Plessis-Hôtel, 25 rue du Grand-Prieuré, 11e. Mo République, Oberkampf (47.00.13.38). A friendly, good-value hotel.

Hôtel Jules César, 52 av Ledru-Rollin, 12e. Mo Gare de Lyon, Bastille, Ledru-Rollin (43.43.15.88). Clean and okay, though the *patronne* is a pain.

Le Central-Hôtel, 1 bis rue du Maine, 14e. Mo Montparnasse, Edgar-Quinet. (43.20.69.15). Very convenient, on a quiet square right behind Montparnasse.

Hôtel du Parc, 6 rue Jolivet, 14e. Mo Montparnasse, Edgar-Quinet. (43.20.95.54). Same square as above. Clean rooms and a very nice *patron*. Try before the Central.

Hôtel de L'Avre, 21 rue de l'Avre, 15e. Mo La Motte-Picquet (45.75.31.63). A basic, but very decent, clean establishment in a quiet side street. Some cheaper CT doubles.

Hôtel Ini, 159 bd Lefebvre, 15e. Mo Porte-de-Vanves (48.28.18.35). Another clean and reasonably-priced hotel, but the location is dull, out on the *périphérique*.

Institut Hôtel, 23 bd Pasteur, 15e. Mo Pasteur (45.67.10.48). Perfectly adequate hotel, on leafy avenue south of the Invalides, with some much cheaper CT doubles.

Hôtel Printania, 142 bd de Grenelle, 15e. Mo Motte-Picquet (45.79.23.97). Overlooking the elevated métro line. A bit worn and dingy, but okay.

Tourisme Hôtel, 66 av de la Motte-Picquet, 15ᵉ. Mᵒ Motte-Picquet (47.34.28.01). Unprepossessing barrack-like building on the corner of bd de Grenelle, but the rooms are fine.

Hôtel des Batignolles, 26–28 rue des Batignolles, 17ᵉ. Mᵒ Rome, place Clichy (43.87.70.40). A quiet and very reasonable establishment in a neighbourhood that prides itself on its village character. Some cheaper rooms.

Lévis-Hotel, 16 rue Lebouteux, 17ᵉ. Mᵒ Villiers (47.63.86.38). Only ten rooms, but very nice; clean and quiet, in a small side street off the rue de Lévis market.

Hôtel André Gill, 4 rue André-Gill, 18ᵉ. Mᵒ Pigalle, Abbesses (42.62.48.48). Prices at bottom of range for very adequate rooms in a great location on the slopes of Montmartre. Quiet too, in a dead-end off rue des Martyrs.

La Résidence Montmartre, 10 rue Burcq, 18ᵉ. Mᵒ Abbesses (46.06.45.28). A comfortable, quiet Montmartre hotel. All rooms have either shower or bath.

Hôtel Maillot, 47 rue de Sablonville, Neuilly. Mᵒ Sablons, Porte Maillot (46.24.23.45). A comfortable, characterful hotel in a converted bourgeois residence. Prices towards the top of the range.

● *250–350F*

A few pricier ones that caught our eye:
Hôtel du Cygne, 3–5 rue du Cygne, 1ᵉʳ. Mᵒ Châtelet-Les-Halles, Etienne-Marcel (42.60.14.16). An attractive renovated 18C building.

Select Hôtel, 20 rue du Temple, 4ᵉ. Mᵒ Hôtel-de-Ville, (48.87.07.70). Clean and quiet.

L'Hôtel du Septième Art, 20 rue St-Paul, 4ᵉ. Mᵒ St-Paul, Pont-Marie. (42.77.04.03). A supposedly cinema ambiance. The beige-brown rooms are disappointing, but the bathrooms live up to the black and white movie style.

Hôtel du Collège de France, 7 rue Thénard, 5ᵉ. Mᵒ Maubert-Mutualité, St-Michel (43.26.78.36). A very nice comfortable place in the heart of the Latin Quarter. TV, hairdriers and all.

Familia Hôtel, 11 rue des Ecoles, 5ᵉ. Mᵒ Jussieu, Cardinal-Lemoine, Maubert-Mutualité (43.54.55.27). Comfortable, and with three- and four-bed rooms available.

Select Hôtel, 1 place de la Sorbonne, 5ᵉ. Mᵒ Luxembourg (46.34.14.80). Great location, on a paved, traffic-free *place* right by the Luxembourg gardens. Very comfortable three-star.

Hôtel des Deux Continents, 25 rue Jacob, 6ᵉ. Mᵒ St-Germain (43.26.72.46). More comfort in an unbeatable location.

Hôtel La Rive Gauche, 25 rue des Saints-Pères, 6ᵉ. Mᵒ St-Germain, Bac (42.60.34.68). Close to the river.

Hôtel de Seine, 52 rue de Seine, 6ᵉ. Mᵒ St-Germain, Odéon, Mabillon. (46.34.22.80). A good and very conveniently situated establishment.

Résidence Latour-Maubourg. 150 rue de Grenelle, 7ᵉ. Mᵒ Latour-Maubourg (45.51.75.28). An elegant, aristocratic building on a pleasant green at the very corner of the Invalides. Some doubles at 214F and a few cheaper singles, but mostly in 300–370F range. Very hard to beat if you want a bit of class.

Hôtel Urbis, 160 rue du Château, 14ᵉ. Mᵒ Pernety (43.22.00.09). Recently modernised hotel on a quiet old street off av du Maine. Doubles at 300F.

Hôtel de Troyes, 153 rue de Vaugirard, 15ᵉ. Mᵒ Pasteur (47.34.56.75). Comfortable, clean and friendly, though the location is a bit dull.

Hôtel Regyn's, 18 place des Abbesses, 18ᵉ. Mᵒ Abbesses (42.54.45.21). Renovated and smartly decorated – hessian and felt on the walls. Superb site, and lovely views across the city.

FOOD AND DRINK

To eat **French food** is as good a reason as any for going to France, but Paris is not the number one place to sample it, unless your budget is unlimited. That's not to say you won't eat well for there's no end to the choice of establishments to serve you. But too many restaurants trade on the low standards – whether real or imagined – of tourists and on the sheer numbers of people dining out that ensures new customers every night. Buying the **ingredients** is another matter – the markets and specialist shops are one of the city's chief delights. And you can try out **different cuisines** that you might not find at home – North African, Vietnamese, Senegalese or Antillais. But whatever new discoveries you make or disappointments you suffer, Paris can be counted on for good **drinking** and entertaining **café-life**.

Breakfast and snacks

Bars and cafés – there's no difference – commonly advertise *les snacks*, or *une cassecroute* (a bite), with pictures of omelettes, fried eggs, hot dogs or various sandwiches. And even when they don't they'll usually do you a half or third of a *baguette* (French bread stick), buttered (*tartine*) or filled with cheese or meat. This, or a croissant, with hot chocolate or coffee, is generally the best way to take **breakfast** – at a fraction of the cost charged by most hotels. **Brasseries** – which do proper meals (see below) – are also possible for cups of coffee, eggs or whatever you fancy on their menu.

If you're standing at the counter, which is cheaper than sitting down, you may see a basket of croissants or some hard-boiled eggs. (They've usually gone by 9.30 or 10). Help yourself – the waiter will keep an eye on how many you've eaten and bill you accordingly.

Coffee is invariably espresso and very strong. *Un café* or *un express* is black; *un crème* is white; *un grand café* or *un grand crème* is a large cup. In the morning you could also ask for *un café au lait* – espresso in a large cup or bowl filled up with hot milk. *Un déca* is decaff, widely available.

Ordinary **tea** (*thé*) is Lipton's 9 times out of 10; to have milk with it, ask for *un peu de lait frais* (some fresh milk).

After overeating, **herb teas** (*infusions*), served in every café, can be soothing. The more common ones are *verveine* (verbena), *tilleul* (lime blossom) and *tisane* (camomile).

Chocolat chaud – hot chocolate – unlike tea, lives up to the high standards of French food and drink and can be had in any café.

Every bar or café displays the full **price list**, usually without the 15 per cent service added, for drinks at the bar (*au comptoir*), sitting down (*la salle*) and on the terrace (*la terrasse*) – all progressively more expensive. You pay when you leave and you can sit for hours over just one cup of coffee.

At **midday** you may find cafés offering a *plat du jour* (chef's daily special) between 25F and 40F or *formules*, i.e. a limited or no choice menu. *Croque*

Monsieurs or *Madames* (toasted sandwiches) are on sale at **cafés**, **brasseries** and many **street stalls**, along with *frites, crêpes, galettes* (fatter pancakes), *gauffres* (waffles), ice-cream (*glace*) and all kinds of fresh sandwiches. For variety, there are Tunisian snacks like *brik à l'oeuf* (a pastry envelope fried with an egg inside), *merguez* (spicy North African sausage), Greek *souvlaki* (kebabs), Egyptian *falafel* (deep fried chick pea balls) and Japanese titbits. **Wine bars** (see last section) are good for French regional meats and cheeses with the choice of brown bread (*pain de campagne*).

For **picnic and takeaway food**, there's nothing to beat the *charcuterie* ready-made dishes – salads, meats and fully prepared main courses – also available at supermarket *charcuterie* counters. You buy by the weight, or you can ask for *une tranche* (a slice), *une barquette* (a carton) or *une part* (a portion).

Alternatively, ***salons de thé***, which open from mid-morning to late evening, do brunches, salads, quiches, etc. as well as cakes and ice-creams and a wide selection of teas. They tend to be a good deal pricier than cafés or brasseries – you're paying for the chi-chi surroundings.

Typical snacks, fillers and takeaways include:

Un sandwich/ une baguette....	A sandwich ...
... jambon	... with ham
... jambon-buerre	... with ham and butter
... fromage	... with cheese
... saucisson	... with sausage
à l'ail/au poivre	... garlic/pepper
... pâté, terrine de campagne	... with pâté .... farmhouse
Croque-Monsieur	Toasted cheese and ham sandwich
Croque-Madame	Toasted cheese and bacon or sausage
Oeufs-au plat	Fried eggs
Oeufs à la coque	Boiled eggs
Oeufs durs	Hard-boiled eggs
Oeufs brouillés	Scrambled eggs
Omelette	Omelette ...
... nature	... plain
... aux fines herbes	... with herbs
... au fromage	... with cheese

Crêpe	Pancake
... au sucre	... with sugar
... au citron	... with lemon
... au miel	... with honey
... à la confiture	... with jam
... aux oeufs	... with eggs
... à la crème de marrons	... with chestnut purée
Carottes rapées	Salad of grated carrots
Salade de	Salad of ...
... tomates	... tomatoes
... betteraves	... beetroot
... concombres	... cucumber

Other fillings/salads:

Anchois	Anchovy
Andouillette	Tripe sausage
Boudin	Black pudding
Coeurs de palmiers	Palm hearts
Epis de maïs	Sweetcorn
Fonds d'artichauts	Artichoke hearts
Hareng	Herring
Langue	Tongue
Poulet	Chicken
Thon	Tuna fish

And some terms:

Chauffé	Heated up
Cuit	Cooked
Cru	Raw
Emballé	Wrapped up
A emporter	Takeaway
Fumé	Smoked
Salé	Salted/savoury
Sucré	Sweet

More serious business

There's no difference between **restaurants** and **brasseries** in terms of quality or price range. The distinction is that brasseries, which resemble cafés, serve quicker meals at most hours of the day, while restaurants tend to stick to the traditional meal times of 12–2 and 7–9.30/10.30. After 9 or so, restaurants often only serve *à la carte* meals – invariably more expensive than eating the set *menu fixe*. For the more upmarket places it's wise to book a table – easily done on the same day. But there are plenty of establishments that stay open till late and a few that don't shut at all, so you won't starve. When hunting, avoid places that are half empty at peak time and treat the business of sizing up different menus as an enjoyable appetiser in itself. If it's getting late, the **drugstores** are an easy option – they work like brasseries.

Prices and what you get for them are posted outside. Normally there is a choice between one or more *menus fixes*, where the number of courses has already been determined, and choice is very limited, and the *carte*. *Service compris* or *s.c.* means the service charge is included. *Service non compris*, *s.n.c.* or *service en sus* means that it isn't and you need to calculate an additional 15%. **Wine** (*vin*) or **a drink** (*boisson*) may be included, though rarely on menus under 60F. When ordering wine, ask for *un quart* (¼), *un demi-litre* (½) or *une carafe* (a litre). You'll normally be given table wine unless you specify otherwise; if you're worried ask for *vin ordinaire*.

In the French sequence of **courses**, any salad (sometimes vegetables too) comes separate from the main dish; cheese precedes dessert; and you will be offered a coffee to finish which is always extra.

At the bottom price-range, *menus fixes* revolve around standard dishes such as steak and chips (*steak frites*), chicken and chips (*poulet frites*) or various offal concoctions. Look out for the *plat du jour* which may be more appealing.

Going *à la carte* offers much greater choice and, in the better restaurants, access to the chef's specialities. You pay for it, of course, though a simple and perfectly legitimate ploy is to have just one course instead of the expected three or four. You can share dishes or just have several starters – a useful strategy for vegetarians. There's no minimum charge.

The current gourmet trend in French cooking has abandoned rich creamy sauces and bloating helpings, concentrating instead on the intrinsic flavours of foods and new combinations where the mix of the colours and textures complements the tastes. The courses are no more than a few mouthfuls, presented with oriental artistry and finely judged to leave you at the end well-fed but not weighed down. Known as *nouvelle cuisine*, this at its best can induce gastronomic ecstasy from an ungarnished leek or carrot. What it does to salmon, lobster or a wild strawberry pastry elevates taste sensation to the power of sound and vision. But alas since this magical method of cooking requires absolutely prime and fresh ingredients and precision skills in every department, *nouvelle cuisine* meals are usually horrendously expensive.

A list of foods and dishes
The **lists** below, though not comprehensive, should help to indicate what you're ordering – both at **French** and **ethnic restaurants**. Most of the latter describe their dishes in French, and standard North African main courses of *cous-cous* (steamed buckwheat with meat or veg) and *tagine* (spiced casserole) are part of French food language. At Indo-Chinese restaurants you'll recognise terms like *dim-sum*, but inevitably, given the wealth of ingredients in all the different cuisines, you'll sometimes have to rely on inspired guess-work.

Soups (*Soupes*)

Bisque	Shellfish soup
Bouillabaisse	Marseillais fish soup
Bouillon	Broth or stock
Bourride	Thick fish soup
Consommé	Clear soup
Pistou	Parmesan, basil and garlic paste sometimes added to soup
Potage	Thick soup, usually vegetable
Rouille	Red pepper, garlic and saffron mayonnaise served with fish soup
Velouté	Thick soup, usually fish or poultry

Starters (*Hors d'Oeuvres*)

Assiette anglaise	Plate of cold meats
Crudités	Raw vegetables with dressings
Hors d'oeuvres variées	Combination of the above plus smoked or marinated fish

Fish (*Poisson*), Seafood (*Fruits de mer*) and Shellfish (*Crustacés or Coquillages*)

Anchois	Anchovies
Anguilles	Eels
Araignée de mer	Spider Crab
Barbue	Brill
Brème	Bream
Cabillaud	Fresh Cod
Calamares	Squid
Carrelet	Plaice
Congre	Conger Eel
Coques	Cockles
Coquilles St-Jacques	Scallops
Crabe	Crab
Crevettes grises	Shrimps
Crevettes roses	Prawns
Daurade	Sea Bream
Ecrevisse	Freshwater Crayfish
Escargots	Snails
Friture	Assorted fried fish
Gambas	King Prawns
Grenouilles (cuisses de)	Frogs (legs)
Hareng	Herring
Homard	Lobster
Huîtres	Oysters
Langoustes	Sea Crayfish
Langoustines	Dublin Bay Prawns (what scampi comes from)
Limande	Lemon sole
Lotte	Burbot
Lotte de mer	Monkfish
Loup de mer	Sea Bass
Maquereau	Mackerel
Merlan	Whiting
Morue	Salt Cod
Moules (marinière)	Mussels (with shallots in wine sauce)
Palourdes	Clams
Praires	Small clams
Raie	Skate
Rouget	Red Mullet
Saumon	Salmon
Sole	Sole
Thon	Tuna
Truite	Trout
Turbot	Turbot

Terms:

Aïoli	Garlic mayonnaise served with salt cod and other fish
Béarnaise	Sauce made with egg yolks, white wine, shallots and vinegar
Beignets	Fritters
La douzaine	The dozen
Frit	Fried
Grillé	Grilled
Hollandaise	Butter and vinegar sauce
À la meunière	In a butter, lemon and parsley sauce

Mousse/mousseiline	Mousse
Plateau de quenelles	Plate of light dumplings
Tourte	Flan

Meat (*Viande*) and Poultry (*Volaille*)

Agneau	Lamb
Agneau de pré-salé	Lamb grazed on salt pastures
Boeuf	Beef
Bifteck	Steak
Caille	Quail
Canard	Duck
Caneton	Duckling
Cervelle	Brains
Châteaubriand	Porterhouse steak
Contrefilet	Sirloin roast
Coquelet	Young coquerel
Dinde, dindon, dindonneau	Turkeys of different ages and genders
Entrecôte	Ribsteak
Faux filet	Sirloin steak
Foie	Liver
Fraises de veau	Veal testicles
Fricadelles	Meatballs
Gigot	Leg of lamb
Gigot de . . .	Leg of another meat
Grillade	Grilled meat
Hâchis	Minced meat or Hamburger
Langue	Tongue
Lapin, lapereau	Rabbit, young rabbit
Lard, lardons	Bacon, diced bacon
Lièvre	Hare
Mouton	Mutton
Oie	Goose
Os	Bone
Porc, pieds de porc	Pork, pig trotters
Poulet	Chicken
Poulette	Young chicken
Poussin	Baby chicken
Ris	Sweetbreads
Rognons	Kidneys
Rognons blancs	Testicles
Sanglier	Wild Boar
Steack	Steak
Tortue	Turtle
Tournedos	Fillet steak
Tripes	Tripe
Veau	Veal
Tête de veau	Calf's head
Museau de veau	Bits of calf's head
Venaison	Venison
Boeuf bourguignon	Beef stew with Burgundy wine, bacon, onion and mushrooms

Canard à l'orange	Roast duck with an orange and wine sauce
Canard périgourdin	Roast duck with prunes, pâté de foie gras and truffles
Cassoulet	A casserole of beans and meat
Choucroute	Pickled cabbage with peppercorns, sausages, bacon and salami
Coq au vin	Chicken cooked till it falls of the bone in a mixture similar to *Boeuf bourguignon*
Steack au poivre (vert/rouge)	Steak in a black (green/red) peppercorn sauce
Steack tartare	Raw minced beef usually accompanied by a raw egg

Terms:

Blanquette, daube, estouffade, hochepôt, navarin and ragoût	All are kinds of stew
Aile	Wing
Blanc	Breast or white meat
Carré	Best end of neck, chops or cutlets
Côte	Chop or cutlet
Cou	Neck
Epaule	Shoulder
Médaillon	Round piece
Pavé	Thick slice
En croûte	In pastry
Farci	Stuffed
Au four	Baked
Garni	With Vegetables
Grillé	Grilled
Mijoté	Stewed
Quenelles	Light dumplings
Rôti	Roast
Sauté	Lightly cooked in butter
Tourte	Flan

For steaks

Bleu	Almost raw
Saignant	Rare
A point	Medium
Bien cuit	Well done

Très bien cuit	Utterly cooked	*Flageolet*	White beans
Brochette	Kebab	*Frisée*	A frizzy type of lettuce
Garnishes and sauces:		*Gingembre*	Ginger
Beurre blanc	Melted butter, vinegar and seasoning	*Haricots*	Beans
		Verts	French
		Rouges	Kidney
Chasseur	White wine, mushrooms and shallots	*Blancs*	White
		Beurres	Butter
		Lentilles	Lentils
Diable	Strong mustard seasoning	*Mangetout*	Snowpeas
		Marjolaine	Majoram
Forestière	With bacon and mushroom	*Menthe*	Mint
		Moutarde	Mustard
Fricassée	Rich, creamy sauce	*Nouilles*	Noodles
Mornay	Cheese sauce	*Oignon*	Onion
Piquante	Gherkins or capers, vinegar and shallots	*Oseille*	Sorrel
		Pâte	Pasta
		Persil	Parsley
Provençale	Tomatoes, garlic, olive oil and herbs	*Petits pois*	Peas
		Pignons	Pine nuts
Véronique	Grapes, wine and cream	*Pissenlits*	Dandelion leaves
		Poireaux	Leeks
		Poivrons	Sweet peppers
		Pommes (de terre)	Potatoes
Vegetables (*Légumes*), Herbs (*Herbes*) and Side dishes: Spices (*Epices*), etc.		*Radis*	Radishes
		Riz	Rice
Ail	Garlic	*Romarin*	Rosemary
Aneth	Dill	*Safran*	Saffron
Anis	Aniseed	*Salade verte*	Lettuce salad
Artichaut	Artichoke	*Tomates*	Tomatoes
Asperges	Asparagus	*Truffes*	Truffles (underground fungi)
Aubergine	Aubergine, eggplant		
Avocat	Avocado pear	**Some dishes**	
Basilic	Basil (almost always fresh)	*Gratin dauphinois*	Potatoes baked in cream and garlic
Betterave	Beetroot	*Pommes Château/ fondantes*	Quartered potatoes fried in butter
Cannelle	Cinnamon		
Carottes	Carrots	*Pommes lyonnaise*	Fried onions and potatoes
Céleri-rave	Celeriac		
Céleri	Celery	*Ratatouille*	Mixture of aubergines, courgettes, tomatoes, garlic
Champignons	Mushrooms		
Types include: *de bois, de Paris, cèpes, chanterelles, girolles, grisets, mousserons*			
Chou (rouge)	(Red) cabbage	*Rémoulade*	A mustard mayonnaise
Choufleur	Cauliflower	*Salade niçoise*	Salad of tomatoes, radishes, cucumber, hard-boiled eggs, anchovies, onion, artichokes, green peppers, beans, basil and garlic (but rarely as generous, even in Nice).
Ciboulettes	Chives		
Citrouille	Pumpkin		
Concombre	Cucumber		
Courgettes	Courgettes, baby marrows		
Cresson	Water cress		
Echalotes	Shallots		
Endive	Chicory		
Epinards	Spinach		
Epis de maïs	Sweet corn	**Terms:**	
Estragon	Tarragon	*à l'anglaise*	Boiled
Fenouil	Fennel	*Farci*	Stuffed
Fèves	Broad beans		

Gratiné	Browned on top with cheese or butter
Jardinière	With a mixture of diced vegetables
Parisienne	With leeks and potatoes
Parmentier	With potatoes
Primeurs	Early vegetables
Sauté	Lightly fried in butter
Tourte	Flan
à la vapeur	steamed

Je suis végétarien(ne). Il y a quelques plats sans viande? – I'm a vegetarian. Are there some non-meat dishes?

Fruits (Fruits)

Abricots	Apricots
Amandes	Almonds
Ananas	Pineapple
Banane	Banana
Brugnon, nectarine	Nectarine
Cantaloup	Round, green melon, orange inside
Cassis	Blackcurrant
Cérises	Cherries
Citron	Lemon
Citron vert	Lime
Dattes	Dates
Figues	Figs
Fraises	Strawberries
Fraises de bois	Wild strawberries
Framboises	Raspberries
Fruit de la Passion	Passion fruit
Grenade	Pomegranite
Groseilles	Red currants and gooseberries
Marrons	Chestnuts
Melon	Melon
Mirabelles	Greengages
Myrtilles	Bilberries
Noix	Nuts
Oranges	Oranges
Pamplemousse	Grapefruit
Pastèque	Water melon
Pêche (blanche)	(White) peach
Poire	Pear
Pomme	Apple
Prune	Plum
Pruneau	Prune
Raisins	Grapes
Rhubarbe	Rhubarb

Terms:

Beignets	Fritters
Compôte	Stewed

Corbeille de fruits	Fruit basket
Coulis	Sauce
Flambé	Set alight in alcohol
Frappé	Iced
Sorbet	Water ice

Desserts (Desserts or Entremets) and Pastries (Pâtisserie)

Bombe	An ice cream dessert made in a round or conical mould
Bonbons	Sweets
Brioche	Sweet, high yeast bread
Clafoutis	Fruit flan, usually with berries
Crème Chantilly	Vanilla flavoured and sweetened whipped cream
Crème fraîche	Soured cream
Crème pâtissière	Thick cream made with eggs
Crêpes suzettes	Pancakes with orange juice and liqeur
Fromage blanc	Cream cheese more akin to strained yoghurt
Glace	Ice cream
Ile flottante	Soft meringues floating on custard
Oeufs à la neige	
Macarons	Macaroons, not necessarily almond
Madeleine	Small sponge cake
Marrons Mont Blanc	Chestnut purée and cream on a rum soaked sponge cake
Palmiers	Caramelised puff pastries
Parfait	Frozen mousse, sometimes just ice cream
Paris-Brest	Pastry cakes filled with crème pâtissière
Pêche Melba	Cooked peaches, vanilla ice cream and a raspberry sauce
Petit Suisse	A smooth mixture of cream and curds
Petits fours	Mouth-sized cakes or pastries
Poires Belle Hélène	Pears and ice cream in chocolate sauce

Religieuse	Coffee or chocolate coated choux pastry puffs, supposedly in the shape of a nun	Knife	*Couteau*
		Spoon	*Cuillère*
		Table	*Table*
		Bill	*L'addition*
Yaourt	Yoghurt		

and many, many more. . . .

Terms:

Barquette	Small boat shaped flan
Bavarois	Refers to the mould, could be a mousse or custard cream
Biscuit	A kind of cake
Chausson	Pastry turnover
Coupe	A serving of ice cream
Crêpes	Pancakes
Galettes	Biscuits or pancakes
Gênoise	Rich sponge cake
Quatre quarts	Type of sponge cake
Sablé	Sort of biscuit
Savarin	In a ring-shaped mould
Tarte	Flan
Tartelette	Small flan
Truffes	Truffles, the chocolate or liqueur variety

Cheese (*Fromage*)

There are over 350 types of **French cheese**, most of them named after their place of origin. *Chèvre* is goat's cheese. *Le plateau de fromages* is the cheeseboard and bread, but not butter, is served with it.

Some useful phrases: *une petite tranche de celui-ci* (a small piece of this one); *je peux le gouter?* (may I taste it?).

Basics

Bread	*Pain*
Butter	*Beurre*
Eggs	*Oeufs*
Milk	*Lait*
Oil	*Huile*
Pepper	*Poivre*
Salt	*Sel*
Sugar	*Sucre*
Vinegar	*Vinaigre*
Bottle	*Bouteille*
Glass	*Verre*
Fork	*Fourchette*

And one final note: always call the waiter or waitress *Monsieur* or *Madame* (*Mademoiselle*, if a girl).

Drinking Where you can eat you can invariably drink and vice versa. **Drinking** is done at a leisurely pace whether it's a prelude to food (*apéritif*), a sequel (*digestif*) or the accompaniment, and **cafés** are the standard venue.

Wine – *vin* – is the standard accompaniment to every meal and all social occasions. Red is *rouge*, white *blanc*, or there's *rosé. Vin de table* – plonk – is generally drinkable and always cheap.

A.C. (Appellation d'Origine Contrôlée) wines are another matter. They can be excellent value at the lower end of the price scale, where favourable French taxes keep prices down to £1 or so a bottle, but move much above this and you're fast paying serious prices for serious bottles.

Restaurant mark-ups of *A.C.* wines can be outrageous. **Popular** *A.C.* **wines** which you find on most restaurant lists include *Côtes du Rhône* (from the Rhône valley), *St-Emilion* and *Médoc* (from Bordeaux), *Beaujolais* and well upmarket Burgundy.

The **basic terms** are *brut*, very dry; *sec*, dry; *demi-sec*, sweet; *doux*, very sweet; *mousseux*, sparkling; *méthode champenoise*, mature and sparkling. There are grape types as well but the complexities of the subject take up volumes.

A **glass of wine** is simply *un rouge* or *un blanc*. If it is an *AC* wine you may have the choice of *un ballon* (a round glass) or a smaller glass (*un verre*). *Un pichet* (a jug) is normally a ¼ litre. **Buying wine** you'll do best at supermarkets unless you want something very special. **Wine bars** offer the patron's personal selection of favourites. Short of doing a tour of the country's vineyards, these are the places to discover new likes or dislikes.

Beer – *bière* – in cafés is never anything but lager with most of the familiar Belgian and German names available plus home-grown from Alsace. Draught (*à la pression*, usually Kronenbourg) is the cheapest drink you can have after coffee and wine – ask for *un* *demi* (¹/₃ litre). For a wider choice of draughts and bottles you need to go to the special beer-drinking establishments, or English-style pubs.

Cocktails are served at most late-night bars, discos and music places, as well as at upmarket hotel bars.

Strong alcohols are drunk from 5am as pre-work fortifiers, right through the day, though the national reputation for drunkenness has lost some of its truth. **Cognac** or **Armagnac** brandies and the dozens of *eaux de vie* (spirits) and **liqueurs** are distilled with the same perfectionism as in the cultivation of vines. Among less familiar names, try *Poire William* (pear liqueur), *marc* (distilled grape debris) or just point to the bottle with the most attractive colour. Measures are generous, but they don't come cheap: the same applies for imported spirits like whisky, always

called *Scotch*. **Pastis**, aniseed drinks such as *Pernod* or *Ricard*, are served diluted with water and ice (*glaçons*) – very refreshing and not expensive. Two drinks designed to stimulate the appetite are *Pineau*, cognac and grape juice, and *Kir*, blackcurrant juice and white wine – or champagne for a *Kir Royal*.

On the **soft drink** front, bottled fruit juices include apricot (*jus d'abricot*), blackcurrant (*cassis*) and so on. You can also get fresh orange and lemon juice (*orange/citron pressé*), otherwise it's the standard fizzy cans, coke (*coca*) and so forth. Bottles of **spring water** (*eau de source*) and **mineral water** (*eau minérale*) – either sparkling (*pétillante*) or still (*eau plate*) – abound, from the best-seller *Perrier* to the obscurest spa product. But there's not much wrong with the tap water, (*l'eau du robinet*).

COMMUNICATIONS – POST, PHONES AND MEDIA

The **main post office** at 52 rue du Louvre, 1er, is the best place to have your letters sent, unless you have a particular branch office already in mind. It's open 24 hours for *Poste Restante* and telephones. Letters should be addressed (preferably with the surname underlined and in capitals):

Poste Restante, 52 rue du Louvre, 75001 Paris.

To collect mail you'll need a passport or other convincing ID, and there'll be a small charge. You should ask for all your names to be checked – filing systems are not brilliant. **American Express** (11 rue Scribe, 9e; Mon-Fri 9–5.30) also provide a *poste restante* facility.

Other **post offices** (*PTT* or *bureau de poste*) are open every day except Sunday from 8–7. For sending letters, you can also buy **stamps** (*timbres*) from *tabacs*.

Local **phone calls** can be made either from a *bureau de poste* or from a *cabine*, if you can find one that works or hasn't been converted for phone cards. At cafés you may need *jetons* rather than coins and may also be obliged to consume something. A 70F **phone card**, obtainable from post offices and *PTT* boutiques, can be convenient if you're likely to make a lot of calls.

You can make **international calls** from any *cabine*, and receive them as

well, if there's a blue logo of a ringing bell. Put the money in first (1F, 5F and, occasionally, 10F pieces), dial 19, wait for a deepish tone, then dial the country code (44 for Britain) and the number minus its initial 0. To avoid fiddling about with piles of coins, it is easier to call from a post office, where you can pay afterwards. For calls within France but **outside Paris**, dial 16, then the 8-digit number, which now includes the old area code.

British newspapers and the *International Herald Tribune* are widely available at central Paris newsstands. Of the **French daily papers**, *Le Monde* is the most intellectual and respected, with no concessions to entertainment (such as pictures), but a correctly-styled French that is probably the easiest to understand. *Libération* (*Libé* for short) is moderately leftwing, independent and more colloquial with good, if choosy, coverage. *L'Humanité* is the Communist party newspaper. With the exception of *Le Matin*, all the other nationals are firmly on the right.

There are no local Paris papers. For extensive **What's On listings** consult *Pariscope*, *L'Officiel des Spectacles* or *7 Jours à Paris* – in French, – though none of them has crits or features of any consequence. For a fuller account of the cultural scene, there's the English-language *Passion Magazine*.

Weeklies on the Newsweek/Time model include the wide-ranging, left-leaning *Le Nouvel Observateur* and its counter-point, *L'Express*. The best investigative journalism is in the weekly satirical paper *Le Canard Enchaîné*, unfortunately unintelligible to non-native speakers. And the foulest rag of the lot is *Minute*, the *Front National's* organ.

'Moral' censorship of the press is rare.

As well as pornography of every shade, you'll find on the newsstands covers featuring drugs, sex, blasphemy and bizarre forms of grossness alongside knitting patterns and DIY. French **comics**, which often indulge these interests, are wonderful. *Charlie-Hebdo* is one with political targets; and *A Suivre*, which wouldn't cause problems at British Customs, has amazing graphic talents.

OPENING HOURS AND HOLIDAYS

Most shops, businesses, information services, museums, and banks in Paris stay open all day. The exceptions are the smaller shops and enterprises. Basic **hours of business** are from 8 or 9 to 6.30 or 7.30. Sunday and Monday are standard **closing days**, though you can always find *boulangeries* and food shops which stay open.

Museums open around 10 and close between 5 and 6. Where summer times differ from winter, we've indicated the summer ones first, thus: 9/10–6/5. Summer hours usually extend from mid-May or June to mid-September. Sometimes they apply only in July and August, occasionally from Palm Sunday to All Saints. Don't forget closing days – again usually Tuesday or Monday, sometimes both. **Admission charges** can be very off-putting – though most state-owned museums have one or two days of the week when they're free, and you can get a big reduction at most places by showing a student card (or passport if

you're under 18/over 60). **Churches and cathedrals** are almost always open all day, with charges only for the crypt, treasures or cloisters, and little fuss about how you're dressed.

One other factor can disrupt your plans. There are thirteen national **holidays** (*jours fériés*), when most shops and businesses, though not museums or restaurants, are closed. They are:

1 January
Easter Sunday
Easter Monday
Ascension Day (forty days after Easter)
Pentecost (7th Sunday after Easter, plus the Monday)
1 May
8 May (VE day)
14 July (Bastille Day)
15 August (Assumption of the Virgin Mary)
1 November (All Saints)
11 November (1918 Armistice Day)
Christmas Day.

FESTIVALS AND EVENTS

With all that's going on in Paris, **festivals** – in the **traditional 'popular'** sense – are no big deal. But there are an impressive array of **arts events**, with an exciting bi-annual climax in the *Biennale* (due next in late 1987), and, not to be missed for the **politically** interested, an inspired internationalist jamboree at the *Fête de l'Humanité*.

Popular festivals/fêtes

Fête de l'Humanité (Autumn, usually September)
Sponsored by the French Communist Party, this annual event just north of Paris at La Courneuve attracts people in their

thousands and of every political persuasion. In terms of countries represented it must be one of the largest international fairs in the world with almost every CP represented. Their stalls, bands, food and literature whether on the well-funded scale of the socialist countries or the shoestring exile efforts create an amazing sensual atmosphere of colours that go with red, of the smell and taste of a hundred different cuisines, and the sound of as many languages. Though there are sessions of speeches, this fête is a celebration rather than a party platform while illustrating with justice the internationalism of communism which no other left-wing party can rival.

Bastille Day (14 July)
The 1789 surrender of the Bastille is celebrated with official pomp in parades of tanks down the Champs-Elysées, firework displays and concerts, but fails to enthuse most of the city's population. It takes something like Mitterand's election to get the people dancing in the streets and an event like that may not happen for a very long time.

Summer Solstice (June 21)
Midsummer's day (June 21) usually sees parades, including the Gay Pride march, street theatre and amusements, even live bands throughout the city. But the present administration disapproves of people milling about on public roads and has already banned one solstice street party.

Mardi Gras (Week before Lent)
The Mardi Gras are avidly celebrated in the south of France but go almost unnoticed in Paris. A few kids, however, take the opportunity to cover unwary passers-by with flour.

Arts festivals

March	**International Festival of Women's Films** (see p.200)
May	**Soirées de St-Aignan** (see p.196)
May/June	**Festival de Musique Ancienne** (see p.196)
June	**Festival du Marais** (see p.204)
	Fête des Photographes
June/July	**Festival 'Foire Saint-Germain'** (see p.204)
June-Aug	**Festival de l'Orangerie de Sceaux** (see p.196)
July	**Rencontre Musique et Jazz des Années 80** (see p.193)
Sept-Dec	**Festival d'Automne** (see p.204)
Oct/Nov	**Festival International de Danse de Paris** (see p.204)
	Festival de Jazz (see p.193)
Every 2 years	**Biennale de Paris**

WORK AND STUDY

The chances of finding **temporary** or **permanent work** in Paris are not good, though EEC citizens now have no problems getting work permits and (if paper work is done in advance; see below) can sign on for up to three months' **unemployment benefit**. Best chances for a permanent post – unless you have some special skill – remain the old standards of teaching English in a language school or living with a family as an au pair. For temporary work, there's no substitute for checking the papers, pounding the streets and keeping an eye on the noticeboards at the British and, especially, American churches.

Much the simplest way of getting a job in a **language school** is to apply from Britain. Check the ads in the *Guardian's* 'Educational Extra' (every Tuesday normally) or in the weekly *Times Educational Supplement* – late summer is usually the most fruitful time. You don't need fluent French to get a post but a *TEFL* (Teaching English as a Foreign Language) qualification is a distinct advantage.

If you apply from home most schools will fix up the necessary papers for you. EEC nationals don't need a work permit, but getting a *carte de séjour* and social security (see p.6) can still be tricky when employers refuse to help. It is – remotely – possible to find a teaching job when you're **already** in **Paris**, though you may have to accept semi-official status and no job security. For the addresses of schools look under *Ecoles de Langues* in the *Professions* directory of the city phone book. Offering **private lessons** (via university noticeboards, small ads) is a swamped market, and it's hard to reach the people who can afford it, but always worth a try.

Although working as an **au pair** is easily fixed up through any number of agencies (lists available from the French Embassy), this sort of work can be a bit desperate even if you're using it to learn the language. Conditions, pay and treatment by your employers is likely to be little short of slavery. If you give it a go, best apply once in Paris, where you can at least meet the family first and check things out.

To **sign on for benefit** in France you

must collect form E303 before leaving home, available in Britain from any DHSS office. The procedure is first to get registered at an *ANPE* office (*Agences Nationales pour l'Emploi*); You then take the form to the local *ASSEDIC* (benefits office) and give them an address which can be a hostel or hotel for the money to be sent. You sign on once a month at the *ANPE* and receive dole a month in arrears up to three months when officially you must leave the country or get a *carte de séjour* (see p.6)

Studying in Paris

It's relatively easy to be a student in France. Foreigners pay no more than French nationals (around 550F a year) **to enrol** for a course and the only problem is supporting yourself through. Your *carte de séjour* and – within the EEC – social security will be assured and you'll be eligible for subsidised lodgings, meals and all the student reductions. Few people want to do first degrees abroad, but for higher degrees or other diplomas, the range of options is enormous. Strict entry requirements including an exam in French only apply for first degrees. Generally, French universities are much less formal than British ones and many people perfect the language while studying. For full **details and prospectuses** go to the Cultural Service of any French Embassy: (see p.11 for addresses).

Language courses are on offer at the *Alliance Française* (101 bd Raspail, 6e) and a number of other establishments, listed in *Cours de Français pour Etudiants Etrangers*, also obtainable from embassy cultural sections.

FEMINISM

The ***Ministère des Droits des Femmes*** (Ministry of Women's Rights), created by the last Socialist government in 1981, has been changed, under Chirac and the Gaullists, to the *Ministère des Droits des Hommes* (Ministry of the Rights of Man). The irony has gone unremarked by government circles and the public in general.

The women's ministry under Yvette Roudy spent the five years in power getting long overdue equal pay and opportunity measures through parliament. Some funding was given to women's groups but the main emphasis was on legislation, including the significant advance of social security payments for abortion. A law against degrading, discriminatory and violence-inciting images of women was thrown out of the National Assembly in a male establishment storm of outrage and hysteria.

Meanwhile the **MFL** (*Mouvement de Libération des Femmes* – Women's Liberation Movement) was declared dead and buried in 1982. There were no more Women's Day marches, no major demonstrations, no direct action. Feminist bookshops and cafés started closing (*Carabosses* in the 11e amongst them), publications reached their last number and polls showed that girls leaving school were only interested in husbands and babies. But despite the low public profile, women were and are still at work – running battered women's homes and rape crisis centres, campaigning in their unions or political parties, gathering information in the first women's news agency, writing, making films, and, as ever, theorising along divergent lines. The movement is fragmented but not in pieces.

As the socialist policies ran out of steam, cuts in public spending and traditional ideas about the male bread-winner, sent more and more women back to their homes and hungry husbands. Now with the new right-wing government, women have lost their ministry and are threatened with losing most of their hard-won rights. The restrictions on abortion are far tighter anyway than in Britain but the prime minister, Jacques Chirac, has consistently spoken of 'redressing the natality balance' in a blatantly racist context. What happens to the abortion and family allowance laws will depend on the balance of forces in parliament where the National Front can easily influence the majority.

Though for the moment, fund-raising is the immediate task in hand for all women's groups, the measures taken by the right-wing government are inspiring new alliances, particularly with the anti-racist movement. There may well be a new era of activity and protest in which coalition and a broader base will take priority over the sectarian divisions and

Paris dominance that have riddled the movement for nearly two decades.

Contacts and information

Maison des Femmes 8 Cité Prost, 11e 43.48.24.91; M° Faidherbe-Chaligny (off rue Chanzy); Mon-Fri 2–8. A meeting place for different organisations including: **MIEL** (Mouvement d'Information et d'Expression des Lesbiennes) – Mon 7pm; les **Nanas Radioteuses** who produce radio programmes on 101.6 Mhz, Wed 6pm–midnight; **les Filministes** who run a film club; and **Paris-Féministes** who run the centre, produce a fortnightly bulletin and organise a wide range of events and actions. Anti-racist groups, North African women's groups, rape crisis and battered women's organisations also meet at the Maison. This is by far the best place to come if you want to make contact with the movement. Don't be put off by the back alley entrance and though English speakers can't be guaranteed, you can count on a friendly reception. There's a cafeteria run by MIEL (Fri & Sat 6 – midnight), occasional open days with exhibitions and concerts or disco's, workshops and self-defence classes, discussions and film shows.

Centre Audio-Visuel Simone de Beauvoir 7 rue Francis de Pressensé, 14e 45.42.21.43; M° Pernety. Wed, Fri & Sat 3–7. An archive of audio-visual works by or about women financed by de Beauvoir in her lifetime and maintained by her bequest. A small fee allows you access to this comprehensive and compelling collection.

Agence Femmes Information 21 rue des Jeûneurs, 2e 42.33.37.47; M° Sentier. Mon-Fri 10–6.30. A women's news agency producing a weekly bulletin as well as providing the local and national press with stories. Their library of cuttings and women's publications is open for consultation for around 35F (reductions for unemployed and students).

Elles Tournent La Page 8 impasse des Trois Soeurs, 11e; 48.06.72.86; M° Voltaire. Mon-Fri 2–6.

A library along with dance, fitness and writing workshops and a weekly kids' atelier, all in a casual and ramshackle building on a southern style courtyard. Some facilities are mixed.

Bibliothèque Marguerite Durand Mairie du 5e, 21 place du Panthéon; 43.26.85.05; M° Cardinal Lemoine. Mon-Fri 2–6. A library covering all written works to do with women.

Publications

There's no equivalent to Spare Rib or Outwrite. Instead every group, just about, produces its own paper or review, some which come out at random intervals held together by staples, others regular and well printed. Of the latter, **Choisir** is published by a reform-based group of the same name that puts up independent candidates at elections (and won a député in 1981). **Cahiers du Féminisme** belongs to the Revolutionary Communist League. **Les Cahiers du Grif**, more a book than a mag, expresses wider, and ultimately more socialist, concerns than most of the feminist press, a product of non-aligned women with a long history in the movement. Communist Party women edited **Elles voient rouge** while women in the Socialist Party expressed themselves in **Mignonnes, allons voir sous la rose**. Both publications are still going though most of the contributors have left their original parties. **Paris Féministes** (see Maison des Femmes above) carries a good cross-section of left-wing feminist debate with a strong emphasis on anti-sexist/anti-racist links.

Courses and workshops

La Mutinerie 19 rue Frédéric-Lemaître, 20e; 43.66.88.52; M° Jourdain. 12.30 & every day. A place for **lesbians** to eat, read and exercise.

Saphonie c/o Elles Tournent La Page (see above). Painting, writing, dance, photography and other workshops for **lesbians**.

Sos

The addresses below are primarily **refuges** for battered women but since there's no centralised rape crisis organisation, they try to help all victims of male violence. English speakers are rare, so they may not be of much use but if things do get bad you will at least get sympathy and an all-women environment whereas going to the police is likely to be as traumatic as the assault (and be as difficult language-wise). The British Embassy (42.66.91.42) has been known to be helpful in rape cases.

Centre Flora Tristan (Femmes Battues) *7 rue de Landy, Clichy; 47.31.51.69; Bus 54 or 74.*
SOS Femmes Alternatives *54 av de Choisy, 13e; 45.85.11.37; Mo Porte de Choisy.*
Halte-Aide aux Femmes Battues *14 rue Mendelssohn, 20e; 43.48.20.40; Mo Porte Montreuil.*

Bookshops, cafés clubs
Feminist, lesbian or sympathetic commercial enterprises are listed in the relevant chapters: **bookshops** p.144; **cafés** p.163; **clubs** p.192.

LESBIAN AND GAY PARIS

Paris is very much the San Francisco of Europe for **gay men**. New bars, clubs, restaurants, saunas and shops open all the time and in Les Halles and the Marais every other address is gay. For a long time the emphasis has been on providing the requisites for a hedonistic life style rather than political campaigning. The Socialist government made an effort to show its recognition of homosexual rights, but with the legal age of consent set at 15, and discrimination and harassment non-routine, protest was not a high priority.

Matters have changed, here as elsewhere, since the outbreak of AIDS (*SIDA* in French). The resulting homophobia has not been as extreme as in Britain or America but has nevertheless increased the suffering in the group statistically most at risk. The Pasteur Institute in Paris is at the forefront of research into the virus and though gay patients have complained of being treated like cattle there, lives have been saved or extended. A group of gay doctors and the association *AIDES* (see *SOS* below) have been providing sympathetic counselling and treatment, and the gay press has done a great deal in disseminating the facts about AIDS, encouraging the use of sheaths, and providing hope and encouragement.

The new government has, inevitably, been less amenable to the gay community. The annual gay ball, usually held on July 14th but recently switched to the summer solstice, has had to contend with banning orders from the *Préfecture*, and the gay film festival (*Ecrans Gais*) was made illegal for under 18's by the Minister of Culture even though only one film had an X certificate. The movement itself is splitting into factions with the oldguard CUARH (*Comité d'Urgence Anti-Répression Homosexuelle*) being contested by the

more militant GPL (*Gais pour les Libertés*) on the left, and MGL (*Mouvement des Gais Libéraux*) on the right.

For **lesbians**, politics have always been a prime concern with separatists often more active than their straight sisters in the women's movement. But too many lesbians have never come out and many of the places run by them don't always publicise the fact for fear of reprisal. On the whole, lesbian organisations fight alongside gays on the general issue of anti-homosexuality while campaigning separately on the far more numerous and varied repressions women are subject to.

Contacts and information
CUARH *1 rue Keller, 11e; 48.06.09.39; Mo Bastille.* The national campaigning group provides a meeting place for various groups including the Paris section, COPARH, CHOP, the western Paris section, and AHLP (*Association des Homosexuels et des Lesbiennes pour la Paix*), a peace group. The centre is open every afternoon, is **mixed** and organises social and other events.
MIEL *c/o Maison des Femmes – see p.36*
Fréquence Gaie *97.2 FM; 24 hours* Gay and lesbian **radio station** with music, news, chats, information on groups and events, etc.
L'Escargot *40 rue Amelot, 11e; Mo St-Sébastien' ring to enter, 1st floor of courtyard staircase.* **Mixed** meeting-place for various groups and open to individuals to drop in.

Publications
The best mixed bookshop is *Les Mots à la Bouche* in the Marais (see p.144 for this and other gay and lesbian bookshops). You'll find here the annual ***Gai Pied Guide*** which is the most compre-

hensive guide to France for gays and includes lesbian sections. The same team produces a very good weekly – **Gai Pied Hebdo** (predominantly male) which is useful for current culture and events. The shop stocks most of the **international gay press** and the English gay guide to the city – **Weaver's Gay Paris**.

Masques has a high reputation as an arty, culture magazine, and comes out every three months. It's written by both male and female homosexuals. The main **lesbian monthly magazine** is **Lesbia**, on sale at most newsagents and unattached to the women's movement. For the diverse **feminist lesbian press** browse through the shelves of the feminist bookshops (see p.144) or pay a

visit to **Archives Recherches et Cultures Lesbiennes** at 48 rue Sedaine, 11e; Mo Voltaire (Wed 4–8 & Fri 6–10).

Sos
SOS Gais Men: 42.61.00.00, Wed & Fri 6–midnight; women: 42.26.61.07, Sat 3–7. Gay switchboard equivalent.
Association des Médecins Gais 45, rue Sedaine, 11e; 48.05.81.71; Mo Voltaire. Wed 6–8 & Sat 2–6.
AIDES 42.72.19.99; 7–11 daily.

Bookshops, cafés, clubs
Gay, lesbian or sympathetic commercial enterprises are listed in the relevant chapters: **bookshops** p.144; **cafés** p.163; **clubs** p.192.

SEXUAL AND RACIAL HARASSMENT

You're bound to come across **sexual harassment** in this city in which everyone makes a habit of looking you up and down, and more often than not, making comments. Generally it is no worse or more vicious than in the UK, but the problems are in judging men without the familiar linguistic and cultural signs. If your French isn't great, how do you tell if he's gabbling at you because you left your purse behind in a shop, or he's inciting you to swear at him in English and be cuffed round the head for the insult? The answer is you can't but there are some pointers. A '*Bonjour*' or '*Bonsoir*' on the street is the standard pick-up opener. If you so much as return the greeting, you've let yourself in for a stream of tenacious chat and a hard shaking-off task. On the other hand, it's not unusal if you're on your own to be offered a drink in a bar and not to be pestered even if you accept. This is rarer in Paris than elsewhere in the country but don't assume that any contact by a Frenchman is a trap.

Last metrós are nowhere near as

unnerving as they are in London, simply because of greater passenger numbers. And unlike London or New York people are more inclined to intervene when nasty scenes develop. Hitch-hiking out of Paris is a risk – as it is anywhere – and few French women do it. If you need help, go to one of the women's organisations (p.37) or to your embassy (p.39) rather than the police.

You may, as a woman, be warned against '*Les Arabes*'. This is simply **French racism**. If you are Arab or look as if you might be, your chances of avoiding unpleasantness are very low. Hotels claiming to be booked up, police demanding your papers and abusive treatment from ordinary people is horribly commonplace. In addition, being black, of whatever ethnic origin, can make entering the country difficult. Recent changes in passport regulations have put an end to outright refusal to let some British holiday-makers in, but customs and immigration officers can still, like their cross-Channel counterparts, be obstructive and malicious.

POLICE AND THIEVES

French police (popularly, *les flics*) are barely polite at the best of times and can be extremely unpleasant if you get on the wrong side of them. In Paris the **city police** have an ugly history of lethal cock-ups, including sporadic shootings

of innocent people, and of savage brutality against suspects – often just ordinary teenagers – taken in for identity checks. Now that law and order issues are in the hands of Chirac's heavies – Minister of Interior Pasqua and friends (see p.240) – there is nothing to restrain them. The old requirement for everyone to carry **identity papers** is being rigorously enforced again – part of the vote-catching campaign to hit out at illegal immigrants, non-conforming youth, the unemployed, homeless and other such alarming threats to middle-class tranquillity – and you can be stopped in the street and required to produce an ID at any time. In fact, this is now the most likely reason for foreigners or tourists having anything to do with the police. If you are stopped, don't be difficult or facetious. Plenty of heads have been broken already.

The other stalwart body of armed and uniformed men you'll see about the streets are the paramilitary *CRS* (*Compagnies Républicaines de Sécurité*). Their job is guarding embassies and other sensitive spots around town, as much from the citizens of Paris as from any outside terrorist threat. They look only too willing to assault anything that moves. It was their tender mercies which turned public opinion to the side of the students during the events of May 1968.

If you need to **report a theft** in order to claim insurance, the police are the people to go to, though there is no guarantee they'll give you the requisite bit of paper. If in need of **general assistance**, ordinary people are at least as likely to help as the police, and if you need someone in authority, best to go to one of the *mairies* (*arrondissement* town-halls) or the Hôtel de Ville. In difficult circumstances, where the police are the only option, it's best to go with someone else, preferably French.

Petty theft is pretty common in crowded hang-outs like Les Halles, so take normal precautions: don't be too flash with money, take out travel insurance, and you've little to worry about. If you should get attacked, hand over the money and start writing to your insurance company. **Drivers** face greater problems, most notoriously from break-ins. Vehicles are rarely stolen, but cassette players as well as luggage left in cars make a tempting target and foreign number plates are easy to spot. Again, good insurance is the only answer, but try not to leave any valuables in the car even so. If you have an accident while driving, you are officially supposed to fill in and sign a *constat à l'aimable* which car insurers are supposed to give you with a policy; in practice, though, few seem to have heard of it.

For non-criminal **driving offences**, speeding etc., the police can impose an on-the-spot fine and be very unpleasant if you don't have immediate means of payment. Should you be arrested on any charge, you have the right to contact your Consulate (see below). Although they're often reluctant to get involved, their duty is to assist you – likewise in the case of losing your passport or all your money.

Anyone caught bringing into the country or possessing any **drugs,** even a few grammes of marijuana, is liable to find themselves in jail and embassies will not be sympathetic. Which is not to say that hard drug-taking isn't a visible activity: there are scores of Parisian kids dealing in *poudre* (heroin) and the authorities are unable to do anything. As for dope, people are no more nor less paranoid about busts than they are in the UK.

OTHER THINGS

ALARM Phone 3688 for a morning call to wake you.

CONSULATES/EMBASSIES American – 2 av Gabriel, 8e (42.96.12.02; Mo Concorde); **Australian** – 4 rue Jean-Rey, 15e (45.75.62.00; Mo Bir-Hakeim); **British** – 109 rue du Faubourg St-Honoré, 1er (42.96.87.19; Mo Pyramides); **Dutch** – 7–9 rue Eblé, 7e (43.06.61.88; Mo St-François-Xavier); **Irish** – 12 av Foch, 16e (45.00.20.87; Mo Etoile); **New Zealand** – 7 rue Léonard-de-Vinci, 16e (45.00.24.11; Mo Victor-Hugo) **Swedish**

– 17 rue Barbet-de-Jouy, 7e (45.55.92.15; Mo Varenne).

CONTRACEPTIVES Condoms (*préservatifs*) have always been available at *pharmacies*, though contraception was only legalised in 1967. You can also get spermicidal cream and jelly (*dose contraceptive*), plus the suppositories (*ovules, suppositoires*) and – with a prescription – the pill (*la pillule*), a diaphragm or IUD (*le sterilet*).

CUSTOMS If you bring in more than 5,000F worth of foreign cash, you need to sign a declaration at customs. There are also restrictions on taking francs out of the country, but the amounts are beyond the concern of most people.

DISABLED TRAVELLERS Paris has no special reputation for ease of access and facilities, but at least information is available. The tourist office has a free booklet, *Touristes Quand Même*, covering accommodation, transport and accessibility of public places as well as particular aids such as buzzer signals on pedestrian crossings. The *ATH* hotel reservation service service in Paris (48.74.88.51) has details of wheelchair access for 3 and 4 star hotels. Crossing the Channel, *Townsend Thoresen* allow registered disabled to take cars free of charge. The *Access Guide* to Paris is available from the Pauline Hephaistos Survey Project, 39 Bradley Gdns, London W13.

ELECTRICITY is 220V and most plugs are two round pins; in out-of-the-way rural districts you may still find 110V.

LAUNDRETTES Self-service places have multiplied in Paris over the last few years and you'll probably find one close by where you're staying. Central locations include: 24 place Marché-St-Honoré, 1er; 1 rue de la Montaigne-Ste-Geneviève, 5e; 91 rue de Seine, 6e; 108 rue du Bac, 7e; 5 rue de la Tour-d'Auvergne, 9e; and 96 rue de la Roquette, 11e.

LEFT LUGGAGE Lockers and longer term *consigne* at all the stations.

LIBRARIES Foreign Cultural Institutes (Britain: 9 rue de Constantine, 7e; US: 10 rue du Général Camou, 7e) have free access libraries, with newspapers, etc. Interesting Parisian collections include the *BPI* at Beaubourg (vast – and with all the foreign press, too), *Forney* (books

being a good excuse if you want to visit the medieval bishop's palace at 1 rue du Figuier in the 4e), and the *Historique de la Ville de Paris*, a 16C mansion housing centuries of texts and picture books on the city (24 rue Pavée, 4e).

LOST PROPERTY 36 rue des Morillons, 5e (Mo Convention); 45.31.14.80; 8.30–5/8 Mon & Tues, cl. w/e).

TALKING CLOCK Phone 3699 for the time of day.

TAMPONS are available from all *pharmacies* but they are much cheaper in supermarkets.

TELEGRAMS by phone. Internal – 3655; English language – 42.33.21.11; other languages – 42.33.44.11.

TIME France is always 1 hour ahead of Britain, except between the end of September and the end of October (when it's the same).

TOILETS are usually to be found downstairs in bars along with the phone, but they're often hole-in-the-ground squats and paper is rare.

TRAFFIC/ROAD CONDITIONS Inter Service Route (24 hrs): 48.58.33.33.

TRAVEL FIRMS *USIT Voyages* (6 rue de Vaugirard, 15e; Mo Odéon) is an excellent and dependable **student-youth agency** – good for buses to London, Dublin, Amsterdam, etc. as well as discount flights. *Nouvelles Frontières* (166 bd Montparnasse, 6e; 43.22.98.28) have some of the cheapest charters going, and **flights** just about anywhere in the world. For national and international **coaches** you can get information and tickets at the main terminus in place Stalingrad (Mo Stalingrad).

WORLD SERVICE You can tune in on 463m MW or on frequencies between 21m and 31m shortwave at intervals throughout the day and night.

FRENCH TERMS AND ACRONYMS: A GLOSSARY

Terms

ARRÊT bus stop

ARRONDISSEMENT district of the city – each has its own townhall

ASSEMBLÉE NATIONALE French parliament

AUBERGE DE JEUNESSE Youth Hostel

AUTOBUS city bus

BANQUE bank

BEAUX ARTS fine arts school

BIBLIOTHÈQUE library

BISTRO (BISTROT) small restaurant or bar

BOIS wood

BOULANGERIE bakery

BRASSERIE café/restaurant

BUREAU D'ACCEUIL tourist accommodation service

BUREAU DE CHANGE money exchange

CAR coach, bus

CARNET book of métro/bus tickets
CARTE ORANGE métro/bus pass
CHARCUTERIE delicatessen
CHÂTEAU mansion, country house or castle
CIMETIÈRE cemetery
CONSIGNE left luggage
DÉGUSTATION tasting (wine/food)
DIRECTION métro route direction – indicated by name of last station on the line
ÉGLISE church
ENTRÉE entrance
FERMETURE closing time/period
FOYER hostel-type accommodation
GARE station
GARE ROUTIÈRE bus station
GARE SNCF train station
GUINGUETTE turn of the century dancehall-cum-restaurant on the riverside
HALLES covered market
HÔPITAL hospital
HÔTEL an hotel – but also an aristocratic townhouse or mansion
HÔTEL DE VILLE townhall
ÎLE island
JOURS FÉRIÉS public holidays
MAIRIE townhall
MAISON literally a house – can be an office/base
MARCHÉ market
MÉTRO underground/subway
OFFICE DE TOURISME tourist office
OUVERTURE opening time/period
PÂTISSERIE pastry shop
PARISCOPE weekly listings magazine

PLACE square
PORTE gate
POSTE post office
QUARTIER quarter of the city
REZ DE CHAUSSÉE ground floor
SALON DE THÉ tea room
SORTIE exit
SYNDICAT D'INITIATIVE tourist office
TABAC bar or shop selling stamps, cigarettes, etc
TOUR tower
ZONE BLEUE parking zone
ZONE PIÉTONNE pedestrian zone

Acronyms
AJ Auberge de Jeunesse (youth hostel)
AJF youth accommodation bureau
CFDT socialist trade union
CGT communist trade union
CODENE French CND (of sorts)
FN Front National (fascist party)
FO Catholic trade union
HLM council housing
PCF French communist party
PS socialist party
PTT post office
RER city and suburban express rail line
RN route nationale (main road)
RPR Gaullist party (in power), led by Paris mayor Jacques Chirac
SNCF French railways
UDF centre right coalition party headed by Giscard d'Estaing

Part two
THE GUIDE

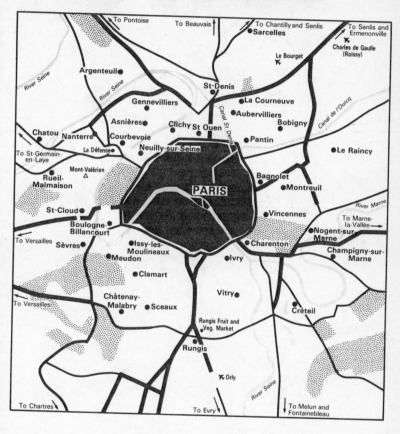

Chapter one
THE CITY

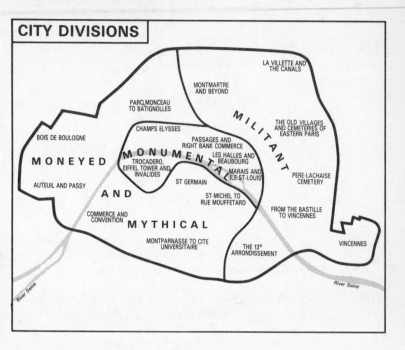

CITY DIVISIONS

LA VILLETTE AND THE CANALS

MONTMARTRE AND BEYOND

PARC MONCEAU TO BATIGNOLLES

CHAMPS ELYSSES

THE OLD VILLAGES AND CEMETERIES OF EASTERN PARIS

M I L I T A N T

BOIS DE BOULOGNE

PASSAGES AND RIGHT BANK COMMERCE

M O N U M E N T A L

LES HALLES AND BEAUBOURG

TROCADERO, EIFFEL TOWER AND INVALIDES

MARAIS AND ILE ST-LOUIS

PERE-LACHAISE CEMETERY

AUTEUIL AND PASSY

ST GERMAIN

M O N E Y E D

A N D

ST-MICHEL TO RUE MOUFFETARD

FROM THE BASTILLE TO VINCENNES

COMMERCE AND CONVENTION

M Y T H I C A L

MONTPARNASSE TO CITE UNIVERSITAIRE

THE 13e ARRONDISSEMENT

VINCENNES

River Seine

River Seine

Monumental, Moneyed and Mythical, and **Militant** are the titles we've given to the three broad divisions of the city. They are distinct geographical areas and they correspond pretty closely to the way the city has evolved through history. The first describes the central **Right Bank** areas, the second the **Left Bank** and wealthy **west**, the third the traditionally working-class districts of the **north** and **east**.

Introductions to each of the divisions outline their particular characteristics – and highlights. The chief unifying factor, which you soon notice, is their remarkable physical homogeneity. All those broad tree-lined boulevards and grey six to seven-storey houses are the work of **Baron Haussman**, the man in charge of Paris under Emperor Napoléon III. He was the inspiration and driving force behind a colossal **redevelopment** programme which wiped out all trace of the medieval city, and fixed the structure and appearance of the capital from the **1850s** to the latter half of the 20C. His influence was so great that little significant was built until the **1960s and 70s**, with the first **high-rise** schemes, **Beaubourg**, and new **expressways** around and across the city. The **current decade** has witnessed a revival of the mammoth **prestige projects** initiated and paid for by the state that have always been dear to the hearts of French rulers – the **Parc de la Villette**, the **pyramid in the Louvre** and, still to come, the new **opera house** at the **Bastille**.

> *At the end of each section of text, you will find a list of cafés, bars, restaurants and salons de thé, arranged alphabetically for cross reference with the reviews in chapter four.*

MONUMENTAL PARIS

Monumental Paris is the French state in essence, and in fact. It contains the government and parliament, the law courts and police HQ, the Bank of France and stock exchange, the top treasures of the nation, the cathedral, the opera and – universal symbol of the city – the Eiffel tower. And what is more, the buildings that house these make up the very fabric of Paris at its centre. It matters not that some are medieval, some are steel, and some are still being built – nothing has scaled down the perspectives or rendered archaic the neo-classical arrangements of a hundred years ago.

It's the Paris you can't help but see, though it's not all majestic masonry and monolithic streets. Parts of the **2e** and **3e** *arrondissements* are definitely seedy; the **Ile St-Louis** and **Marais** are cool, quiet and free of boulevards; the best of food and fashion is to found near the **Champs-Elysées**; jazz clubs haunt **Les Halles**. Cars and people are on the move 24 hours a day and there's plenty to entertain diverse tastes.

THE CHAMPS-ELYSEES

La Voie Triomphale, or Triumphal way, stretches in a dead straight line from the eastern end of the Louvre to the modern complex of skyscrapers at **La Défense** nine kilometres away, incorporating some of the city's most famous landmarks – the Champs-Elysées, the Arc de Triomphe, the Louvre and the Tuileries. Its monumental constructions have been erected over the centuries by kings and emperors, presidents and corporations, to propagate French power and prestige. The message has stood and stands loud and clear, and unchanging (despite valiant efforts by revolutionaries to ransack the Louvre in 1789 and the successful burning down of the Tuileries Palace by the 1871 Commune). Mitterand had planned a further overstatement in the form of an immense cubic arch of brilliant white to head the western end at La Défense. With more pressing needs of tax cuts and the like, prime minister Chirac has shelved this project. But the glass pyramid entrance in the central courtyard of the Louvre is well on its way. And in its wake the original medieval fortress on the site of the Cour Carrée has just been excavated.

The best view of this grandiose and simple geometry of kings to capital is from the top of the **Arc de Triomphe,** Napoléon's homage to the armies of France and himself (10–6/5 in winter; 30F). The emperor and his two royal successors spent 10 million francs between them on this edifice, which victorious foreign armies would use to humiliate the French. After the Prussians' triumphal march in 1871 the Parisians lit bonfires beneath the arch and down the Champs-Elysées to purify the stain of German boots. From 1941 to 1944 Hitler's troops paraded daily around the swastika-strewn monument – de Gaulle's arrival at the scene come Liberation was probably less effective than the earlier ashes and flames.

Assuming there are no armies in sight (on Bastille Day the president plus tanks, guns and flags process down the Champs-Elysées), your attention is most likely to be caught not by the view but by the mesmerising traffic movements around **place de l'Etoile** – the world's first organised roundabout – directly below you. Of the twelve fat avenues making up the star (*étoile*) the one that disgorges and gobbles the most motors is the **avenue des Champs-Elysées.** Its graceful gradients like a landing flight-path finish up eastwards at **place de la Concorde** where the same crazy vehicles make crossing over to the middle a death-defying task.

As it happens, some 1,300 people did die here between 1793 and 1795, beneath the Revolutionary guillotine: Louis XVI, Marie-Antoinette, Danton and Robespierre among them. The centre-piece of the *place,* chosen like its name to make no comment on these events, is an **obelisk** from the temple of Luxor, offered as a favour-currying gesture by the viceroy of Egypt in 1829. It serves merely to pivot more geometry: the alignment of the French parliament, the **Chambre des Deputés,** on the far side of the Seine with the church of the **Madeleine*** to the north. Needless to say, it cuts the Voie Triomphale at a precise and predictable right-angle. And the symmetry continues beyond the *place* in the formal layout of the **Tuileries gardens,** disrupted only by the bodies lounging on the grass, kids chasing their boats round the ponds, and gays cruising near the **Orangerie** at one end of the western terrace.

Back to the west, between Concorde and the Rond-Point roundabout whose Lalique glass fountains disappeared during the German occupation, the Champs-Elysées is bordered by chestnut trees and municipal flower-beds, pleasant enough to stroll among but not sufficiently dense to muffle the discomforting squeal of accelerating tyres. The two massive buildings rising above the greenery to the south are the **Grand** and **Petit Palais,** with their overloaded neoclassical exteriors, railway station roofs and exuberantly optimistic flying statuary. On the north side, combat

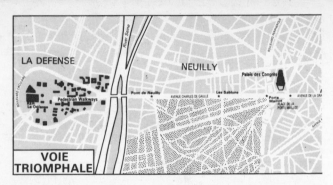

police guard the high walls round the presidential **Elysée palace** and the line of ministries and embassies ending with the US in prime position on the corner of place de la Concorde. On Thursdays and weekends you can see a stranger manifestation of the self-images of states in the postage **stamp market** at the corner of avenues Gabriel and Marigny.

Though the glamour of the Champs-Elysées is not what it was, with airline offices, car showrooms and bright light shopping arcades now dominant, there's still the Lido cabaret, Fouquet's high-class bar and restaurant, plenty of cinemas and outrageously priced cafés to bring the punters in. At Christmas this is where the fairy lights go and on 31 December it's the equivalent of Trafalgar Square with everyone happily jammed, in their cars, hooting in the New Year.

To reach **La Défense** at the extreme western end of the Voie Triomphale make one stop on the RER from Etoile – there you follow the signs for *Parvis*, avoiding at all costs the snare of the *Quatre Temps* hypermarket. Once on the *parvis*, you have before you and above you a perfect monument to the wastefulness and inhumanity of capital production. There is no formal pattern to the arrangement of towers. Token apartment blocks, offices of ELF, Esso, IBM, banks and other businesses compete for size, dazzle of surface and ability to make you dizzy. Mercifully, **bizarre art works** transform the nightmare into comic entertainment. Jean Miro's giant wobbly creatures despair at their misfit status beneath the biting edges and curveless heights of the buildings. Opposite, Alexander Calder's red iron offering is a *stabile* rather than a mobile and between them a black marble metronome shape without a beat releases a goal-less line across the *parvis*. A classic war memorial perches on a concrete plinth in front of a plastic coloured waterfall and nearer the river disembodied people clutch each other round endlessly repeated concrete flowerbeds.

Cafés/bars: Brasserie de l'Etoile, L'Ecluse, The Look, Broadside
Restaurants: Bistro de la Gare, Bistro Romain,
Salons de thé/snacks: Fauchon, Lord Sandwich
Drugstores: Champs-Elysées, Matignon

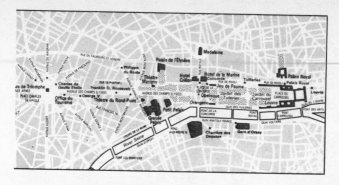

THE PASSAGES AND RIGHT BANK COMMERCE

In the narrow streets of the 1er and 2e *arrondissements*, **between the Louvre and bds des Italiens, Montmartre and Poissonnière,** the grandiose financial, cultural and political state institutions are surrounded by smaller businesses – the ragtrade, newspapers, sex and old-fashioned shopping. In greatest contrast to the hulks of the Bourse, Banque de France, Bibliothèque Nationale, etc. are the crumbling and secretive **Passages,** shopping arcades with glass roofs, tiled floors and unobtrusive entrances that predate the need for pedestrian precincts. Some are being done up and leased to travel agencies, beauticians and the like, such as **Galerie Vivienne** (between rue Vivienne and rue des Petits-Champs) with its flamboyant décor of Grecian and marine motifs. The neighbouring **Galerie Colbert,** gorgeously lit by bunches of bulbous lamps, has become a showcase extension for the Bibliothèque Nationale.

North of rue St-Marc the decline of the *passages* from their 19C chic is more noticeable. The grid of half-abandoned arcades round **passage des Panoramas** have a typical combination of bric-à-brac shops, bars, stamp dealers and an upper-crust printer, established 1867, with intricately carved shop-fittings of the same period. In **passage Jouffroy** across bd Montmartre, a Monsieur Segas sells walking canes and theatrical antiques opposite a North African and Asian carpet emporium. Further on, beyond the next street, you can hunt for old comics and cameras in **passage Verdeau.** The tiny **passage des Princes** at the top of rue Richelieu is where to look for hand-made smokers' pipes. Its erstwhile neighbour, the passage de l'Opéra, described in surreal detail by Louis Aragon in *Paris Peasant,* was eaten up by the completion of Haussmann's boulevards.

The best stylistically are the dilapidated three-story **passage du Grand-Cerf** (at the bottom of rue St-Denis) and **Galerie Véro-Dodat** (off rue Croix-des-Petits-Champs) named after the two pork butchers who set it up in 1824. This last is the most homogeneous and aristocratic of the *passages,* with painted ceilings and panelled shop-fronts divided by black marble columns. At no 26 Monsieur Capia keeps a collection of antique dolls in a shop piled high with miscellaneous curios.

Place du Caire is the centre of the ragtrade district, where frenetic trading and deliveries of cloth, the food market on rue des Petits-Carreaux, and general to-ing and fro-ing make a lively change from the office-bound quarters further west. Beneath an extraordinary pseudo-Egyptian façade of grotesque Pharaonic heads (a celebration of Napoléon's conquest of Egypt), an archway opens on to a series of arcades, the **Passage du Caire**. These, contrary to any visible evidence, are the oldest of them all, and entirely monopolised by wholesale clothes shops.

The garment business gets progressively more upmarket westwards from the trade area. Louis XIV's **place des Victoires**, adjoined to the north by the appealingly unsymmetrical **place des Petits-Pères**, is a centre for designer clothes, displayed to deter all those without the necessary funds. Another autocratic square, **place Vendôme**, with Napoléon high on a column clad with recycled Austro-Russian canons (the felling of which was a major morale boost during the Commune), now offers the fashionable accessories for haute couture – jewellery, perfumes, the original Ritz, a Rothschilds office and the Law and Order ministry. The boutiques on **rue St-Honoré** and its Faubourg extension reach the same class, paralleled across the Champs-Elysées by **rue François 1er** where **Dior** has at least four blocks on the corner with av Montaigne. After clothes, bodies are the most evident commodity on sale in this area, on rue St-Denis above all. In the mid 70s prostitutes from all over Paris occupied churches and marched down this street demanding, amongst other things, union recognition. That they got, but the power of the pimps has never been broken and the opiate-glazed eyes of so many of the women indicate the doubly vicious bind they're trapped in. On rue Ste-Anne business is much less blatant, being gay, transvestite and unde-rage. For the kids, reaching the age of 13 or 14 means redundancy. Such are the libertarian delights of Paris streetlife.

In the centre of the 2e stands the **Bourse** – the scene for dealing in stocks and shares, dollars and gold. The classical order of the façade utterly belies the scene within, like an unruly boys' public school, with creaking floors, tottering pigeon-holes and people scuttling about with bits of paper. There's hardly a micro in sight and the real financial sharks go elsewhere for their deals. The status of the City of London is the French no 2 grudge after the dominance of the English language, so plans to modernise the Bourse are always being promised. In the meantime the efficiency of the antennae-topped building of the French news agency AFP overshadowing the Bourse from the south is far more convincing.

Another obese Napoleonic structure on the classical temple model is the **church of the Madeleine** which serves for snob society weddings and for the perspective across place de la Concorde. There's a **flower market** every day except Monday along the east side of the church and a luxurious Art Nouveau loo by the métro at the junction of place and bd Madeleine. But the greatest appeal of the square is for rich or window-gazing gourmets. In the north-east corner are two blocks of the best food display in Paris – at *Fauchon's* – and down the west side the smaller *Hédiard's* plus caviar, truffle and spirit specialists (see p.150). If you just want a cheap midday meal, try rue des Capucines off bd Madeleine at the point where it becomes bd des Capucines.

It was at 35 bd des Capucines, in Nadar's studio, that the first Impressionist exhibition was shown to an outraged art world. As one critic said of Monet's *Impression: Soleil Levant* 'it was worse than anyone had hitherto dared to paint'. That was in 1874, only a year before the most preposterous building in Paris, at the far end of the boulevard, was finally completed – the **Paris Opéra**. Its architect, Charles Garnier, looks suitably foolish in a golden statue on the rue Auber side of his edifice, that so perfectly suited the by then defunct court of Napoléon III. Excessively ornate and covering three acres in extent, it provided ample space for aristocratic preening, ceremonial pomp and the social intercourse of

opera-goers, for whom the performance itself was a very secondary matter. Contemporary lovers of the art who can't afford a £30–60 ticket have to queue all night. By day you can visit the **interior** (11–5), including the auditorium, where the ceiling is the work of Chagall. The classic horror movie, *The Phantom of the Opéra*, was set, though never filmed, here and underground a stream lends credence to the tale.

The av de l'Opéra, was built at the same time – bereft of trees which might mask the vista of the Opéra. It leads down to the **Palais Royal**, originally Richelieu's residence, which now houses various government and constitutional bodies and the **Comédie Française** where the classics of French theatre are performed. The **palace gardens** to the north were once the gastronomic, gambling and amusement hotspot of Paris. There was even a *café mécanique* where you sat at a table and sent your order down one of its legs and were served via the other. The prohibition on public gambling in 1838 put an end to the fun but the flats above the empty cafés remained desirable lodgings, for the likes of Cocteau and Colette.

Folly has returned to the palace in the form of zebra pillars in different sizes standing amidst flowing water in the main courtyard. The artist responsible, Daniel Buren, was commissioned in 1982 by the socialist Minister of Culture – his successor's permission for the work to continue caused paroxysms amongst self-styled guardians of the city's heritage and set an interesting precedent. After a legal wrangle, the decision was taken on the grounds that artists had the right to complete their creation.

These monochrome Brighton rock look-a-likes might have been better in the gardens which are now no more than a useful shortcut from the Louvre to rue des Petits-Champs, though a certain charm lurks about rue Beaujolais bordering the northern end with its corner café looking on the Théâtre du Palais Royal and short arcades leading up to the main street. Here, just to the left on the other side of the road is the forbidding wall of the **Bibliothèque Nationale**, the French equivalent of the British Museum library. They have a public display of coins and ancient treasures (open 1–5), so you can at least enter the building should you feel so inclined.

Cafés/bars: *Blue Fox, Aux Bons Crus, Champsmeslé, L'Ecluse, Harry's New York Bar, de la Paix, Le Rubis, Willi's, Le Grand Café.*

Restaurants: *Baalbek, Bistro Romain, Aux Crus de Bourgogne, Le Grand Cerf, Ile de la Réunion, Les Muses, La Savane, Tyr, Le Vaudeville, Drouot.*

Salons de thé/snacks: *Angelina's, A Priori Thé, Ladurée, Lord Sandwich, Pandora, Ramen-Tei, Rose Thé.*

LES HALLES AND BEAUBOURG

In 1969 the main **Les Halles** market was moved out to the suburbs after more than 800 years in the heart of the city. There was widespread opposition to the destruction of Victor Baltard's 19C pavilions and considerable disquiet at what renovation of the area would mean. The authorities' excuse was the RER and métro interchange they had to have below. Digging began in 1971 and the hole has yet to be entirely filled. Hardly any trace remains of the working-class quarter with its night bars and bistros serving the market traders. Rents now rival the 16e and the all-night places serve and profit from salaried and speed-popping types. Les Halles is constantly promoted as the in-spot of Paris where the cool and famous congregate. In fact anyone with any sense and money hangs out in the traditional bourgeois *quartiers* to the west.

From Châtelet-Les Halles RER, you surface only after ascending levels – 4 to 0 of the **Forum des Halles** shopping centre. These aquarium-like arcades are enclosed by glass buttocks with white steel creases sliding down to an imprisoned patio. To cover up for all this commerce, poetry, arts and crafts pavilions top two sides of the Forum in a simple construction – save for the mirrors – that just manages to be out of sync with the curves and hollows below. From the terrace you can see an aimless sequence of metal arches on which plants resolutely refuse to flourish, alongside concrete trunks for water to dribble down, and, at the edge of the endless worksite, the Gothic monkeys' rock of **St-Eustache** (where a woman 'preached' the abolition of marriage during the Commune) and the rotunda of the **Bourse du Commerce**. Visions of the completed ensemble with half a dozen more major structures are too horrible to contemplate. Better to join the throng around the **Fontaine des Innocents** and watch and listen to water cascading down perfect Renaissance proportions.

There are always hundreds of people around the Forum, filling in time, hustling or just loafing about. Pick-pocketing and sexual harassment are pretty routine, the law plus canine arm are often in evidence and at night it can be quite tense. The supposedly trendy streets on the eastern side have about as much appeal as contemporary Carnaby Street. The area southwards to **place du Châtelet**, however, teems with jazz bars, night clubs and restaurants (see chs 6 and 5) and is far more crowded at 2am than 2pm. To the north, however, and strictly not for vegetarians, some old food businesses survive at the bottom of **rues Montmartre, Montorgueil** and **Turbigo**. Retreating back towards the Louvre, streets like **de l'Arbre-Sec** and **du Roule** revive the gentler attractions of window-shopping, with shop-fronts decorated to suit the wares inside and secluded *salons de thé* (see chs 4 and 5). Or you can take a look at the Art

Nouveau gold, green, and glass décor of the **Samaritaine** department store on the riverfront.

In the daytime the main flow of feet is to and from Les Halles and **Beaubourg**, the **Georges Pompidou national art and culture centre**. At least this building, whether you like it or not, is unlike any other – including the rest of architects Panzi and Rogers' work. (Though for a much earlier example of an external metal frame, look at 124 rue Réaumur, built in 1903.) Beaubourg is big, complicated and colourful and, unfortunately, in frequent need of new coats of paint. The colours match the codes used on architectural drawings to distinguish the loads of different pipes, ducts and cables – all, of course, visible in this structure. Some say it's a cartoon, others that it's six piled sheds. It's damned for being undynamic and for mocking its surroundings. But it is the most popular building in Paris and no matter what is going on inside, buskers of mime, magic, music and fire entertain the crowds outside in a permanent, shifting spectacle.

The centre is open, free, every day except Tuesday, from 12–8 and until 10 at weekends; for galleries, cinema, kids, etc. see pp. 107, 200, 133. On the ground floor the postcard selection and art bookshop betters anything on the streets outside (and there are free loos). The escalator is usually one long queue, but you must ride up this glass intestine once. As the circles of spectators on the plaza recede, a horizontal skyline appears: the Sacré-Coeur, St-Eustache, the Eiffel Tower, Notre-Dame, the Panthéon, the Tour St-Jacques with its solitary gargoyle and La Défense menacing in the distance. From the platform at the top you can look down on the château-style chimneys of the Hôtel de Ville with their flowerpot offspring sprouting all over the lower rooftops.

Back on the ground, **visual entertainments** around Beaubourg don't appeal to every taste. There's the clanking gold *Défenseur du Temps* clock in the Quartier de l'Horloge, courtesy of Jacques Chirac; a *trompe l'oeil* as you look along rue Aubry-le-Boucher from Beaubourg; and sculptures and fountains by Tinguely and Nicky de St-Phalle in the pool between the centre and Eglise St-Merri, which pay homage to Stravinsky and show scant respect for passers-by. The locality is much favoured by small commercial art galleries, St-Martin, Quincampoix and Beaubourg being the most popular streets.

Rue Renard, the continuation of rue Beaubourg, runs down to **place de l'Hôtel de Ville** where the oppressively vertical, gleaming and gargantuan mansion is the seat of the city's local government. An illustrated history of the edifice, which has always been a prime target in riots and revol-utions, is displayed along the platform of the Châtelet métro on the Neuilly-Vincennes line. The opponents to the establishments of kings and emperors created their alternative municipal governments at this building in 1789, 1848 and 1870 – the last occasion seeing Gambetta proclaim the third French republic to the crowd below while standing on a window ledge. With the defeat of the Commune, the bourgeoisie, back in control, concluded that the Parisian municipal authority had to go if order, property, morality and the suppression of the working class were to be maintained. So for 100 years Paris was ruled directly by the government. The next head of an independent municipality after the leaders of the Commune was Jacques Chirac, who became mayor in 1977. Hardly posing the same threat to the establishment, Chirac did however compete in status with President Giscard, rule Paris with scant disregard for his other councillors, and built up a power base that in 1986 helped him into the premiership and gives him an edge over his rivals for the 1988

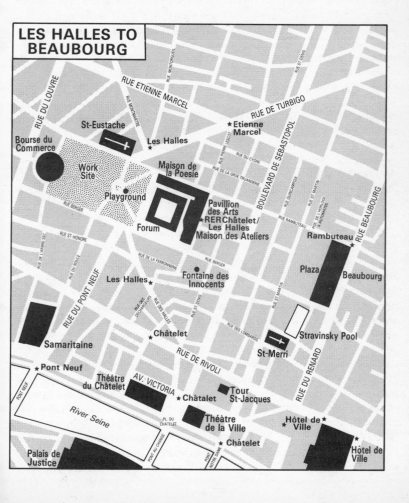

presidentials. He is still Mayor of Paris as well as head of the French government – something no 19C revolutionary ever achieved and the power wielded in this Hôtel de Ville is still crucial, though not for the forces of progress.

Cafés/bars: *Costes, Guinness Tavern, Magnetic Terrace, Pacific Palissades, La Pointe St-Eustache, Tribulum,*
Restaurants: *Bistro de la Gare, Les Deux Saules, Kinkeliba, Le Petit Ramoneur, Au Pied de Cochon, Le Potiron, Les Alsaces aux Halles*
Snacks: *Self-Service de la Samaritaine.*

THE MARAIS AND THE ILE ST-LOUIS

Jack Kerouac translates **rue des Francs-Bourgeois** as 'street of the outspoken middle classes'. The original owners of the mansions that line its length would not have taken kindly to such a slight on their blue-bloodedness. The name's origin is medieval and it was not until the 16C and 17C that the **Marais**, as the area between Beaubourg and the Bastille is known, became a fashionable aristocratic district. After the revolution it was abandoned to the masses who, up until some fifteen years ago, were living ten to a room on unserviced, squalid streets. Since then, gentrification has preceded apace and the middle classes are finally ensconced – mostly media, arty or gay, and with little need to be outspoken. The renovated mansions, their grandeur concealed by the narrow streets, have become museums, libraries, offices and chic flats flanked by shops selling designer clothes, house & garden accoutrements and one-off trinkets.

Though cornered by Haussmann's boulevards, the Marais itself was spared the Baron's heavy touch and very little has been pulled down in the recent upmarketing. It is Paris at its most seductive – old, secluded, as unthreatening by night as it is by day, and with as many little shops, bars and places to eat as you could wish for. A few low-rent pockets still exist to the east and around **rue des Rosiers**, the main Jewish quarter of the city. Local proprietors have taken to keeping flats empty, not for rent speculation, but to try to stem the trendy bourgeois invasion.

There have been several bomb attacks in the last few years on synagogues here and on Goldenburg's deli/restaurant, at no 7, and FN spray-cans periodically eject their obscenities on walls and shop-fronts. Not suprisingly the reception given to strangers is rather stiff, but you can shrug off hostility in the **Hammam St-Paul** or in the deep armchairs of **Le Loir dans la Théière** *salon de thé*, both on rue des Rosiers, (see pp.137/168). The peeling streets between **rues de Sévigné** and **Turenne** near rue St-Antoine are worth walking through just for contrast with the area west of rue de Sévigné to rue des Archives on and above rue des Francs-Bourgeois.

And even more so in relation to **place des Vosges**. This vast square of stone and brick symmetry was built for the majesty of Henri IV and Louis XIII, whose statue is hidden by trees in the middle of the grass and gravel gardens. Toddlers and octogenarians, lunch-break workers and schoolchildren come to sit or play here, in the only green space of any size in the Marais.

If you wander northwards from the posh Marais you're bound to end up at the grimly barren **place de la République**, one of the largest roundabouts in Paris. Dominated on the north side by army barracks and joining seven major streets all penetrating through the then-surrounding areas of rebellious dissent, this is the most blatant example of Napoléon III's political town planning. In order to build it Haussmann destroyed a number of popular theatres including the *Funambules* of *Les Enfants du Paradis* fame and Daguerre's unique diorama.

Just below République is the **quartier du Temple**, a good night-life area (see p.185) and lively by day as well with streets of wholesale clothes shops and the Carreau-du-Temple clothes market.

To the other side of the Marais, below rue de Rivoli/St-Antoine, the crooked steps and lanterns of rue Cloche-Perce, the tottering timbered houses of rue François-Miron, the medieval *Acceuil de France* buildings behind St-Gervais-et-Protais and the smell of flowers and incense on rue des Barres are all good indulgence in Paris picturesque. But shift eastwards to the next tangle of streets and you'll find the modern, chi-chi flats of the 'Village St-Paul' with outrageously expensive antique shops centring round rue St-Paul. This part of the Marais suffered a post-war hatchet job and though 17C and 18C magnificence is still in evidence it lacks the architectural cohesion of the Marais to the north. The 15C **Hôtel de Sens** on the rue de Figuier (now a public library) looks somewhat bizarre in its isolation. On rue du Petit-Muse there is an entertaining combination of 30's modernism and florid 19C additions in the Hôtel Fieubert (now a school); just around the corner is the café *Le Temps des Cérises*.

The bottom south-east corner of the 4ᵉ *arrondissement* is rather different, taken up since the last century by the Céléstine barracks and previously by the Arsenal which used to overlook a third island in the Seine. Bd Morland was built in 1843 covering over the arm of the river which formed the Ile de Louviers. The mad poet Gérard de Nerval escaped here as a boy and lived for days in a log cabin he made from the island's timberyards. In the 1830s his more extrovert contemporaries – Victor Hugo, Liszt, Delacroix, Alexandre Dumas and co. – were using the library in the former residence of Louis XIV's artillery chief as a meeting place. (You can see three showpiece rooms, but not the books, in the one remaining bit of the Arsenal on Wed & Thurs at 2.30; 1st floor, 1 rue de Sully.) While the literati discussed turning art into a revolutionary form the locals were on the streets giving the authorities reason to build more barracks.

Another Bohemian hangout a decade or so later was the **Hôtel Lauzun** at 17 quai d'Anjou on the **Ile St-Louis**. The Hashashins club met here monthly and Baudelaire lived for a while in the attic which it was said he had decorated with stuffed snakes and crocodiles. Nowadays you have your home on the island if you're the Aga Khan, the Pretender to the French throne or equivalent. Unlike its larger neighbour, the Ile St-Louis has no monuments or museums, just high houses on single-lane streets, a school, church and the best sorbets in the world chez *M.Berthillon*. You can seek even greater seclusion on the *quais*, tightly clutching a triple

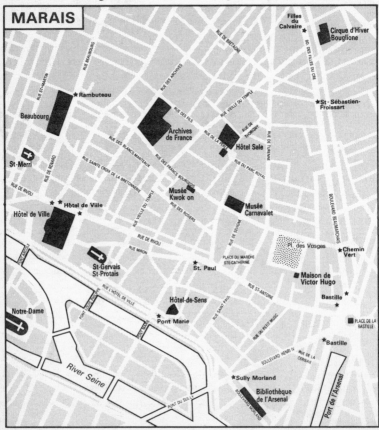

cornet of sorbets as you descend the various steps down or climb over the low gate on the right of the garden across bd Henri IV to reach the best sunbathing spot in Paris. Nothing can rival the taste of iced passion or kiwi fruit, guava, melon or whichever flavour – a sensation that ripe, fresh-picked fruit is only a shadow of. But even when Bertillon and his six concessionaries are closed, the island and its *quais* have their own very considerable charm.

Cafés/bars: *Bleu Nuit, H.L.M., Ma Bourgogne, La Tartine, Le Taxi Jaune, Le Temps des Cérises, Le Duplex, Le Sling, Le Swing, Hôtel Central.*
Salons de thé/snacks: *Bertillon, Centre Culturel du Marais, La Crêpe St-Louis, Dattes et Noix, L'Ebouillanté, Eurydice, Fleur de Lotus, Le Loir dans la Théière, Musée Picasso, L'Oiseau Bariolé, Le Roi de Falafel, Le Salon des Thés, Piccolo Théâtre.*
Restaurants: *Anahi, Bistro du Marais, Brasserie Bedhet Valette, Goldenberg's, Hassan, L'Orient Express, Au Franc Pinot, La Petite Chaumière, Restaurant Végétarien.*

ILE DE LA CITE

The Ile de la Cité is where Paris began. The earliest settlements were sited here, as was the small Gallic town of Lutetia overrun by Julius Caesar's troops in 52BC. A natural defensive site commanding a major east-west river trade route, it was an obvious candidate for a bright future. The Romans garrisoned it and laid out one of their standard military town plans, overlapping on to the Left Bank. While it never achieved any great political importance, they endowed it with an administrative centre which became the palace of the Merovingian kings in 508, then of the counts of Paris, who in 987 became kings of France. So from the very beginning the Ile has been close to the administrative heart of France.

Today the lure of the island lies in its tail-end – the **square du Vert-Galant,** the *quais,* **place Dauphine** and the **cathedral of Notre-Dame** itself. Haussmann demolished the central section in the 19C, displacing some 25,000 people and virtually breaking the island's back with four vast edifices in bland Baronial-Bureaucratick, largely given over to housing the law. He also perpetrated the litter-blown space in front of the cathedral, though that at least has the virtue of allowing a full-frontal view.

If you arrive on the island by the **Pont-Neuf,** the city's oldest bridge, recently gift-wrapped for a fortnight in 44,000 square metres of straw-coloured nylon by the Bulgarian artist Christo, you will see a statue of

Henri IV, the king who commissioned it. He was a Protestant country boy from the Pyrenees, who renounced his faith for the throne; 'Paris is worth a Mass,' he said. It was he who guaranteed the civil rights of the sizeable Protestant minority in 1598. When Louis XIV abrogated those guarantees nearly 100 years later, the Protestants scattered across the world from Holland to the New World. As many of them were highly skilled craftsmen, their departure was a blow to the economy, as was the death and exile of so many *Communards* 200 years later, for they too were largely the working-class elite.

Behind his statue a flight of steps goes down to the *quais* and the square du Vert-Galant, a small tree-lined green enclosed within the triangular stern of the island. The prime spot to occupy is the extreme point beneath a weeping-willow – haunt of lovers, sparrows and sunbathers.

On the other side of the bridge, across the street from the king, 17C houses flank the entrance to the sanded, chestnut-shaded **place Dauphine**, one of the city's most secluded and exclusive squares, where Simone Signoret lived, next to the *salon de thé Fanny Tea*, until her death in 1985. Opposite is a much sought-after cheap hotel, called the *Henri IV*. The further end of the square is blocked by the dull mass of the **Palais de Justice**, which swallowed up the palace that was home to the French kings until Etienne Marcel's bloody revolt in 1358 frightened them off to the greater security of the Louvre. In earlier times it had been the Roman governors' residence too.

The only part of the older complex that remains in its entirety is Louis IX's **Sainte Chapelle**, built to house a collection of holy relics he had bought at extortionate rates from the bankrupt empire of Byzantium. It stands in a courtyard to the left of the main entrance (bd du Palais), looking somewhat squeezed by the proximity of the 19C lawcourts, which incidentally anyone is free to sit in on. Though much restored, the chapel remains one of the finest achievements of French Gothic (consecrated in 1248). Very tall in relation to its length it looks like a cathedral choir lopped off and transformed into an independent building. Its most radical feature is its fragility: the reduction of structural masonry to a minimum to make way for a huge expanse of stunning **stained glass**. The impression inside is of being enclosed within the wings of a myriad of butterflies – the predominant colours blue and red, and, in the later rose window, grass-green and blue. It pays to get there as early as possible (open 10–6/5 from 1 Oct–31 Mar; half price Sun & hols). It is a terrible tourist trap, and expensive: 30F with the ticket for the **Conciergerie**, the old prison where Marie-Antoinette and, in their turn, the leading figures of the Revolution were incarcerated before execution. The chief interest of the Conciergerie is the enormous late Gothic Salle des Gens d'Arme, canteen and recreation room of the royal household staff. You are missing little in not seeing Marie-Antoinette's cell and various other macabre mementoes of the guillotine's victims.

For the loveliest view of what the whole ensemble once looked like you need to get hold of the postcard of the June illustration from the 15C Book of Hours known as Les Très Riches Heures du Duc de Berry (see Musée Condé, p.217), the most mouthwatering of all medieval illuminated manuscripts. It shows the palace with towers and chimneys and trellised rose garden and the Sainte Chapelle touching the sky in the right-hand corner. The Seine laps the curtain wall where now the quai des Orfèvres (goldsmiths) runs. In the foreground pollarded willows line the Left Bank, while barefoot peasant girls rake hay in stooks and their menfolk scythe light green swathes up the rue Dauphine. No sign of the square du Vert-Galant: it was just a swampy islet then, not to be joined to the rest of the Cité for another hundred years and more.

If you keep along the north side of the island from the Conciergerie you come to **place Lépine**, named for the police boss who gave Paris's coppers their white truncheons and whistles. There is a **flower market** six days a week, with birds on Sundays. Next bridge but one is the Pont d'Arcole, named for a young revolutionary killed in an attack on the Hôtel de Ville in the 1830 rising (see p.234), and beyond that the only bit of the Cité that survived Haussmann's attentions. In the streets hereabouts once flourished the cathedral school of Notre-Dame, forerunner of the Sorbonne. Around the year 1200 one of the teachers was Peter Abélard, of Héloïse fame. A philosophical whizz-kid and cocker of snooks at the establishment intellectuals of his time, he was very popular with his students and not at all with the authorities, who thought they caught a distinct whiff of heresy. Forced to leave the cathedral school, he set up

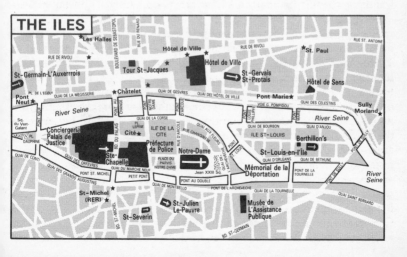

shop on the Left Bank with his disciples and, in effect, founded the university of Paris. His love life was less successful, though much better known. While living near the rue Chanoinesse behind the cathedral he fell violently in love with his landlord's niece, Héloïse, and she with him. She had a baby. Uncle had him castrated and the story ended in convents, lifelong separation and lengthy correspondence. Today their tomb lies in the cemetery of Père Lachaise (see p.98).

Close by, the **Cathédrale de Notre-Dame** itself is so much photographed that even seeing it for the first time the edge of your response is somewhat dulled by familiarity. Yet it is truly impresssive, that great H-shaped west front, with its strong vertical divisions counterbalanced by the horizontal emphasis of gallery and frieze, all centred by the rose window. It demands to be seen as a whole, though that can scarcely have been possible when the medieval houses clustered close about it. It is a solid, no-nonsense design, confessing its Romanesque ancestry. For the more fantastical kind of Gothic, look rather at the **north transept façade** with its crocketed gables and huge fretted window-space.

Notre-Dame was begun in 1160 under the auspices of Bishop de Sully and completed c1245. In the 19C, Viollet-le-Duc carried out extensive renovation work, including remaking most of the statuary – the entire frieze of kings, for instance – and adding the steeple and baleful-looking gargoyles, which you can see close-up if you brave the ascent of the towers (10–5.45/4.45; half price Sun & hols).

Inside the immediately striking feature, if you can ignore the noise and movement, is the dramatic contrast between the darkness of the nave and the light falling on the first great clustered pillars of the choir, emphasising the special nature of the sanctuary. It is the end walls of the transepts which admit all this light, nearly two-thirds glass, including two magnificent **rose windows** coloured in imperial purple. These, the vaulting, the soaring shafts reaching to the springs of the vaults, are all definite Gothic elements, yet, inside as out, there remains a strong sense of Romanesque in the stout round pillars of the nave and the general sense of four-squareness.

Before you leave, walk round to the public garden at the east end for a view of the **flying buttresses** supporting the choir, and then along the riverside under the south transept, where you can sit in springtime with the cherry blossom drifting down. And say a prayer of gratitude that the city fathers had the sense to throw out President 'Paris-must-adapt-itself-to-the-automobile' Pompidou's scheme for extending the quayside expressway along here.

Out in front of the cathedral, in the plaza separating it from Haussmann's police HQ, is what appears to be and smells like the entrance to an underground toilet. It is, in fact, a very well displayed and interesting museum, the **crypte archéologique** (10–6/5; 25F, but half-price Sun), in which are revealed the remains of the original cathedral, as well as streets and houses of the Cité back as far as the Roman era.

On the pavement by the cathedral west door is a spot known as **kilomètre zéro,** from which all main road distances in France are calculated. For the Ile de la Cité is the symbolic heart of the country, or at least of the France that in the school books fights wars, undergoes revolutions and launches space rockets. So it is fitting that the island should also be the symbolic tomb of the 200,000 French men and women who died in the Nazi concentration camps during the Second World War – Resistance fighters, Jews, forced labourers. Their moving memorial, **Le Mémorial de la Déportation**, is a kind of bunker-crypt, scarcely visible above ground, at the extreme eastern tip of the island. Stairs scarcely shoulder-wide descend into a space like a prison yard. A single aperture overlooks the brown waters of the Seine, barred by a grill whose spiky ends evoke the torments of the torture chamber. Above, nothing is visible but the sky and, dead centre, the spire of Notre-Dame. Inside, the crypt is a tunnel-like chamber, its sides studded in thousands of points of light representing the dead. Floor and ceiling are black and it ends in black – in a raw hole, with a single naked bulb hanging in the middle. Either side are empty barred cells. 'They went to the other ends of the Earth and they have not returned. 200,000 French men and women swallowed up, exterminated in the mists and darkness of the Nazi camps.' Above the exit, the words: 'Forgive. Do not forget . . .'

Cafés/bars:	*Taverne Henri IV*
Salons de thé/Snacks:	*Fanny Tea.*

TROCADERO, EIFFEL TOWER AND LES INVALIDES

The vistas are splendid, from the terrace of the **Palais de Chaillot** (place du Trocadéro) across the river to the Tour Eiffel and Ecole Militaire, from the ornate 1900 Pont Alexandre III along the grassy Esplanade to the Hôtel des Invalides. But once you have said to yourself, 'How splendid!', there is little reason to get any closer. This is town-planning on the despotic scale, an assertion of power that takes no account of the small-scale interests and details of everyday lives.

The Palais de Chaillot, like a latterday Pharaoh's mausoleum (1937), is, however, home to several interesting **museums** (see p.121f) and a theatre used for diverse but usually radical productions. And the **Tour Eiffel,** though no conventional beauty, is nonetheless an amazing structure. When completed in 1889 it was the tallest building in the world at 300m. Its 7,000 tons of steel, in terms of pressure, sit as lightly on the ground as a child in a chair. Reactions to it were violent:

'(We) protest with all our force, with all our indignation, in the name of unappreciated French taste, in the name of menaced French art and history, against the erection, in the very heart of our capital, of the useless and monstrous Eiffel Tower . . . Is Paris going to be associated with the grotesque, mercantile imaginings of a constructor of machines?'

Eiffel himself thought it was beautiful. 'The first principle of architectural aesthetics,' he said, 'prescribes that the basic lines of a structure must correspond precisely to its specified use . . . To a certain extent the tower was formed by the wind itself.' Needless to say, it stole the show at the 1889 Exposition, for which it had been constructed. **Going to the top** (10–11/10.30am) costs 37F – only worth it on a really clear day.

Stretching back from the legs of the tower the long rectangular gardens of the **Champs de Mars** lead to the 18C buildings of the **Ecole Militaire**, now the Staff College. No prizes for guessing who the most famous graduate was. A less illustrious but better loved French soldier has his name remembered in a neighbouring street and square: Cambronne. He commanded the last surviving unit of Napoléon's Imperial Guard at Waterloo. Called on to surrender by the English, although surrounded and reduced to a bare handful of men, he shouted back into the darkness one word: '*Merde*' – Shit! the commonest French swear word, known euphemistically ever since as *le mot de Cambronne*.

The surrounding *quartier* is expensive and sought after as an address, but uninteresting to look at, like the **UNESCO building** at the back of the Ecole Militaire. Controversial at the time of its construction in 1958, it just looks pedestrian, and badly weathered, today. Most unexpected, therefore, to discover the wedge of **early 19C streets between av Bosquet and the Invalides**. Chief among them is the market street, **rue Cler**, with its attractive cross streets, rue de Grenelle and rue St-Dominique, full of classy little shops, including a couple of *boulangeries* with their original painted glass panels.

Out on the river bank at **quai d'Orsay** the **American church** rubs shoulders with the South African embassy. Very different institutions, though. The church, together with the American College in nearby av Bosquet (no31), is a nodal point in the well-organised life of the large American community. The noticeboard is plastered with job offers and demands. The people are friendly and helpful in all kinds of ways.

The other quayside attraction is the **sewers**, *les égouts* (entrance at the south-east corner of Pont de l'Alma; 2–5, Mons, Weds & last Sat of the month). Your nose will tell you, if not the cadaverous pallor of the superannuated sewermen who wait on you. The guide books always bill this as an outing for kids; I doubt it. The visit consists of an unilluminating film, a small museum and a very brief look at some tunnels with a lot of smelly water swirling about. Cloacal appetites will get much more satisfaction from **Victor Hugo's description** in *Les Misérables*: 20 pages on the value of human excrement as manure (25 million francs' worth down the plug hole in the 1860s) and the history, ancient and modern, including the sewage flood of 1802 and the first perilous survey of the system in 1805 and what it found – a piece of Marat's winding sheet and the skeleton of an orang-outan, among other things.

The film show is a laugh, for its evasive gentility. It opens with misty sunrises, portraits of monarchs and a breathless voice saying, 'Paris, do you remember when you were little?' before relating how three million *baguettes*, 1,000 tons of fruit, 100 tons of fish etc go a daily progress through the guts of the city and end up in the sewers. As for the museum, serious students of urban planning could find some interesting items, if they were only allowed the time to look. In fact, I'd say, stay in the museum and skip the tour. Among other things there is an appropriate memorial to Louis Napoléon: an inscription beginning, 'In the reign of His Majesty Napoléon III, Emperor of the French, the sewer of the rue de Rivoli . . .'

Les Invalides

The **Esplanade des Invalides**, striking due south from **Pont Alexandre III**, is a more attractive and uncluttered vista than Chaillot-Ecole Militaire. The wide façade of the **Hôtel des Invalides**, overtopped by its distinctive dome, fills the whole of the further end of the Esplanade. It was built as a home for invalided soldiers on the orders of Louis XIV. Under the dome are two churches, one for the soldiers, the other intended as a mausoleum for the king but now containing the mortal remains of Napoléon. The Hôtel (*son et lumière* in English from April to September) houses the vast **Musée de l'Armée** (see p.124).

Both churches are cold and dreary inside. The **Eglise du Dôme**, in particular, is a supreme example of architectural pomposity. Corinthian columns and pilasters abound. The dome – pleasing enough from outside – is covered with paintings and flanked by four round chapels displaying the tombs of various luminaries. Napoléon himself lies in a hole in the floor in a cold smooth sarcophagus of red porphyry, enclosed within a gallery decorated with friezes of execrable taste and grovelling piety, captioned with quotations of awesome conceit from the great man: 'Cooperate with the plans I have laid for the welfare of peoples'; 'By its simplicity my code of law has done more good in France than all the laws which have preceded me'; 'Wherever the shadow of my rule has fallen, it has left lasting traces of its value.'

Immediately east of the Invalides is the **Musêe Rodin** (see p.120), on the corner of **rue de Varenne**, housed in a beautiful 18C mansion, which the sculptor leased from the state in return for the gift of all his work at

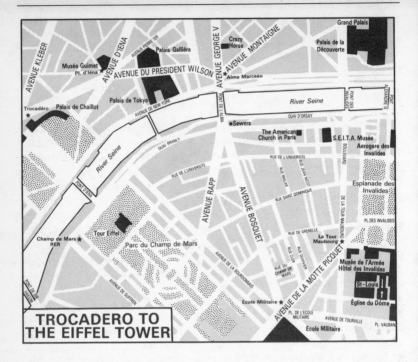

TROCADERO TO THE EIFFEL TOWER

his death. The garden, planted with sculptures, is quite as pretty as the house, with a pond and flowering shrubs and a superb view of the Invalides dome rising above the trees. The rest of the street, and the parallel **rue de Grenelle**, is full of aristocratic mansions, including the **Hôtel Matignon**, the Prime Minister's residence. At the further end the **rue du Bac** leads right into rue de Sèvres, cutting across **rue de Babylone**, another of the *quartier*'s livelier streets, with a couple of very agreeable and reasonable restaurants, *Au Babylone* and the tiny *Au Pied de Fouet*, and the crazy, rich man's folly, **La Pagode**, down on the left beyond the barracks (see p.168).

Cafés/bars: *Au Bon Accueil, Kléber*
Salons de thé/snacks: *La Pagode, Le Relais du Village, Palais de Tokyo snack bar*
Restaurants: *Au Babylone, Restaurant Lyly, Au Pied de Fouet, Aux Délices de Széchuen, Escale de Saigon, Le 18 AM.*

MYTHICAL AND MONEYED PARIS

That sedulously cultivated image of luxurious chic and stylish radicalism – the **Myth of Paris** – is best reflected in the life and manners of the Left Bank districts of Saint-Michel, Saint-Germain and Montparnasse and the Right Bank 16e and 17e *arrondissements*. On the Left Bank, the myth-makers gather, the writers, painters, philosophers, movie-makers, politicians, journalists, designers: the people who tell the city what it is. On the Right Bank, in the fashionable districts of the so-called *beaux quartiers*, their paymasters live, the people Reago-Thatcherism admiringly calls the wealth-creators, the descendants of those eager 19C capitalists who needed little encouragement to follow Foreign Minister Guizot's mid-century injunction to get rich quick: '*Enrichissez-vous par le travail et l'épargne.*' It's the land of Hermès scarves, Lacoste sports shirts and weekend *rallyes* or meets, where the children of the upper classes forega-ther to slide a chaste hand round a tender waist in anticipation of some future advantageous match. *Bon chic, bon genre (BCBG)*, they're called: elegant and eligible – the equivalents of London's Sloane Rangers.

There's not much to see in the streets of the *beaux quartiers*. There are three first-rate museums in the **Marmottan, Arts et Traditions Popul-aires** and the **Palais de Tokyo**. The old villages of **Auteuil** and **Passy** and the **Bois de Boulogne** make for some rewarding walks, as does the seedy eastern half of the 17e towards Montmartre. The most visitable territory covered in this section is the **Left Bank**, for its sights, shops, people, cafés, **Luxembourg gardens, Cluny** and **Rodin** museums and general atmos-phere. Then there's a large chunk of territory towards the south and west periphery of the city which, despite its geographical position, does not count as Left Bank with a capital L. This is the big 15e *arrondissement* and the shabbier parts of the 14e beyond Montparnasse, sightless both, but fertile country for glimpses into other people's street life.

THE LEFT BANK

The term **Left Bank** (*rive gauche*) connotes Bohemian, dissident, intellec-tual – the radical student type, whether 18 years of age or 80. As a topographical term it refers particularly to their traditional haunts – the warren of medieval lanes round the **boulevards St-Michel** and **St-Germain**, known as the **Quartier Latin** because that was the language of the university sited there right up until 1789. In modern times its reputation for turbulence and innovation has been renewed by the activities of painters and writers like Picasso, Apollinaire, Breton, Henry Miller, Anaïs Nin and Hemingway after the First World War, Camus, Sartre, Juliette Greco and the Existentialists after the Second, and the political turmoil of 1968 which escalated from student demonstrations and barricades to factory occupations, massive strikes and the near-overthrow of de Gaulle's presidency. This is not to say that the whole of Paris south of the Seine is the exclusive territory of revolutionaries and avant-gardists. It does, however, have a different and distinctive feel and appearance, noticeable as soon as you cross the river.

St-Michel to rue Mouffetard

The pivotal point of the Quartier Latin is **place St-Michel,** where the tree-lined **boulevard St-Michel** begins. It has lost its radical penniless chic now, preferring harder commercial values. The cafés and shops are jammed with people, mainly young and in summer largely foreign. All the world's bobby-soxers unload here – just a Canon's throw from Notre-Dame. The fountain in the *place* is a favourite meeting, not to say pick-up, spot. **Rue de la Huchette,** once the Mecca of avant-gardists, with its theatre still showing Ionesco's *Cantatrice Chauve* 25 years on, is now given over to Greek restaurants of indifferent quality and inflated price, as is the adjoining rue Xavier-Privas, with the odd *couscous* joint thrown in. Connecting it to the riverside is the city's narrowest street, the Chat-qui-Pêche, alarmingly evocative of what Paris at its medieval worst must have looked like.

Things improve, however, as you move away from the boulevard. At the end of rue de la Huchette, **rue St-Jacques,** is aligned on the main street of Roman Paris. It gets its name from the medieval pilgrimage to the shrine of St-Jacques/St James at Compostela in northern Spain. This bit of hill was the first taste of the road for the millions who set out from the church of St-Jacques (only the tower remains) just across the river. A short distance to the right **St-Séverin,** one of the more attractive Parisian churches (mainly 15C), boasts some splendidly virtuoso chiselwork in the pillars of the choir.

Back towards the river, **square Viviani** with its welcome patch of grass and trees provides the most flattering of all views of Notre-Dame. The mutilated little church in the corner, **St-Julien-le-Pauvre,** is the same age, though no longer much to look at. It used to be the venue for university assemblies until some rumbustious students tore it apart in the 1500s. Round to the left on rue de la Bûcherie the English bookshop, **Shakespeare and Co.,** is haunted by the shades of James Joyce and other great expatriate literati, though only by proxy, as Sylvia Beach, publisher of Joyce's *Ulysses,* had her original shop on rue de l'Odéon. Despite their romantic reputation, the riverside *quais* hereabouts are not much fun to walk because of the traffic, unless you get right down by the water's edge.

The best strolling area this side of bd St-Michel is the slopes of the **Montagne Ste-Geneviève**, the hill on which the Panthéon stands. The best way in is either from **place Maubert** (good **market** Tues, Thurs and Sat am) or from the crossroads of boulevards St-Michel and St-Germain, where the walls of the 3C **Roman baths** are visible in the garden of the **Hôtel de Cluny**. A 16C mansion resembling an Oxford or Cambridge college, the hôtel was built by the abbots of the powerful Cluny monastery as their Paris pied-à-terre. It now houses a very beautiful museum of medieval art (see p.116). There is no charge for entry to the quiet shady courtyard.

The grim-looking buildings on the other side of rue des Ecoles are the **Sorbonne, Collège de France**, and **Lycée Louis le Grand**, all major constituents of the brilliant and mandarin world of French intellectual activity. You can put your nose in the Sorbonne courtyard without anyone objecting. The **Richelieu chapel**, dominating the uphill end, was the first Roman-influenced building in 17C Paris and set the trend for subsequent developments. Nearby the traffic-free **place de la Sorbonne** with its lime trees, cafés and student habitués is a lovely place to sit.

Further up the hill the broad rue Soufflot provides an appropriately grand perspective on the domed and porticoed **Panthéon**, Louis XIV's thankyou to Sainte Geneviève, patron saint of Paris, for curing him of illness. Imposing enough at a distance, it is cold and uninteresting close to – not a friendly detail for the eye to rest on. The Revolution transformed it into a mausoleum for the great. It is deadly inside (10–6/4, cl. Tues). There are, however, several cafés to warm the heart's cockles down towards the Luxembourg gardens.

More interesting than the Panthéon is the mainly 16C church of **St-Etienne-du-Mont** on the corner of rue Clovis, with a façade combining Gothic, Renaissance and Baroque elements. The interior, if not exactly beautiful, is highly unexpected. The space is divided into three aisles by free-standing pillars connected by a narrow catwalk and flooded with light by an exceptionally tall clerestory. Again, unusually – for they mainly fell victim to the destructive anti-clericalism of the Revolution – the church still possesses its rood screen, a broad low arch supporting a gallery reached by twining spiral stairs. There is some good 17C glass in the cloister. Further down rue Clovis a huge piece of Philippe Auguste's 12C city walls emerges from among the houses.

Just a step **south from the place du Panthéon**, in the quiet rue des Fossés-St-Jacques, the kerbside tables of the **Café de la Nouvelle Mairie** wine bar make an excellent lunch stop, while at the end of the street on rue St-Jacques there are several cheap restaurants, mainly Chinese. There is not much point in going further south on rue St-Jacques. The area is

dull and lifeless once you are over the Gay-Lussac intersection, though
Baroque enthusiasts might like to take a look at the 17C church of **Val-de-Grâce** with its pedimented front and ornate cupola copied from St
Peter's in Rome, while round the corner on **bd de Port-Royal** is another
big market and several brasseries, including the *Académie de la Bière* (see
p.166).

More enticing wandering is to be had in the villagey streets **east of
the Panthéon. Rue de la Montagne-Ste-Geneviève** climbs up from place
Maubert across rue des Ecoles to the gates of what used to be the **Ecole
Polytechnique**, one of the prestigious academies for entry to the top
echelons of state power. The school has just decamped to the surburbs
leaving its buildings to become the Ministry of Research and Technology.

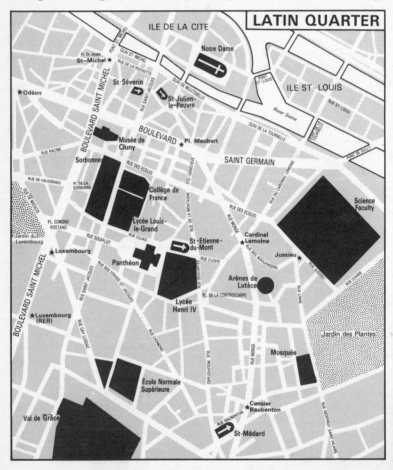

A trip down memory lane for many of its staff, no doubt. There's a sunny little café outside the gate and several cheap restaurants in rue de l'Ecole Polytechnique facing the new ministry, as well as *L'Harmottan*, a publisher and bookshop specialising in African and Third World affairs.

From here, rue Descartes runs into the medieval **rue Mouffetard**, a cobbled lane winding downhill to the church of **St-Médard**, once a country parish beside the now covered river Bièvre. The bottom half of the street with its fruit and veg stalls is still attractive. The upper half is all eating places, mostly Greek and little better than in rue de la Huchette. Like any place wholly devoted to the entertainment of tourists, it has lost its soul. The tiny **place de la Contrescarpe** half-way down was once an arty hangout, where Hemingway wrote and Georges Brassens sang. It is a dossers' rendez-vous now.

A little **further east**, across rue Monge, however, are some of the city's most agreeable surprises. Down rue Daubenton, past a delightful Arab shop selling sweets, spices, and gaudy tea-glasses you come to the crenelated walls of the Paris **mosque**, overtopped by greenery and a great square minaret. You can walk in the sunken garden and patios with their polychrome tiles and carved ceilings, but not the prayer room (9–12, 2–6; cl. Fri and Muslim hols). There is a **tearoom** too, open to all, and a **hammam** (see pp.168/136).

Opposite the mosque is an entrance to the **Jardin des Plantes**, with a small, cramped, expensive zoo, botanical gardens, hothouses and museums of paleontology and mineralogy – a pretty space of greenery to while away the middle of a day. By the rue Cuvier exit is a fine Cedar of Lebanon planted in 1734, raised from seed sent over from Oxford Botanical Gardens, and a slice of an American sequoia more than 2,000 years old with Christ's birth and other historical events its life has encompassed marked on its rings. In the nearby physics labs Henri Becquerel discovered radioactivity in 1896, and two years later the Curies discovered radium – unwitting ancestors of the *force de frappe* (the French nuclear deterrent). Pierre ended his days under the wheels of a brewer's dray on rue Dauphine.

A short distance away, with an entrance in rue de Navarre and another through a passage on rue Monge, is Paris's other Roman remain, the **Arènes de Lutèce**, an unexpected backwater hidden from the street. It is a partly restored amphitheatre, with a *boules* pitch in the centre, benches, gardens and a kids' playground behind.

Cafés/bars: Café de Cluny, La Chope, Café Notre-Dame, La Périgourdine, Polly Magoo, Le Crocodile, L'Ecluse, Café de la Nouvelle Mairie, Académie de la Bière, La Gueuse, Mayflower Pub
Salons de thé/snacks: Café de la Mosquée, La Fourmi Ailée, La Passion du Fruit

> **Restaurants:** Les Balkans, Le Baptiste, Le Grenier de Notre-Dame,
> Le Liban à la Mouff, Perraudin, Quan Nho, Aux Savoyards, Le Tire-
> Bouchon, Brasserie Balzar, Chez Nacef, Pizza Roma, Restaurant A,
> La Vallée des Bambous, Le Paprika, Sud-Ouest, Aux Abeilles d'Or

St-Germain

The northern half of the 6ᵉ *arrondissement*, unsymmetrically centred on
place St-Germain-des-Prés is the most physically attractive, lively and
stimulating square kilometre in the entire city. It's got the money, elegance
and sophistication, but with it, also, an easygoing tolerance and simplicity
that comes from a long association with the mould-breakers and trend-
setters in the arts, philosophy, politics and sciences. The aspiring and
expiring are equally at home.

The most dramatic approach is to cross the river from the Louvre by
the **Pont des Arts**, with the classic upstream view of the Ile de la Cité,
with barges moored at the quai de Conti and the Tour St-Jacques and
Hôtel de Ville breaking the Right Bank skyline. The dome and pediment
at the end of the bridge belong to the **Institut de France**, seat of the
Académie Française, an august body of writers and scholars whose
mission is to safeguard the purity of the French language. This is the
grandiose bit of the Left Bank riverfront. To the left is the **Hôtel des
Monnaies,** redesigned as the Mint in the late 18C. To the right is the
Beaux-Arts, the school of Fine Art, whose students throng the *quais* on
sunny days, sketch pads on knee. Further down is the ornate **Gare d'Orsay**
now transformed into a museum for the Jeu de Paume's Impressionist
collection and other of the capital's art treasures (see p.113).

The **riverside part of the quarter** is cut lengthwise by **rue St-André-des-
Arts** and **rue Jacob**. It is full of bookshops, galleries, antique shops, cafés
and restaurants. Poke your nose into courtyards and sidestreets. The
houses are four to six storeys high, 17C and 18C, some noble, some stiff,
some bulging and skew, all painted in infinite gradations of grey, pearl
and off-white. Broadly speaking, the further west the posher. Historical
associations are legion. Picasso painted *Guernica* in rue des Grands-
Augustins. Molière started his career in rue Mazarine. Robespierre and
co. split ideological hairs at the *café Procope* in rue de l'Ancienne-
Comédie. In rue Visconti, Racine died, Delacroix painted and Balzac's
printing business went bust. In the parallel rue des Beaux-Arts, Oscar
Wilde died, Corot and Ampère, father of amps, lived and the crazy poet,
Gérard de Nerval, went walking with a lobster on a lead.

If you're looking for lunch, **place** and **rue St-André-des-Arts** offer a
tempting concentration of places – from Tunisian sandwich joints to
seafood extravagance – and a brilliant food market in rue Buci up towards

bd St-Germain. Before you get to Buci, there is an intriguing little passage on the left, **Cour du Commerce**, between a *crêperie* and the café, *Le Mazet*. Marat had his printing press in the passage, while Dr Guillotin perfected his notorious machine by lopping sheep's heads in the loft next door. A couple of smaller courtyards open off it, revealing another stretch of Philippe Auguste's wall.

An alternative corner for midday food or quiet is around rue de l'Abbaye (vegetarian meals here at *Guenmai*) and **place Furstemberg**, a tiny square where **Delacroix's old studio** overlooking a secret garden has been converted into a museum (at no 6; see p.121). This is also the beginning of some very upmarket **shopping territory**, in **rue Jacob** and **rue Bonaparte** in particular. At 53 rue Jacob you can peer through the grill at the house where Benjamin Franklin, David Hartley and others signed the Treaty of Independence between Britain and the U.S. on 23 September 1783. There are also cheap eating places at this end of the street, serving the university medical school by the intersection with rue des Saints-Pères.

Place St-Germain-des-Prés, the hub of the *quartier*, is only a stone's throw away, with the *Deux Magots* café on the corner and *Flore* just down the street. Both are renowned for the number of philosophico-politico-poetico-literary backsides that have shined their seats, like the snootier *Brasserie Lipp* across the boulevard, long-time haunt of the more successful practitioners of these trades. Only the chosen are permitted to enter. The proprietor stands guard at his door, more like a po-faced gnome of Zurich than the terrible Cerberus he's reputed to be, and decides at a glance whether you come up to scratch.

The tower opposite the *Deux Magots* belongs to the **church of St-Germain**, all that remains of an enormous Benedictine monastery. There has been a church on the site since the 6C. The interior is best, its pure Romanesque lines still clear under the deforming paint of 19C frescoes. In the corner of the churchyard by the rue Bonaparte there is a little Picasso head of the poet Apollinaire.

South of bd St-Germain the streets round St-Sulpice are calm and classy. **Rue Mabillon** is pretty, with a row of old houses set back below the level of the modern street. There are two or three restaurants, including the old-fashioned *Aux Charpentiers*, decorated with models of rafters and roof-trees; it is the property of the Guild of Carpenters. On the left are the **halles St-Germain**, on the site of a 15C market. Rue St-Sulpice, with a delicious *pâtisserie* and a shop called *L'Estrelle* specialising in teas, coffees and jams, leads through to the front of the enormous **church of St-Sulpice**, with the popular *Café de la Mairie* on the sunny north side of the square.

The church, erected either side of 1700, is austerely classical, with a Doric colonnade surmounted by an Ionic, and Corinthian pilasters in the

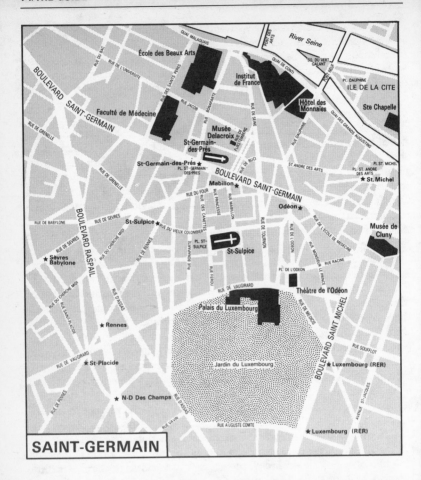

SAINT-GERMAIN

towers, only one of which is finished. The interior (some Delacroix frescoes in the first chapel on the right) is not to my taste. But softened by the chestnut-trees and fountain of the square, the ensemble is peaceful and harmonious. To the south, rue Férou, where a gentleman called Pottier composed the Internationale in 1776, connects with **rue de Vaugirard**, Paris's longest street, and the **Luxembourg gardens** (see below).

The main attraction of **place St-Sulpice** is **Yves Saint Laurent Rive Gauche**, the most elegant fashion boutique on the Left Bank. That's on the corner of the ancient **rue des Canettes**. Further along the same side of the *place* there's Saint Laurent for men, and then it's Consume, Consume all the way, with your triple-gilt uranium-plated credit card, down rues Bonaparte, Madame, de Sèvres, de Grenelle, du Four, des

Saints-Pères . . . Hard to believe now, but smack in the middle of all this at the Carrefour de la Croix Rouge, there was a major barricade in 1871, fiercely defended by Eugène Varlin, one of the Commune's leading lights, later betrayed by a priest, half-beaten to death and shot by government troops on Montmartre hill.

But it will be till-shock, not shell-shock, you'll be suffering from. You may feel safer in rue Princesse at the small, friendly and well-stocked American bookshop, *The Village Voice*, where you can browse through the latest poetry over coffee and snacks.

The least posh bit of the *quartier* is the eastern edge, where the university is firmly implanted, along bd St-Michel, with attendant scientific and medical bookshops, skeletons and instruments of torture as well as a couple of weird and wonderful shops in rue Racine. But there is really no escape from elegance round here, as you'll see in rue Tournon and rue de l'Odéon, which leads to the Doric portico of the **Théâtre de l'Odéon** and back to the Luxembourg gardens by the rue de Médicis.

It was Marie de Médicis, Henri IV's widow, who had the **Jardin and Palais du Luxembourg** built to remind her of the Palazzo Pitti and Giardino Boboli of her native Florence. The palace forms yet another of those familiar Parisian backdrops that no one pays much attention to, though there would be outrage if they were to disappear. The gardens are the chief lung and recreation ground of the Left Bank, with tennis courts, pony rides, children's playground, *boules* pitch, yachts to hire on the pond and in the wilder south-east corner a miniature orchard of elaborately espaliered pear trees. With its strollers and mooners and garish parterres it has a distinctly Mediterranean air on summer days, when the most contested spot is the shady **Fontaine de Médicis** in the north-east corner.

Cafés/bars: Le Bonaparte, Café de la Mairie, Les Deux Magots, Le Flore, Le Mandarin, Au Petit Suisse, Sam Kearney's, The Village Voice, Georges, Le Petit Bacchus, Au Sauvignon, Bedford Arms, London Tavern, La Pinte, Pub Saint-Germain, La Taverne de Nesle, Twickenham, Drugstore Saint-Germain
Salons de thé/snacks: A la Cour de Rohan, La Table d'Italie.
Restaurants: Restaurant des Arts, Restaurant des Beaux-Arts, Miniferme, Le Petit Bistro, Le Petit Mabillon, Le Petit St-Benoît, Aux Charpentiers, Drugstore Saint-Germain, Brasserie Lipp, La Maison de la Lozère, La Mascareigne, Le Muniche, Le Petit Zinc, Polidor, Le Tchaika, Au Vieux Paris, Village Bulgare, Restaurant des Saints-Pères.

Montparnasse to the Cité Universitaire

Like other Left Bank *quartiers* **Montparnasse** still trades on its association with the wild characters of the inter-war artistic and literary boom, habitués of the cafés *Select, Coupole, Dôme, Rotonde* and *Closerie des Lilas*, all still going strong on **bd du Montparnasse**. The clientèle still belongs, at least partly, to the world of the arts and politics – fatter wallets than the old days, though.

Another major sub-community in the *quartier* in the early years of the century were the outlawed Russian revolutionaries. They were so many that the Tsarist police ran a special Paris section to keep tabs on them. **Lenin** and **Trotsky** both lodged in the area. Trotsky lived in **rue de la Gaîté** near the cemetery, now a seedy street of sex shops, dangerous undies and cinemas showing titles that are both disgusting and laughable, like *Salopes Inassouvies avec Super Poitrines* (Untamed Bitches with Big Tits), *Culs pour Sodomies en Chaine* (Bums for Buggery Assembly-line style) and *Défonce-moi, chéri* (Shove it in me, darling).

Most of the life of the quarter is concentrated round the station end of boulevard du Montparnasse, where the colossal **Tour du Montparnasse** has become one of the city's principal landmarks – at its best at night when the red staple-shaped corner lights give it a certain elegance. At 56 storeys it holds the record as Europe's tallest office building. You can go up on a tour for less than the Eiffel Tower (9.30/10–11/10; 40F, children half-price), though it makes more sense to spend the money on a drink at the top-floor bar – the lift ride up comes free.

It is much reviled as a building, not because it is particularly ugly – it's in the bland tombstone style – but because it should not be there at all, totally out of scale with its surroundings. Worse, it's breeding a rash of workers' barracks in the area behind it. But no one is too bothered about that: it's the other side of the tracks . . . In front of it, on **place du 18 juin 1940**, is an enormous, largely subterranean shopping complex, with a Galeries Lafayette, C & A, boutiques galore, snack bars, sports centre and what have you. Very convenient, if you like shopping underground.

On the front of the complex a plaque records the fact that here General Leclerc of the Free French forces received the surrender of von Choltitz, the German general commanding Paris, on 25 August 1944. Under orders from Hitler to destroy the city before abandoning it, he luckily decided to disobey. And the name of the *place* is also significant in French wartime history. It commemorates the date, 18 June, 1940, when de Gaulle broadcast from London, calling on the people of France to continue the struggle in spite of the armistice signed with the Germans by Marshal Pétain.

The animated part of bd du Montparnasse ends at bd Raspail, where **Rodin's** *Balzac* broods over the traffic, though literary curiosity might take you down as far as the *Closerie des Lilas*, on the corner of the treelined avenue connecting the Observatory and Luxembourg gardens. Hemingway used to come here to write, and Marshal Ney, one of Napoléon's most glamorous generals, was killed by royalist firing squad on the pavement outside in 1815. He's still there, waving his sword, in idealised stone.

Boulevard du Montparnasse marks the boundary between the 6e and 14e *arrondissements* and is still a class divide. On the north side the streets are sedate and bourgeois, to the south they are working-class and increasingly derelict, especially between avenue du Maine and the railway tracks, which in years gone by sucked thousands of émigré Bretons into the city.

The change is clear as you soon come to the **market in bd Edgar-Quinet**, where the cafés are full of stall-holders. Just off to one side is the main entrance to the **Montparnasse cemetery**, a gloomy city of the dead, with ranks of miniature temples, dreary and bizarre, and plenty of illustrious names for spotters, from Baudelaire to Sartre and André Citroën to Saint-Saens. In the south-west corner is an old windmill, one of the 17C taverns frequented by the carousing, versifying students who gave the district its name of Parnassus. If you are determined to spend your time among the dear departed, you can also get down into the **catacombs** (Tues-Fri 2–4, Sat and Sun 9–11/2–4) in nearby **place Denfert-Rochereau**, formerly place d'Enfer – Hell Square. These are abandoned quarries stacked with millions of bones cleared from the old charnel houses in 1785 – claustrophobic in the extreme, and cold. Punks and art-students recently developed a taste for this as a party location – something the authorities, alas, soon put paid to.

Having surfaced, you will find yourself on rue Rémy-Dumoncel. From here you can stroll back over av du Général-Leclerc to the quiet little streets of clothes and crafts shops and cheap flats bordered by the cemetery and av du Maine (with a food market on rue Daguerre as well). Or you can follow rue la Tombe-Issoire to the **Observatoire de Paris**, where there's a garden open on summer afternoons in which to sit and admire the dome. From the 1660's, when the observatory was constructed, to 1884, all French maps had the zero meridian running through the middle of this building. After that date, they reluctantly agreed that 0° longitude should pass through a village in Brittany that happens to be due south of Greenwich. Visiting the Observatoire is a complicated procedure and all you'll see are old maps and instruments.

If you head south, you'll pass Ste-Anne's psychiatric hospital where one of the greatest living political philosophers, Louis Althusser, is committed, for murdering his wife. One block further on, at the bottom of av Réné-Coty, is the **Parc Montsouris**, with a marker of the old meridian on the far side near bd Jourdan. It looks a tempting place to collapse but you'll be up against the city's obsessionally whistling park police the moment you touch the grass. A beautiful reproduction of the Bardo palace in Tunis, built for the 1867 *exposition universelle*, is being allowed to decay. Lenin used to take strolls here when he was living nearby, as, no doubt, did Dali, Lurgat, Miller, Durrell and other artists who found homes in the tiny cobbled street of **Villa Seurat** off rue de la Tombe-Issoire just across the reservoirs from the park.

On the other side of bd Jourdan, several thousand students from over 100 different countries live in the curious array of buildings of the **Cité Universitaire**. The central *Maison Internationale* resembles the Marlin-spike of Tintin books. The others reflect in their mixture of styles the diversity of the nations and peoples willing to subsidise foreign study.

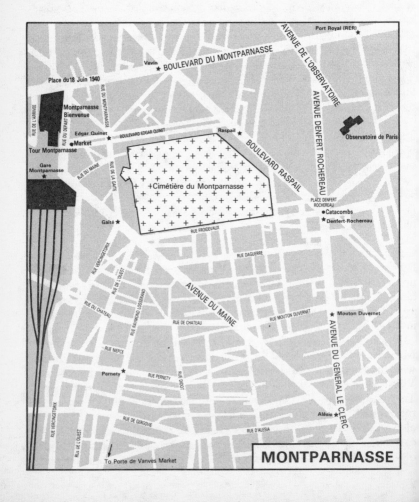

MONTPARNASSE

Armenia, Cuba, Indo-China and Monaco are neighbours at one end; Cambodia, guarded by startling stone creatures, has been boarded up since the country became Kampuchea; an extradition debate closed Spain; Switzerland (designed by Le Corbusier in his stilts phase) and the US are the most popular for their relatively luxurious rooms; and the Collège Franco-Britannique is a red-brick monster. The atmosphere is far from internationalist, but there are films, shows and other events (check the *Maison Internationale*) and you can eat cheaply in the cafeterias if you have a student card.

Beyond the tracks

Once **over avenue du Maine** to the west, you are into a very different world. The small-scale buildings, courtyards and cobbled alleys with their mixture of housing, shops and workshops recall a much older conception of urban planning and social organisation. Dirty and dilapidated though they are, especially along **rue de l'Ouest** and **rue Vercingétorix**, they provide a disquieting contrast with the public greenery and industrial housing units that face them. It is too early to say that gentrification has hit the *quartier*, but something is happening. Off-beat shops have begun to appear, so have restaurants and jazz clubs.

Rue Raymond-Losserand cuts through the *quartier* to hit the exterior boulevard at Porte de Vanves, where the city fortifications used to run until the 1920s, when despite talk of a green belt most of the space gained by their demolition was given over to speculative building. Porte de Vanves itself is a windy desert, and the workers' flats along the boulevard will never be candidates for the yuppies. In the back, however, on av Marc-Sangnier and av Georges-Lafenestre, one of the city's best junk markets takes place on Saturdays and Sundays.

Commerce and Convention: the 15e

Between the Montparnasse railway tracks and the river lies the big, unfashionable *15e arrondissement*, home of the city's least visible inhabitants. It was in the **rue du Commerce** here that George Orwell worked as a dish-washer in a White Russian restaurant in the late 20s, described in his *Down and Out in Paris and London*.

If you start walking, say, in **av de la Motte-Picquet** by the Ecole Militaire, you'll get the full flavour of the *quartier*. That's the staid end, with the brasseries full of officers from the Ecole and the rather dreary **Village Suisse** with its 150 expensive antique shops (open daily except Tues and Wed) – all Louis Quinze and Second Empire. The nature of the *quartier* changes at **bd de Grenelle** where the métro runs on iron piers above the street. Seedy hotels rent rooms by the month and the corner cafés offer cheap *plats du jour*. **Rue du Commerce** begins here, a lively, old-fashioned high street full of small shops and peeling, shuttered houses.

Scale and architecture give it a sunny, friendly atmosphere. There are cheap eating places in rues Tiphaine and Letellier. The best known establishment is **Le Commerce** at no. 51 (see p.171).

Towards the end of the street, **place du Commerce** with an Art Nouveau butcher's on the corner and a bandstand in the middle is a model of old-fashioned petty-bourgeois respectability. It might be a frozen frame from a 1930s movie.

If you carry on south, **rue de la Croix-Nivert** brings you to the **Porte de Versailles** where, at an informer's signal, government troops first entered the city in their final assault on the Commune on 21 May 1871. Today it is the site of several large **exhibition halls** where the *Foires* are held – Agricultural Show, Ideal Home Exhibition and the like.

Not very far away, in **passage Dantzig** off rue Dantzig, in a delightful secluded garden is an unusual polygonal building known as **La Rûche**, the Beehive. It was designed by Eiffel as the wine pavillion for the 1900 trade fair and transported here from its original site in the Champs de Mars. It has been used ever since as artists' studios, rented by some of the biggest names in 20C art, starting with Chagall, Modigliani and Léger.

The **western edge** of the *arrondissement* fronts the Seine from the **Port de Javel** to the Eiffel Tower. Most of the river bank is marred by a sort of mini-Défense development of half-cocked futuristic towers and uninviting Panoramas and Perspectives. Out in midstream a narrow island, the **Allée des Cygnes**, a pleasant place to walk, joins the Pont de Grenelle and Pont de Bir-Hakeim. A scaled-down version of the **Statue of Liberty** stands at the downstream end, while just off Pont de Bir-Hakeim in the beginning of bd de Grenelle, at no 8, a plaque on the wall commemorates the notorious *rafle du Vel d'Hiv*: the Nazi round-up of 12,884 Parisian Jews in July 1942. 9,000 of them were interned here at the cycle track for a week, including 4,000 children, before being carted off to Auschwitz. Thirty adults were the only survivors.

Cafés/bars: *Le Boulevard, Le Chien qui Fume, La Coupole, Le Dôme, La Rotonde, Le Select, Ciel de Paris, La Closerie des Lilas, Au Père Tranquille, Le Rallye*
Salons de thé/snacks: *JeThéMe.*
Restaurants: *Bistro de la Gare, Le Commerce, Chez Marcel, Café-Restaurant à l'Observatoire, Yakitori, Bergamote, Le Bernica, Le Bistro Romain, Boeuf Gros Sel, Le Golestan de Perse, M'Zadette M'Foua, La Route du Château.*

BEAUX QUARTIERS AND BOIS DE BOULOGNE

The **Beaux Quartiers** are essentially the 16e and 17e *arrondissements*. The 16e is aristocratic and rich, the 17e, or at least the southern part of it, bourgeois and rich, embodying the staid, cautious values of the 19C manufacturing and trading classes.

The northern half of the 16e towards place Victor Hugo and place de l'Etoile is leafy and distinctly metropolitan in feel. The southern part, round the old villages of **Auteuil** and **Passy**, has an almost provincial air, and is full of pleasant surprises for the walker. A good peg to hang a walk on is a visit to the **Musée Marmottan** (see p.117) in av Raphael, with its marvellous collection of late Monets. There are also several interesting pieces of **20C architecture** scattered through the district, especially by Hector Guimard, designer of the swirly green Art Nouveau métro stations, le Corbusier and Mallet-Stevens, architects of the first 'cubist' buildings.

A good place to start is the **Eglise d'Auteuil** métro station with several **Guimard** buildings in the vicinity for aficionados: 34 rue Boileau, 8 av de la Villa-de-la-Réunion, 41 rue Lagache-Chardon, 192 av de Versailles and 39 bd Exelmans. From the métro exit, the old village high street, **rue d'Auteuil**, leads to **place Lorrain** with a Saturday market. More Guimard houses are to be found at the further end of rue La Fontaine, which begins here; no 60 is perhaps the best in the city. In rue Poussin, just off the *place*, carriage gates open on to **Villa Montmorency**, a typical 16e 'villa', a sort of private village of leafy lanes and English-style gardens. Gide and the Goncourt brothers of Prix fame lived in this one. Behind it is rue du Dr-Blanche (see below) where, in a cul-de-sac on the right, are **Le Corbusier's** first private houses (1923), one of them now the *Fondation Le Corbusier* (10–1 & 2–6; cl. weekends and Aug). Built in strictly cubistic style, very plain, with windows in bands, the only extravagance is the raising of one wing on piers and a curved frontage. They look commonplace enough now, but what a contrast to anything that had gone before. Further along Dr-Blanche, the tiny rue Mallet-Stevens was built entirely by Mallet-Stevens also in 'cubist' style. To continue on to the Musée Marmottan, there's a subway under the now disused *Petite Ceinture* railway, which brings you out by av Raphael.

Passy too offers scope for a good meandering walk, from place du Trocadéro to Balzac's house and up rue de Passy to the spectacles museum. If you start in rue Franklin, take a left after place de Costa-Rica and go down the steps into **square Alboni** – a patch of garden enclosed by tall apartment buildings as solid as banks. Here the métro line emerges from the once vine-covered hillside beneath your feet at the Passy stop – more like a country station – before rumbling out across the river by the Pont de Bir-Hakeim. Below the station, in **rue des Eaux**, Parisians used to come to take the Passy waters. It too is enclosed by another canyon of capitalist apartments, which dwarf the 18C houses of **square Charles Dickens**. In one of them, burrowing back into the cellars of a vanished monastery, the **Musée du Vin** charges 20F for a disappointing display of viticultural odds and bobs (*dégustation*, if you need it). Its vaults connect with the ancient quarry tunnels – not visitable – from which the stone for Notre-Dame was hewn.

If you keep along the foot of the Passy hill, down the back of the Ministry of *urbanisme* and *logement*, whose appearance does not bode well for the aesthetics of its works, you arrive in the cobbled **rue d'Ankara** at the gates of an 18C château half-hidden by greenery and screened by a high wall. It's a brave punter who will march resolutely up to the gate and peer in with the confident air of the connoisseur. And you'd better make it convincing, for all the time your nose is pressed between the bars, at least four CRS are watching the small of your back intently, fingers on the trigger. This is the Turkish embassy. Not a parked car, nothing to obstruct the field of fire. It was once a clinic where the pioneering Dr Blanche tried to treat the mad Maupassant and Gérard de Nerval, among others; before that it was the home of Marie-Antoinette's friend, the Princesse de Lamballe.

From the gates **rue Berton**, a cobbled path with its gas lights still in place follows round the ivy-covered garden wall. By an old green-shuttered house a boundary stone bears the date 1731. Apart from the embassy security there is nothing to say that it is not still 1731 in this tiny backwater. The **house was Balzac's** in the 1840s, and now contains memorabilia and a library (see p.126). The entrance is from rue Raynouard, down a flight of steps into a dank garden overshadowed at one end by a singularly unattractive block of flats built, and lived in, by the architect Auguste Perret, father of French concrete.

Just across the road, **rue de l'Annonciation** gives more of the flavour of old Passy. You may not want your Bechstein repaired or your furniture lacquered, but as you approach the end of the street there'll be no holding back the saliva glands. Sacks of herbs, wheels of cheese, coffees and teas, figs, dates and nuts, pheasant and venison, salmon and lobster . . . and health foods, for the morning after.

At **place de Passy**, you join the old high street, **rue de Passy**, and a parade of eye-catching boutiques: Daniel Hechter, Fikipsy, Manoukian, Caroll Wembley, Kickers for kids, Guérlain etc, stretching up to **métro La Muette**. There in an opticians' shop at 2 av Mozart, is an intriguing and beautiful collection of specs, lorgnettes, binoculars and sundry other lenses, known as the **Musée des Lunettes et Lorgnettes de Jadis** (see p. 123).

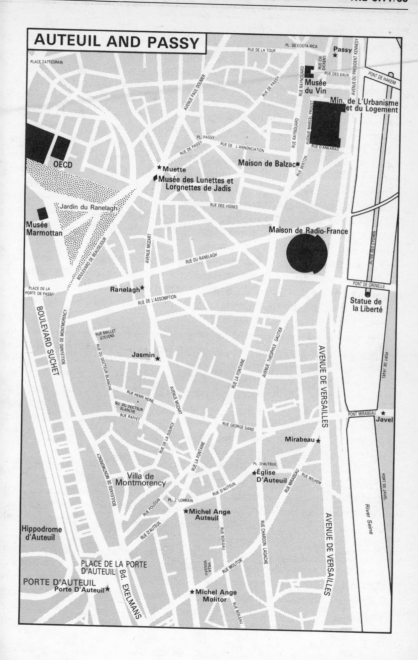

AUTEUIL AND PASSY

Bois de Boulogne

The **Bois de Boulogne**, running all down the west side of the 16ᵉ, is supposedly modelled on Hyde Park, though it is a very French interpretation. It offers all sorts of facilities: the **Jardin d'Acclimatation** with lots of attractions for kids (see p.131); the excellent **Musée National des Arts et Traditions Populaires** (p.125); the **Parc de Bagatelle**, with beautiful displays of tulips, hyacinths and daffodils in the first half of April, irises in May, waterlilies and roses at the end of June; a riding school; **bike hire** at the entrance to the Jardin d'Acclimatation; **boating** on the Lac Inférieur; **race courses** at Longchamp and Auteuil. The best, and wildest, part for walking is towards the south-west corner. When it was opened to the public in the 18C, people said of it, '*Les mariages du bois de Boulogne ne se font pas devant Monsieur le Curé*' – 'Unions cemented in the Bois de Boulogne do not take place in the presence of a priest.' Today's after-dark unions are no less disreputable, the speciality in particular of Brazilian transvestites.

Chaster and tenderer encounters take place not too far away in the secret gardens of Mr Kahn, banker and very worthy philanthropist. The entrance to the **Jardin Albert Kahn**, as it's called, is in rue des Abondances, the last turning on the right as you approach the Pont de St-Cloud from

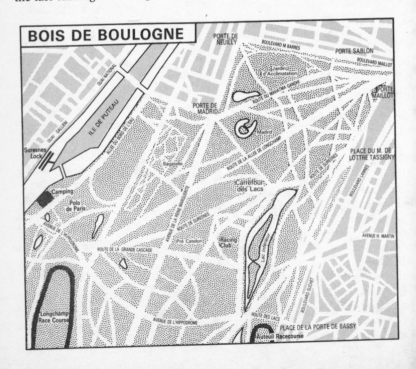

Porte de St-Cloud (open mid-March to mid-Nov, 9.30–12.30, 2–6/7 from April to Sept; M° Pont de St-Cloud; bus 72 to Rhin-et Danube stop). Maybe you wouldn't make it a special expedition, but it is an enchanting place, with gaudy rhodendrons under blue cedars, palm house and rose garden, forest and hillock, and a Japanese garden complete with pagoda, tea house, streams and maples.

Parc Monceau to Batignolles

The 17e *arrondissement* is most interesting in its eastern half. The smarter western end is cold and soulless, cut by too many wide and uniform boulevards. A route that takes in the best of it would be from **place des Ternes** with its cafés and flower market through **parc Monceau** and on to the **'village' of Batignolles** on the wrong side of the St-Lazare railway tracks.

The nearest *parc* entrance is from av Hoche through enormous gilded gates. There's a roller-skating rink and kids' play facilities, but basically it's a formal garden with antique colonnades, grots and the like. Half the people who command the heights of the French economy spent their infancy there, promenaded in prams by proper nannies. In av Velasquez on the far side the **Musée Cernuschi** houses a small collection of ancient Chinese art (see p.121) bequeathed to the state by the banker, Cernuschi, who nearly lost his life for giving money to the Commune. From there a left turn on bd Malesherbes, followed by a right on rue Legendre brings you to **place de Lévis**, already much more interesting than the sedate streets you have left behind. **Rue de Lévis** has one of the city's most strident, colourful and appetising **food markets**, every day of the week except Monday. It's a good area for restaurants too, both cheap and not so, particularly around **rue des Dames**, which leads across the railway line to **rue des Batignolles**, the heart of Batignolles 'village', now sufficiently conscious of its uniqueness to have formed an association for the preservation of its *caractère villageois*. At the northern end a semi-circular *place* with cafés and restaurants frames a colonnaded church, behind which the tired and trampled greenery of **square Batignolles** stretches back to the big marshalling yards. The long **rue des Moines** leads north-east towards Guy-Moquet. This is the working-class Paris of the movies, all small, animated, friendly shops, four- to five-storeyed houses in shades of peeling grey, brown-stained bars where men drink standing at the 'zinc'. If you come back on av de St-Ouen, go through **rue du Capitaine-Madon**, a cobbled alley with washing strung at the windows, leading to the wall of the **Montmartre cemetery**, on the offchance that Hôtel Beau-Lieu still exists. Run by a 90-year-old, who has just died, it has remained unchanged for sixty years. Ramshackle, peeling, on a tiny courtyard full of plants . . . it epitomises the kind-hearted, no-nonsense, instinctively arty, sepia Paris that every romantic visitor secretly cherishes. Most of the guests have been there fifteen years or more! The new owner plans to refurbish it, so its days are probably numbered.

Salons de thé/snacks: Le Coquelin Aîné
Restaurants: Au Bon Accueil, La Guinguette de Neuilly, Le Mouton Blanc, Natasha, Le Petit Poucet, Zerda.

MILITANT PARIS

For all the bulldozing and gentrification, the areas from **Pigalle** *and* **Montmartre** in the **north, eastwards** down to the **13e** *arrondissement*, still belong to the immigrant and French working class. It may not be for long, if the developers and planning authorities have their way. For the steady flight from the city's unaffordable rents shows no sign of letting up.

It was in these streets that the **great rebellions** of the 19C were fomented and fought: the insurrections of 1830, 1848, and the short-lived **Commune** of 1871, that divided the city in two, with the centre and west battling to preserve the status quo against the oppressed and radical east. Even in the 1789 revolution, when Belleville, Ménilmontant and Montmartre were still just villages, the most progressive demands came from the artisans of Faubourg-St-Antoine. By the middle of the 19C, **Baron Haussmann** had incorporated all of Militant Paris within the city boundaries and his own authoritarian street plan.

Today, precious little stands in remembrance of these events. The *Mur des Fédérés* in Père Lachaise cemetery records the death of 147 *Communards*; the Bastille column and its inscription commemorate 1830 and 1848; a few streets bear the names of the people's leaders. But nothing in the 11e, for instance, suggests its history as the most fought-over *arrondissement* in the city.

What hasn't yet disappeared completely is the physical backdrop: the blocks of narrow streets and artisan houses of **Belleville, Ménilmontant,** the **rue de Flandres** and the **Butte aux Cailles,** and the remnants of old trades around **Canal St-Martin.** The abattoirs and factories of **La Villette,** however, have been cleared for the new Arts, Science and Leisure complex – a transformation of this forgotten corner of the city.

The hill of **Montmartre** – the *Butte* – with its literary and artistic links, its **Sacré-Coeur** and open, airy feel, provides the main tourist focus. **Père Lachaise,** too, over in the east, draws its devotees – though the charms of the higher *quartiers* beyond are less often explored. Out on the edge, the **Bois de Vincennes** is more or less a mirror image of the Bois de Boulogne, without the high society history; it is a good place to take children, not least for its excellent zoo. So too – or for casual wandering – is the hilly **Parc des Buttes-Chaumont**.

MONTMARTRE AND BEYOND

Montmartre lies in the middle of the largely petty-bourgeois and working-class 18ᵉ *arrondissement*, respectable round the slopes of the *Butte* (hill), distinctly less so towards the **Gare du Nord** and **Gare de l'Est**. Beyond the tracks of the Gare de l'Est you're into the slums, rotting and depressed.

The **Butte** itself has a relaxed, sunny, countrified air. **Pigalle**, though, at the foot of the hill, has lost its stuffing. You won't find the golden-hearted whores and Bohemian artists of popular tradition. It's all sex shops and peep shows, the women tired and bored in the doorways. Like any red-light district, the tourists have to be shown it, or so their masters of ceremonies think.

The Butte

Everyone goes up via the rue de Steinkerque and the steps below the Sacré-Coeur. If you approach from the west or south-west via **rue Lepic**, **place des Abbesses**, or the **cemetery** in a quiet hollow below rue Caulaincourt (graves of Berlioz, Degas, Stendhal, Zola . . .), you can still have the streets to yourself.

Place des Abbesses is postcard pretty, with one of the few complete surviving Guimard métro entrances: the glass porch as well as the railings and the slightly obscene orange-tongued lanterns. There is a nice bookshop in rue Yvonne-Le-Tac, the street where St-Denis, the first bishop of Paris, had his head chopped off by the Romans c250. Legend has it that he carried his head until he dropped, where the cathedral of St-Denis now stands (see p.213), in a traditionally Communist suburb north of the city. **Place Dullin**, a bit further over, is also a beauty.

Artistic associations abound hereabouts. Zola, Berlioz, Turgenev, Seurat, Degas, Van Gogh lived in the area. Toulouse-Lautrec's *Moulin Rouge* – a feeble shadow of it former self – is down on bd de Clichy, with the *Moulin de la Galette* windmill painted by Renoir and Utrillo on rue Lepic. Picasso, Braque and Juan Gris invented Cubism in the **Bateau-Lavoir** studios in rue Ravignan, while Apollinaire and Max Jacob were hauling poetry into the 20C.

But it is decades now since the serious artists decamped. The **Musée de Montmartre** on rue Cortot just over the brow of the hill tries to recapture something of the feel of those pioneering days, but the exhibits are a disappointment. The house itself, rented at various times by Renoir,

Dufy, Suzanne Valadon and her mad son, Utrillo, is worth visiting for the view over the neat terraces of the **Montmartre vineyard** and the north side of the Butte. The entrance to the vineyard is on the steep rue des Saules: harvest time, the beginning of October.

The heart of tourist Montmartre is **place du Tertre**, photogenic but totally bogus, jammed with overpriced restaurants and 'artists' doing quick portraits while you wait. Here, on 18 March 1871, Montmartre's most illustrious mayor, a future Prime Minister of France, Georges Clemenceau, flapped about trying to prevent the bloodshed that started that terrible and long-divisive civil war between the Commune and Thiers' Third Republic, between the radical, Communist, urban, muddled Left and the frightened, unwilling or reactionary Rest.

France had provoked a disastrous war with Bismarck's Germany. The emperor, Napoléon III, had been captured and Paris surrounded. The Germans would not accept surrender from any but a properly elected government. A cautious and reactionary government was duly elected and promptly capitulated, handing over Alsace and Lorraine. Frightened of Paris in arms, they tried to get hold of the artillery still in the hands of the National Guard. When, however, government troops went to fetch the guns parked at Montmartre, the people, fearing another restoration of empire or monarchy such as has happened after the 1848 revolution, persuaded them to take no action. Two of their generals were seized and shot against the wall in rue du Chevalier-de-la-Barre behind the Sacré Coeur, where a few weeks later Thiers' people took revenge by shooting Eugène Varlin, founder member of the First International. The terrified government fled to Versailles leaving the Commune master of Paris.

Divided among themselves and isolated from the rest of France, the *Communards* fought for their city street by street against government attack for a week between 21 and 28 May. No one knows how many died, certainly no fewer than 20,000 with another 10,000 executed or deported. A working-class revolt, as the particulars of those involved clearly demonstrate, but it hardly had time to be as socialist as subsequent mythologising would have it. The terrible cost of repression had long-term effects on the French working-class movement, both in terms of numbers lost and psychologically. And after it, not being revolutionary could only appear a betrayal of the dead.

Between place du Tertre and the Sacré-Coeur, the old church of **St-Pierre**, is all that remains of the Benedictine convent that occupied the Butte Montmartre from the 12C on. Though much altered, it still retains its Romanesque and early Gothic feel. In it are four ancient columns, two by the door, two in the choir, leftovers from a Roman shrine that stood on the hill – 'mons mercurii', Mercury's Hill, the Romans called it.

As for **Sacré-Coeur** itself, graceless and vulgar pastiche though it is, its white pimply domes are an essential part of the Paris skyline. The best thing about it is the **view from the top** (9.30–12.30 & 1–5.30). It costs next to nothing, is almost as high as the Eiffel Tower, and you can see across virtually the whole city.

If you go down the north side of the Butte by the long **rue du Mont-Cenis**, where Berlioz lived, across the quiet and agreeable rue Caulaincourt, you come eventually to **Porte de Clignancourt**, where the main *marché aux puces*, or **flea-market**, is located under the *boulevard périphérique*. You won't find many bargains, but it is an entertaining trip to wander round the stalls and shacks selling jeans, bags, shirts, leather jackets, furniture and assorted junk (Sat, Sun and Mon, mornings mainly). *Chez Lisette*, a scruffy *restaurant-buvette* in the centre, is where the great gypsy jazz guitarist, Django Reinhardt, sometimes played. Just outside the market, at 126 av Michelet, *La Cigale*, a slightly seedy bar-restaurant, serves a decent meal (with affordable mussels) to the wheeze of an old accordion.

The **eastern slopes** of the Butte drop steeply down through a reposeful public garden to the recently renovated *halles*-like structure of the **Marché Saint-Pierre**, where African, Arab and French women jostle in colourful quest of some of the best fabric and textile bargains in town. Outside in rue Ronsard, masked by a fringe of overhanging greenery, are the now-sealed entrances to the quarries where plaster of Paris was extracted.

Further downhill towards bd Rochechouart and its junction with bd Barbès, where the métro clatters by on iron trellises, the mingling of cultures becomes more marked.

East from here, along the north side of bd de la Chapelle, stretches the poetically named and picturesque-squalid quarter of the **Goutte d'Or** – the Drop of Gold: a name that derives from the vineyard that occupied the site in the Middle Ages. Since the First World War, when large numbers of North Africans were first imported to replenish the ranks of Frenchmen dying in the trenches, it has gradually become an immigrant ghetto. In the late 1950s and early 1960s, during the Algerian war, its reputation struck terror in respectable middle-class hearts, as much for the clandestine political activity and settling of scores as its low dives, brothels and drugs. Though less ferocious now that the political tension has gone, its buildings remain in a lamentable state of decay, prostitutes linger in evil-smelling courtyards and there's a good chance you'll be offered dope if you appear aimless and irresolute on the street – offers best ignored as the quality is notoriously poor and there's almost certainly a plain-clothes *flic* keeping watch nearby.

With artists, writers and others moving in, attracted by the only affordable property left in the city, and the municipal authorities, directed by mayor-Prime Minister Chirac, going ahead with a programme of closing down, pulling down and cleaning up, the character of the area is clearly set to change. For the moment, however, the daytime appearance of rue de la Goutte-d'Or and its tributary lanes (especially to the north: Myrha,

Léon, the Marché Dejean) remains distinctly Oriental. The textile shops are hung with *djellabas* and gaudy fabrics. The windows of the *pâtisseries* are stacked with trays of equally gaudy cakes and pastries. Sheep's heads grin from the slabs of the Hallal butchers, the grocers shovel their wares from barrels and sacks and the plangent, evocative sounds of Arab music blare forth from the record shops. But despite these exotic elements there is a sense of watching and waiting in the atmosphere which makes most outsiders reluctant to linger, and the cafés certainly give the impression

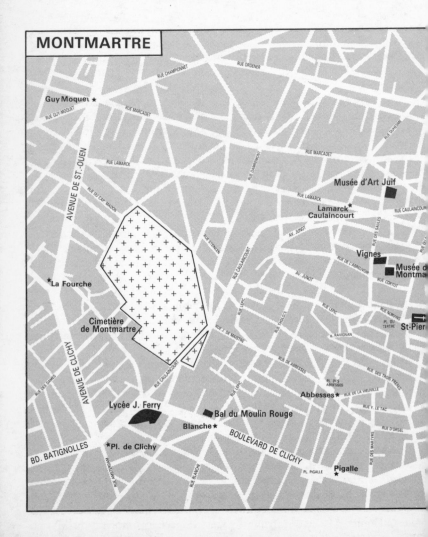

you would not be welcome. It's a neighbourhood to be treated with caution and sensitivity.

Cabarets and sex: around Pigalle

For many foreigners, Paris is still synonymous with a use of the stage perpetuated by those mythical names the *Moulin Rouge, Folies Bergères* and *Lido*. These **cabarets**, which flash their presence in the 9e and 18e, from bd de Clichy to bd Montmartre, predate the film industry, though

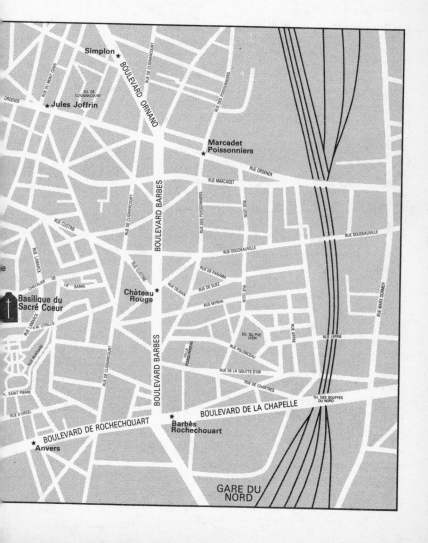

it appears as if the glittering Hollywood musicals of the 1930s are their inspiration rather than their offspring. They define an area of pornography that would have trouble titillating a prudish Anglo-Saxon and though the audience is mainly male, the whole event is to live sex shows what glossy fashion reviews are to 'girly' mags. Apart from seeing a lot of bare breasts, your average coached-in tourist may well feel he has not got what he paid, rather excessively, for. All the more easy prey for the pimps of Pigalle.

The *Lido*, for example, takes breaks from multi-coloured plumage and illuminated distant flesh to bring on a conjuror to play tricks with the clothes and possessions of the audience. Then back come the computer-choreographed 'Bluebell Girls', in a technical tour de force of light show, music and a moving stage transporting the thighs and breasts to more far away exotica – the sea, a volcano, ice or Pacific island. The scale is far too spectacular to be a dirty macs night-out.

The oldest cabaret, unique in attracting a local audience, is similar but makes no attempt, even in the production, to be modern. What turned the punters on at the *Folies Bergères* in the 1860s keeps them happy today – the cancan, some *ancien régime* waltzing, flouncing, frilly and extravagant costumes, songs and standard cabaret routines. If you're curious this is the one to waste least money on (around 200F – see *Pariscope*, etc. for details). The cancan, they say, is nothing now to the days when Toulouse Lautrec painted the *Moulin Rouge*. The singers, acrobats and comedians provide the dubious talent to the show that is advertised as 'women, women, women'.

At the *Crazy Horse* the theatrical experience convinces the very bourgeois audience that they are watching art and the prettiest girls in Paris. In the ranks of defences for using images of female bits to promote, sell, lure and exploit, Frenchmen are particular in putting 'art and beauty' in the front line. In upholding the body suspendered and pouting, weak and whimpering, usually nude and always immaculate, they claim to protect the femininity, beauty and desirability of the Frenchwoman as she would wish it herself.

Moving from the glamour cabarets to the **'Life Sex'** venues (never 'Live Sex' for some reason) is to leave the world of elegant gloss and exportable Frenchness for a world of sealed-cover porn that knows no cultural borders. As in London, Los Angeles or Lagos, the sort of acts where sex and violence are wilfully combined take place behind locked doors in private clubs. On the open market, besides the standard strip shows, you have 'ultra-hard life sex'. Some of these specialise in the pornographic language to accompany the sex, goading the audience with desire for what they cannot quite reach. The one that bills itself as 'the most intelligent sex show in Paris' is no more than a script and half a story line to eke out the show between bouts of very straightforward and heterosexual fucking. In a contest of offensiveness, the audience would always win hands down.

Cafés/bars: *Cave Drouot, Aux Négociants, Bar Belge, Au Général de Lafayette, Le Pigalle.*
Restaurants: *Casa Miguel, Chartier, La Cigale, Fouta Toro, Le Maquis, Port de Pidjiguiti, L'Auberge des Temples, Eléphant Blanc, Au Grain de Folie, Kazatchok, Au Petit Moulin, Au Petit Riche, A la Pomponnette, Antalya, Baalbeck, Les Chants du Piano, Brasserie Flo, Brasserie Julien, Au Ras du Pavé, Terminus Nord, Mary's Restaurant, Au Gratin de Folie, La Corossol Doudou.*

LA VILLETTE AND THE CANALS

The **bassin de La Villette** and the canals at the north-eastern gate of the city were for generations the centre of a densely populated working-class district. The jobs were in the main meat market and abattoirs of Paris or in the many interlinked industries that spread around the waterways. The amusements were skating or swimming, betting on cockfights or eating at the numerous restaurants famed for their fresh meat. Now La Villette is the wonderworld of high-tech culture, the pride of Giscard and Mitterand, and the recipient of £½ billion worth of public spending.

The largest of the market halls – an ironframe structure designed by Baltard, the engineer of the vanished Les Halles pavilions – has become a vast and brilliant exhibition space, the **Grande Salle**. Close by it, near the Porte de Pantin métro, is a theatre and cinema, and the site of a music conservatory yet to be built. Away to the east, beyond the Grande Salle is the Zenith rock venue inflatable (see p.199). The surrounding worksite and mud tracks will soon become a recreation park with all the trappings of organised leisure: covered galleries. restaurants, playgrounds, swimming pools, saunas, plants probably, games and more besides.

But the major extravagance is the new **Science, Industry and Technology Museum** built onto the concrete hulk of the abandoned abattoirs building at the Porte de la Villette end of the site. Three times the size of Beaubourg, this is no happily coloured oil refinery. A laboratory maybe, cold, clinical, complicated and, in appearance at least, hardly user-friendly. Walls of glass hang beneath a dark blue lattice of steel. White rod walkways accelerate into the building which emerges reluctantly from the ground like the Pentagon. But in front of it balances the **Géode**, a bubble of reflecting steel dropped from an intergalactic *boules* game, landing there as if by fluke. Inside, half the sphere is a projection screen – the largest currently existing on the planet – for film and lasers and space for holograms. The Géode isn't a perfect round and the pool in which the chopped off base sits is too shallow to make believe it is. But from any distance this dome of mirrored steel is magical and near redeems the macro-chip behind. On a slope to the west is a very different toy, the **dragon slide**, made from recycled cable drums and pipes and just for children.

For details of the exhibitions and activities in the Géode and Cité des Sciences et de l'Industrie see p. 200/114. The information centre for the complex is on your right as you approach the Grande Salle from Porte de Pantin métro and may still be showing their publicity film which is an experience in itself.

Canal St-Martin

The **Canal St-Martin** was built as a shortcut to lop off the great western loop of the Seine round Paris. It runs underground at the Bastille to surface again in bd Jules Ferry by the rue du Faubourg-du-Temple, another key point in the annals of revolutionary street fighting. Barricaded by the *Communards* in 1871 and the *quarante-huitards* in 1848, it is now a peacable, populous, rundown street of small shops, cafés, Arab sweatshops and crummy passages (bargain prices on fruit and veg). Much of it obviously has not changed: the poverty, at least in relative terms, and the physical dilapidation too.

The **southern stretch** of the canal is the most attractive. Plane trees line the cobbled *quais* and elegant high-arched footbridges punctuate the spaces between the locks. The houses are solid bourgeois-looking residences of the mid-19C, many with hide-merchants' shops at street level, for leather was the *quartier*'s principal trade until the craftsmen went out of business. But gentrification and modernisation are on the way. An 18-floor tower with orange-tinted balconies has already elbowed in among the traditional 4 to 6 storeys. The idea of canal frontage has clearly put a light in the developers' eyes, but at least it has not been turned into the motorway that Pompidou suggested.

Ancient corners do continue to exist. Down the steps to **rue des Vinai-griers**, the shoemakers' union has its HQ, *Fédération Nationale des Artisans de la Chaussure*, behind a Second Empire shop front. Fluted wooden pilasters flank the door, crowned with capitals of grapes and a gilded Bacchus. A lion ramps above the lintel. Pineapple finials top the railings, while across the street the surely geriatric *Cercle National des Garibaldiens* still has a meeting place. At no 35 Poursin has been making brass buckles in the same premises since 1830.

Across the lock, in the rustic-sounding **rue de la Grange-aux-Belles**, two café names evoke the canal's more vigorous youth: *Le Pont-Tournant* – the Swing-Bridge, – and *L'Ancre de Marine*. Traditionally, the bargees came from the north, whence the name of the famous **Hôtel du Nord** at

102 quai de Jemappes (lots of Revolutionary and socialist street names in eastern Paris), the setting for Michel Carné's film. There has been talk of transforming it into a movie museum, but for the moment it remains a cheap and incredibly squalid hotel.

The more drastic changes have taken place north of the rue des Recollets, where both banks are up for redevelopment, the Jemappes side in particular. 'It's not what it used to be,' a café owner complained. 'The factories and workshops are closed, the craftsmen gone. The quays used to be swarming with people in the evenings after work. They're empty now. Paris is just becoming a dormitory.'

At **place de Stalingrad** you have to make a brief detour away from the canalside. In the middle of the *place*, squashed up against the overhead métro line, there's a peculiarly Roman-looking building. It was one of the **toll-houses** in Louis XVI's tax wall, where taxes were levied on all goods coming into the city – a major irritant in the run-up to the 1789 Revolution.

Beyond the *place* begins the now defunct **Bassin de la Villette** dock – Paris used to be the first port in France. The people you meet along the abandoned quays are anglers, dog-walkers, lonelyhearts and the occasional glue-sniffer. At the further end, the rundown **rue de Crimée** crosses a unique hydraulic bridge (1885) operated by the canal water. The streets to your left are in the last stages of decrepitude, full of close, decaying houses with burrowing smelly passages into courtyards held together by improvised repairs. The film, *Diva*, was shot hereabouts. It is petty-crook, no-hope territory, both sides of the **rue de Flandres**. And the high-rise estate on the west side of the street does not hold much promise of a brighter future either. Another immigrant ghetto, it is mainly North African this side of rue de Tanger and place du Maroc, predominantly African round rue d'Aubervilliers.

THE OLD VILLAGES AND CEMETERIES OF EASTERN PARIS

At the northern end of the Belleville heights, a short walk from La Villette is the **parc des Buttes-Chaumont** (M° Buttes-Chaumont or Botzaris) constructed under Haussman in the 1860s to camouflage what until then had been a desolate warren of disused quarries, rubbish dumps and miserable shacks. The sculpted, beak-shaped park stays open all night and, equally rarely for Paris, you're not cautioned off the grass.

At its centre is a huge rock upholding a delicate Corinthian temple and surrounded by a lake which you cross via a suspension bridge or the shorter '*Pont des Suicides*'. This, according to Louis Aragon, the literary grand old man of the French Communist party, 'before metal grills were erected along its sides, claimed victims even from passers-by who had had no intention whatsoever of killing themselves but were suddenly tempted by the abyss. . . . And just see how docile people turn out to be: no one any longer jumps off this easily negotiable parapet'. (*Le Paysan de Paris*).

Perhaps the attraction for suicides and roving Commie writers is the unlikeliness of this park, with its views of the Sacré-Coeur and beyond, its grotto of stalactites, the fences of concrete moulded to imitate wood and its very existence in this corner of a city so badly deprived of green space. There are enticements for kids and other lovers of life (see p.132).

From Buttes-Chaumont to Père-Lachaise and eastwards is the one-time village of **Belleville** and its hamlet **Ménilmontant**, while south and east of the cemetery **Charonne** was once little more than orchards and market gardens. They were all incorporated into Paris in the 1860s. As the poorest working-class quarters of the city, there was near-on unanimous and active support for the Paris Commune. And it was here that the *Communards* took their last stand having retreated back to their homes from the merciless counter-revolutionary offensive. For several decades following the fall of the Commune, building works in Charonne would strike mass graves of the *Fédérés*. The eastern *arrondissements* are still amongst the poorest of the city and there is still a pride in their revolutionary past.

Belleville and Ménilmontant now have large immigrant populations – Yugoslavs, Jews, Portuguese, Chinese, Arabs and Africans – and, inevitably, a reputation for danger among western Parisians. Various municipal schemes are afoot to 'ameliorate' the area 'while preserving its identity' – i.e. gentrification jobs. Round every corner the narrow streets are blocked by bulldozers and concrete mixers. There is already a massive amount of 1960s and 1970s high-rise and in all probability Belleville will end up looking more like the suburbs than Paris proper. But there remain odd little *villas* (cul-de-sacs of terraced houses): *Castel*, rue du Transvaal; *Olivier-Métra*, rue Olivier-Métra; *Ermitage*, rue de l'Ermitage and rue des Pyrénées, or streets just wide enough for a tricyle of the sort the roving knife-grinders still use – passage de la Duée, 17 rue de la Duée; or narrowing to stairways and foot bridges – rue de la Mare, rue de la Voulze. And nothing can block all the brilliant views over the city.

The first main street you cross coming down from Buttes-Chaumont, **rue de Belleville**, could be the main street of any French town, save for the Vietnamese and Chinese restaurants dominating the lower end. *Boulangeries* and *charcuteries* proliferate the length of the street and there's a market at the unfestive **place des Fêtes**, once the village green, just off to the north half way up. Edith Piaf was born at no 72 – on the steps. At the bottom end, just south-east of the crossroads with bd de

Belleville is a small sequence of streets and passages doomed for demolition. Rue Ramponneau was where the last *Communard* on the last barricade held out alone for 15 minutes. Now this area is the nearest Belleville comes to living up to its slums-of-Tunis image.

The public gardens on nearby rue Piat give a good view downwards, but it's the next main street, **rue de Ménilmontant**, that is most spectacular – just before it kinks above rue de l'Ermitage. The rooftop of Beaubourg is the infinity meeting point of the sides of the street as it descends into rue Oberkampf. Further up, no 140 rue de Ménilmontant is the entrance to a monolithic workers' estate of the 1920s and a few yards on is one of the best bakers in Paris, Ganachaud (see p.151). A beautiful building that may not be preserved for long is *La Bellevilloise* at 25 rue Boyer which runs south off rue de Ménilmontant opposite rue de l'Ermitage. Now taken over by sweatshops, it was built for the *PCF* in the 1920s

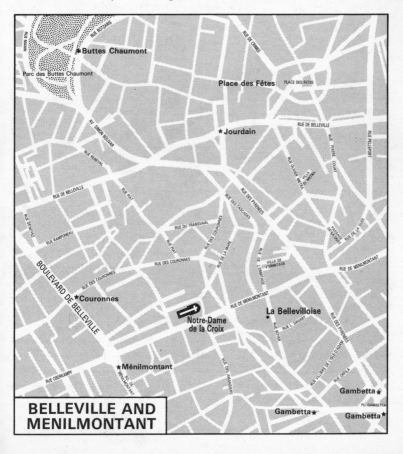

BELLEVILLE AND
MENILMONTANT

with a mosaiced and sculpted constructivist façade celebrating 50 years of work and science.

If you like churches and need a reason to wander around Charonne, **St-Germain-de-Charonne** on place St-Blaise has changed little since it served a village, and the belfry not at all since the 13C. It has its own graveyard – unique in Paris churches save for St-Pierre in Montmartre. Charnel houses were the norm with the bones emptied into the catacombs (see p.77) as more space was required. It was not until the 19C that public cemeteries appeared on the scene, the most famous being one block away from St-Germain-de-Charonne.

Restaurants: A la Bonne Humeur, Oaj-Djerba, Plateau Gourmand.

Père-Lachaise Cemetery

The **cimetière Père-Lachaise** is like a miniature city devastated by a neutron bomb: a great number of dead, empty houses and temples of every size and style, and exhausted survivors, some congregating aimlessly, some searching persistently. The first response manifests itself best around Jim Morrison's tomb, where French hippies roll joints against a backdrop of Doors' lyrics and declarations of love and drug consumption graffitied in every western language on every stone in sight. The alternative response, the searchers, are everywhere, looking for their favourite famous dead in an arrangement of numbered divisions that is neither entirely haphazard nor strictly systematic. A safe bet for a high score is to head for the south-eastern corner (near the rue de la Réunion entrance). There you will find memorials to concentration camp victims and executed Resistance fighters of the last war, Communist Party general-secretaries, Laura Marx and the *Mur des Fédérés*, where troops of the Paris Commune were lined up and shot in the last days of the battle.

Defeat is everywhere. The oppressed and their oppressors interred with the same ritual. Abélard and Heloïse side by side in prayer, still chastely separate, the relative riches and fame as unequal among the tombs of the dead as in the lives of the living. The cemetery is open from 7.30–6 every day.

FROM THE BASTILLE TO VINCENNES

The column with the 'Spirit of Liberty' on **place de la Bastille** was erected not to commemorate the surrender of the prison in 1789, but the July Revolution of 1830 which replaced the autocratic Charles X with the 'Citizen King' Louis-Philippe. When Louis-Philippe fled in the much more

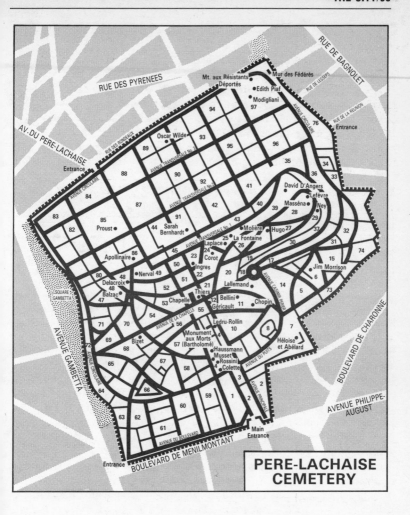

PERE-LACHAISE
CEMETERY

significant 1848 revolution his throne was burnt beside the column and
a new inscription added. The Liberal and Socialist provisional government
introduced universal male suffrage and the right to free education and a
job. Revolt had spread across all Europe but the victors of the 1789
French Revolution were not now going to make concessions to the Paris
working-class. Reaction set in and, four months after the birth of the
Second Republic, the workers took to the streets. All of eastern Paris was
barricaded, with the fiercest fighting on rue du Faubourg St-Antoine.

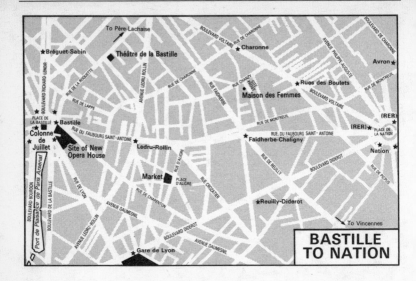

BASTILLE
TO NATION

The rebellion was quelled with the usual massacres and deportation of survivors, and it is still the 1789 Bastille Day that France celebrates.

The present government's current project for dissatisfying the demands of the populace is a new opera house being built to jut on to the Bastille between rues de Charenton and de Lyon and scheduled to open on the bicentennial of the bourgeois revolution of 1789. It will, naturally, be enormous and has already destroyed no mean amount of low-rent housing – speculation on the neighbouring blocks is rife. The Bassin de l'Arsenal between the Seine and Bastille has already become a marina. Ignored local protest centres round the nearby **place d'Aligre** – a daily market place and one of the best for bargains.

In the quieter backwaters to the north of rue du Faubourg-St-Antoine, on **rue de Lappe**, there are remnants of a very Parisian tradition – the *bals musettes*, or music halls of 1930s 'gai Paris', frequented between the wars by Piaf, Jean Gabin and Rita Hayworth. The most famous is *Balajo*, founded by one Jo de France, who introduced glitter and spectacle into what were then seedy gangster dives and brought Parisians from the other side of the city to the rue de Lappe low-life.

There is nothing very special about the passages and ragged streets above rue du Faubourg St-Antoine or indeed throughout the boulevard-crossed 11ᵉ *arrondissement*. Except that they are utterly Parisian with the odd detail of a building, the obscurity of a shop's speciality, the display of veg at an ordinary greengrocer's, the sunlight on a café table or the grafitti on a Second Empire street fountain to charm an aimless wander.

The 12ᵉ is less appealing and much better suited to bus travel. No 29 from Bastille takes you down av Daumesnil past the ebullient *Mairie* of the 12e and, almost opposite, the old Reuilly freight station, then on to the smug lions of place Félix Eboué. The disused railway line has been earmarked for a green promenade and bicycle track from Bastille to the Bois de Vincennes but no one can predict the completion date. The one finished creation in this part of town is the **Palais des Omnisports de Bercy** (see p.197), remarkable for its lawn-clad sides. The new Ministry of Finance is being built alongside and this stretch of the riverside by the pont de Bercy, recently nothing but warehouses, is all set to become pricey executive land. Back towards the centre, along quai de la Rapée, office blocks have long been ensconced, belittling a classic 19C building behind them, the **Gare de Lyon**.

Vincennes

From Faubourg St-Antoine, various buses will take you out **towards the Bois de Vincennes**. No 86 crosses **place de la Nation**, another much barricaded junction, decorated with the bizarre ensemble of two medieval monarchs, looking very small and sheepish in pens on the top of two high columns and below, in bronze, the Triumph of the Republic. Bus 46, with the same destination, crosses place Félix Eboué and passes the **Musée des Arts Africains et Océaniens** (see p.116) with its 1930s colonial façade of jungles, hard-working natives and the place names of the French Empire representing the 'overseas contribution to the capital'. The bus's next stop is the **Parc Zoologique**, which was one of the first zoos to replace cages with ditches and give the animals room to exercise themselves. It's far superior to its London equivalent. Hours are 9–6/5.30; admission 40F.

In the **Bois de Vincennes** itself, you can spend an afternoon **boating** on Lac Daumesnil (just by the zoo) or hire a bike from the same place and take some stale *baguette* to the ducks on Lac des Minimes on the other side of the wood (or bus 112 from Vincennes métro).

The fenced enclave on the southern side of Lac Daumesnil is a **Buddhist centre** with a Tibetan temple, Vietnamese chapel and international pagoda, all of which you can visit. As far as real woods go, the *bois* opens out and flowers once you're east of av de St-Maurice, but the area is so overrun with roads that countryside sensations don't stand much of a chance. The largest road-free space, between routes de la Tourelle and Dauphine, is currently fenced off for tree planting, following demolition of the open **university of Vincennes**, a traditional centre of subversion razed to the ground in 1980 and incorporated in reduced form with Nanterre on the other side of La Défense.

Any straggling collections of middle-aged men you see lurking between route de la Tourelle and av du Polygone will be engaged in the innocent activity of a *boules* concourse. Organised amongst themselves, this is one

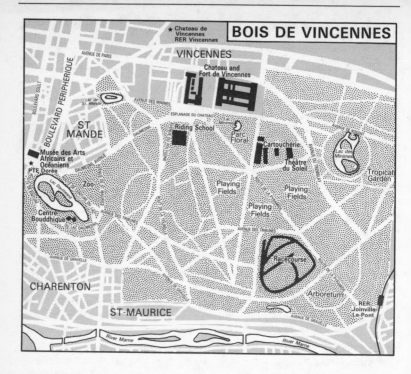

of the few activities in the *Bois* that doesn't conform to the French love of institutionalising leisure. To the north, near the château, the **Parc Floral** (Bus 112 from Vincennes métro) testifies to the French lack of flair in landscape gardening, but there are some fun things for kids (see p. 131). Despite this being a wood, tree lovers are encouraged to visit the **arboretum** (Mon, Wed, Fri; 1–4.30; route de la Pyramide: RER Joinville-le-Pont) where 80 different species of greenery are tended.

To the east of the Parc Floral is the **Cartoucherie de Vincennes**, an old ammunitions factory, now home to four theatre companies including the radical *Théâtre du Soleil* (see p.201).

On the northern edge of the *Bois*, the **Château de Vincennes**, royal medieval residence, then state prison, porcelain factory, weapons dump and military training school, is still undergoing restoration work started by Napoléon III. A real behemoth of a building, no amount of stone-scrubbing and removal of 19C gun positions is likely to greatly beautify it.

Cafés/bars: *Le Baron Rouge, Le Clown, La Mousson, Le Baron Rouge.*

Restaurants: *Anjou-Normande, Bar Sassia, Bofinger, La Cracovia, Le Cyrnos, Douchka, Kin Malebo, Pour le Plaisir, Les Trois Claudes, La Mansouria, Le Train Bleu.*

THE 13ᵉ ARRONDISSEMENT

The south-east quarter of Paris, **the 13ᵉ** has similarities with the south-east boroughs of London. The tightly-knit community on and around rue Nationale between bd Vincent-Auriol and the inner ring road never had much to hope for. But they made do with their overcrowded, rat-ridden, ramshackle slums not just because they had no choice but because life at least could be lived on the street – in the shops, the cafés (of which there were 48 on rue Nationale alone), and with the neighbours who all shared the same conditions. Paris was another place, rarely ventured to. But come the 1950s and 1960s, the city planners, here as elsewhere, came up with their sense-defying solution to housing problems. Much of the region now resembles Lower East Side, Manhattan. Each tower block flat is hygienic, secure, expensive to run and there's only a couple of cafés left on rue Nationale. The person next door is no longer a school-fellow and work-mate but a well-dressed office worker from north of the river. It's a sad part of town and only the Dunois jazz venue (see p.195) or, for Le Corbusier fans, the Salvation army hostel at 12 rue Cantagrel, is likely to tempt you down here.

West a bit, between av d'Italie, rue Tolbiac and bd Masséna, is the **Chinatown** of Paris, with the same concrete eruptions and every variety of Far Eastern cuisine, movies, tapes and publications on sale. A **market** between av de Choisy and d'Ivry (every day except Monday) makes even the French look unimaginative in their choice of food.

Nearer to the city centre, above bd Vincent-Auriol, the buildings are ornate and bourgeois, dominated by the immense **Hôpital de la Salpê-trière**, built under Louis XIV to dispose of the dispossessed. It later became a psychiatric hospital, fulfilling the same function. Jean Charcot, who believed that susceptibility to hypnosis was proof of hysteria, staged his theatrical demonstrations here, with Freud one of his greatly interested witnesses. If you ask very nicely in the *Bibliothèque Charcot* (block 6, red route), the librarian may show you a book of photographs of the poor female victims of these experiments. For a more positive statement on women, take a look at the building at 5 rue Jules Breton which declares in large letters on its façade, 'In humanity, woman has the same duties as man. She must have the same rights in the family and in society' – a female Masonic lodge, as it happens.

West of av d'Italie small houses with fancy brickwork or decorative

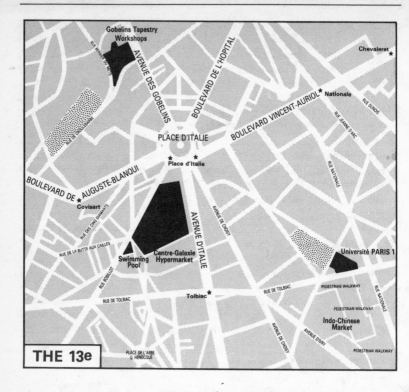

THE 13e

timbers have remained intact: around place de l'Abbé-Henocque, rue Dr-Leray, the Cité Floral between rues Boussingault and Brillat-Savarin and the villa Daviel. Closer to place d'Italie there's a rare taste of pre-tower block life in the **Butte aux Cailles** *quartier* around the street of the same name. You'll find on it book and food shops, one of the green Art Nouveau municipal drinking fountains, a community action centre, a workers' co-operative jazz bar (*La Merle Moqueur* at no 11), an excellent second-hand clothes and crockery shop (at no 58) and bars and bistros open till midnight. The *Bar des Sports* (no 15) occasionally announces crocodile and turtle on the day's menu. And there's a food market nearby on bd Auguste-Blanqui.

Place d'Italie was the scene of one short-lived victory of the Left in the 1848 revolution. A government general and his officers were allowed through the barricade and immediately surrounded and dragged off to the police station where the commander was persuaded to write an order to his troops to retreat and a letter to the effect that 3 million francs had been voted by parliament for the poor of Paris. Needless to say, neither was honoured and the reprisals were heavy. Many of the people involved would have been tanners, laundry-workers or dye-makers with their work-place the banks of the Bièvre river. This was covered over in 1910 (creating rues Berbier-du-Mets and Croulebarbe) as a health hazard, the main source of pollution being the dyes from the **Gobelins tapestry workshops**, in operation here some 400 years. Tapestries are still being made by the same methods on cartoons by contemporary painters – a painfully slow process which you can watch (Tues, Wed & Thurs; 2–3.30; guided visit; 42, av des Gobelins).

Restaurants: *Bar des sports, Le Bol en Bois, Jadorie, La Nouvelle Gare*

Chapter two
GALLERIES AND MUSEUMS

You may find there is sufficient visual stimulation just wandering around Paris streets without exploring what's to be seen in the city's **galleries and museums**. It's certainly questionable whether the Louvre, for example, can compete in pleasure with the Marais, the *quais* or parts of the Latin quarter. But if established art appeals at all, the Paris collections are not to be missed.

The most popular are the various **museums of modern art:** in the **Beaubourg Pompidou Centre, Palais de Tokyo** and new **Musée Picasso,** and, for the brilliantly represented opening stages, in the **Orangerie, Marmottan** and newly opened **Musée d'Orsay.** Since Paris was the well-rocked cradle of Impressionism, Fauvism, Cubism, Surrealism and Symbolism, there's both justice and relevance in such a multitutde of works being here. No less breathtaking, going back to earlier cultural roots, are some of the **medieval works** in the **Musée Cluny,** including the glorious *La Dame à la Licorne* tapestry.

Among the city's extraordinary number of **technical, historical, social and applied art museums,** pride of place must go to the dazzling new **Cité des Sciences museum,** radical in both concept and architecture – and fun. Entertaining too, if more conventional, is the **Musée National des Arts et Traditions Populaires,** its equivalent for the past. Some of the smaller ones are dedicated to a **single person** – Balzac, Hugo, Piaf – and others to very **particular subjects** – **spectacles, counterfeits, tobacco.** We've detailed all but a very few of the smallest and most highly specialised, like the **freemasonry** and **lawyers'** museums, details of which can be obtained from the tourist office. A few others, like **Le Corbusier, Montmartre** and the **Bibliothèque Nationale** have been incorporated in the text (p.81, 87, 52).

The **Big Four** – Louvre, Beaubourg, d'Orsay and Cité des Sciences – are described first. The remainder follow under five headings: **Art, Fashion and Fripperies, History, Performance Arts and Literature** and **Science and Industry.**

Admission prices vary: some, like the Marmottan and Cité des Sciences, are fairly expensive, pushing 30F but most are in the 10–20F range and they all offer student reductions if you've got a card. The Louvre and other state-owned museums **close on Tuesdays** and have **free days** – usually crowded out – on Wednesdays and/or Sundays.

Lastly, keep an eye out for **temporary exhibitions** – some of which match any of Paris's regular museums – held in Beaubourg and the Grand Palais; these are usually well advertised by posters or there are full details in *Pariscope* and the other listings magazines. The same goes for the numerous **commercial galleries**, heavily concentrated in the Beaubourg and St-Germain areas, which of course you can visit without charge.

THE BIG FOUR

Beaubourg: Musée National d'Art Moderne
Centre Beaubourg, rue Beaubourg, 4ᵉ; Mᵒ Rambuteau/Hôtel-de-Ville. Open 12am–10pm, wk/ends 10–10, cl Tues, free Sun.
The Musée National d'Art Moderne on the 3rd and 4th floors of Beaubourg is second to none. The art is exclusively 20C and constantly expanding. Contempoary movements and works dated the year before last find their place here along with the late-Impressionists, Fauvists, Cubists, Figuratives, Abstractionists and the rest of this century's First World art trends. The recent rearrangement of the galleries has made the light and space conditions even better.

One of the earliest paintings in the **main gallery** is Henri Rousseau's *La Charmeuse de Serpent* (1907), an extraordinary, idiosyncratic beginning. In a different world, Picasso's *Femme Assise* of 1909 brings in the reduced colours and double dimensions of **Cubism**, presented in its fuller development by Braque's *L'Homme à la Guitare* (1914) and, later, in Léger's solid balancing act, *Les Acrobates en Gris* (1942–4). Among **Abstracts**, there's the sensuous rhythm of colour in Sonia Delaunay's *Prismes Electriques* (1914) and a good number of Kandinskys at his most harmonious and playful. Dali disturbs, amuses or infuriates with *Six apparitions de Lénine sur un piano* (1931) and there are more surrealist images from Magritte and de Chirico. Moving to the **Expressionists**, one of the most compulsive pictures – of 1920s female emancipation as viewed by a male contemporary – is the portrait of the journalist Sylvia von Harden by Otto Dix. The gender of the sleeping woman in *Le Rêve* by Matisse has no importance – it is the human body at its most relaxed that the artist has painted. Jumping forward, to Francis Bacon, you find the tension and the torment of the human body and mind in the portraits, and – no matter that the figure is minute – in *Van Gogh in Landscape* (1957). Squashed-up cars, lines and squares, wrapped-up grand pianos and Warhol's *Electric chair* (1966) are there to see and for a reminder that **contemporary** art can still hold its roots, there's the classic subject of *Le Peintre et son modèle* by Balthus in 1980–1.

There are temporary exhibitions of photographs, drawings, collages and prints in the **Salle d'Art Graphique** and **Salon Photo**, part of the permanent collections of the museum. If your grasp of French is sufficient you can take advantage of the **audio-visual presentations** on the major

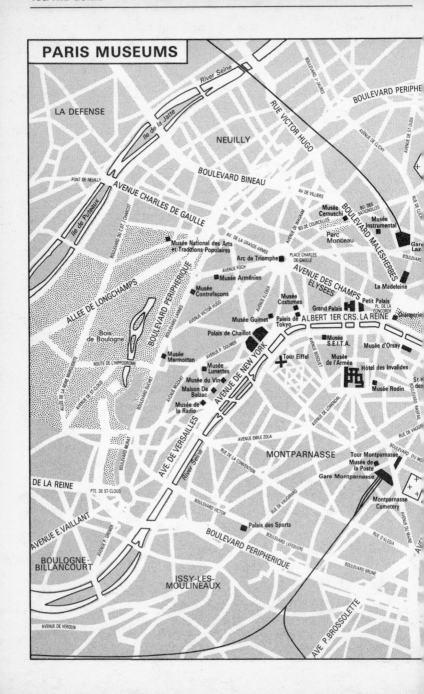

PARIS MUSEUMS

River Seine

LA DEFENSE

NEUILLY

RUE VICTOR HUGO

BOULEVARD PERIPHE

BOULEVARD J. JAURES

AVENUE DE ST-OUEN

AVENUE DE CLICHY

Ile de la Jatte

PONT DE NEUILLY

AVENUE CHARLES DE GAULLE

BOULEVARD BINEAU

AV. DE VILLIERS

BD. DES BATIGNOLLES

RUE DE CLICH

Ile de Puteaux

BOULEVARD DU LT. CHARCOT

Musée Cernuschi

Musée Instrumental

Gare Laz

AV. DE WAGRAM

AVENUE DE COURCELLES

BOULEVARD MALESHERBES

BOULEVARD

Musée National des Arts
et Traditions Populaires

AV. DE LA GRANDE ARMEE

Parc Monceau

ALLEE DE LONGCHAMPS

BOULEVARD PERIPHERIQUE

Arc de Triomphe

PLACE CHARLES
DE GAULLE

AVENUE DES CHAMPS
ELYSEES

La Madeleine

AVENUE FOCH

Musée Arménien

Bois
de Boulogne

BOULEVARD LANNES

AVENUE VICTOR HUGO

Musée
Contrefaçons

AVENUE KLEBER

Musée
Costumes

Petit Palais

Grand Palais

PL. DE LA
CONCORDE

ROUTE DE L'HIPPODROME

Musée Guimet

AVENUE P. DOUMER

Palais de
Tokyo

ALBERT 1ER CRS. LA REINE

Orangerie

Palais de Chaillot

AVENUE DE NEW YORK

Musée
S.E.I.T.A.

Musée d'Orsay

AVENUE BOSQUET

Musée Marmottan

Musée
Lunettes

Tour Eiffel

Musée
de l'Armée

Hôtel des Invalides

AVENUE MOZART

Musée du Vin

St-

BOULEVARD SUCHET

Maison De
Balzac

Musée Rodin

des

ALLEE DE LA REINE MARGUERITE

AVENUE DE ST CLOUD

Musée de
la Radio

AVENUE DE LOWENDAL

BOULEVARD RASPAIL

BOULEVARD MURAT

AVE. DE VERSAILLES

AVENUE EMILE ZOLA

RUE DE VAUG

MONTPARNASSE

BOULEVARD DU MO

DE LA REINE

PTE. DE ST-CLOUD

River Seine

RUE DE LA CONVENTION

Tour Montparnasse

Musée de
la Poste

Gare Montparnasse

Montparnasse
Cemetery

AVENUE DU MAINE

AVENUE E. VAILLANT

AVENUE F. ORDIER

BOULEVARD VICTOR

Palais des Sports

BOULEVARD LEFEBVRE

RUE DE VALGRAND

RUE D'ALESIA

BOULOGNE-
BILLANCOURT

BOULEVARD PERIPHERIQUE

BOULEVARD BRUNE

ISSY-LES-
MOULINEAUX

AVENUE DE VERDUN

AVE. P. BROSSOLETTE

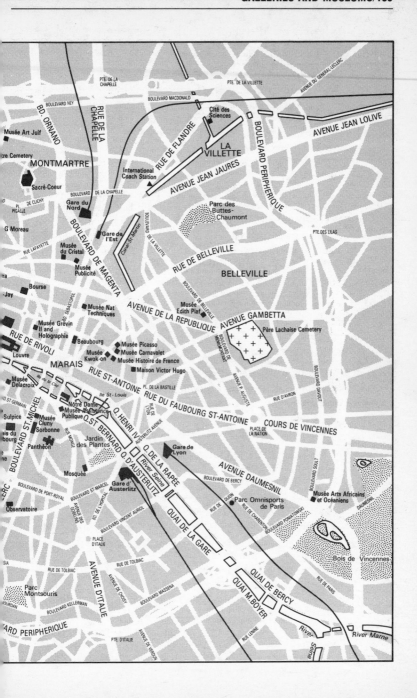

artistic movements of this century, or the **films**, projected several times daily, on contemporary art, on current exhibitions or as experimental art in themselves.

On the mezzanine floor (down the stairs to the right of the plaza doors) are the **Galeries Contemporaines** where the overspill of the museum's contemporary collection gets rotated and young artists get a viewing. The **Grande Galerie** right at the top of the building is where the big-time expositions are held. They usually last several months, are extremely well publicised, and can, occasionally, be brilliant. Yet more temporary shows on equally diverse themes are to be seen in the basement **Centre de Création Industrielle**.

Entry to the Centre is free but the Museum and Galeries Contemporaines have admission charges (except on Sundays) as do the major exhibitions. Given the amount to see it may be worth getting a daypass.

Beaubourg also has an excellent **cinema** (see p.200), a **reference library** including foreign newspapers open to all, a **record library** where you can take a music break, a **snackbar** and **restaurant** (with seating on the roof), a **bookshop**, **contemporary music centre** (see p.195), **dance** and **theatre space** and **kids' workshop** (see p.133).

The Louvre
Palais du Louvre, 1ᵉʳ; Mᵒ Palais-Royal, Louvre. Open 9.45–6.30; cl. Tues; free Sun & Wed.

> 'You walked for a quarter of a mile through works of fine art; the very floors echoed the sounds of immortality. . . . It was the crowning and consecration of art. . . . These works instead of being taken from their respective countries were given to the world and to the mind and heart of man from whence they sprung. . . .'

William Hazlitt, writing of the Louvre in 1802, goes on, in equally florid style, to claim for this museum the beginning of a new age when artistic masterpieces would be the inheritance of all, no longer the preserve of kings and nobility. Novel the Louvre certainly was. The palace, hung with the private collections of monarchs and their ministers, was first opened to the public in 1793, during the Revolution. Within a decade Napoléon had made it the largest art collection on earth with takings from his empire.

However inspiring it might have been then, for most tourists these days going round the Louvre is an atonement for all the fun times in Paris. The museum is in fact in the process of being completely transformed. The plan is to transfer all post-1850 paintings to the new Musée d'Orsay (the paintings have already left the Louvre) and to use the space thus liberated, plus the whole of the north wing hitherto occupied by the Ministry of Finance, to redeploy the existing collections as well as a host of material at present in storage in a more logical and coherent manner. At the same time a vast new subterranean service area is being built under the *Cour Napoléon*, to accommodate an information centre, ticket offices, bookshop, banks, cloakrooms and the like, with direct access by escalator and lift – the whole to be roofed by an elegant glass pyramid designed by the Chinese-American architect, I. M. Pei. When exactly the project will be complete is hard to predict. The Chirac government, for instance, in a move that looks like sour grapes obstruction has just decided to reinstate the Ministry of Finance offices in the north wing after they had already been dismantled, pending the completion of their new home at Bercy. But the final result should remove the need for heroic will-power and stamina in the search for one work you like, or are looking for, amongst the 300,000. For the moment, with the alterations in progress, it's even worse than before. With all the galleries switched about it's virtually impossible to give a guide.

A bonus from the building works has been the opportunity to excavate the remains of the medieval Louvre – Philippe Auguste's 12C fortress and Charles V's 14C palace conversion – under the *Cour Carrée* and some houses and streets under the *Cour Napoléon*. The former will remain on view, incorporated into special underground galleries.

The museum's collections will continue to be arranged in seven basic divisions: three lots of antiquities, sculpture, painting, applied and graphic

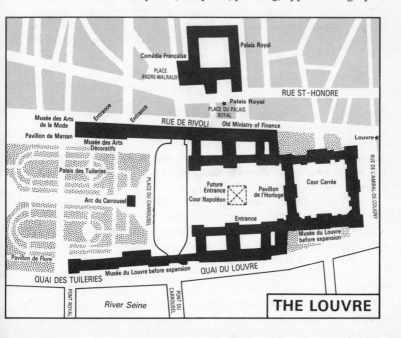

arts. **Oriental Antiquities** cover the Sumerian, Babylonian, Assyrian and Phoenician civilisations, plus the art of ancient Persia. **Egyptian Antiquities** contains jewellery, domestic objects, sandals, sarcophagi and dozens of examples of the delicate naturalism of Egyptian decorative technique, like the wall tiles depicting a piebald calf galloping through fields of papyrus and a duck taking off from a marsh. Some of the major exhibits are: the pink granite *Mastaba sphinx*, the *Kneeling Scribe* statue, a wooden statue of *chancellor Nakhti*, the *god Amon*, protector of Tutankhamen, *Sethi I* and the *goddess Hathor*, a bust of *Amenophis IV*. The **Greek and Roman Antiquities** include the *Winged Victory of Samothrace* and the *Venus de Milo*, biggest crowd-pullers in the museum after the Mona Lisa. Venus, striking a classic model's pose, is one of the great sex pots of all time. She dates from the late 2C BC. Her antecedents are all on display too, from the delightful *Dame d'Auxerre* of 7C BC to the 5C BC bronze *Apollo of Piombino*, still looking straight ahead in the archaic manner, to the classical perfection of the *Athlete of Benevento* and the beautiful *Ephebe of Agde*. In the Roman section are some very attractive mosaics from Asia Minor and luminous frescoes from Pompeii and Herculanum, which already seem to foreshadow the decorative lightness of touch of a Botticelli still 1,000 years and more away.

The **Applied Arts** collection is heavily weighted on the side of vulgar imperial opulence. Beautifully crafted and extravagantly expensive pieces of furniture, which arouse no aesthetic response whatever, just an appalled calculation of the cost. The same has to be said of the renowned cabinet-maker, Boulle's, work (active round 1700), immediately recognisable by the heavy square shapes and lavish use of inlays in copper, bronze and pewter and such ecologically catastrophic exuberance as entire doors of tortoise shell. There are also several acres of tapestry – all of the very first quality and workmanship, but a chore to look at. Relief has to be sought in the smaller, less public items: Marie-Antoinette's travelling case, for example, fitted up with the intricacy of a jigsaw to take an array of bottles, vials and other queenly necessaries. Or, the carved Parisian ivories of the 13C: angels with rouged cheeks and the Virgin pulling a sharp little tit from her dress to suckle the Babe. Or, the Limoges enamels and even earlier Byzantine ivories.

The **Sculpture** section covers the entire development of the art in France from Romanesque to Rodin and includes Michelangelo's *Slaves* designed for the tomb of Pope Julius II. But once you have seen the Greeks, you are not likely to want to linger over many of the items here.

The largest and most indigestible section by far is the **paintings** – French from the year dot to mid-19C, with Italians, Dutch, Germans, Flemish and Spanish represented too. Among them are many paintings so familiar from reproduction in advertisements and on chocolate boxes that it is a surprise to see them on a wall in a frame. And unless you are an art historian, the parade of mythological scenes, classical ruins, piteous piety, acrobatic saints and sheer dry academicism is hard to make much sense of. A portrait, a domestic scene, a still life, is a real relief. Walking by with eyes selectively shut is probably the best advice. The early Italians are the most interesting part of the collection, at least up to Leonardo and the 16C. Giotto, Fra Angelico, Uccello's *Battle of San Romano*, Mantegna, Botticelli, Filippo Lippi, Raphael . . . all the big names are represented. It is partly their period, but there is still an innate classical restraint which is more appealing to modern taste than the exuberance and grandiloquence of the 18C and 19C. If you want to get near the *Mona Lisa*, go first or last thing in the day. No one, incidentally, pays the slightest bit of attention to the other Leonardos right alongside, including the *Virgin of the Rocks*.

If you're likely to be back in Paris in a few years, wait till the **glass pyramid** is in place and all the buildings works finished. Then you'll be able to glide down below the courtyard, consult computers, audio-visuals and multi-lingual 'hostesses' before taking ambulators and escalators to the relevant section, and sit down with a cup of coffee in between the galleries of a much enlarged museum.

Musée d'Orsay

Quai Anatole France, 7e; M° Gare d'Orsay. Open 10.30–6; cl. Mon.
The conversion of the disused railway station, the Gare d'Orsay, into the spanking new *Musée d'Orsay* marks a major advance in the reorganis-ation of the capital's art collections. It houses the painting and sculpture of the immediately pre-modern period, 1848–1914, bridging the gap between the Louvre and the Centre Beaubourg. Its focus is the cobweb-clearing, eye-cleansing collection of **Impressionists** rescued from the cramped corridors of the Jeu de Paume, though not, unavoidably, from the coach parties and gangs of brats. Scarcely less electrifying are the works of the **Post-Impressionists** brought in from the Palais de Tokyo.

The general layout is as follows. On the **ground floor**, the mid-19C sculptors, including Barye, caster of super-naturalistic bronze animals, occupy the centre gallery. To their right, a few canvases by Ingres and Delacroix (the bulk of whose work is in the Louvre) serve to illustrate the transition from the early 19C. Puvis de Chavannes, Gustave Moreau, the Symbolists and early Degas follow, while in the galleries to the left Daumier, Corot, Millet and the realist school lead on to the first Impressionist works, including Manet's *Déjeuner sur l'Herbe*, which sent the critics into apoplexies of rage and disgust when it appeared in 1863. *Olympia* is here too, equally controversial – for the colour contrasts and sensual surfaces, rather than the content, though the black cat was thought peculiar.

To get the chronological continuation you have to go straight up to the top level, where numerous landscapes and outdoor scenes by Renoir, Sisley, Pissarro and Monet owe much of their brilliance to the novel practice of setting up easels in the open to catch a momentary light. Monet's waterlilies are here in abundance, too, along with five of his Rouen cathedral series, each painted in different light conditions.

Le Berceau (1872), by Morisot, the only woman in the early group of Impressionists, is one of the few to have a complex human emotion as its subject – perfectly synthesized with the classic techniques of the movement. A very different touch, all shimmering light and wide brush strokes, is to be seen in Renoir's depiction of a good time being had by all in *Le Moulin de la Galette* – a favourite Sunday afternoon out on the Butte Montmartre.

Cézanne, a step removed from the preoccupations of the mainstream Impressionists, is also wonderfully represented. One of the canvases most revealing of his art is *Still life with apples and oranges* (1895–1900), in which the background abandons perspective and the fruit has an extraordinary reality.

The rest of this level is given over to the various offspring of Impressionism. Among a number of pointilliste works by Seurat and others is Signac's horrible *Entrée du Port de Marseille*. There's Gauguin, post- and pre-Tahiti, as well as some very attractive derivatives like Georges Lacombe's carved wood panels; several superb Bonnards and Vuillards and lots of Toulouse-Lautrec at his caricaturial night-clubbing best – one large canvas including a rear view of Oscar Wilde at his grossest. Plus all the blinding colours and disturbing rhythms of the Van Goghs.

The **middle level** takes in Rodin and other late 19C sculptors, three rooms of Art Nouveau furniture and *objets* and, lastly, some Matisses and Klimts to mark the transition to the moderns in the Beaubourg collection.

As if these exhibition riches weren't enough, **the building** is itself a handsome structure, especially the interior, a huge vault of glass and steel, pusillanimously disguised by a façade of bourgeois stone. It was inaugurated in time for the 1900 World Fair and continued to serve the stations of south-west France until 1939. Orson Welles used it as the setting for his film of Kafka's *Trial*, and de Gaulle used it announce his coup d'état of 19 May 1958, his messianic return to power to save the *patrie* from disintegration over the Algerian liberation war. Notwithstanding this illustrious history it was only saved from a hotel developer's bulldozer by the colossal wave of public indignation and remorse at the destruction of Les Halles.

Cité des Sciences et de l'Industrie.
Porte de la Villette, 18ᵉ; Mᵒ Porte de la Villette. Open Tues-Fri 2–10; Sat, Sun & hols 12–10; cl. Mon.
The science museum, in fact. It would be worth visiting for the interior

of the building alone: all glass and stainless steel, crowsnests and cantilevered platforms, bridges and suspended walkways, the different levels linked by a lift and escalator – in the intestinal style of Richard Rogers of Beaubourg fame. The **permanent exhibition**, called *Explora*, is arranged in clusters of related units on galleries that surround a huge central space open to the full 40-metre height of the roof. Its themes/sectors are four: Earth and the Universe, the Adventure of Life, Matter and Human Labour, Language and Communication – the last three currently in the process of expansion.

This is not at all the conventional museum-repository, where Knowledge is represented by the accumulation of objects. As the exhibition title suggests, the keynote is exploring, the continuing process of finding out. Farming the seas, agriculture, plant biology, the origins of humankind, the nature of sound and speech, meteorology, the movement of planets, space and the oceans . . . it's all here, to be explored and enjoyed actively, for this is the participatory museum par excellence. You can play games, manipulate blips on screens, watch videos, listen to tapes to your heart's content. And if you've got the time to stand and stare you can watch two slabs of wall part company at the rate of 2cm a year; set in motion on 13 March 1986, they enact the gradual estrangement of Europe and the US – this particular aspect of the process apparently unaffected by White House incumbency. In fact, the whole experience resembles

nothing so much as an animated and personal version of the frozen events you witness through the portholes of the model space laboratory suspended near the cafeteria on level 2, where there is a just-opened planetarium.

Additional attractions are a **resources centre** (*médiathèque*), **kids' activity centre** (*inventorium* – yes, there's a fair bit of word-coinage in deference to the age of computerspeak), a changing exhibition of contemporary French **high-tech** industrial achievements (*la maison de l'industrie*) and a whole programme of **temporary exhibitions**.

Admission is a bit steep, but there is enough here to keep the young of all ages busy for several days. English-language audio-guides are available.

THE REST OF THE ART

Musée des Arts Africains et Océaniens
283 av Daumesnil, 12ᵉ; Mᵒ Porte-Dorée. Open 9.45–12 & 1.30–5.15; cl. Tues.
This strange museum – one of the cheapest and least crowded in the city – has an African gold brooch of curled-up sleeping crocodiles on one floor and, in the basement, five live crocodiles in a tiny pit surrounded by tanks of tropical fishes. Imperialism is much in evidence in a gathering of culture and creatures from the old French colonies: hardly any of the black African artefacts are dated – the collection predates European acknowledgment of history on that continent – and the captions are a bit suspicious too. These masks and statues, furniture, adornments and tools should be exhibited with paintings by Expressionists, Cubists and Surrealists to see in which direction inspiration went. Picasso and friends certainly came here often. And though the casual tourist might not respond with a bit of painting or sculpture, there is enjoyment enough to be had.

Musée de Cluny
Place Paul-Painlevé, 5ᶜ (off rue des Ecoles); Mᵒ Odéon, St-Michel. Open 9.45–12.30 & 2–5.15; cl. Mon.
If you have always found tapestries boring, this treasure house of medieval art may well provide the flash of enlightenment. There are numerous beauties: a marvellous depiction of the grape harvest; a Resurrection embroidered in gold and silver thread, with sleeping guards in medieval armour; a room of 16C Dutch tapestries, full of flowers and birds, a woman spinning while a cat plays with the end of the thread, a lover making advances, a pretty woman in her bath, overflowing into a duck pond. But the greatest wonder of all is *La Dame à la Licorne. The Lady with the Unicorn*: six enigmatic scenes featuring a beautiful woman

flanked by a lion and a unicorn, late 15C, perhaps made in Brussels. Quite simply, it is the most stunning piece of art you are likely to see in many a long day. The ground of each panel is a delicate red worked with a thousand tiny flowers, birds and animals. In the centre is a green island, equally flowery, framed by stylised trees, and here the scene is enacted. The young woman plays a portable organ, takes a sweet from a proffered box, makes a necklace of carnations while a pet monkey, perched on the rim of a basket of flowers, holds one to his nose . . .

Grand and Petit Palais

Av W-Churchill, 8ᵉ; Mᵒ Champs-Elysées/Clemenceau. Grand Palais open 10–8 (Wed till 10); cl. Tues. Petit Palais open 10–5.40; cl. Mon; free Sun.

The **Grand Palais Galeries** hold major temporary art exhibitions, good ones being evident from the queues stretching down av Churchill. *Pariscope* and co. will have details and you'll probably see plenty of posters around.

In the **Petit Palais**, whose entrance hall is a brazenly extravagant painted dome, you'll find the *Beaux Arts* museum, which seems to be a collection of leftovers – from all periods – after the other main galleries had taken their pick. There's a certain interest – you can compare the ugliness of an Art Nouveau dining room with the effete 18C furniture in the *Salles Tuck* – but this collection shouldn't be at the top of your list. And that despite its considerable section of 19C French painting.

At the back of the Grand Palais (av Roosevelt) is the **Palais de la Découverte** which has become an anachronism now that La Villette is open. Presumably troops of French schoolchildren will still be taken round this stuffy traditional science museum, given demonstrations of classic experiments and given a break in the planetarium. But no one else need set foot.

Musée Guimet

6 place d'Iena, 16ᵉ; Mᵒ Iéna. Open 9.45–12 & 1.30–5.15; cl. Tues.

Little visited, this features a huge and beautifully displayed collection of Oriental art, from China, India, Japan, Tibet and south-east Asia. There is a particularly fine collection of Chinese porcelain on the top floor.

Musée Marmottan

2 rue Louis-Boilly, 16ᵉ (off av Raphael); Mᵒ Muette. Open 10–6; cl. Mon; expensive admission.

The Marmottan house itself is interesting, with some splendid pieces of First Empire pomposity, chairs with golden sphinxes for armrests, candelabra of complicated headdresses and twining serpents. There is a small and beautiful collection of 13–16C manuscript illuminations, but the star of the show is the collection of **Monet paintings** bequeathed by the artist's son. Among them used to be a canvas entitled *Impression, Soleil Levant (Impression, Sunrise)*, an 1872 rendering of a misty sunrise over Le Havre, whose title the critics usurped to give the Impressionist movement its name. It was stolen from the gallery in October 1985, along with four other Monets, two Renoirs, a Berthe Morisot and a Naruse. All the paintings so well-known they can't possibly be resold on the open market. Presumably it was a contract job and the paintings now hang in the private fortress of some pathological millionaire. Still, despite this anti-social act, the best paintings remain on the walls: a dazzling collection of canvases from Monet's last years at Giverny (see p.224). They include several *Nymphéas* (Water-lilies), *Le Pont Japonais, L'Allée des Rosiers, La Saule Pleureur*, where rich colours are laid on in thick, excited whorls and lines. Marks on white canvas: form dissolves. To all intents and purposes, these are abstractions – so much more 'advanced' than the work of, say, a Renoir, Monet's exact contemporary.

The Orangerie
Place de la Concorde. 1er: Mo Concorde, Open 9.45–5.15; cl. Tues; free Wed.
The **Orangerie**, on the south side of the Tuileries terrace overlooking place de la Concorde, reopened in 1985 after everyone had forgotten what it had inside, to reveal its two oval rooms arranged by **Monet** as panoramas for his largest waterlily paintings. In addition there are works by no more than a dozen other **Impressionist** artists – Matisse, Cézanne, Utrillo, Modigliani, Renoir, Soutine and Sisley amongst them. This is a private collection, inherited by the state with the stipulation that it should always stay together. Consequently the pictures won't move to the Musée d'Orsay and the Orangerie will remain one of the top treats of Paris art museums. Cézanne's southern landscapes, the portraits by Van Dongen, Utrillo and Derain of Paul Guillaume and Jean Walter, whose taste this collection represents, the massive nudes of Picasso, Monet's *Argenteuil* and Sisley's *Le Chemin de Montbuisson*, are the cherries on the cake of this visual feast. What's more, you don't need marathon endurance to cover the lot and get back to your favourites for a second look. The only black mark is the gilt heaviness of the frames.

Palais de Tokyo
Av du Président-Wilson, 16e; Mo Iéna, Alma-Marceau. Musée d'Art Moderne de la Ville de Paris, open 10–5.40; cl. Mon. Centre National de la Photographie, open 9.45–5.15; cl. Tues.
In the east wing, the **Musée d'Art Moderne de la Ville de Paris** has a large permanent collection of works by Vlaminck, Zadkine, Picasso, Braque, Juan Gris, Valadon, Matisse, Dufy, Utrillo, both Delaunays,

Chagall, Modigliani, Léger and many others, as well as sculpture and painting by contemporary artists. The most spectacular room is one devoted to four huge Robert Delaunays – great whirling wheels and cogs of rainbow colour – with the pale figures of Matisse's *La Danse* leaping off their long arcaded canvas across the end wall. Next door, Dufy's enormous mural, *La Fée Electricité* (done for the electricity board), illustrates the story of electricity from Aristotle to the then modern power station in 250 lyrical, colourful panels filling three entire walls. And a little number worth checking out: the shop in the foyer, which, among other artists' designs, sells a set of Sonia Delaunay's playing cards, guaranteed to rejuvenate the most jaded cardsharp.

The west wing of the Palais, which used to house the Musée d'Art et d'Essai and a collection of post-Impressionists, both now installed in the Musée d'Orsay, is being reorganised as the Centre National de la Photographie. Parts of it are already (mid-1986) open. The policy is to mount temporary exhibitions of past and contemporary work.

Musée Picasso
5, rue de Thorigny, 3ᵉ; Mᵒ St-Paul/Filles-du-Calvaire. Open 9.45–5.15; Wed late opening to 10; cl. Tues.

The French are justly proud of their newest art museum. The grandiloquent 17C mansion, the Hôtel Salé, has been restored and restructured at a cost to the government of £¾m. The spacious but undaunting interior is admirably suited to its contents; a large proportion of the works personally owned by Picasso at the time of his death on which the state had first option in lieu of taxes owed. This is the largest collection of Picassos anywhere. It includes all the different mediums he used, the paintings he bought or was given by his contemporaries, his African masks and sculptures, photographs, letters and other personal memorabilia.

All of which said, I found myself disappointed. These are not Picasso's most enjoyable works – the museums of the Côte d'Azur and the Picasso gallery in Barcelona are more exciting. But the collection does leave you with a definite sense of the man and his life in conjunction with his production. This is partly because these were the works he wanted to keep. The paintings of his wives, lovers and families are some of the gentlest and most endearing: the portrait of *Marie-Thérèse and Claude dessinant, Françoise et Paloma*. This one is accompanied by a photo of Picasso drawing with his kids Claude and Paloma. Throughout the chronological sequence, the photographs are vital in showing this charismatic (and highly photogenic) man seen at work and at play by friends and family.

The portrait of *Dora Maar*, like that of Marie-Thérèse, was painted in 1937, during the Spanish Civil War when Picasso was going through his worst personal and political crises. This is the period when emotion and passion play hardest on his paintings and they are by far the best, even though you have to go to Madrid to see *Guernica*. A decade later, Picasso was a member of the Communist Party – his cards are on show along with a drawing entitled *Staline à la Santé* (Here's to Stalin), and his delegate credentials for the 1948 World Congress of Peace. The *Massacre en Corée* (1951) demonstrates the pacifist commitment in his work.

Temporary exhibitions will bring to the Hôtel Salé works from the periods least represented: the Pink Period, Cubism (despite some fine examples here, including a large collection of collages), the immediate post-war period and the 1950s and 1960s.

The modern museological accoutrements are all provided: audio-visuals and films in a special cinema; biographical and critical details displayed in each room, a library, and a good and not too expensive restaurant/tea-room. The museum opened in September 1985; the crowds of visitors have yet to start thinning out.

Musée Rodin
77 rue de Varenne, 7ᵉ (just to the east of the Invalides); Mᵒ Varenne. Open 10–6; cl. Tues; half-price Sun.
This collection represents the whole of Rodin's work. Major projects like *Les Bourgeois de Calais, Le Penseur, Balzac, La Porte de l'Enfer, Ugolini et fils*, are exhibited in the garden – the latter forming the centrepiece of the ornamental pond. Indoors (very crowded) are works in marble like *Le Baiser, La Main de Dieu, La Cathédrale* – those two perfectly poised, almost sentient, hands. There is something particularly fascinating about the works, like *Romeo and Juliet* and *La Centauresse*, which are only, as it were, half-created, not totally liberated from the raw block of stone.

INDIVIDUAL ARTIST OR SMALLER MUSEUMS

Institut Français d'Architecture
6 rue de Tournon, 6ᵉ; Mᵒ Odéon. Open 10.30–7; cl. Mon and Sun.
Very interesting temporary exhibitions.

Musée d'Art Juif
42, rue des Saules, 18ᵉ; Mᵒ Lamarck-Caulaincourt. Open 3–6; wkdays only; cl. Aug.
Some contemporary art, models of the great synagogues, and numerous objects to do with worship.

Atelier d'Henri Bouchard
25, rue de l'Yvette, 16ᵉ; Mᵒ Jasmin. Open 2–7 Wed & Sat only.
Another studio of a sculptor (1875–1960), with works in bronze, stone, wood and marble exhibited.

Musée Bourdelle
16, rue Antoine-Bourdelle, 15ᵉ; Mᵒ Montparnasse/Falguière. Open 10–5,40; cl. Mon.
The work of the early 20C sculptor, including casts, drawings and tools, in the studio and house where he lived.

Musée Cernuschi
7 av Velasquez, 17ᵉ (by east gate of Parc Monceau); Mᵒ Monceau/Villiers. Open 10–5.40; cl. Mon.
A small collection of ancient Chinese art with some exquisite pieces, but of fairly specialised interest.

Musée Cognacq-Jay
25, bd des Capucines, 2ᵉ; Mᵒ Opéra. Open 10–5,40; cl. Mon.
For lovers of European art of the 18C – Canaletto, Fragonard, Tiepolo – and early Rembrandt. Also porcelain, furniture and aristocratic trinkets in a matching setting of wood panelled rooms.

Musée Delacroix
6 place de Furstemburg, 6ᵉ; Mᵒ St-Germain-des-Prés. Open 9.45–5.15; cl. Tues.
Some attractive watercolours, illustrations from *Hamlet* and a couple of versions of a lion hunt hang in the painter's old studio, but there's nothing much in the way of major work.

Musée Ernest Hébert
85, rue due Cherche-Midi, 6ᵉ; Mᵒ Duroc/Vaneau. Open 2–6; cl. Tues.
Pics and drawings by the painter Ernest Hébert (1817–1908).

Musée de l'Holographie
Niveau 1, Forum des Halles, 1ᵉ; Mᵒ Les Halles. Open 10.30–7; Sun/Mon 1–7.
Like most holography museums to date, this one is less exciting than you expect, the fault lying with the state of the art. But there are a couple of holograms more inspired than women winking as you pass, and works where artists have combined holograms with painting. The most impressive technically are the reproductions of museum treasures which just like the originals you can't touch.

Musée des Monuments Français,
Palais de Chaillot, place du Trocadéro, 16ᵉ; Mᵒ Trocadéro. Open 9.45–12.30 2–5; cl. Tues.
In the east wing of the Palais, the Musée des Monuments Français comprises full-scale reproductions of the most important church sculpture from Romanesque to Renaissance. All the major sites are represented.

This is the place to come to familiarise yourself with the styles and periods of monumental sculpture in France. Also included are repros of the major frescoes.

Musée Gustave Moreau
14 rue de la Rochefoucauld, 9e; M° Trinité. Open 10–12.45; cl. Mon, Tues & holidays.
An out-of-the-way bizarre, overcrowded collection of cluttered, joyless paintings by the Symbolist, Gustave Moreau. If you know you like him, go along. Otherwise, give it a miss.

Musée Valentin-Haûy
5, rue Duroc, 7e; M° Duroc, Open 2.30–5 Tues & Wed only; cl. July and Aug; free.
Not for the blind but about them – the aids devised over the years as well as art and objects made by blind people.

Musée Zadkine
100 bis rue d'Assas, 6e; M° Vavin. Open 10–5.40; cl. Mon.
Studio, garden and works of the Cubist sculptor, Ossip Zadkine.

FASHION AND FRIPPERIES

Musée des Arts de la Mode
109, rue de Rivoli, 1er; M° Palais-Royal. Open Wed-Sat 12.30–6,30. Sun 11–5; cl. Mon & Tues.
The newest fashion museum of Paris is part of the *Arts Décoratifs* set up in the north wing of the Louvre (but with a separate entrance and admission charge). The circular roof windows of the building look out on the Eiffel Tower, the Sacré-Coeur, Beaubourg, and the line of the Louvre disappearing down rue de Rivoli – the best views on offer so far in this unimaginative display. Some of the costumes on dummies have a certain camp appeal, and there are a couple of scenes set, but no suggestion of why fashions change nor anything post-1940. That was the opening exhibition – it may get better, but it's unlikely to join the ranks of the city's modern museum marvels.

Musée du Cristal
30 bis, rue de Paradis, 10e; M° Poissonnière. Open 10–12 & 2–5; wkdays only; free.
The most intricate and beautiful examples of crystal glass from the manufacturers Baccarat.

Arts Décoratifs
Same address/hours as the Louvre, see p.110.
Taking up the end of the Louvre's north wing, this museum is not one

to tackle if you've just slogged your way through the rest of the building. It covers tables and chairs, timepieces, cloth and toys – in fact anything that illustrates the decorative skills from the Middle Ages to the 1980s. On the whole, furniture dominates, though with none of it looking as if it's ever been used. The contemporary section is rather meagre given the availability, though there is a fabulous table by Totem. The one outstanding section is the 1900–1925 period: Art Nouveau twirling hair combs and twisting bed heads; a 1920s bathroom with outrageous ocelot loo seat cover; Futurist cigarette cases; and several entire rooms recreated.

Intercoiffure
11 bis rue Jean-Goujon, 8ᵉ; Mᵒ Champs-Elysées. Open Tues & Fri 2–6.
Alexandre, the hairdresser for those who shop at the neighbouring *haute couturiers*, has set up this gallery of *haute coiffure:* pins and tiaras, pictures of hairstyles, combs and razors and jewellery made of hair.

Musée des Lunettes et Lorgnettes de Jadis
2 av Mozart, 16ᵉ; Mᵒ La Muette. Open 9–1 & 2–7; cl. Sun/Mon.
Don't look for a museum. This superb collection of focusing aids resides in an ordinary commercial optician's shop, with nothing on the outside to advertise its existence. The exhibits span pretty much the whole history of the subject, from the first medieval corrective lenses to modern times, taking in binoculars, microscopes and telescopes on the way. Many items are miniature masterpieces: bejewelled, inlaid, enamelled and embroidered – an intricate art that readily accommodated itself to the gimmickry its rich patrons demanded. There are, for example, lenses set in the hinges of fans and the pommels of gentlemen's canes, and a lorgnette case that pops open to reveal an 18C dame sitting on a swing above a waterfall. A special collection consists of pieces that have sat upon the bridges of the famous: Audrey Hepburn, the Dalai Lama, Sophia Loren and ex-President Giscard.

Musée de la Mode et du Costume
10 av Pierre 1ᵉ-de-Serbie, 16ᵉ; Mᵒ Léna/Alma-Marceau. Open 10–5.40; cl. Mon.
Clothes and fashion accessories from the 18C to today exhibited in temporary thematic exhibitions. They last about six months and during changeovers (usually May-Nov) the museum is closed.

Musée de la Parfumerie
9, rue Scribe, 9ᵉʳ; Mᵒ Opéra or RER Auber. Open 9.30–5,30; cl. Sun; free.
The early origins of perfume manufacture, the traditional techniques of the French business, plus containers and labels.

Musée de la Publicité
18 rue du Paradis, 10ᵉ; Mᵒ Château-d'Eau. Open 12–6, cl. Tues.
Publicity posters, adverts and TV and radio commercials are presented in monthly exhibitions, concentrating either on the art, the product or the politics. There's an excellent selection of postcards for sale and very beautiful surroundings of Art Nouveau tiles and wrought iron.

SEITA
12 rue Surcrouf, 7ᵉ; Mᵒ Invalides/Latour-Maubourg. Open 11–6; cl. Sun; free.
The state tobacco company has this small and delightful museum in its offices, presenting the pleasures of smoking with pipes and pouches from every continent – early Gauloise packets, painted *tabac* signs and, best of all, a slide show of tobacco in painting from the 17C to now.

Musée du Vin
Rue des Eaux, 16ᵉ; Mᵒ Passy. Open 12–6; cl. Mon.
20F badly spent! The collection of paraphernalia connected with the wine trade-supposedly the museum's *raison d'être*, – is thoroughly uncon-vincing. The setting – the cellars and tunnels of an erstwhile monastery and quarry – is waxwork-twee. What with the restaurant, *dégustation* and wines for sale, it is clear that profit is the goal, not information. Leave to the manacled coach parties.

HISTORY

Musée de l'Armée
Hôtel des Invalides, 7ᵉ; Mᵒ Invalides, Latour-Maubourg, Ecole-Militaire. Open 10–6/5.
France's national war museum is enormous. By far the largest part is devoted to the uniforms and weaponry of Napoléon's armies. There are numerous personal items of Napoléon's, including his campaign tent and bed, and even his dog – stuffed. Later French wars are illustrated, too, through paintings, maps and engravings. Sections on the two world wars are good, with deportation and resistance covered as well as battles. Some of the oddest exhibits are Secret Service sabotage devices, for instance, a rat and a lump of coal stuffed with explosives.

Musée Arménien and Musée d'Ennery
59, av Foch, 16ᵉ; Mᵒ Porte-Dauphine. Open 2–5; Sun & Thurs; Musée Arménien Sun only; free.
On the ground floor artefacts, art and historical documents of the Armenian people from the Middle Ages to the genocide at the start of this century. On the floors above, the personal acquisitions of a 19C

popular novelist – Chinese and Japanese objects including thousands of painted and sculpted buttons.

Musée National des Arts et Traditions Populaires

6 rte du Mahatma Gandhi, Bois de Boulogne, 16e (beside main entrance to Jardin d'Acclimatation); Mᵒ Les Sablons/Porte-Maillot. Open 10–5.15; cl. Tues.

If you have any interest in the beautiful and highly specialised skills, techniques and artefacts developed in the long ages that preceded industrialisation, standardisation and mass-production, then you should find this museum fascinating. Boat-building, shepherding, farming, weaving, blacksmithing, pottery, stone-cutting, games, clairvoyance . . . all beautifully illustrated and displayed. Downstairs, there is a study section – cases and cases of implements of different kinds, with cubicles where you can call up explanatory slide shows at the touch of a switch.

Musée de l'Assistance Publique

Hôtel de Miramion, 47 quai de la Tournelle, 5e; Mᵒ Maubert. Open 10–5; cl. Mon & Tues.

This covers the history of Paris hospitals from the Middle Ages to the present with pictures, pharmaceutical containers, surgical instruments and decrees relating to public health.

Musée Carnavalet

23 rue de Sévigné, 3e; Mᵒ St-Paul. Open 10–5.40; cl. Mon.

A Renaissance mansion in the Marais presents the **history of Paris** as viewed and lived in by royalty, aristocrats and the bourgeoisie – from François I to 1900. The rooms for 1789–95 are full of sacred mementoes: models of the Bastille, original *Declarations of the Rights of Man and the Citizen*, tricolours and liberty caps, sculpted allegories of Reason, crockery with revolutionary slogans, glorious models of the guillotine and execution orders to make you shed a tear for the royalists as well. In the rest of the gilded rooms, the display of paintings, maps and models of Paris is too exhaustive to give you an overall picture of the city changing. And unless you have the historical details to hand, it's hard to get intrigued by any one period.

Musée Grévin I

10 bd Montmartre, 9e; Mᵒ Montmartre. Open 1–7, during school hols 10–7; no admissions after 6; very expensive.

The main Paris waxworks are nothing like as extensive as London's and only worth it if you are desperate to do something with the kids. The ticket includes a 10-minute conjuring act.

Musée Grévin II
Niveau 1, Forum des Halles, 1er; M° Les Halles. Open 10.30–8; equally expensive.

One up on the wax statue parade of the parent museum but typically didactic. It shows a series of wax model scenes of French brilliance at the turn of the century, with automatically opening and closing doors around each montage to prevent you from skipping any part of the voice-over and animation.

Musée de l'Histoire de France
Archives Nationales, 60 rue des Francs-Bourgeois, 3e; M° Rambuteau. Open 2–5, cl. Tues; Weds free.

The **Archives Nationales** have on show some of the authentic bits of paper that fill the vaults: edicts, wills and papal bulls; a medieval English monarch's challenge to his French counterpart to stake his kingdom on a duel; Henry VIII's RSVP to the Field of the Cloth of Gold invite; fragile cross-Channel treaties; Joan of Arc's trial proceedings with a doodled impression of her in the margin; and more recent legislation and consti-tutions. The Revolution section includes Marie-Antoinette's book of samples from which she chose her dress each morning and a Republican children's alphabet where J stands for Jean-Jacques Rousseau and L for labourer. It's scholastic stuff (and no English translations), but the early documents are very pretty, dangling seals and penned in a delicate and illegible hand.

Musée de la Marine
Palais de Chaillot, place du Trocadéro, 16e; M° Trocadéro. Open 10–6; cl. Tues.

Dozens of beautiful models of French ships, ancient and modern, warlike and commercial.

Musée de la Préfecture de Police
1 bis, rue des Carmes, 5e; M° Maubert. Open 2–5; cl. Wed & Thurs; free.

The history of the Paris police force as presented in this collection of uniforms, arms and papers, stops at 1944 and is, as you might expect, all of the legendary criminals variety.

PERFORMANCE ARTS AND LITERATURE

Maison de Balzac
47 rue Raynouard, 16e; M° Passy/La Muette. Open 10–5.40; cl. Mon; free Sun.

Contains several portraits and caricatures of the writer and a library of works of his authorship, his contemporaries' and his critics'. Balzac lived here between 1840 and 1847, but literary grandees seem to share the common fate of not leaving ghosts.

Musée du Cinema
Palais de Chaillot, place du Trocadéro, 16e; Mo Trocadéro. Open for guided tours only at 10,11,12,2,3, and 4; cl. Mon.
Costumes, sets, cameras, projectors, etc., from the early days on.

Centre Culturel des Halles
Terrasse du Forum des Halles, 101 rue Rambuteau, 1er; Mo Les Halles.
Temporary exhibitions, events and workshops of poetry, crafts and arts take cover beneath the queasy strictured structures above the Forum: in the **Maison de la Poésie, Pavillon des Arts** and **Maison des Ateliers**. There's also a school of theatre and dance with a performance space to come. An auditorium, libraries for video, records and children's books and a photography centre are on their way. Information about these and every other official cultural event in town can be had Monday to Saturday 10–8 from the **Maison d'Information Culturelle** on the ground floor by the main RER entrance (rue Pierre-Lescot).

Maison de Victor Hugo
6 place des Vosges, 4e; Mo Bastille. Open 10–5.40; cl. Mondays.
This museum is saved by the fact that Hugo decorated and drew, as well as wrote. Many of his ink drawings are exhibited and there's an extraordinary Japanese dining room he put together for his lover's house. Otherwise the usual pictures, manuscripts and memorabilia shed sparse light on the man and his work.

Musée Instrumental
14 rue Madrid, 8e; Mo Europe. Open 2–6; cl. Sun, Mon & Tues.
The Paris Conservatoire has on show several thousand musical instruments dating from the Renaissance onwards, many of which have been played by the classical greats.

Instruments de Musique Mécanique
Impasse Berthaud, 3e; Mo Rambuteau. Open 2–7; weekends only.
Barrel organs, gramophones and automatons with demonstrations.

Musée Kwok-On
41 rue des Francs-Bourgeois, 4e; Mo Rambuteau/St-Paul. Open 12–6, wkdays only.
Changing exhibitions feature the popular art of southern Asia – the musical instruments, festival decorations, religious objects, and, most of

all, the costumes, puppets, masks and stage models for theatre, in eleven different countries stretching from Japan to Turkey. The collection includes such things as figures for the Indonesian and Indian Theatres of Shadows, Peking Opera costumes and story-tellers' scrolls from Bengal. The colour is overwhelming and the unfamiliarity shaming – much recommended.

Musée Adam Mickiewicz
6 quai d'Orléans, 4ᵉ; Mᵒ Pont-Marie. Open Thurs 3–6 or by appointment (43. 54. 35. 61); free.
A tiny museum dedicated to one of the greatest Polish poets, a Romantic and nationalist who came to France in 1832 unable to bear the partitioned non-existence of his homeland. A collection of 19C and early 20C paintings by Polish artists who spent some time in France is evidence of the long-lasting Franco-Polish connection.

Musée Edith Piaf
5 rue Créspin-du-Gast, 11ᵉ; Mᵒ Ménilmontant/St-Maur. Admission by appointment only: 43.55.52.72. Open Mon-Thurs afternoons only; cl. July; free.
For the fans of the great cabaret singer: her clothes and letters; posters, photographs and all the existing recordings.

Musée Renan-Scheffer
16 rue Chaptal, 9ᵉ; Mᵒ Pigalle/St-Georges. Open 10–5.40; cl. Mon.
The life of intellectuals and literati in the 19C is the subject of changing exhibitions in this museum. The permanent collection has to do with just one thinker, writer and activist of that century – George Sand. Her jewels and trinkets are on show, rather than her manuscripts but there are some beautiful drawings, by Delacroix, Ingres and Sand herself.

SCIENCE AND INDUSTRY

Musée Branly
21 rue d'Assas, 6ᵉ; Mᵒ St-Placide. Open 9–12 & 2–5; wkdays only; cl. Aug; free.
In the 1890s Marconi used Branly's invention of an electric wave detector – the first coherer – to set up the startling system of communication which didn't need wires. The coherer in question is exhibited along with other pieces from the physicist's experiments.

Musée de la Contrefaçon
16 rue de la Faisanderie, 16ᵉ, Mᵒ Porte-Dauphine. Open 8.30–5; wkdays only.

One of the odder ones – examples of imitation products, labels and brand marks trying to pass off as the 'genuine article'.

Musée de l'Homme
Palais de Chaillot, place du Trocadéro, 16e; Mo Trocadéro. Open 9.45–5; cl. Tues.
Contains displays illustrating the way of life, costumes, characteristic occupations, etc. of numerous countries in all parts of the world and is beginning to look a little dilapidated.

Jardin des Plantes
5e; Mo Austerlitz, Jussieu. Open 1.30–5, Sun 10.30–5; cl. Tues.
There are three museums in the *jardin:* paleontology, botany and mineralogy of which the best is paleontology with a great collection of fossils, pickled bits and pieces and things dinosaurian.

Musée de la Poste
34 bd de Vaugirard, 15e; Mo Montparnasse. Open 10–5; cl. Sun.
Not just stamps, though plenty of those. Also the history of sending messages, from the earliest times to the high-tech inefficient present.

Musée de Radio-France
116 av du Président Kennedy, 16e; Mo Passy. Open 10–12 & 2–5; cl. Mon; guided visits.
Models, machines and documents covering the history of broadcasting in the national TV and radio building.

Musée de la Serrure
1 rue de la Perle, 3e; Mo Chemin-Vert/Rambuteau. Open 10–12 & 2–5; cl. Sun & Mon.
This collection of elaborate and artistic lock-making throughout the ages includes the Napoleonic fittings for his palace doors – the one for the Tuileries bashed in by revolutionaries – locks that trapped your hand or shot your head off if you tried a false key and a 17C masterpiece made by a craftsman under lock and key for four years. The rest of the exhibits are pretty boring, though the setting in a Marais mansion is some compensation.

Musée National des Techniques
270 rue St-Martin, 3e; Mo Réaumur-Sébastopol/Arts-et-Métiers. Open Tues-Sat 1–5.30; Sun (free) 10–5.15.
Utterly traditional and stuffy glass-case museum with thousands of technical things from fridges to flutes, clocks and trains. The only exceptional part is the entrance – an early Gothic church filled with engines, aeroplanes, cars and bikes.

Chapter three

KIDS STUFF AND DAYTIME AMUSEMENTS

When it's cold, wet and grey and you've peered enough at museums, monuments and the dripping panes of shop fronts and café vistas, don't despair or retreat back to your hotel. There are **Golden Oldie movies** to be seen, **music halls** are playing the tango for anyone to dance to, there are **saunas** to soak in, **ice rinks** to fall on, **bowling alleys, billiards, swimming pools** and **gyms**.

And when the weather isn't so bad, you can go for a **ride in a boat**, or even a **helicopter** after a successful flutter on the horses in the Bois de Boulogne. The two-wheeled and essentially French **trotting races** take place in the Bois de Vincennes and both woods are good places for cycling, jogging or just lying about.

Our first category below, of things for **kids**, doesn't exclude adults – you'll find **zoos, circuses** and **parks** listed as well as the playthings for which age limits are in force.

MAINLY FOR KIDS

Parisians with children complain that the capital is a strictly adult city with nothing for energetic 4 to 12-year-olds to do. But when they cross the Channel they find to their horror that you can't even have your offspring with you while you drink. People's **attitude** here to children, in bars, restaurants, hotels and museums, is almost always welcoming, though a certain amount of discipline is expected. And where the Parisian parent may have suggested the same outing a hundred times, the novelty for visiting kids should keep them going for a while at least. One thing they won't find in abundance are adventure playgrounds, and certain activities may be too over-organised for Anglo-Saxon tastes. That apart, younger children are not too badly catered for – although the problem of amusing early to mid-teenagers is as hard as it is anywhere.

The most useful **source of information**, for current shows, exhibitions and events, are the special sections in the listings magazines, *'pour les* *jeunes'* in *Pariscope*, 'Enfants' in *7 à Paris* and 'Jeunes' in *L'Officiel des Spectacles*.

The *Mairie* of each *arrondissement* will provide the address of the local *MJC* which offers various sports facilities, usually a ping-pong table, and courses in anything from videos to pottery. You may have to take out a subscription but it shouldn't be too much despite the new government's dislike of these *Maisons de la Jeunesse et de la Culture*.

Two other places where you can get details of youthful leisure activities are the *CIDJ*, 101 quai Branly, 15e and *Loisirs-Jeunes*, 36 rue de Ponthieu, 8e.

OUTDOOR AMUSEMENTS

The star attraction for young children is the **Jardin d'Acclimatation** (Mo Porte-Maillot) in the Bois de Boulogne, open every day from 9–6.30 with special attractions Wed, Sat and Sun and all week during school holidays. It's a cross between funfair, zoo and amusement park. There's a small entrance charge plus separate tickets for nearly every activity – some very expensive. The temptations include bumper-cars, go-karts, pony and camel rides, sealions, birds, bears and monkeys, a toy-town train ride from Porte Maillot (pm only), a magical mini-canal ride, distorting mirrors, scaled-down farm buildings, and a superb collection of antique dolls at the **Grande Maison des Poupées**. Astérix and friends may still be explaining life in their Gaulish village – created by archaeologists in the **Musée en Herbe**. If not, there'll be another kid-compelling exhibition with game sheets (in English), workshops and demonstrations of traditional crafts. And if they just want to watch and listen, the **Théâtre du Jardin pour l'Enfance et la Jeunesse** puts on musicals and ballets.

Outside the *jardin*, in the **Bois de Boulogne**, older children can amuse themselves with **mini-golf** and **bowling**, or **boating** on the *Lac Inférieur*. By the entrance to the *jardin* there's a **bike hire** for roaming the wood's cycle trails.

Other places you can let kids off the leash are the **Jardin des Plantes** (Mo Jussieu/Monge) with a small **zoo** (9–5.30) and **Natural History Museum** (10–5.30; cl Tues). The best **zoo** – and both are expensive – is in the **Bois de Vincennes** (9–6/5.30 in winter; Mo Porte-Dorée, see p.101). On the other side of the wood, on rte de la Pyramide, fun and games are to be had at the **Parc Floral** (9.30–6/8, Sat to 10, in summer; free for under sixes). A little train tours all the gardens, there's an excellent **playground** with **clowns**, **puppets** and **magicians** on summer weekends, an electric car circuit and a children's theatre, the **Théâtre Astral**. Most of the activities are free and in general you'll be far less out of pocket after an afternoon here than at the Jardin d'Acclimatation.

Back in the centre of town, if you want to lose your charges for the odd hour at **Les Halles**, send them into the small but intriguing playground where plants grow into elephants. It's just west of the Forum, near St-Eustache and professional child-carers are there to encourage and keep watch.

Numbers of squares and public gardens have play areas with sand-pits and slides but the best climbing and slithering experience is to be had on the **Dragon slide** in the **Parc de la Villette** (see p.93). And if they're not in the mood for dragons and want something soft, cuddly and real, take them a short way down av Jean-Jaurès from Mᵒ Porte-de-Pantin. At no 184, at weekends, a sheep joins two alsatian friends on a bed of straw in the porch of a restaurant.

Parc Monceau in the 17ᵉ has a roller-skating rink; there's a puppet theatre in **Parc Montsouris** in the 14ᵉ; the **Luxembourg gardens** have a large playground, pony rides, toyboat hire and puppets; the **Buttes-Chaumont** park has ducks to feed, donkey-drawn carts to ride in, puppets and grassy slopes to roll down. Yet another **puppet-show** takes place in the gardens on the north side of the Champs-Elysées at the Rond-Point (same days as at Buttes-Chaumont: Wed, Sat and Sun).

One last outdoor thrill – **funfairs** – are, alas, few and far between. The odd carousel appears from time to time, at the Forum des Halles or beneath Tour St-Jacques at Châtelet. Rue de Rivoli around Mᵒ St-Paul sometimes hosts a mini-fairground, but the municipal authorities have never been too keen on showpeople. At Christmas 1985, big wheels, dodgems and stalls squatted in the Tuileries gardens in protest at the lack of venues and the general decline in funfair-going thanks to television. The then Minister for Culture, the maverick Jack Lang, was all for letting them stay, but apoplexy in the museums department eventually won out.

INDOORS AND UNDERGROUND

Unlike funfairs, **circuses** are seen as culture and there are several venues including the 19C *Cirque d'Hiver Bouglione* (110 rue Amelot, 11ᵉ). The strolling players and fairy lights beneath the dome welcome circus-goers from October to January (and TV and fashion shows the rest of the year). Other places to check out (see *Pariscope*) are: *Dakotas Show* (square Amiral-Bruix, 16ᵉ; Mᵒ Porte-Maillot); *Cirque de Paris*, (quai Henri IV, 4ᵉ; Mᵒ Quai-de-la-Rapée); *Cirque Pauwels* (Jardin d'Acclimatation, Bois de Boulogne; Mᵒ Sablons); *Cirque Zavatta-Fils* (square Réjane, Cours-de-Vincennes, 20ᵉ; Mᵒ Nation).

Several **theatres**, apart from *Astral* and *du Jardin* (see above), occasionally put on shows for children and where it's mime, dance and music, comprehension won't be frustrated. *Le Dunois 28* (28 rue Dunois, 13ᵉ; Mᵒ Chevaleret) has a special kids' slot, though this may be over-verbal; Wed and Sun at 3pm, October-March. Many **cinemas** show kids' films, though inevitably they'll be in French – with cartoons this might not matter.

Given kids' particular and sometimes peculiar tastes, the choice of **museums and monuments** had better be left to them. But don't forget the gargoyles of **Notre-Dame**, the aquariums at the **Musée des Arts Africains et Océaniens** (see p.116) and beneath the Palais de Chaillot (Trocadéro, 16e; open 10–5.30). And avoid the **Musée des Enfants** which boringly purveys sentimental images of childhood. **Beaubourg** should score well and also offers a **children's workshop**, the *Atelier des Enfants*, free for visitors 10–11.30 on Wed; 2–3.30 & 3.45–5 on Wed and Sat. While you visit the exhibitions, your offspring can dance, paint, sculpt and play games with English-speaking organisers. At the **Parc de la Villette** in the 19e, screen addicts should be given the treat of the **Géode**'s 180° projection – don't worry about language, it's a visual knockout and the commentary is naff anyway. For details, turn to the cinema section on p.200. The **Cité des Sciences et de l'Industrie** is guaranteed to grab most children and has areas specially designed for them. Very highly recommended – see p.114.

The ghoulish and horror fanatics should get a really satisfying shudder from the **Catacombs** (2–4, w/e 9–11 & 2–4; cl. Mon; but read p.77 first), while the architypal pre-teen fixation might find fulfilment in the **sewers** – *Les Egouts* (tours Mon, Wed and the last Saturday of the month, 2–5; see p.64).

SHOPS

If they've run out of **things to read**, the English bookshops, *Brentano's* (37 av de l'Opéra, 2e), *WH Smith* (248 rue de Rivoli, 1er) and *Galignani* (224 rue de Rivoli, 1er) all have good children's sections.

For **toys and games**, even if you've no intention of buying them anything, kids will try their hardest looking around some of these shops:
Alfa Paris, 48 rue des Francs-Bourgeois, 3e. Soft toys for young kids – a few under 50F, mostly around 100F.
Ali Baba, 29 av de Tourville, 7e. 10–1 & 2–7; cl. Sun. A big 3–storey cavern – good for all ages.
Baby Train, 9 rue du Petit-Pont, 5e. 9.30–6.30; cl. Sun. The best collection of electric trains, radio-controlled planes, buggies and boats.
Le Canard à Roulettes, 60 rue Mazarine, 6e. 1–6; cl. Sun, Mon, August and September. Beautifully made miniature furniture, and dolls' house accessories.
Carambol, 20 rue des Francs-Bourgeois, 4e. Wooden toys and kaleidoscopes.
Les Cousins d'Alice, corner rues Lalande/Daguerre, 14e. 10–1 & 3–7; cl.

Sun, Mon & Aug. Alice in Wonderland decorations, plus a general range of books and records.

Françoise Cousseau, 52 rue St-André-des-Arts, 6e. Puppets, marionettes, masks, pencil boxes, jack-in-the-boxes.

Deyrolle, 46 rue du Bac, 7e. 9–12.30, 2–6.30; cl. Sun. *The* taxidermist: insects, butterflies, stuffed animals – from the biggest to the smallest, plus rocks and fossils. Fun to look at.

Magic Toys, Centre Beaugrenelle, 16 rue Linois, 15e; 10–7.30 (Mon from 11); cl. Sun. The biggest toyshop in Paris – good for half a day.

La Maison de la Peluche, 74 rue de Seine, 6e. 10–7.30; cl. Sun. More lovely stuffed animals, of the cuddly type.

Le Monde en Marche, 34 rue Dauphine, 6e. 10.30–7.30; cl. Sun, Mon, Aug. Wooden toys of all sorts, from puzzles to dolls' houses.

Puzzles, 118 rue du Château, 14e. Exactly what it says; with workshop on the premises.

Rigodon, 13 rue Racine, 6e 10.30–7; cl. Sun. & Aug. A weird and wonderful wizard's cave of marionettes, puppets, horror-masks and other spooks.

Parisian **kids' clothes shops** can also be fun – and considerably more imaginative than their British or American equivalents, particularly in the shoes line. Rewarding stops/browsings might include the kids' sections in the big department and discount stores (see p.149) and any of the following specialists:

Agnès B, 2/3 rue du Jour, 1er; 13 rue Michelet, 6e, 17 av Pierre 1er-de-Serbie, 16e. 10.30–7; cl. Sun. Fashionable and entertaining.

Baby Dior, 28 av Montaigne, 8e. 9.30–6.30 (Mon & Sat 10–1 & 2.30–6.30); cl. Sun. Not perhaps for buying – it's part of the main Dior shop – but you could all have a good laugh at the prices.

Michel Bachoz, 98 rue de Rennes, 6e 10–7; cl. Sun. French Benetton for kids' equivalent but better quality.

Gullipy, 66 rue de Babylone, 7e. 9–7 (Sat 11–1 & 2–7); cl. Sun. Fun accessories as well as clothes – satchels, bags, wallets etc.

La Petite Gaminerie, 28/32 rue du Four, 6e; 10–7; cl. Sun (& Mon in Aug). Designer clothes – New Man, Cacharel, Hechter, Kickers. Good stuff, though not cheap.

Pom d'Api, 13 rue du Jour, 1er; 10.30–7 (Sat 10.30–7.30); cl. Sun. Colourful and sometimes bizarre-looking shoes for kids of all ages. Well worth a look.

FOOD, BABYSITTING AND ESSENTIALS

Restaurants are usually good at providing small portions or allowing children to share dishes. *Chantegrill* (18 rue St Denis, 1er) has a special children's menu and comic books appear between courses. Similar attractions come with American food at *Yankel*'s (102 rue Réaumur, 2ᵉ; cl. Sat).

The two main **babysitting** agencies are *ABABA, La Maman en Plus!* (43.22.22.11; 8–10 every day; includes English speakers) and *Allo Maman Poule* (47.47.78.78; 24 hrs every day). Apart from these, you could try the *Association Générale des Etudiants en Médicine de Paris* – medical students (105 bd de l'Hôpital, 13ᵉ; 45.86.19.42) or if you know someone with their own phone, dial up *Babysitting* on '*Elletel*' via their *minitel*. Charges are around 20F per hour plus agency fees and taxis home when the métro's stopped running.

You will have little problem in getting hold of **essentials for babies.** Familiar brands of babyfood are available in the supermarkets, as well as disposable nappies (*couches à jeter*) etc. After hours, you can get most goods from late night chemists (see p.13).

MORE FOR ADULTS

Paris's range of both **spectator and participatory amusements** is outlined below. For **additional possibilities** – sports events in particular (and the French currently play beautiful **football**) – check *Pariscope*, etc. or *Figaro*.

WORK-OUTS, SWIMMING AND SAUNAS

The transatlantic craze for twisting, stretching and straining muscles, while competing in style rather than scores, has, predictably, caught on with the Parisians. **Aerobics, dance work-outs** and anti-stress **fitness programmes** are big business, along with the trans-Pacific activities of **yoga, tai-chi** and **martial arts.** Since almost all of these are organised in courses or involve a minimum month's subscription, it's advisable to enjoy your holiday, guilt-free, without them.

An exception is the *Centre de Danse du Marais* (41 rue du Temple, 4ᵉ; Mᵒ Hôtel-de-Ville; open 9–7). Here you can take single lessons in Rock 'n Roll, folkloric dances from the East, tap-dancing, modern dance, physical expression, and West Coast aerobics courtesy of the California Club at the same address. Expect to pay around 50F per session.

Back across bd Sebastopol, for 100F plus, fanatics can spend a day doing every kind of tendon-shattering gyration at *Espace Vit'Halle* (48 rue Rambuteau, 3ᵉ; MᵒRER Châtelet-Halles). It's open Mon-Fri 9–10; Sat 10–6; Sun 11–3; and it's divided into four 'work zones' – the parquet, the gym floor, the body-building room, and the multi-gym room. '*Détente*' is also provided for with a sauna, hammam, solarium and diet bar.

For straightforward exercise, and for under 10F you can go **swimming** in any of the municipal baths, but check first in *Pariscope* for opening times (under *Piscines*) as varying hours are given over to schools and clubs. *Butte aux Cailles* (5 pl Verlaine, 13ᵉ: Mᵒ Place d'Italie) is housed in a bizarre brick building and generally hassle-free. *Henry-de-Montherlant* (31 bd Lannes, 15ᵉ; Mᵒ Porte-Dauphine) has a warm pool at 271°C and **solarium**. UV tanning is also on offer at *Bernard-Lafay* (70 rue de la Jonquière, 17ᵉ; Mᵒ Guy-Moquet) and *Clignancourt* (12 rue René-Binet, 18ᵉ; Mᵒ Clignancourt). Of the non-municipal, and therefore more expensive, pools, there's *Pontoise* (19 rue de Pontoise, 5ᵉ; Mᵒ Maubert-Mutualité) and *Jean Taris* (16 rue de Thouin, 5ᵉ; Mᵒ Cardinal-Lemoine) in the centre of the Latin Quarter. For outside bathing try *Molitor* (2–8 av de la Porte-Molitor; Mᵒ Porte-d'Auteuil) on the edge of the Bois de Boulogne. Or the crowded *Deligny* (25 quai Anatole-France, 7ᵉ; Mᵒ Chambre-des-Deputés) with the amusing, if expensive, spectacle of rich bodies sunning themselves on the vast deck above the Seine. Most of the extras at *Roger-Le Gall* (34 bd Carnot, 12ᵉ; Mᵒ Porte-de-Vincennes) are reserved for club members but anyone can swim in the pool which has the unique feature of a collapsible roof.

If it's your ankles and shock absorbers you want to exercise, get on the ice at one of the city's two **icerinks**. The *Patinoire de la Gaîté Montparnasse* (27 rue du Commandant-Mouchotte, 15ᵉ; Mᵒ Montparnasse) is the more crowded generally. The other is the *Patinoire des Buttes-Chaumont* (30 rue Edouard-Pailleron, 19ᵉ; Mᵒ Bolivar) and a bit cheaper – around 30F including skate hire. **Roller-skating** has a special rink at *La Main Jaune* (pl de la Porte-de-Champerret, 17ᵉ; Mᵒ Champerret) which costs a good bit more – 45F to 80F for evening sessions. There are occasional free nights, for men with guests as well as for women, and the scene is more social than sportive. For opening hours, see *Pariscope* and co.

One final word on serious exercise: the **Paris Marathon** is held in May and running or jogging is now an all-year-round preoccupation. Take great care, however, with the traffic, even in the Bois de Boulogne and Bois de Vincennes – drivers may run themselves, but they'll mow you down at the flick of a light.

A steam bath and a massage may be as necessary after a trip to the Louvre as after an hour and half's workout. The **Hammams**, or Turkish baths, are one of the unexpected delights of Paris. Much more luxurious than the standard Swedish sauna, these are places to linger and chat. At the *Hammam de la Mosquée* (39 rue Geoffroy-St-Hilaire, 5ᵉ; Mᵒ Censier-Daubenton), you can order mint tea and honey cakes after your baths, around a fountain in a marble and cedar wood-covered courtyard. Open 10–7; women: Mon, Thurs & Sat; men: Fri & Sun; cl. Aug; and very good value for around 50F (massage 40F extra). The *Hammam de St-Paul* (4 rue des Rosiers, 4ᵉ; Mᵒ St-Paul) is less exotic but still a treat with a bar and plates of pâtisserie, beauty treatments of all descriptions, and a summer garden atmosphere with the wickerwork and greenery. Open 10–10; women Wed & Fri; men Thurs & Sat; around 80F; massage, manicure, etc. 50–70F extra.

For a cosmetic-conscious **sauna**, women can try out *La Fourche* (10 rue de la Condamine, 17ᵉ; Mᵒ Rome) which lays on videos, music and a bar to accompany sunbeds, beauty treatments – including make-up – and massage. At a price. For other solariums, see swimming pools above.

BOWLING, BILLIARDS, BETTING . . . AND HORSES

There's nothing particularly Parisian about **bowling alleys**, but they exist and they're popular, should the urge to scuttle skittles take you. Prices vary around 12F a session, double where you have to hire shoes, and more at weekends.

The *Gaîté-Montparnasse complex* (see icerinks above) has 16 lanes, operating from 10 in the morning to 2 at night, and until 4 Fri & Sat. Entertainment is complete, with bar, brasserie, pool tables and video games. An active and young clientele rolls the balls in Chinatown at the *Stadium* (66 av d'Ivry, 13ᵉ; Mᵒ Tolbiac), open 2–2, Sun 10–2am. Bar-billiards and pool alongside. Students favour *Bowling Mouffetard* (73 rue Mouffetard, 5ᵉ; Mᵒ Monge), the cheapest one in town, while the chic types west of town go to *Bowling de Paris* (Jardin d'Acclimatation, Bois de Boulogne; Mᵒ Sablons). For other venues see *Pariscope*.

Billiards, unlike bowling, is an original, and ancient, French game. Unlike the English or American versions, the table has no pockets. If you want to watch or try your hand, here are three places which will cost you nothing: *Académie de Clichy-Montmartre* (84 rue de Clichy, 9ᵉ; Mᵒ Clichy; open 1.30–11.30); *Académie de Paris* (47 av de Wagram, 17ᵉ; Mᵒ Ternes; open 12.30–11, w/e 2–11); *Café Les Sports* (108 bd Jourdan, 14ᵉ; Mᵒ Porte-d'Orléans; open 7.30am–11.30pm, cl. Thurs).

For **pool**, see bowling venues above, and for **pinball** – every café has one. As for the classic French game involving balls, **boules**, or *pétanque*, is more a southern pastime in sleepy town squares, but you may well see it played in Paris, in any of the parks.

On a completely different track, being a spectator at a **horse race** could make a healthy change from looking at art treasures. If you want to fathom the **betting system**, any bar or café with the letters PMU will take your money on a three-horse bet, known as *le tiercé*. The **biggest races** are the *Prix de la République* and the *Grand Prix de L'Arc de Triomphe* on the first and last Sundays in October at Longchamp. The week starting the last Sunday in June sees nine big events, at Auteuil, Longchamp, St-Cloud and Chantilly (see p.216). **Trotting races** with the jockeys in chariots run from August to September on the *Route de la Ferme* in the Bois de Vincennes. St-Cloud *champ de courses* is in the park off Allée de Chamillard. Auteuil is off the rte d'Auteuil, and Longchamp off the rte des Tribunes, both in the Bois de Boulogne. *L'Humanité* and *Paris-Turf* carry details, and admission charges are around 12F.

If you want to **get on a horse yourself**, you need to have come already equipped with a hat, boots and crop. Secondly, you have to buy a licence, the *Carte Nationale de Cavalier* – around 70F, before you can mount. This can be got from the *Fédération Equestre Française* (164 rue du Faubourg-St-Honoré, 8e) or from the clubs which may charge a bit more for it. *Bayard UCPA* on av du Polygone in the Bois de Vincennes (Mo/RER Vincennes) offers trail rides and lessons for around 60F. On the other side of town and a little bit more expensive is *Manège de Neuilly* (19 rue d'Orléans, Neuilly; Mo Sablons) for canters in the Bois de Boulogne.

BOAT TRIPS AND HELI RIDES

From the *quais* or the bridges, after the light has fallen, the sudden appearance of a bulging **Bateau-Mouche**, blaring multi-lingual commentaries, its dazzling floodlights catching you head on and blinding, for a moment at least, the ugly sight of its hulking hull, might make you wonder what it would take to sink the entire fleet. But rather than going off to local manufacturers of Exocets or asking the Intelligence agencies for mining advice, the problem can be solved, individually at least, by getting on the boat yourself. You can't escape the commentary, but the evening rides certainly give the best close-up glamorous gazing at the classic Seine-side buildings and are even said to be quite fun.

Bateaux-Mouches start from the *Embarcadère du Pont de l'Alma* on the right bank in the 8e; rides (1¼ hrs) every half-hour between 8.30–10pm (around 30F) or in the day from 10–12 & 2–6 (around 20F); winter departures at 11, 2.30, 4 & 9 only. Outrageously priced dinners and extravagant lunches are offered on board, to those 'correctly' dressed. *Bateaux-Mouches'* **competitors** are *Bateaux Parisiens* and *Bateaux Vedettes Pont Neuf / Tour Eiffel* and *de Paris Ile-de-France*. The last one does day cruises out of Paris; otherwise they're much of a muchness and detailed in *Pariscope* etc under *Promenades*.

Less blatantly tourist fodder are the **canal boat trips**. *Canauxrama* chugs up and down between the Port de l'Arsenal (opposite 50 bd de la Bastille 12e; Mo Bastille) and the Bassin de la Villette (5 bis quai de la Loire, 19e; Mo Jaurès) on the Canal St-Martin. At the Bastille end is a long tunnel from which you don't surface till the 10e *arrondissement*.

The ride lasts 3hrs – not a bad bargain at 60F in the morning and 75F afternoon. The company also run day trips along the Canal de l'Ourcq, west as far as Meaux, with a coach back.

But by far the classiest boat to take is the catamaran of *La Patache Eautobus*, in which, when not on deck, you sit in a little green and white house with windowboxes full of geraniums. Its journey, lasting 3 hrs, takes you from quai Anatole-France in the 7ᵉ (opposite no 15) up the Seine and into Canal St-Martin. Or you can start at the other end, at 212 av Jean-Jaurès, 20ᵉ, in the Parc de la Villette. It leaves quai Anatole-France at 9.30, and La Villette at 2.30, every day from April to November, and costs around 85F, 40F for under-12s, free for under-6s. It's also vital to reserve – tel: 48. 74. 75. 30.

Having seen Paris from the water, the next step up is Paris from the air. A tour above all the city's sights is somewhat prohibitive at over 400F. But if **helicopter rides** turn you on as much or more than a good meal, a stalls seat at the theatre or two catamaran rides, then a whirl around La Défense is on. The two companies operating are *Héli-France* (9–7.30) and *Hélicap* (8.45–7.30), both at the Héliport de Paris, 4 av de la Porte-de-Sèvres, 15ᵉ.

AFTERNOON TANGOS

One pastime to fill the afternoon hours that might not cross your mind: the *bals musettes*. These dancehalls – the between-the-wars solution in the down-and-out parts of *Gai Paris* to depression, dole and the demise of the Popular Front – are still going strong. Three or four generations of owners later, they still attract a mainly working-class clientele, and run both afternoon and evening sessions. The evening sessions may have become a bit of a cross-town affair, but that was true when Jo de France opened *Balajo*, rue de Lappe in the 1930s. Film stars and jaded aristocrats came to indulge in a bit of rough. *Balajo, La Boule Rouge* and others became part of the ethos of that period, though *bals musettes* themselves had been going since the turn of the century. And now, in the multi-national, management-style bourgeois boredom of the 1980s, you'll find people dancing to abandon, cheek-to-cheek, couple squashed against couple, on a weekday afternoon in the rue de Lappe. Their clothes aren't smart, their French isn't academy, men dance with women, and everyone drinks.

Balajo (9 rue de Lappe, 11ᵉ; Mᵒ Bastille) opens at 3 and closes at 6.30 before reopening at 10 for the evening session (see p.189). The music, all recorded, is a mixture of waltz, tango, java, disco and rock. Admission price of around 40F includes one drink. *La Boule Rouge*, down the street at no 8 is free – you only have to drink.

Away from rue de Lappe, in another down-market *quartier*, is *Tchatch au Tango* (13 rue au Maire, 3e; Mo Arts-et-Metiers), open 2.30–6.30. Entry is free – just cloakroom and drinks to pay for. It's one of the oldest dance halls in town with an ancient jumble of décors to prove it. Teenagers, septuagarians and every age in between, waltz, tango and cha-cha, none of them chic and no-one seriously on the pick-up.

Chapter four

SHOPS AND MARKETS

Even if you don't plan – or can't afford – to buy, Parisian **shops** are still an important part of the cityscape. There is an amazing density of them, given even greater emphasis by the compactness and walkability of the *quartiers* and, not least, by the French knack for creating in their display a dazzling illusion of glamour and gloss.

Markets, too, are grand spectacle. Mouth-watering arrays of **food** enliven even the drabbest parts of the city, intoxicating in their varieties of colour, shape and smell. And they are not only French in appearance: North Africa dominates Belleville and the Goutte d'Or, South East Asia the 13ᵉ *arrondissement*. Though the food is perhaps the best quality of Paris markets, there are also street markets dedicated to **secondhand goods** (the *marchés aux puces*), **clothes and textiles, flowers, birds, books** and **stamps**.

SHOPS

The most distinctive and unusual **shopping area** is the 2ᵉ *arrondissement* with its 19C arcades – the *passages* (see p.49) – some neglected, some smartly renovated, with hundreds of small shops ranging from the down-at-heel to the chi-chi or plain eccentric. On the streets proper, the square kilometre around **place St-Germain-des-Prés** is hard to beat, packed with books, antiques, gorgeous garments, artworks and playthings. **Les Halles** is another well-shopped district, with its focus the submarine shopping complex of the *Forum des Halles*, a kind of Parisian Covent Garden good for everything from records through to designer clothes. And the aristocratic **Marais**, to the east, is filling up with dinky little boutiques, arty and specialist shops and galleries. For window-shopping the really **moneyed** Parisian *haute couture*, your Hermès and suchlike, the two traditional areas are **rue Faubourg-St Honoré** (8ᵉ) and **av Victor Hugo** (16ᵉ).

Shop **opening hours** are variable throughout the city, but most tend to stay open later than their London equivalents – through to 7 or 8 as often as not – and to close for a lunch hour (1–2 or 2–3). For **late-night shopping** there's a 24hr Monday to Saturday supermarket, *As Eco*, by

Beaubourg, as well as a chain of three *Drugstores* (open 10–2am, every day; see p.169 for addresses) selling books, papers, tobacco and all kinds of gift gadgetry.

For **food and essentials**, the cheapest supermarket chains are *Ed-Discount* and *Franprix:* also good places to go if you're looking for value-for-money wines to carry home. Other **last-minute or convenience shopping** is probably best at FNAC shops (for books and records) and the big department stores (for practically everything else).

ART AND DESIGN

For an idea of what is going on in the world of contemporary art, the best thing is to take a look at the **commercial art galleries**. They are concentrated in three main areas: bd Haussmann-av Matignon in the 8ᵉ, near the Pompidou Centre (especially, rue Quincampoix) in the 4ᵉ, and in Saint-Germain – the latter being particularly good on the contemporary scene. Anyone can go in – free, of course – and look around for as long as they like without having to reach for the credit cards. *Pariscope* carries details of the major exhibitions every week, under *Expositions* and *Galeries*.

Of the places listed below, the **VIA** – Paris's equivalent of London's Design Centre – is a powerhouse in the field of contemporary furniture, lighting and other aspects of **design**.

Alain Blondel, 4 rue Aubry-le-Boucher and 50 rue du Temple, 4ᵉ. 11–7, Sat 2–7; closed Sun, Mon and August. A specialist in *trompe-l'oeil* art works, plus excursions into contemporary paintings with no tricks.

Duo sur Canapé, 3 rue Turbigo, 1ᵉʳ and 36 rue Etienne-Marcel, 2ᵉ. Contemporary furniture for streamlined penthouses, with occasional stuff by the Lyon fantasists, Totem.

Ecart, 111 rue St-Antoine, 4ᵉ. Recreation of early 20C furniture designs: beautiful constructivist and *art déco* carpets, Mallet-Stevens chairs, angular desks etc – mostly £1000 and over.

Lutherie Ancienne Moderne, 4 rue Elzévir, 3ᵉ. In an ancient house, the selling, buying and restoration of stringed instruments goes on.

Les Virtuoses de la Réclame, 5 rue St-Paul, 4ᵉ. Shop signs, enamel adverts, ashtrays and bottles that were once two a penny and are now, here, outrageously overpriced, but fun to look at.

Tête d'Affiche, 5 rue Caron, 4ᵉ Posters, postcards, etc.

VIA, place Ste-Opportune, 1ᵉʳ. The Design Centre, promoter of the best contemporary work.

BIKES

Raleigh (no 36), Peugeot (no 72) and other big boys are to be found in

av de la Grande Armée, 17ᵉ. But for the enthusiast, these three **specialists** are more interesting:
CNC, 184 rue du Faubourg-St-Denis, 10ᵉ. 9.30–12.30, 1–6.45/2–6 Sat; closed Sunday.
La Maison du Vélo, 8 rue de Belzunce, 10ᵉ. 10–1, 2–7; closed weekends.
La Roue d'Or, 7 rue de la Fidelité, 10ᵉ. 9–12.30, 2–6.30; closed weekends and August.

BOOKS

Books are not cheap in France – foreign books least of all. But don't let that stop you browsing. The best areas are the Seine *quais* with their rows of **stalls** perched against the river parapet and the narrow streets of the *Quartier Latin*.

For **English books**, try:
Brentano's, 37 av de l'Opéra, 2ᵉ. 10–7; cl. Sun. English and American books. Good section for kids.
Galignani, 224 rue de Rivoli, 1ᵉʳ. 9.30–6.30; cl. Sun. Children's books as well.
Shakespeare & Co, 37 rue de la Bûcherie, 5ᵉ. 12–12 every day. A cosy, friendly, literary haunt, with the biggest selection of second-hand English books in town. Also, poetry readings and such.
WH Smith, 248 rue de Rivoli, 1ᵉʳ. 9–6.30; cl. Sun. Wide range of books and newspapers for children, too. *Salon de thé* upstairs.
Village Voice, 6 rue Princesse, 6ᵉ. Tues, Fri, Sat 11–8; Wed, Thurs 11–10; cl. Sun & Mon. Principally poetry and modern literature, both English and American. A very agreeable atmosphere: you're free to browse and read in the café at the back.

For **French books**, the biggest and most convenient shop is the *FNAC* at the Forum des Halles, level – 2, 1ᵉʳ, with lots of *Bandes Dessinées*, guide books and maps among everything else (also, 136 rue de Rennes, 6ᵉ). For a less pressurised browse, good **general bookshops** include:
Le Divan, 37 rue Bonaparte, 6ᵉ.
Gallimard, 15 bd Raspail, 7ᵉ.
Gibert Jeune, 5 place St-Michel, 5ᵉ, and 27 quai St-Michel, 5ᵉ. With lots of sales – and some English books.
La Hune, 170 bd St-Germain, 6ᵉ (beside the *Café Deux Magots*). One of the biggest and best.
Le Magnard, bd St Germain, 6ᵉ (opposite Mᵒ Odéon). Open seven days a week, up till midnight.

For **secondhand**:
L'Introuvable, 25 rue Juliette-Dodu, 10ᵉ. 11–1, 3–7; cl. Sun. and Mon. All sorts stocked.

La Terrasse de Gutenberg, 76 av Ledru-Rollin, 12e, 10–7.30; Monday 2–7; cl. Mon. morning only. Big stock, and a gallery upstairs.

Plus the stalls along the banks of the Seine.

Specialist bookshops

African/Third World
L'Harmattan, 16 rue des Ecoles, 5e. 10–12.30 & 1.15–7; cl. Sun. Excellent, very knowledgeable bookshop – especially good for Arab/North African literature (in French).

Art and Architecture
Artcurial, 9 av Matignon, 8e. 10.30–7.15; cl. Sun & Mon. French and foreign art books, plus a gallery.
Librairie du Musée des Arts Décoratifs, 107 rue de Rivoli, 1er. 10–7. Design, posters, architecture, graphics, etc.
Librairie du Musée d'Art Moderne de la Ville de Paris, Palais de Tokyo, 11 av du Président-Wilson, 16e. 10–5.40; cl. Mon. Specialist publications on modern art, including foreign works.
Librairie de l'Ecole des Beaux Arts, 13 quai Malaquais, 6e. 10–6; cl. Sat, Sun and Aug. Beaux Arts publications, plus posters, postcards, etc.
Librairie du Musée du Louvre, place du Carrousel, 1er 10.45–5.15; cl. Tues.

Autographs
Librairie de l'Abbaye, 27 rue Bonaparte, 6e. 9.45–12.30, 2–7; cl. Sun. and August. Signatures of the famous. Good for a browse.

Cinema
Les Feux de la Rampe, 2 rue de Lynes, 7e. 11–1, 2.15–7; cl. Sun. Mon. and most of August. Books, scripts, photos, etc.

Comics/*Bandes Dessinées*
Album, 6–8 rue Dante, 5e. 10–9; cl. Sun.
Boulinier, 20 bd St-Michel, 6e. 10–7.30; cl. Sun. New and second-hand and long-out-of-print.
Virgule, 2 rue des Tournelles, 4e. Back copies of all the bizarre and familiar French comics.

Feminist
La Brèche, 9 rue de Tunis, 12e. The best place to find feminist and lesbian literature.
La Fourmi Ailée, 8 rue du Fouarre, 6e. Left-wing bookshop and *salon de thé*, stocking most feminist reviews.
Librairie Anima, 3 rue Ravignan, 18e.
Librairie Pluriel, 58 rue de la Roquette, 11e. The ex-Carabosse bookshop

(see p.35) – without the café, but still selling feminist periodicals and radical women's books, more in the arty-literary line than political.
Des Femmes Librairie-Galerie, 74 rue de Seine, 6ᵉ. A Psyche et Po bookshop.

Gay
Les Mots à la Bouche, 6 rue Ste-Croix-de-la-Bretonnerie, 4ᵉ. 11–8; cl. Sun. Literature, psychology etc: books and magazines – some in English.

Leftist/Avant-garde
Actualités, 38 rue Dauphine, 6ᵉ. 11–1, 2–7; cl. Sun. Literature, philosophy, *bandes dessinées*, etc.
Parallèles, 47 rue St-Honoré, 1ᵉʳ. 10–7; cl. Sun. French and foreign: solar energy, conservation, underground, etc. See also *Feminism* (above).

Music
Hamm, 135 rue de Rennes, 6ᵉ. 10–1, 2–7; cl. Sun and Mon. Song books, scores, manuals, librettos – French and foreign. And musical instruments.
Librairie Musicale de Paris, 68bis rue Réaumur, 3ᵉ. Huge selection of books, on music and of music: Baroque oratorios to heavy metal.

Occult
Librairie de Médicis, 3 rue de Médicis, 6ᵉ. 9.30–7; cl. Sun. and Mon. Astrology, alchemy, Zen, mysticism . . .

Poetry
L'Envers du Miroir, 19 rue de Seine, 6ᵉ. 12–7.30; cl. Sun. Mon. and August, Some fine and rare editions of modern poetry, as well as periodicals.
Le Pont Traversé, 62 rue de Vaugirard, 6ᵉ. 12–7; cl. Sun. and Mon. Modern French poetry, surrealist works, etc, in a very attractive old shop.

Theatre and Dance
Librairie Bonaparte, 39 rue Bonaparte, 6ᵉ. 11–1, 3.30–7; cl. Sun and August.
Librairie du Spectacle, 39 rue de Seine, 6ᵉ. 11–12.30, 2–7; cl. Sun.

Travel
L'Astrolabe, 46 rue de Provence, 9ᵉ. 10–7; cl. Sun. Every conceivable map, French and foreign climbing and hiking guides, sailing, natural history.
Institut Géographique National (IGN), rue La Boétie, 8ᵉ. 9–6.20; cl. Sun. The French Ordnance Survey: the best for maps of France.
Ulysse, 35 rue St-Louis-en-l'Ile, 4ᵉ. 2–8; cl. Sunday and Mon. Travel books, maps, guides.

Au Vieux Campeur, 2 rue de Latran, 5ᵉ. 9.30–8.30 (Mon 2–7; Sat 9.30–8) cl. Sun. Maps, guides, climbing, hiking, ski gear, camping, etc. And a kids' climbing wall.

CLOTHES

There's nothing to prevent you trying on fabulously expensive creations by **famous couturiers** in rue du Faubourg-St-Honoré, av François 1ᵉʳ and av Victor-Hugo, apart from the intimidating scorn of the assistants and the awesome chill of the marble portals. Likewise, you can treat the **younger designers** round place des Victoires and in the Saint-Germain area as sightseeing.

But **if you want to buy**, the best area is **the 6ᵉ**: round rue de Rennes, rue de Sèvres and, in particular, rue St-Placide, which has a very high concentration of shops selling end of line and last year's models at 30–50% reductions, as has rue St-Dominique in the neighbouring 7ᵉ. Second best is **Les Halles**, but beware the rip-offs in the Forum. More individual boutiques are to be found in the **Marais** – in rue du Temple and rue Quincampoix in particular. This end of rue Rivoli also has plenty of chain stores, including a Monoprix supermarket for essentials, or you can get even better bargains in the **rag-trade district** round place du Caire or **place de la République**, with a *Printemps* on the north side, *Tati* on the south and the adjacent rues Meslay and Notre-Dame de Nazareth full of **shoe and clothes shops** respectively. **For jewellery** – gems and plastic – try rue du Temple and rue Montmorency.

The **sales** take place from mid-July through August and, best of all, from mid-December through January, with up to 40% reductions, including *haute couture* sales. Two common signs, *vente en gros* and *vente en détail* or *vente aux particuliers* mean wholesale and retail, respectively.

We've given the main or most convenient branch of the big names.

Designers
Many of these have prices well into the stratosphere: for possible alternatives see the *Discount* section below. The biggest general collection of designers is to be found at the **Galeries Lafayette** department store (see p.149).
Agnès B, 13 rue Michelet, 6ᵉ.
Arnys, 14 rue de Sèvres, 7ᵉ.
Giorgio Armani, 31 rue du Four, 6ᵉ.
Balenciaga, 10 av Georges V, 8ᵉ.
Balmain, 44 rue François 1ᵉʳ, 8ᵉ.
Anne-Marie Beretta, 24 rue St-Sulpice, 6ᵉ.
Biba, rue de Sèvres, 7ᵉ.
Cacharel, 62 (& 165) rue de Rennes, 6ᵉ.

Pierre Cardin, 29 & 83 rue du Faubourg-St-Honoré, 8e.
Castelbajac, 31 place du Marché-St-Honoré, 1er.
Cerruti 1881, 39 av Victor Hugo, 16e.
Chanel, 31 rue Cambon, 1er & 42 av Montaigne, 8e.
Chloé, 60 rue du Faubourg-St-Honoré, 8e.
Chris R, 28 rue de Grenelle, 7e.
Comme des Garçons, 42 rue Etienne-Marcel, 2e.
Courrèges, 49 rue de Rennes, 6e.
Dior, 30 av Montaigne, 8e.
Dorothée Bis, 33 rue de Sèvres, 6e.
Louis Féraud, 47 rue Bonaparte, 6e.
J-P Gaultier, 6 rue Vivienne, 2e.
Givenchy, 3 & 8 av Georges V, 8e.
Daniel Hechter, Forum des Halles level – 1, 1er and 146 bd St-Germain, 6e.
Kenzo, 3 place des Victoires, 1er.
Emanuelle Khan, 2 rue du Tournon, 6e and 10 rue de Grenelle, 7e.
Michel Klein, 39 rue de Grenelle, 6e.
Lanvin, 2 rue Cambon & 8 rue du Faubourg-St-Honoré, 8e.
Lacoste, 2 & 44 rue St-Placide, 6e.
Ted Lapidus, 52 rue Bonaparte, 6e.
Guy Laroche, 47 rue de Rennes, 6e.
Miyake, 201 bd St-Germain, 6e.
Claude Montana, 31 rue de Grenelle, 6e.
Hanae Mori, 17–19 av Montaigne, 8e.
Thierry Mugler, 10 place des Victoires, 2e.
Per Spook, 59 bis rue Bonaparte, 6e.
Paco Rabanne, 7 rue du Cherche-Midi, 6e.
Georges Rech, 54 rue Bonaparte, 6e.
Nina Ricci, 39 av Montaigne, 8e.
Sonia Rykiel, 4–6 rue de Grenelle, 6e.
Saint-Laurent, 6 place St-Sulpice, 6e and 38 rue du Faubourg-St-Honoré, 8e.
Jean-Louis Scherrer, 31 rue de Tournon, 6e.
Ungaro, 25 rue du Faubourg-St-Honoré, 8e.
Yamamoto, 25 rue du Louvre, 1er.

Discount

There are a great many shops where last year's designer numbers are sold off at big reductions. Though before you get too excited, remember that 20% off £500 still leaves a hefty bill. Not that all items are as expensive as that. Most of the shops listed here deal in clothes from several different houses.
La Clef des Soldes, 99 rue St-Dominique, 7e and 33 rue Vavin, 6^e
9.45–2.15, 3.15–7; cl. Sun & Mon a.m. Men, women and kids.

Cacharel Stock, 114 rue d'Alésia, 14ᵉ. 10–7.30; cl. Sun. Men, women and kids.

Discount R, 37 rue St-Placide, 6ᵉ.

Dorothée Bis, 76 rue d'Alésia, 14ᵉ. Cl. Sun. Women and kids.

La Grange des Soldes, 159 rue de Rennes, 6ᵉ. 9.30–7.30; cl. Sun & Mon.

Halles Bys, 60 rue Richelieu, 2ᵉ. Men, women and kids.

King Soldes, 24 rue St-Placide, 6ᵉ and 102 rue d'Alésia, 14ᵉ. 9.45–7; cl. Sun & Mon a.m.

Le Mouton à Cinq Pattes, 8 rue St-Placide, 6ᵉ for women and no 48 for men. 10–9; cl Sun & Mon.

Stock Michel Bachoz, 74 rue d'Alésia, 14ᵉ. Cl. Sun.

Stock Austerlitz, 16 bd de l'Hôpital, 13ᵉ. Daniel Hechter, for men, women and children.

Stock System 110–112 rue d'Alésia, 14ᵉ. 10–7; cl. Sun & Mon. Men and women.

Toutes Griffes Dehors, 76 rue St-Dominique, 7ᵉ and 84 rue de Sèvres, 6ᵉ. Women.

Hats/jewellery

Divine, 39 rue Daguerre, 14ᵉ. 10.30–1, 3–7.30; closed Monday. Flamboyant hats, belts, jewellery, carnival masks, etc.

Exactement Fauve, 5 rue Princesse, 6ᵉ. More glorious fantasy jewellery, some of it affordable.

Schmock Broc, 15 rue Racine, 6ᵉ. A cavern of bizarre hats, veils, dresses, jewellery – all your Art Nouveau or thereabouts.

Toumain, 56 rue de Lanery, 10ᵉ. Jewellery workshop/shop selling a wide selection of really cheap and interesting pieces.

Secondhand and *rétro*

Rétro means period clothes, mostly unsold factory stock from the 1950s and 1960s, though some shops specialise in expensive high fashion articles from as far back as the 1920s. Plain **secondhand** stuff is referred to as **fripe** – not specially interesting compared with London and dominated by the US combat jacket style. The best place to look is probably the Porte de Montreuil flea market (see p.158).

Anouchka, 27 rue de la Grande-Truanderie, 1ᵉʳ. Specialises in 1950s.

Brocante, 58 rue de la Butte-aux-Cailles, 13ᵉ. *Fripe*, crockery and oddments.

Chic et Pas Cher, 17 rue des Quatre-Vents, 6ᵉ and 42 rue Grégoire-de-Tours, 6ᵉ. 1940s and 1960s factory stock – not cheap in spite of the name.

Duo 29, 29 rue du Roi-de-Sicile, 4ᵉ. Precious 1920s and 1930s dresses, and shirts and jackets from east Europe.

Hébé, 41 rue de l'Arbe-Sec, 1ᵉʳ. Hats and stockings, plus some older *rétro*: expensive, though.

Rag Time, 23 rue du Roule, 1ᵉʳ. p.m. only. A veritable museum of superb dresses and high fashion articles from 1920s to the 1950s. Expensive.
Réciproque, 95, 101 & 123 rue de la Pompe, 16ᵉ. 10–6.45; cl. Sun & Mon.
Rétro Activité, 38 rue du Vertbois, 3ᵉ. 12–7; cl. Sun. *Fripe*.
Square, 26bis rue Charles-Baudelaire, 12ᵉ. 10.30–1, 3–7; cl. Sun p.m. & Mon. *Fripe*.
Violence et Passion, 1 rue Keller, 11ᵉ. 11–7; cl. Sun. 1950s and 1960s *rétro* and *fripe* – run by two women who wouldn't look out of place in London.

Shoes
Childebert, 14 rue Custine, 18ᵉ. Stacks and stacks of end-of-line shoes, if you have the patience to open all the boxes.
Sabotine, 35 rue de la Roquette, 11ᵉ & 13bis rue Custine, 18ᵉ. Permanent sales.

Tati
Tati is in a class by itself, the cheapest of cheap clothes stores. And there are real bargains to be found among the masses of junk. The press of people is too much for ditherers. Addresses are 4–30 bd Rochechouart, 18ᵉ; 140 rue de Rennes, 6ᵉ*; 13 place de la République, 11ᵉ.

DEPARTMENT STORES AND HYPERMARKETS

The two largest **department stores**, *Printemps* and *Galeries Lafayette*, are right next door to each other – and between them there's not much they don't have. For eats, *Printemps* has the edge with its restaurant set below an amazing starred glass dome.
Au Bon Marché, 38 rue de Sèvres, 7ᵉ. 9.30–6.45; cl. Sun. Paris's oldest department store – founded in 1852. The prices are lower on average than at the chicer *Galeries Lafayette* and *Printemps*, but then the tone is more mass-market middle class. It has an excellent kids' department and an enormous food hall.
Galeries Lafayette, 40 bd Haussmann, 9ᵉ (9.30–6.30; cl. Sun) and Centre Commercial Maine-Montparnasse, 15ᵉ (9.45–7.15; cl. Sun). The bd Haussmann branch is the original shop. The store's forte is, above all, high fashion. Two complete floors are given over to the latest creations by leading designers for men, women and kids. Then there's household stuff, tableware, furniture, a host of big names in men and women's accessories, a huge *parfumerie*, etc.
Au Printemps, 64 bd Haussmann, 9ᵉ. 9.35–6.30; cl. Sun. Books, records,

* This branch was a target in the Autumn 86 bombing campaign: a deliberately murderous attack which resulted in several deaths.

a *parfumerie* even bigger than the rival *Galeries Lafayette*, excellent fashion departments for women and men.
La Samaritaine, 75 rue de Rivoli, 1er. 7.30–7/8.30 Tues and Fri; cl. Sun. The biggest of the department stores, whose boast is to provide anything anyone could possibly want. It aims down-market of the previous two. Superb view of the Seine from the tenth-floor terrace – closed from October to March.

Paris too has its share of **hypermarkets**, giant shopping complexes, of which the Forum des Halles and Centre Maine-Montparnasse are the most successful.
Forum des Halles, rue Pierre Lescot, 1er.
Centre Maine-Montparnasse, 17 rue de l'Arrivée, 15e.
Palais des Congrès, place de la Porte-Maillot, 17e, mainly upmarket shops to complement the conference and concert facilities.
Quatre-Saisons, La Défense, directly over the RER station.
Centre Galaxie, Place d' Italie, 13e.

FOOD

Food markets are detailed in the final section of this chapter. These listings are for the **specialist places**, palaces of gluttony, many of them, and some with prices to match. The equivalents of Harrods' foodhall are to be found at *Fauchon's* and *Hédiard's*, on the place de la Madeleine: each has exhibits to rival the best of the capital's museums. Among smaller collections, don't miss *Poilâne's* – the world's most sought-after bakery, the *Barthélémy* cheese shop, *La Maison de l'Escargot*, or the amazing provincial confectioneries of *Specialités de France*. Wines are most startlingly extensive at the English-run *La Cave de la Madeleine*.

Buying food with a view to **economic eating**, you will be invariably best off shopping at the **street markets** or **supermarkets** – though save your bread buying at least for the local *boulangerie* and let yourself be tempted once in a while by the apple *chaussons, pains aux raisins, pains au chocolat, tartes aux fraises* and countless other goodies. Useful **supermarket addresses** are:
As Eco, 11 rue Brantôme, 3e. Open 24 hours.
Ed-Discount – an enormous cheap chain. If you ring 46.87.33.60 they'll tell where the nearest branch is. Same goes for *Franprix*, on 45.76.96.00. Others, marginally more expensive, include *Félix Potin, Prisunic, Monoprix*, etc.

The palaces . . .
Fauchon, 26 place de la Madeleine, 8e. 9.40–7; cl. Sun. Carries an amazing range of super-plus groceries, almost anything you can think of. Just the place for presents of tea, jam, truffles, chocolates, exotic vinegars

and mustards, etc. They also have an extensive wine cellar. And it is worth bearing in mind that some of Fauchon's products can be had for less than Madeleine prices at the rather out-of-the-way *Torréfaction Gambetta*, 273 rue des Pyrénées, in the 20e *arrondissement* (8–12.45, 2.45–5.15; cl. Sun & Mon).

Hédiard, 21 place de la Madeleine, 8e. 9–7.30; cl. Sun. Since 1850, the aristocrat's grocer, with sales staff as deferential as servants, as long as you don't try to reach down items for yourself. Other branches at 126 rue du Bac, 7e; 106 bd de Courcelles, 17e; Forum des Halles, level – 1, and some more.

and a few specialists

Bread
Ganachaud, 150–154 rue de Ménilmontant, 20e. 7.30–8.30; Tues, p.m. only; Sun, a.m. only; cl. Mon. Special for its wide range of traditional cakes and different types of bread.

Poilâne, 8 rue du Cherche-Midi, 7e (7.15–8.15; cl. Sun) and 49 bd de Grenelle, 7e (7.15–8.15; cl. Mon). Bakes to ancient and secret family recipes, but there is always a queue. If you're impatient you could try the brother's establishment at 87 rue Brancion, 15e – no love lost, but the same recipes.

A personal favourite is at 45 rue Ste-Croix-de-la-Bretonnerie in the 4e, with wonderful *florentines* and chocolate and coffee macaroons.

Charcuterie
Divay, 50 rue du Faubourg-St-Denis, 10e – for *foie gras*, *choucroute*, *saucisson* and such.

Aux Ducs de Gascogne, an excellent chain with numerous south-western products like preserved fruits in Armagnac, *foie gras*, conserves, hams and all the rest. Some branch addresses: 4 rue du Marché-St-Honoré, 1er; 31 rue Monge, 5e; 176 rue de Grenelle, 7e; 112 bd Haussmann, 8e; 29 rue des Martyrs, 9e; 44 rue de Lévis, 17e. Opening hours are 10–7; cl. Sun and August.

Goldenberg's, 7 rue des Rosiers, 4e. 10 a.m.–11 p.m. Superlative Jewish deli - and restaurant.

Labeyrie, 6 rue Montmartre, 1er. 7.30–12.30; 2–6; cl. Sun & Mon. Specialist in products from the Landes region: Bayonne hams, goose and duck *pâtés*, conserves, etc.

Maison de la Truffe, 19 place de la Madeleine, 8e. 9–8; cl. Sun. Truffles, of course, and more from the Dordogne and Landes.

St-Maur, 63 rue St-Maur, 11e. A popular *charcuterie de quartier* with lots of cheese and *plats du jour* to take away.

Cheese

Androuet, 41 rue d'Amsterdam, 8ᵉ. 8.30–6.45; cl. Sun. A huge selection, plus *dégustation* in the restaurant.

Barthélémy, 51 rue de Grenelle, 7ᵉ. 8.30–1, 4–7.15; cl. Sun, Mon & August.

Carmes, 24 rue de Lévis, 17ᵉ. 8.15–1, 4–7.30; cl. Sun p.m., Mon and August. In the rue de Lévis market.

Maison du Fromage, 62 rue de Sèvres, 6ᵉ. 8.45–1, 4.15–7.45; cl. Sun, Mon and August.

Chocolates, sweets, teas and such

Debauve and Gallais, 30 rue des Saints-Pères, 6ᵉ. 10–1, 2–7; cl. Sun, Mon and August. All sorts of goodies behind a beautiful old shop front near the Medical School.

Estrella, 34 rue St-Sulpice, 6ᵉ. A handsome French Anglo-style shop right under the church of St-Sulpice, selling an infinite variety of exotic teas, and jams.

A la Mère de Famille, 35 rue du Faubourg-Montmartre, 9ᵉ. 7.30–1.30, 3–7; cl. Sun, Mon and August. *Marrons glacés*, prunes from Agen, dried fruit, sweets, chocolates and even some wines.

Spécialités de France, 44 av Montaigne, 8ᵉ 9–6.45; cl. Sun. Traditional delicacies from every province in France.

La Petite Fabrique, 12 rue Daval, 11ᵉ (cl. Sun and Wed) and 91 rue Lemercier, 17ᵉ (cl. Sun p.m. and Mon). Beautiful homemade chocolates, especially the bars, nuts, nougat, and the dark stuff, all elegantly wrapped. Ice cream too from the 11ᵉ branch.

Herbs and Spices

Aux Cinq Continents, 75 rue de la Roquette, 11ᵉ. Boxes, trays, sacks of rice, pulses, herbs, spices, tarama, vine leaves, etc, from the world over. 8–1, 3–8; cl. Sat & Sun p.m.

L'Herbier de Provence, 25 rue de l'Annonciation, 16ᵉ. 10.30–1.30, 2.30–7; cl. Sun, Mon and second half of August. Herbs, spices, *tisanes* in sacks and jars. A second branch at 19 rue Daguerre, 14ᵉ, open 10–1, 4–7.30; cl. Sun, Mon and August.

Pâtisseries

There are dozens of them, not to mention the *boulangeries*, but a good chain to look out for is *Le Moule à Gâteaux*, open 9–1.30, 4–7.30. Addresses: 47 rue St-Louis-en-L'Ile, 4ᵉ; 111 rue Mouffetard, 5ᵉ; 51 rue Cler, 7ᵉ; 17 rue Daguerre, 14ᵉ; 25 rue de Lévis, 17ᵉ, 53 rue des Abbesses, 18ᵉ.

Salmon, seafood and caviar

Aux Cinq Etoiles, 46 rue Cler, 7ᵉ. 8–1, 3–7.30; cl. Sun p.m. and Mon.

Fish, shells and lobster, hot from the Atlantic coast.
Comptoir de Saumon et Cie, 60 rue François-Miron, 4ᵉ. 10.30–1.30,
3.30–8; cl. Sun, Mon and second half of August. A Norwegian shop full
of salmon and other fishy things from the North, at better prices than
elsewhere.
Fenouil, 18 and 51 rue de Lévis, 17ᵉ. 7.30–1, 4–7.30; cl. Sun p.m. and
Mon. More delectable fruits of the sea.
Kaspia, 17 place de la Madeleine, 8ᵉ and *Petrossian*, 18 bd de la Tour-
Maubourg, 7ᵉ for the gilt-edge fish eggs. And there's more caviar and
truffles in rues Montorgueil and Montmartre.

Snails
La Maison de l'Escargot, 79 rue Fondary, 15ᵉ. 8.30–8; cl. Mon and mid-
July to mid-August. They even sauce them and re-shell them while you
wait. Of interest to zoologists as well as gourmets.

Vegetarian
Diététique Régime, 45 rue St-Paul, 4ᵉ. 9.30–1.15, 2–30–7.30; cl. Sun
and Mon. Dietary, macrobiotic, vegetarian ... one of the city's oldest
specialists.

Wine
Les Caves St-Antoine, 95 rue St-Antoine, 4ᵉ. A personal favourite.
Les Caves de la Madeleine, Cité Berryer, 25 rue Royale, 8ᵉ. 9–7/Sat 10–2;
cl. Sun. A suit and tie and Oxbridge accent would go down well here. It
may be expensive but is definitely one of the best-stocked cellars in Paris.
If you want to discuss your purchase, the proprietor is Steven Spurrier
of wine bar fame and three of his 'boys' are English.
Club Amical du Vin Jean-Christophe Estève, 10 rue de la Cerisaie, 4ᵉ;
cl. Sun, Mon and August.
Oddbins, 25 rue des Ecoles, 5ᵉ; 64 rue Rambuteau, 3ᵉ; 129 bd Voltaire,
11ᵉ.

RECORDS

Records are not a particularly cheap buy in Paris but you may come
across selections that are novel enough to tempt you. Like the live music
to be heard, Brazilian, Caribbean, Antillais, African and Arab albums
that would be **specialist** rarities in London, as well as every kind of **jazz**,
abound in Paris. Secondhand bargains can be scratchy treats – anything
from the Red Army choir singing the *Marseillaise* to African drummers on
skins made from spider ovaries. The **flea markets**, Porte de Clignancourt
especially, are good places to look for ready-played discs. In the **classical**
department, the choice of interpretations is very generous and un-

xenophobic. For all new and mainstream records FNAC usually has the best prices.

Afro-Rhythms, 65 passage Brady, 10ᵉ. African music specialists.
Crocodisc, 42 rue des Ecoles, 5ᵉ. 11–7; cl. Sun & Mon. Jazz, blues, and reggae with reduced prices on many.
Disques, 17 rue de Lappe, 11ᵉ. New-Wave and Afro-Samba.
Le Disque Arabe, 116bis bd de la Chapelle, 18ᵉ. Good range of Arab music.
Dream Store, 4 place St-Michel, 6ᵉ. 9.30 (1.30 Mon) – 7; cl. Sun. Jazz, rock, folk.
FNAC, Forum des Halles, level – 2, 1ᵉʳ; 136 rue de Rennes, 6ᵉ; 26 av de Wagram, 8ᵉ. 10–7.30; cl. Sun & Mon, except the Forum shop, which is open 1–7.30 on Mon. A wide selection of records and at the best prices too.
Joseph Gibert, 26 bd St-Michel, 6ᵉ. 10–7; cl. Sun. Big selection of second-hand records.
Lido Musique, 68 av des Champs-Elysées, 8ᵉ. 10–2a.m. (Sun 1.30–8.30). A late-night expensive Champs-Elysées scram, but a good range of music – funk, disco, classical . . . and videos.
Les Mondes du Jazz, 2 rue de la Petite-Truanderie, 1ᵉʳ. 11–7; cl. Sun & Mon. *The* jazz shop for French and imported records.
New Rose, 6 rue Pierre-Sarrazin, 6ᵉ. Another good record shop.
Parallèles, 47 rue St-Honoré, 1ᵉʳ. The book shop (see p.145), but also does records.
Paris Musique, 10 bd St-Michel, 6ᵉ. 10.30–11 (midnight Sat & Fri); Sun 2–8. Second-hand, bootlegs and new – jazz, classical and rock. The chief advantage is late hours and weekend opening.

TRIVIA AND MISCELLANEOUS

Some of the most entertaining and tempting Parisian shops are those small cluttered affairs which reflect their owners' **particular passions**. Among the strangest are some of those in the *Passages* – sculpted canes in Passage Jouffroy, old comics in Passage Verdeau, pipes in Passage des Princes (see p.49) . . . but you'll find traders in off-beat merchandise all over the place.
A Combes, 45 rue de la Roquette, 11ᵉ. Mon-Sat 2–7. An odd collection of little toys, postcards, stamps, old jugs, chairs and all sorts.
A l'Image du Grenier sur l'Eau, 45 rue des Francs-Bourgeois, 4ᵉ. 1900s postcards.
Atelier des Brikezolces, 21 rue Liancourt, 14ᵉ. Ceramics.
Bois Lacté, 106 rue du Château, 14ᵉ. Nothing but dried flowers.
Caractère, 99 rue St-Maur, 11ᵉ. 11–7, Tues-Sat. Coins, music scores,

syringes, cacti and coloured pebbles, lightshades, shells – all set in solid glass.

Au Chat Dormant, 15 rue du Cherche-Midi, 6ᵉ. Everything to do with cats or made in the likeness of cats.

Chic et Choc, by Rambuteau exit of Les Halles RER station. Towels, wallets, lighters, etc., all with the métro ticket emblem. The owner is the Paris transport authority.

Le Drapeau Français, 10 rue de la Cerisaie, 4ᵉ (2nd floor). 8.30–12, 1–5.15, Mon-Thurs; Fri 8.30–12, 1–4.15. A ridiculous place to hire or buy national flags – the hammer and sickle, union jack, tricolour or even ones in red, green, black and white or green, gold and orange, that aren't on their list.

Herboristerie du Palais-Royal, 11 rue des Petits-Champs, 1ᵉʳ. 8–7; cl. Sat, Sun and August. Every medicinal plant, organic perfume, facecream and dietary food.

Papeterie St-Sabin 14 rue St-Sabin, 11ᵉ. If you're in the area – pens, files, notebooks . . . what the Parisians are good at, and reasonably priced here.

La Tisseranderie, 12 rue de Sévigné, 4ᵉ. 10–7, Tues-Sat. A wool shop, with accessories of beads and jewellery, displayed to mesmerising effect.

L'Usine, 9 rue de la Roquette, 11ᵉ. Excellent and original selections of furniture, a few clothes, crockery, earrings and assorted bits and pieces. Not too expensive either.

For **toyshops**, see Kids Stuff (p.133).

MARKETS

Several of the markets are described in the text of the *City* chapter. These, however, are the details – and the highlights.

FLEA MARKETS (*MARCHES AUX PUCES*)

Paris has half a dozen flea markets – most of them of ancient descent, gathered about the old gates of the city. They are no longer the haunts of the flamboyant gipsies and petty crooks of literary tradition, but they are usually good entertainment value and if you go early enough you might just find something special.

Place d'Aligre, 12ᵉ. *Daily, except Mon, till 1 p.m.* Clothes, books, prints, crockery, junk and a solid foodstall presence too.

Belleville, place des Fêtes, 20ᵉ. *Sundays only*. In the main North African quarter of town. Good for cheap clothes.

PARIS MARKETS

LA DEFENSE

River Seine

Ile de la Jatte

NEUILLY

BOULEVARD J.-JAURES

RUE VICTOR HUGO

BOULEVARD PERIPHER

AVENUE DE CLICHY

BOULEVARD BINEAU

AV. DE VILLIERS

Rue de Lévis

PONT DE NEUILLY

Ile de Puteaux

AVENUE CHARLES DE GAULLE

BOULEVARD DU LOT TOMBOT

AVENUE DE WAGRAM

AVENUE DE BD DE COURCELLES

AV. DE LA GRANDE ARMEE

Place des Ternes

Parc Monceau

BD. DES BATIGNOLLES

BOULEVARD MALESHERBES

RUE DE CLICHY

Gare Laza

Arc de Triomphe

PLACE CHARLES DE GAULLE

AVENUE DES CHAMPS ELYSEES

BOULEVARD

ALLEE DE LONGCHAMPS

BOULEVARD PERIPHERIQUE

BOULEVARD LANNES

AVENUE FOCH

AVENUE KLEBER

AVENUE VICTOR HUGO

Stamp Market

La Madeleine

Place de la Madeleine

Bois de Boulogne

Grand Palais

Petit Palais

PL. DE LA CONCORDE

ALBERT 1ER CRS. LA REINE

Palais de Chaillot

AVENUE P. DOUMER

ROUTE DE L'HIPPODROME

AVENUE DE LA REINE MARGUERITE

ALLEE DE ST CLOUD

AVENUE BOSQUET

Tour Eiffel

AVENUE DE NEW YORK

Rue Cler

Hôtel des Invalides

St

des

St

BOULEVARD MURAT

AVENUE MOZART

BOULEVARD SUCHET

AVE. DE VERSAILLES

River Seine

Avenue Emile Zola

RUE DE LA CONVENTION

AVENUE DE CONGRAL

AVENUE DE RASPAIL

Raspail

RUE DE VAUGIRARD

BOULEVARD DU M

MONTPARNASSE

Tour Montparnasse

Edgar Quine

DE LA REINE

PTE. DE ST-CLOUD

Convention

RUE DE VAUGIRARD

Gare Montparnasse

Montparnasse Cemetery

AVENUE E.VAILLANT

AVENUE P. GRENIER

BOULEVARD VICTOR

Palais des Sports

BOULEVARD LEFEBVRE

RUE D'ALESIA

AVENUE DU MAINE

BOULEVARD BRUNE

BOULOGNE-BILLANCOURT

BOULEVARD PERIPHERIQUE

ISSY-LES-MOULINEAUX

Porte-de-Vanves

AVENUE DE VERDUN

AVE. P.BROSSOLETTE

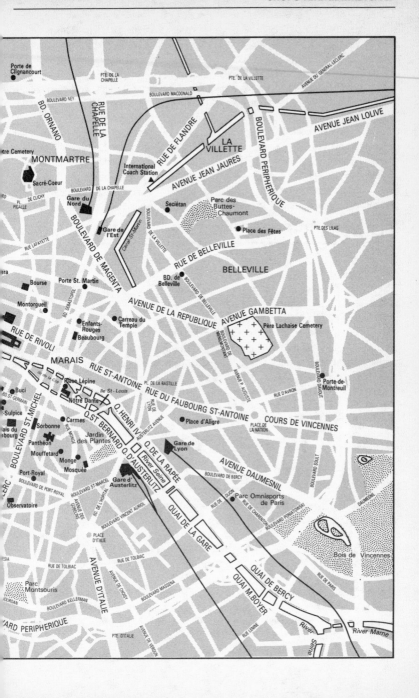

Carreau du Temple, between rue Perrée and rue du Petit-Thouars, 3ᵉ. *Daily, except Mons till 12 (1 p.m. at wkends)*. A beautifully renovated *halles* (covered market) which sells plain, practical new clothes.

Porte de Clignancourt, 18ᵉ. *Sat, Sun, Mon 7–7*. The biggest and most touristy, with stalls selling clothes, shoes, records, books and junk of all sorts as well as expensive antiques (often shipped over from the north of England). Enjoyable for all that – and despite the crowds and prices.

Porte de Montreuil, 20ᵉ. *Sat, Sun, Mon 7–7*. Best of the flea markets for secondhand clothes – cheapest on the Monday when leftovers from the weekend are sold off.

Porte de Vanves, av Georges-Lafenestre/av Marc-Sangnier, 14ᵉ. *Sat, Sun 7–7*. The obvious choice for bric-à-brac searching, with amateurs spreading wares on the pavement as well as the professional dealers.

FLOWERS, BIRDS, BOOKS AND STAMPS

There used to be innumerable **flower markets** around the streets but today just three remain.

Place des Ternes, 8ᵉ. *Daily*.

Place de la Madeleine, 8ᵉ. *Mon-Sat*.

Place Lépine, Ile de la Cité, 1ᵉʳ. *Mon-Sat*.

The **place Lépine** transforms into a **bird and pet market** every *Sunday* – worth a look, though it is dwarfed by the concentration of **plant and pet shops** along the **quai de la Megisserie** between Pont Neuf and Pont au Change.

Other specialised gatherings include the **secondhand bookstalls** (*daily*) along the **Seine** *quais* in the Quartier Latin, and a **stamp market** (*Thurs. Sat, Sun*) probably familiar from a number of old movies, at the junction of avenues Marigny and Gabriel, on the north side of **place Clemenceau** in the 8ᵉ.

FOOD MARKETS

The **mainly-for-food street markets** provide one of the capital's more exacting tests of will-power. At the top end of the scale, there are the Satanic arrays in **rue de Lévis** in the 17ᵉ and **rue Cler** in the 7ᵉ, both of which are more market street than street market, with their stalls mostly metarmorphosed into permanent shops. More for ordinary mortals, the real street markets include a tempting scattering in the **Left Bank** – **rue de Buci** (the most photographed) near St-Germain-des-Prés, **rue Mouffetard**, **place Maubert** and **place Monge**. Bigger ones at **Montparnasse** in **bd Edgar-Quintet** and opposite Val-de-Grâce in **bd Port-Royal**, the biggest in **rue de la Convention** in the 15ᵉ. For a different feel – the unfamiliar goods – try also the Mediterranean/Oriental displays in **bd de Belleville** and **rue d'Aligre**. And finally, for architecture as much as provisions, the ancient covered **halles** of **Château-d'Eau, St-Germain** and **av de Secrétan**.

Locations and hours/days are:

Belleville, bd de Belleville, 20ᵉ. *Tues & Fri.*

Buci, rue de Buci and rue de Seine, 6ᵉ. *Tues-Sun.*

Carmes, place Maubert, 5ᵉ. *Tues, Thurs & Sat.*

Rue Cler, 7ᵉ. *Tues-Sat.*

Convention, rue de la Convention, 15ᵉ. *Tues, Thurs & Sun.*

Edgar-Quinet, bd Edgar-Quinet, 14ᵉ. *Wed & Sat.*

Enfants-Rouges, 39 rue de Bretagne, 3ᵉ. *Tues-Sat 8–1, 4–7.30; Sun 8–1.*

Rue de Lévis, 17ᵉ. *Tues-Sun.*

Monge, place Monge, 5ᵉ. *Wed, Fri, Sun.*

Montorgueil, rue Montorgueil and rue Montmartre, 1ᵉʳ. *Daily.*

Mouffetard, rue Mouffetard, 5ᵉ. *Daily.*

Porte-St-Martin, rue du Château-d'Eau, 10ᵉ. *Tues-Sat 8–1, 4–7.30; Sun 8–1.*

Port-Royal, bd Port-Royal, 5ᵉ – near Val-de-Grâce. *Tues, Thurs, Sat.*

Raspail, bd Raspail, 6ᵉ – between rue du Cherche-Midi and rue de Rennes. *Tues and Fri.*

Secrétan, av Secrétan/rue Riquet, 19ᵉ. *Tues-Sat 8–1, 4–7.30; Sun 8–1.*

Saint-Germain, rue Mabillon, 6ᵉ. *Tues-Sat 8–1, 4–7.30; Sun 8–1.*

Ternes, rue Lemercier, 17ᵉ. *Tues-Sat 8–1, 4–7.30; Sun 8–1.*

Chapter five

DRINKING AND EATING

The French never segregate the major pleasures of **food and drink**. With tens of thousands of establishments specialising in one or the other, while dedicated to both, your choice of a meal, a snack, a glass of wine or a cup of coffee could be overwhelming.

The different places – **restaurants**, **wine bars**, **cafés** and so forth – are listed **by area** at the end of each section in the *City chapter*. You'll find them here **by category** in alphabetical order, with cross references for *ethnic, vegetarian and late-night possibilities* at the end of the chapter. For a general **introduction** to the business, and some assistance with vocabulary and how to go about getting what you want, turn to the *Food and Drink* section of *Basics* (pp.24–32).

CAFÉS AND BARS

Cafés are all over the place, big ones, small ones, scruffy ones, stylish ones, snobby ones, arty ones. Crossroads and intersections are where they chiefly like to congregate, often side by side with the look-alike *brasseries*.

The most enjoyable are often ordinary, local places, but there are particular **areas** which café-lizards head for. **Boulevards Montparnasse** and **St-Germain** on the Left Bank are favoured ones. There you'll find the *Select*, *Coupole*, *Closerie des Lilas*, *Deux Magots* and *Flore* – the erstwhile hangouts of Apollinaire, Picasso, Hemingway, Sartre, de Beauvoir and most other literary-intellectual figures of the last six decades. Most of them are still frequented by the big, though not yet legendary, names in the Parisian world of art and letters, cinema, politics and thought, as well as by their hangers-on and other lesser mortals.

The location of other lively **Left Bank café concentrations** is determined by the geography of the university. Art students from the Beaux Arts school patronise the old-time *La Palette* on the corner of rue Jacques-Callot. Science students gravitate towards the cafés in rue Linne by the Jardin des Plantes. The Humanities gather in the newly planted place de la Sorbonne and rue Soufflot. And all the world – especially non-Parisians

– finds its way to the place St-André-des-Arts and the downhill end of bd St-Michel.

The **Bastille** is another good area to tour – always lively at night, as is **Les Halles**, though the latter's trade is principally the transient out-of-towners up for the bright lights. The much-publicised *Café Costes* is here, Mecca of the self-conscious and committed trendies (*branchés* – plugged in – as they're called in French). A recent clone is the *Café de la Jatte* on rich, smart **Neuilly's** off-shore island. Other trendy hangouts, **more cocktail bar than café**, include *La Mousson*, *Tribulum*, and the American-style *Pacific Palissades* and *Magnetic Terrace*.

All the main squares and boulevards have cafés spreading on to the pavements, always more expensive than those a little removed from the thoroughfares. The smarter or more touristy *arrondissements* set **prices** souring. The Champs-Elysées and rue de Rivoli, for instance, are best avoided at double or triple the price of a Belleville, Villette or lower 14ᵉ café.

CAFÉS

Au Bon Accueil, 15 rue Babylone, 7ᵉ. A cosy characterful old-timer, right next door to a good lunch-time restaurant, *Au Babylone*.

Le Bonaparte, corner rue Bonaparte and place St-Germain-des-Prés. Quieter and less touristy than *Deux Magots* or *Flore*.

Le Boulevard, 73 bd du Montparnasse, 6ᵉ. Gorgeous, grotesque ices and cheaper than the neighbours.

Brasserie de l'Etoile, north side of Champs-Elysées, close to Etoile. Still going strong at 6 am, if you want to make a night of it.

Café de Cluny, corner of bd St-Michel and bd St-Germain, 5ᵉ. Very crowded, but a convenient meeting place. Go upstairs for some peace and quiet. Open till 2 am.

Café Costes, 4 rue Berger, 1ᵉʳ. Tedious, overpriced, shallow and ugly. The design of the bogs is original but has failed to take account of the effect water smears have on glass.

Café de la Mairie, place St-Sulpice, 6ᵉ. A peaceful, pleasant, youthful café on the sunny north side of the square.

Café de la Paix, 12 bd des Capucines, 9ᵉ. Open till 2 am. On place de l'Opéra, it is decoracted in the sumptuous, vulgar Imperial style perfected by Garnier, architect of the Opéra. It has a fast restaurant as well, *Relais Capucines*. Prices not the cheapest.

Le Chien Qui Fume, 19 bd du Montparnasse, 14ᵉ. Named after a real dog, it's an old and ordinary café – a refuge from its tourist-haunted famous neighbours.

La Chope, place de la Contrescarpe, 5ᵉ. Hemingway was a regular and Juliette Greco and George Brassens used to sing. Now swamped by tourists in summer but perfect for sunny winter days.

La Chope du Croissant, corner of rue du Croissant and rue Montmartre, 2ᵉ. On 31 July 1914 the Socialist leader, Jean Jaurès, was assassinated here for his anti-war activities. The table he was sitting at still remains.

Le Clown, 114 rue Amelot, 11ᵉ. Rendezvous for professional circus artistes.

La Coupole, 102 bd de Montparnasse, 14ᵉ. Open till 2 am; closed in August. Still the haunt of the chic and successful. Café, bar and restaurant – dancing, too, in the afternoons and evenings – its prices are middling.

Les Deux Magots, 170 bd St-Germain, 6ᵉ. Open till 2 am. Cl. August. Right on the corner of place St-Germain-des-Prés, it too owes its reputation to the *intellos* of the Left Bank, past and present. In summertime it picks up a lot of foreigners seeking the exact location of the spirit of French culture, and buskers galore play to the packed terrace.

Le Dôme, 108 bd du Montparnasse, 6ᵉ. Open to 1 am. Cl. Mon. Its reputation is the same as the above, but it has become more of a restaurant than café nowadays. Drinks only on the terrace.

Le Flore, 172 bd St-Germain, 6ᵉ. Open till 2 am. Cl. July. The great rival and immediate neighbour of *Deux Magots* with a very similar clientele.

Le Fouquet's, 99 av des Champs-Elysées, 8ᵉ. 9–2 am. A long-established and expensive watering-hole for aging stars, rich Lebanese and anyone else who has anything to hide behind dark glasses.

Le Grand Café, 40 bd des Capucines, 9ᵉ. A favourite all-nighter.

Kléber, place du Trocadéro, 16ᵉ. Open till dawn. Good for cinematic views of the Eiffel Tower catching the first light or morning mist filling the valley of the Seine.

Ma Bourgogne, 19 place des Vosges, 3ᵉ. A quiet and agreeable stopover on the corner of the square – with proper meals too.

Le Mandarin, 148 bd St-Germain, 6ᵉ. Berthillon ices.

Café Notre-Dame, corner of quai St-Michel and rue St-Jacques, 5ᵉ. With a view right across to the cathedral. Lenin used to drink here.

La Périgourdine, corner of quai des Grands-Augustins and place St-Michel, 5ᵉ. A classic cane-chaired corner café, big and busy.

Le Petit Lappe, 20 rue de Lappe, 11ᵉ. A simple café with a beautifully painted exterior opposite the *Chapelle des Lombards*.

Au Petit Suisse, place Claudel, 6ᵉ. An attractive small café on the corner of rue de Médicis by some excellent antiquarian bookshops.

Le Pigalle, 22 bd de Clichy, 9ᵉ. 24hr. bar, brasserie and *tabac*.

La Pointe St-Eustache, 1 rue Montorgueil, 1ᵉʳ. Alongside the church of St-Eustache, it has the advantage of being just an ordinary café-brasserie on the edge of the Les Halles hype.

Polly Magoo, 11 rue St-Jacques, 5ᵉ. A scruffy all-nighter frequented by chess addicts.

La Rotonde, 105 bd du Montparnasse, 6ᵉ. Another of the Montparnasse grand old names, with the names of the departed famous on the menu – Lenin, Trotsky, etc.

Sam Kearney's, rue Princesse, 6ᵉ. An American café-bar in the same small quiet street as the *Village Voice*.

Le Select, 99 bd du Montparnasse, 6ᵉ. The least spoilt of the Montparnasse cafés and more of a traditional café than the rest. Open till 3 am.

Le Taxi Jaune, 13 rue Chapon, 3ᵉ. Open till 2 am. Cl. Sun. An ordinary café, made special by the odd poster, good taped rock and new wave music, food till 11.30 and the occasional concert.

Le Temps des Cérises, 31 rue de la Cerisaie, 4ᵉ. It is hard to say what it is so appealing about this café, with its dirty yellow décor, old posters and prints of *vieux Paris*, save that the *patronne* knows most of the clientele, who are young, relaxed and not the dreaded *branchés*. There's a cheap *menu fixe* at midday.

The Village Voice, 6 rue Princesse, 6ᵉ. Cl. Sun. and Mon. It's a bookshop with an extensive selection of American and British books, especially poetry, with a café and a few snacks in the back. Visiting literati seem to find their way here, and there's a noticeboard advertising English-language activities.

MORE BAR THAN CAFÉ

Though cafés are called *bars* or *cafés* without distinction, some drinking places are definitely more **bar-ish**, with cocktails, music, and sometimes a transatlantic, gay or starlet flavour. All of them serve coffee though, and food.

Bleue Nuit, 9 rue des Vertus, 3ᵉ. 8.30–2am. Starts filling up around 11ish. The half-French, half-English Cyril behind the bar serves unextravagant cocktails and keeps the New Wave tapes turning. The décor changes every year and there's a restaurant next door (cl. Sun).

Broadside, 13 rue de la Ferronnerie, 1ᵉʳ; 6–1am. Cocktails, snacks and a favourite gay pick-up place.

Hôtel Central, 33 rue Vieille-du-Temple, 4ᵉ; midday–2am. One of the most popular gay bars in the Marais, women excluded.

Ciel de Paris, Tour Montparnasse, 33 av du Maine, 15ᵉ. 12–2am. Popular with tourists, the bar has a tremendous view over the western part of the city and into the setting sun. Better to go to the bar than take the tour – no lift fee.

La Champmeslé, 4 rue Chabanais, 2ᵉ; Mᵒ Pyramides. 6–2am. A mixed bar with a backroom reserved for lesbians and not very friendly to outsiders. Cocktails and picture/photo exhibitions.

La Closerie des Lilas, 171 bd du Montparnasse, 6ᵉ. 12–2am. A smart, arty, fashionable bar with good cocktails. No bum's paradise – it's pricey. The tables are name-plated after its celebrated habitués and there's a pianist in residence.

Conways, 73 rue St-Denis, 10ᵉ. Open till 1 am. A New York-style bar with photos of boxers and gyms on the walls and trans-Atlantic food in the restaurant. Brunch on Sunday. A relaxed friendly atmosphere without being stuffy or dull. An oasis in the Les Halles neighbourhood. Reasonable prices without being cheap.

Hôtel Crillon, 10 place de la Concorde, 8ᵉ. 12–2 am. Very classy surroundings where English rock stars in Paris are likely to drink after their gigs.

Le Crocodile, 6 rue Royer-Collard, 5ᵉ. 10.30–2 am; cl. Sun and August. Small, cosy, old-fashioned bar, where a stooping old proprietor fixes cocktails to the sounds of Kinks and Beatles.

Le Duplex, 25 rue Michel le Comte, 3ᵉ; 8–2 am. Young gay and lesbian bar with an arty flavour and friendly.

Harry's New York Bar, 5 rue Daunou, 2ᵉ. 10.30–4 am. Sporty American décor. Frequented by Fitzgerald and Hemingway in their time, and lots of their posthumous groupies.

H.L.M., 3 rue des Haudriettes, 3ᵉ 11–1 am/2 am at weekends. A late-night bar decorated in the somewhat unlikely style of an HLM, or French council flat – doilies, figurines and loud checks. But there's no guarantee it won't have changed by the time you get there. 1970s rock videos, cheapish cocktails, 50F menu until 10 pm.

The Look, 49 rue St-Honoré, 1ᵉʳ; Mᵒ Louvre; 6–2 am; cl. Mon. A smart and spacious gay bar. There's music, and women and straight men are welcome.

Magnetic Terrace, 12 rue de la Cossonnerie, 1ᵉʳ. Californian super-trendy, but a bit passé now.

La Mousson, 9 rue de la Bastille, 4ᵉ. Open till 2 am. Colonial-style décor – its name means monsoon. Young and trendy – advertising, magazine people, etc. Excellent cocktails for reasonable prices. Comfy armchairs and background sounds of 1940s jazz.

Pacific Palissades, 51 rue Quincampoix, 4ᵉ. 12–3; 8–2 am. Like Magnetic Terrace . . . and was frequented by the pin-ups and their groupies.

Le Sling, 10 rue du Perche, 3ᵉ; Mᵒ Filles-de-Calvaire; 6 – 2 am. Leather video-bar, exclusively for men.

Le Swing, 42 rue Vieille-du-Temple, 4ᵉ. 12 – 2 am. Gays, lesbians and heteros amuse themselves in this 1950s style bar, with newspapers to read and early rock and roll in the background.

Tribulum, 62 rue St-Denis, 1ᵉʳ. Wooden horses, masks, statues, magicaı signs . . . They'll fix you an astrological cocktail made from alcohol derived from plants associated with your zodiacal sign!

WINE BARS

Wine bars have been something of a growth industry in recent years, with the Ecluse chain adding new links, and the English leading the way at *Willi's*, the *Blue Fox* and *Petit Bacchus*. The attention to wine is serious and scholarly and the object of the exercise is to make really good or interesting wines available by selling them by the glass. Traditional *bistrots à vin* like *Le Rubis* and *La Tartine* cater for everyone, but the newer generation have a distinctly yuppish flavour, and are not cheap.

Le Baron Rouge, 1 rue Théophile-Roussel, 12ᵉ. 9.30 – 1.30; 4.30 – 7.30. Cl. Sun afternoon and Mon. Cheese, *charcuterie* and wines to taste and still leave you enough money for bargains at the nearby place d'Aligre market.

Blue Fox, Cité Berryer, 25 rue Royale, 8ᵉ. 12 – 3; 7 – 10.30. Cl. Sat. evening and Sun. Run by English wine expert, Steven Spurrier, who more or less invented the 'new' Parisian wine bar. He changes his selection of by-the-glass wines frequently. The speciality is wine from the *côtes du Rhone*. Food too.

Aux Bons Crus, 7 rue des Petits-Champs, 1ᵉʳ. A relaxed workaday place, with blue collars and white, and much cheaper than the neighbours. A *plat*, cheese and a quarter of Bordeaux works out about 45F.

Ma Bourgogne, 133 bd Haussmann, 8ᵉ. 7 – 8.30; cl. weekends and August. Not the establishment on the place des Vosges, but a place for pre-siesta glasses of Burgundy (*plats du jour* as well).

Cave Drouot, 8 rue Drouot, 9ᵉ. 7.30 – 9. Cl. Sun. and Sat. from July 14 – Sept 1. By the Drouot auction rooms. Excellent wines and a reasonably priced restaurant with *plats du jour* and *charcuterie*.

L'Ecluse, 15 quai des Grands-Augustins, 6ᵉ. 12 – 2 am. Forerunner of the new generation of wine bars, with décor and atmosphere in authentic traditional style – just lacking the workmen to spit on the floor. Small and intimate: a very agreeable place to sit and sip – not cheap, though. It has spawned offspring at: rue Mondétour, 1ᵉʳ; 64 rue François 1ᵉʳ, 8ᵉ; and 15 place de la Madeleine, 8ᵉ.

Georges, 11 rue des Canettes, 6ᵉ. 12 – 2 am; cl. Sun. and Mon, and July 14 – August 15. An attractive place in the spit-on-the-floor mould, with its old shop front still intact in a narrow leaning street off place St-Sulpice.

Aux Négociants, 27 rue Lambert, 18ᵉ. 11.30 – 9. Cl. weekends and July 15 – August 15. Cheap good wines and snacks. Popular with journalists and not at all snobby.

Café de la Nouvelle Mairie, 19 rue des Fosses-St-Jacques, 5ᵉ. 10.30 – 8.30; cl. Sat and Sun. A small sawdusted bar in a quiet Latin Quarter street close to the Panthéon, with good wines, *saucisson* and sandwiches. Three or four tables on the street. A perfect place for serious discussion. The clientele is literary-academic.

Au Père Tranquille, 30 av du Maine, 15ᵉ. 10 – 8; cl. Sun and Mon. Pleasant little place close to the Montparnasse tower.

Le Petit Bacchus, 13 rue du Cherche-Midi, 6ᵉ. 9 – 7.30; cl. Sun and Mon. Elegant quiet situation for elegant quiet people. Another Steven Spurrier outfit with changing selection of wines . . . and snacks. Opposite Poilâne's bakery.

La Rallye, 6 rue Daguerre, 14ᵉ. 9.30 – 8.30/7 on Saturday; cl. Sun, Mon and August. A good place to recover from the Catacombs or Montparnasse cemetery. The *patron* offers a bottle for tasting, but gulping the lot would be considered bad form. Good cheese and *saucisson*.

Le Rubis, 10 rue du Marché-St-Honoré, 1ᵉʳ. 7 – 10; cl. Sat, Sun and 2 weeks in August. One of the oldest wine bars, it enjoys a reputation for having among the best wines, plus excellent snacks and *plats du jour*. Very crowded.

Au Sauvignon, 80 rue des Sts-Pères, 6ᵉ. 9 – 10; cl. Sun, hols and August. Very small and decorated with Alsatian posters and murals, and a relaxed, unpretentious atmosphere.

La Tartine, 24 rue de Rivoli, 4ᵉ. Open till 10; cl. Tues, August and Christmas. The genuine 1900s article, which still cuts class boundaries in its clientele. A good selection of affordable wines, plus excellent cheese, and *saucisson* with *pain de campagne*.

Taverne Henri IV, 13 place du Pont-Neuf, 1ᵉʳ. 11.30 – 9.30; cl. wkends and August 15 – September 15. Another of the good older bars, opposite Henri IV's statue. Yves Montand used to come here, when Simone Signoret lived in the adjacent place Dauphine. Full of lawyers from the Palais de Justice. The food is good, but a bit pricey.

Willi's, 13 rue des Petits-Champs, 1ᵉʳ. 11 – 10; cl. weekends. Another English-run bar, frequented by journalists, stockbrokers, the posh and less so. If you don't want to eat you can stand at the bar. The English staff are friendly and can give you advice on what wines to try. Prices are middling.

BEER CELLARS AND PUBS

As their names and décor suggest, **beer-drinking** establishments owe their inspiration chiefly to the cross-Channel cousins. Most stock at least some British draught beers and a host of international bottles.

Académie de la Bière, 88 bis bd de Port-Royal, 5ᵉ. 3.30 – 2 am. Cl. Sun and August. 120 and more beers from 22 countries. Also food – good mussels and chips. Crowded.

Bar Belge, 75 av de St-Ouen, 17ᵉ. 3.30 – 1 am. Cl. Mon. Belgian beers.

Bedford Arms, 17 rue Princesse. 6ᵉ. Open till dawn. Darts and Guinness . . .

Au Général La Fayette, 52 rue La Fayette, 9ᵉ· 11 (Sat 3) – 2 am. Cl. Sun. A dozen draughts, including Guinness, and many more bottled. Belle Epoque décor and mixed clientele.

Guinness Tavern, 31 rue des Lombards, 1ᵉʳ. 6 – 4 am. Music (piano and live folk, jazz, rock on Mon, Tues and Thurs) . . . and Guinness.
London Tavern, 3 rue du Sabot, 6ᵉ. 10 (Sun 6) – 2am (Sat 3). Watney's and Heineken, plus piano (from 5pm on Sunday, 9pm other days) and jazz.
La Gueuse, 19 rue Soufflot, 5ᵉ. Same enterprise as *L'Académie* above.
Mayflower Pub, 49 rue Descartes, 5ᵉ. All nighter. International beers and loads of students.
La Pinte, 13 carrefour de l'Odéon, 6ᵉ. 6.30 – 2am. Cl. August. Boozy and crowded, with piano and jazz.
Pub Saint-Germain, 17 rue de l'Ancienne-Comédie, 6ᵉ. 24 hours. 21 draught beers and hundreds of bottles – literally. Huge and crowded. Hot food at meal times, otherwise cold snacks.
La Taverne de Nesle, 32 rue Dauphine, 6ᵉ. 7 – 2am (stays open later if trade warrants it). Vast selection of beers. Full of local nightbirds.
Twickenham, 70 rue des Sts-Pères, 6ᵉ. 12 – 2am (Sat, opens at 7pm only); cl. Sunday. Rugger pub. Wood and brass, on the corner on rue de Grenelle.
Pub Winston Churchill, 5 rue de Presbourg, 16ᵉ. 9 – 2am. (Sat and Sun 2.30am). Edwardian brass and panelling. English breakfast, and roast beef and Yorkshire at lunchtime – reasonable prices.

SALONS DE THE, SNACKS AND ICES

Tearoom does not quite conjure up the chic and feminine atmosphere of the *salons de thé* that crop up wherever a new part of town has been gentrified as well as in the established *BCBG* (see p.67) haunts. The oldest is *Angelina's* with its marble icing sugar exterior. More relaxed and exotic are *La Pagode* and *La Mosquée*, in the two least Parisian buildings of the city. **Snacks** and **light midday meals** are easy to find and unlikely to disappoint. As well as the places listed below there are all the cafés and *brasseries* to choose from. The classier cafés sell concoctions of cake and **icecream**, as do the drugstores; the supreme sorbet experience is *Berthillon's* on Ile St-Louis.

Salons de thé
A la Cour de Rohan, 59 – 61 rue St-André-des-Arts, 6ᵉ. 12(3pm at weekends) – 7. Cl. Mon and August. A genteel chintzy drawing-room atmosphere in a picturesque 18C alley. Cakes, *tartes*, poached eggs, etc. Close to bd St-Germain.
Angelina, 226 rue de Rivoli, 1ᵉʳ. 10 – 7; closed August. A long-established gilded cage for the well-coiffed to sip the best hot chocolate in town, plus *pâtisseries* and puds of the same high quality. About 35F for tea and a cake.

A Priori Thé, 35–37 galerie Vivienne, 2ᵉ. 12 – 7; cl. Sunday. Sip your tea outside but under cover in the watery lighting of a *passage*.

Berthillon, 31 rue St-Louis-en-l'Ile, 4ᵉ. 10 – 8; cl. Mon and Tues. The very best ice creams and sorbets made and sold here on the Ile St-Louis. Also available at *Lady Jane* and *Le Flore-en-l'Ile*, both on quai d'Orleans, as well as four other island sites listed on the door.

Café de la Mosquée, rue Geoffroy-St-Hilaire, 5ᵉ. 10 – 9.30; cl. Fri. In fine weather you can drink mint tea by fig trees and fountain in the courtyard of the Paris mosque – a delightful haven of calm. The interior of the *salon* is a little gloomy.

Centre Culturel du Marais, 20 rue des Francs-Bourgeois, 3ᵉ. Art bookshop with *salon de thé*.

Le Coquelin Aîné, 67 rue de Passy, 16ᵉ. 9 – 6.30; cl. Sun and Mon. Right on place Passy, meeting place of gilded youth and age. Excellent salads, *tartes*, cakes . . . Not for paupers.

Dattes et Noix, 4 rue de Parc-Royal, 3ᵉ. 12 – 12. Not the most appealing of décors, but good cakes and salads.

L'Ebouillanté, 6 rue des Barres, 4ᵉ. 12 – 9; closed Monday. Very small, with reasonable prices and simple fare – choc cakes and *pâtisseries* as well as savoury dishes.

Eurydice, 10 place des Vosges, 4ᵉ. 12 – 7 (10 in summer); cl. Mon and Tues. On the east side of the *place* and desirable for the summer tables under the arcade, if you can get one. Cakes, salads, meat dishes and seafood, with an east European touch, and the possibility of accompanying vodka. Brunch on Sunday.

Fanny Tea, 20 place Dauphine, 1ᵉʳ. 1 – 7.30; cl. Mon and August. Savoury snacks, tarts, etc, as well as tea and cakes. Very small. In summer, tables outside in the beautiful 17C *place*.

La Fourmi Ailée, 8 rue Fouarre, 5ᵉ.
Part of the bookshop (see p.144) serving scones and apple crumble as well as the usual fare.

JeThéMe, 4 rue d'Alleray, 15ᵉ. 12 – 7; cl. Sun and August. Obnoxious name and nostalgic décor, and the usual sweets, salads and snacks, served at reasonable prices and with rare grace. Also sells coffee, tea and chocolate to take away.

Ladurée, 16 rue Royale, 8ᵉ. 8.30 – 7; cl. Sun and August. For the dainty and affected. Best to buy the chocolate and coffee macaroons to take away. Does lunch for around 60F.

Le Loir dans la Théière, rue des Rosiers, 4ᵉ. 12 – 7; Sun. 11 – 7. Cl. Mon and August. The name means the dormouse in the teapot and the only point to the place is the mural of the Mad Hatter's Teaparty. Sunday brunch, midday *tartes* and omelettes, fruit teas of every description and cakes all day.

La Pagode, 57 bis rue de Babylone, 7ᵉ. 4 – 10. A real-life pagoda (see p.199) – one of the most beautiful buildings in Paris in which to have tea. Tables in the Chinese garden in summer.

Pandora, 24 passage Choiseul, 2ᵉ. 11.30 – 7; cl. Sat and July 15 – August 15. Another *passages* stop-off with excellent food.

La Passion du Fruit, 71 quai de la Tournelle, 5ᵉ and 31 av de Suffren, 7ᵉ. 12 – 1.30am; Mon and Tues 6 – 1.30am. Juice, sorbets, salads, milk shakes and teas – all of fruit. The quai Tournelle version has an attractive *terrasse* opposite Notre-Dame with a few tables in the garden.

Piccolo Teatro, 6 rue des Écouffes, 4ᵉ. Open till 12.30am; cl. Tues. Vegetarian *salon de thé*-cum-restaurant. An extremely comfortable place serving delicious edibles with pedantic names.

Le Relais du Village, Village Suisse, 51 av de la Motte-Picquet, 15ᵉ. In among the antique shops, if you should just happen to be on the lookout for a Louis XV bureau.

Rose Thé, 91 rue St-Honoré, 1ᵉʳ. 12 – 7 weekdays only. Calm and tranquil, in a courtyard of antique shops and faded bric-à-brac. Teas, milk shakes, *tartes aux fruits*, salads, etc. Reasonable prices.

Le Salon des Thés, 4 rue du Roi-de-Sicile, 4ᵉ. 12 – 7; cl. Mon. Yet another Marais tea shop – mixed salads and brunch.

Snacks

La Boutique à Sandwiches, 12 rue du Colisée, 8ᵉ. 11.45 – 11.30; cl. Sun and August. The best sandwiches in town, though certainly not the cheapest. If you go for something like the *maison's* speciality – the Alsatian *pickelfleish* – you're getting a whole meal and paying for it.

La Crêpe St-Louis, 86 rue St-Louis-en-l'Ile, 4ᵉ. 12 – 12. Breton *crêpes* with cider.

Drugstore Elysées, 133 av des Champs-Elysées, 8ᵉ; Mᵒ Etoile; 9am – 2am. *Drugstore Matignon*, 1 av Matignon, 8ᵉ; Mᵒ Franklin-Roosevelt, 10am – 2am and *Drugstore Saint-Germain* 149 bd St-Germain, 6ᵉ; Mᵒ St-Germain-des-Prés; 10am – 2am. All day salads, sandwiches, *plats du jour*, full blown meals and huge, delicious desserts, are available from the three drugstores, along with books, newspapers, tobacco and a multitude of fripperies. Prices are reasonable and the food much better than the décor would suggest.

Fauchon, 24 place de la Madeleine, 8ᵉ. 9.45 – 6.30; cl. Sun. Narrow and uncomfortable counters at which to gobble wonderful *pâtisseries*, *plats du jour* and sandwiches – at a price.

Fleur de Lotus, 2 rue du Roi-de-Sicile, 4ᵉ. 10 – 9. Cheap Vietnamese dishes, heated up while you wait – to take away or eat on the premises.

Lord Sandwich, 276 rue St-Honoré, 1ᵉʳ and 134 rue du Faubourg-St-Honoré, 8ᵉ. A New York-style choice of bread and filler combinations.

Restaurant du Musée Picasso, Hôtel Salé, 5 rue de Thorigny. 10 – 5.15

You may have to wait for a table. Reasonable prices and reliable luchtime fare.

L'Oiseau Bariolé, 16 rue Ste-Croix-de-la-Bretonnerie, 4ᵉ. Small and friendly, with *plats du jour* at 30F, salads at 20F, Breton cider, omelettes etc.

Palais de Tokyo, av du Président-Wilson, 16ᵉ. Good food in the museum snack bar.

Ramen-Tei, 163 rue St-Honoré, 1ᵉʳ. 11.30 – 1. Japanese snack bar without a trace of Frenchness. Pay before you eat and take pot luck.

Le Roi Falafel, 34 rue des Rosiers, 4ᵉ. Takeaway Egyptian.

Self-Service de la Samaritaine, 2 quai du Louvre, 1ᵉʳ. 11.30 – 6; cl. Sunday. In the number two *magasin*. More for the view over the Seine than the food.

La Table d'Italie, 69 rue de Seine, 6ᵉ. Italian pasta, snacks, etc at the counter, plus a grocery selling *pasta* and other Italian delicatessen products.

RESTAURANTS AND BRASSERIES

Contrary to what you might expect, eating out in Paris need not be an enormous extravagance. There are numerous **fixed price menus under 50F** providing simple but well-cooked fare, and at *Casa Miguel* you can have a whole meal for just 5F. Paying a little **more than 50F** gives the chance to try out a greater range of dishes and once **over 150F** you should be getting some serious gourmet satisfaction. Our classification into these three main categories is based on the cheapest fixed price menu on offer and doesn't include drink. If you choose from the *carte* bear in mind that you may well boost the bill into the next price category.

Ethnic restaurants, of which there are a great many in Paris, are listed first in their price category with full details, then again at the end of the section according to the origin of the food they serve. **Vegetarian** places are also listed twice for ease of identification. For **late-night** restaurants, see the checklist at the end of this chapter.

AROUND 50F

Restaurant des Arts, 73 rue de Seine, 6ᵉ. Cl. Fri night, Sat, Sun and August. Menu at 45F including service. A small, crowded, *sympa* place with simple, homely fare. Young and old, well-heeled and not at all.

Au Babylone, 13 rue de Babylone, 7ᵉ. Midday only; cl. Sun. Murky, with lots of old-fashioned charm. Under 50F, and there's an equally old-fashioned café next door.

Les Balkans, 3 rue de la Harpe, 5e; cl. Wed. Good standby cheapie – *couscous*, goulash, etc. – for around 40F.

Le Baptiste, 11 rue des Boulangers, 5e. 12 – 2.30, 7.30 – 10.30; cl. Sat night and Sun. 45F with wine. Warm, friendly and noisy, a place to rub elbows with the neighbours. The food is simple and good.

Restaurant des Beaux-Arts, 11 rue Bonaparte, 6e. Cl. Mon and August. Menu at 45F, including wine. The choice is wide, the portions generous, and the queues long in tourist time. A matey, warm-hearted place.

Brasserie Bedhet Valette, rue St-Louis-en-l'Ile (Notre-Dame end), 4e. A cheaper and less tourist-ridden choice than the *brasserie* on quai de Bourbon.

Bistro de la Gare, 59 bd du Montparnasse, 6e (with others at 30 rue St-Denis, 1er and 73 Champs-Elysées, 8e). 12 – 3, 6 – 1am every day. The Montparnasse one has the 1900 décor. The food is okay, if slightly plastic. Service is fast – the kind of place people go en route to the movies or theatre. If you want a leisurely meal, avoid them.

Bistro du Marais, 15 rue Ste-Croix-de-la-Bretonnerie, 3e. A pleasant cheap local.

Le Bol en Bois, 35 rue Pascal, 13e. Till 9.30; cl. Sun. A rather austere macrobiotic restaurant, with *plats du jour* around 39F, and a veggie grocery next door.

A la Bonne Humeur, 26 rue Orfila, 20e. A pleasant old *restaurant de quartier* with a menu at 40F, if you're in the area at lunchtime.

Casa Miguel, 48 rue St-Georges, 9e. 12 – 1, 7 – 8; cl. Sun evening. A meal with wine for 5F.

Chartier, 7 rue du Faubourg-Montmartre, 9e. Every day till 9.30. Brown lino floor, dark-stained woodwork, brass hatracks, clusters of white globes suspended from the high ceiling, mirrors, and waiters in long aprons. Meals for the populace in a turn-of-the-century soup kitchen. Worth seeing and, though crowded and rushed, the food is not bad.

La Cigale, 126 av Michelet, St-Ouen, just outside the Porte de Clignancourt, by the flea market. Nicely scruffy bar with wheezy accordion music and cheap mussels and lamb.

Le Commerce, 51 rue du Commerce, 15e. 11– 3, 6 – 9.30, every day. The same management as Chartier, but smaller, less touristy, less rushed . . . and some way off the beaten track. Menu at 46F. The décor is interesting: green bamboo wallpaper, pea green pillars, green gallery railings . . . and mirrors.

Le Cyrnos, 228 rue de Charenton, 12e. Small and *sympa*, with a menu at 34F and *paella* on Friday evenings.

Aux Deux Saules, 91 rue St-Denis, 1er; Mo Les Halles/Etienne-Marcel. Very cheap omelettes, sausages, chips and the like.

Drouot, 103 rue de Richelieu, 2ᵉ. Admirably cheap and satisfying food served at a frantic pace, in an Art Nouveau décor. Same management as the better known Chartier.

Fouta Toro, 3 rue du Nord, 18ᵉ. Cl. Sunday. Senegalese dishes for around 50F, including *thiep*, the national dish.

Au Grain de Folie, 24 rue La Vieuville, 18ᵉ. Evenings only, till 10.30. Good, unpretentious vegetarian cheapie.

Le Grand Cerf, 10–12 passage du Grand Cerf (145 rue St-Denis), 2ᵉ. 12 – 10; cl. Sun and August. An old-fashioned cheapie with a menu at 32F. Spanish as well as French fare.

Le Grenier de Notre Dame, 18 rue de la Bûcherie, 5ᵉ. Macro specialities right on the river opposite Notre Dame.

El Karnak, 13 rue Louvel-Tessier, 10ᵉ. Till 12.30am every day. Menus at 35F and 45F. Egyptian.

Restaurant Lyly, rue Bosquet, 7ᵉ. 12 – 2.30, 7 – 10.30. Simple local Vietnamese, with menu at 39F.

Le Liban à la Mouff, 18 rue Mouffetard, 5ᵉ. A pleasant and unusually cheap Lebanese.

Le Maquis, 69 rue Caulaincourt, 18ᵉ. Till 11pm; cl. Sunday. Brilliant lunchtime menu for 47F, which you can eat out of doors in summer.

Chez Marcel, 16–18 rue Lalande, 14ᵉ. Good value *menu fixe* until 9pm. Very friendly. Excellent *couscous* at all times.

Mary's Restaurant, 9 rue de Turenne, 9ᵉ. Till 10pm. As English as the name – reasonably priced vegetarian gourmet flans and tarts.

Miniferme, 29 rue St-André-des-Arts, 6ᵉ. 11 – 11; cl. Sun. Over 100 omlettes from 10–36F and a menu at 42F.

La Nouvelle Gare, 49 bd Vincent-Auriol, 13ᵉ. 24hrs; cl. Sat midday and Sun. For people coming off night shifts. The lowest late night prices and a great atmosphere.

Oaj-Djerba, 110 rue de Belleville, 20ᵉ. Till midnight; cl. Fri and Sat midday. Basic Tunisian-Jewish.

Café-Restaurant à l'Observatoire, 63 av Denfert-Rochereau, 14ᵉ. Cl. Sunday. A straightforward quick eating place with *steack frites* and the like at their most basic and best. Very crowded at lunchtime.

Le Petit Bistro, 2 rue du Sabot, 6ᵉ. Unpretentious little place with a menu at 46F – without service, though.

Le Petit Mabillon, 6 rue Mabillon, 6ᵉ. Till 11.30; cl. Sun and midday Mon. An attractive place in an attractive street: under 50F.

Le Petit Ramoneur, 74 rue St-Denis, 1ᵉʳ. Till 9.30; cl. weekends and August. A basic 41F menu in good bistro tradition, with cheap wine that's better than plonk. Crowded, but a welcome and genuine relief in Les Halles.

Le Petit Saint-Benoît, 4 rue Saint-Benoît, 6ᵉ. Till 10; cl. weekends. Solid traditional fare for around 60F.

Perraudin, 157 rue St-Jacques, 5ᵉ. Till 9pm; cl. Sat night and Sun. Good cheap fare for 38F.

Au Pied de Fouet, 45 rue de Babylone, 7ᵉ. 2 – 4, 7 – 8.50; cl. Sat night, Sun and August. Good food and a great little place – little being the operative word; there are just four tables and no reservations.

Port de Pidjiguiti, 28 rue Etex, 18ᵉ. Cl. Mon. Very *sympa* and excellent food for about 50F. It is run by a village in Guinea-Bissau, whose inhabitants take turns in manning the restaurant; the proceeds go to the village.

Quan Nho, 5 rue du Sommerard, 5ᵉ. A real cheap Vietnamese in the Latin Quarter.

Aux Savoyards, 14 rue des Boulangers, 5ᵉ. Till 10.30; cl. Sat night and Sun. A delightfully friendly and wholesome place, but on the map and likely to be packed. 45F all in.

Bar des Sports, 15 rue de la Butte-aux-Cailles, 13ᵉ; Mᵒ Corvisart/Place d'Italie. A local bistro with unusual and unecological fare (crocodile, sometimes turtle).

Le Tire-Bouchon, 47 rue Descartes, 5ᵉ. Basic fare, plus *fondues*, for under 50F.

Restaurant Végétarien, 2 place du Marché Ste-Cathérine, 4ᵉ. 11 – 6; cl. Sun. Small, quiet and inexpensive.

Yakitori, 64 rue Montparnasse, 14ᵉ. Every day till 11pm. Japanese: *brochettes* served with a variety of piquant sauces.

UP TO 130F

Le 18AM, 18 rue Amélie, 7ᵉ. A small and unintimidating place run by women for a mainly but not exclusively female clientele.

Anahi, 49 rue Volta, 3ᵉ. 7.30 – midnight. Cl. Wed. A restaurant specialising in South American cuisine: *empanadas*, *cururu de camerao*, Argentinian grills . . . and prices at the top of the range.

Brasserie Les Alsaces aux Halles, 6 rue Coquillière, 1ᵉʳ. All night brasserie.

Anjou-Normande, 13 rue de-la-Folie-Méricourt, 11ᵉ. Cl. Wed and Mon evening. Traditional cooking – *artisanal*, as they like to put it – with no colourings or other additives.

L'Auberge des Temples, 74 rue de Dunkerque, 10ᵉ. Till 10.30. Choice of Chinese, Vietnamese, Thai, Cambodian and Japanese dishes all under one roof.

Brasserie Les Alsaces aux Halles, 6 rue Coquillière, 1ᵉʳ. All night *brasserie*.

Anjou-Normande, 13 rue de-la-Folie-Méricourt, 11ᵉ. Cl. Wed and Mon evening. Traditional cooking – *artisanal*, as they like to put it – with no colourings or other additives.

Il Barone, 5 rue Léopold-Robert, 14ᵉ. Good Italian food for around 100F.

Bergamote, 1 rue Niepce, 14ᵉ. 43.22.79.47. Till 11pm; cl Sun and Mon. A small and *sympa* bistro-style restaurant, in a scruffy street off rue de l'Ouest. Only about ten tables; you need to book at weekends. There's a 55F menu available until 9pm and an 80F menu. The *carte* will be around 125F.

Le Bernica, 4 impasse de la Gaîté, 14ᵉ. 43.20.39.02. Cl. Sun. Cuisine from Ile de la Réunion. Friendly and interesting.

Le Bistro Romain, 103 bd du Montparnasse, 6ᵉ. 43.25.25.25. A slightly posher, vaguely Italian, version of the Bistro de la Gare. The advertised 50F menus are a bit deceptive. Okay for a quick meal, but not recommended for intimate chats. Other establishments at: 9 bd des Italiens, 2ᵉ (42.97.49.55); 122 Champs-Elysées, 8ᵉ (43.59.93.31); place Victor-Hugo, 16ᵉ (45.00.65.94); 9 av des Ternes, 17ᵉ (47.64.17.38).

Boeuf Gros Sel, 299 rue Lecourbe, 15ᵉ. 45.57.16.33. Till 10pm. Cl. Sun and Mon midday. Around 100F. An old favourite.

Le Bol en Bois, 35 rue Pascal, 13ᵉ. Till 10pm; cl. Sun. Japanese-inspired vegetarian.

Au Bon Accueil, corner av de Versailles and rue Wilhem, 16ᵉ. A local bistro in a part of the world where there are not many such, though the address makes the prices steeper than they would be otherwise.

Café de la Jatte, 67 bd de Levallois, Ile de la Jatte – off the coast of Neuilly, where most of the fashionable and rich who frequent it live, or aspire to. The locale is unbeatable, in a courtyard off a leafy street lined with small workshops and idiosyncratic houses. The building is a converted manège: airy and spacious, with potted palms, spotless linen and wicker chairs. The food is excellent – around 70F for an enormous lunchtime salad – and the staff, both male and female, just as tasty.

Aux Charpentiers, 10 rue Mabillon, 6ᵉ. 43.26.30.05. Till 11.30. Cl. Sun. A friendly old-fashioned place belonging to the *Compagnons des Charpentiers* (Carpenters Guild), with appropriate décor of roof-trees and tie beams. Traditional *plats du jour* are their forte.

La Coupole, 102 bd du Montparnasse, 14ᵉ. 43.20.14.20; Mᵒ Vavin. Cl. midday Sun and Aug. Open till 1.45. One of the best *brasserie* menus in an arch-Parisian hang-out.

La Corossol Doudou, 1 rue de la Ferrière, 9ᵉ. Till 7am. Antillais all-nighter.

La Cracovia, 10 rue Alexandre-Dumas, 11ᵉ. Solid and reliable Polish bistro.

Aux Crus de Bourgogne, 2 rue Bachaumont, 2ᵉ. 42.33.48. 24. Good Burgundy cuisine at reasonable prices including lobster.

Aux Délices de Széchuen, 40 av Duquesne, 7ᵉ. 43.06.22.55. Till 10.30; cl. Mon and 2 weeks in August. High quality and reasonably priced Chinese food served to the elegant inhabitants of an elegant *quartier*. A menu at 77F.

Drugstore Saint-Germain, 149 bd St-Germain, 6ᵉ. Till 2 am. The best of the drugstores for food. Basics like *steack tartare* and *langoustines* done to a T.

Eléphant Blanc, 33 rue des Trois-Frères, 18ᵉ. Cuisine from Laos and Thailand.

Escale de Saigon, 24 rue Bosquet, 7ᵉ. 45.51.60.14. Small, good, local Vietnamese.

Goldenberg's, 7 rue des Rosiers, 4ᵉ. 48.87.20.16. Daily to 11pm. Around 100F. This is the best known Jewish restaurant in the capital. Its *bortsch, blinis*, potato *strudels, zakovski* and other central European dishes are a treat.

Le Golestan de Perse, 4 rue Severo, 14ᵉ. Iranian, with an excellent *menu fixe* for around 50F.

Au Grain de Folie, 24 rue de Vieuville, 18ᵉ. 42.58.15.57. 7 – 10. Vegetarian, with a menu at 45F.

La Guinguette de Neuilly, 12 bd de Levallois, Ile de la Jatte. 46.24.25.04. Crowded with the same well-heeled, well-fed set as the other Jatte establishments. Excellent food – best on a sunny day at one of the outside tables.

Hassan, 27 rue de Turbigo, 3ᵉ. Till midnight; cl. Mon. Moroccan: North African food at its best and most beautiful.

Ile de la Réunion, 119 rue St-Honoré, 1ᵉʳ. 42.33.30.95. Cl. Sun. Very simple and plain, and the food is passable.

Kazatchok, 7 rue Manuel, 9ᵉ. 48.78.74.81. Till 2am; cl. Sun. Most Parisian Russian restaurants are high-class establishments run by old aristos. This isn't: a small friendly place with great smoked salmon *blinis, kotlet Kievski*, and other Slav specials.

Kinkeliba, 5 rue des Déchargeurs, 1ᵉʳ. 45.08.96.61. A Gabonese restaurant, catering for European fantasies of sunny Africa. Smoked fish, *yassa* chicken, stuffed crab, buffalo and antelope, palm wine, etc. Around 100F.

Kin Malebo, 2 Passage Louis-Philippe, 11ᵉ. Till 2am. Zairean cuisine.

Lipp, 151 bd St-Germain, 6ᵉ. 45.48.53.91. Open till 12.45am; cl. Mon, July and two weeks at Christmas and Easter. A 1900s *brasserie*, one of the best-known establishments on the Left Bank, haunt of the successful and famous. It's entertaining, but don't be downcast if the po-faced owner gives you the thumbs-down. He scrutinises all-comers and if he doesn't rate you tells you there won't be a table for 90 minutes, and never mind the ten empty places under your nose. Once in, you can get away with about 120F.

La Maison de la Lozère, 4 rue Hautefeuille, 6ᵉ. 43.54.26.64. Till 10pm. Cl. Sun, Mon and August. A scrubbed wood restaurant serving up the cuisine, cheeses, etc of the Lozère *département*. A menu at 61F, including wine. Crowded with office workers at lunchtime.

La Mansouria, 11 rue Faidherbe-Chaligny, 11ᵉ. 43.71.00.16. Mᵒ Faidherbe-Chaligny. A feminist restaurant close to the Maison des Femmes.

La Mascareigne, 8 rue du Dragon, 6ᵉ. 45.44.12.53. Cl. Mon. A Réunion restaurant, with an Antillais band after 11pm.

Le Mouton Blanc, 40 rue d'Auteuil, 16ᵉ. 42.88.02.21. Good traditional food at around 120F. The establishment was once patronised by Molière, Racine, La Fontaine and other literary aces of the time. It is now an agreeable local for the *quartier's* well-off residents.

Le Muniche, 27 rue de Buci, 6ᵉ. 46.33.62.09. Open till 3am. A crowded old-style brasserie specialising particularly in seafood – bang in the middle of the Saint-Germain nightlife. Prices at the top of the range.

M'Zadette M'Foua, 152 rue du Château, 14ᵉ. 43.22.00.16. Till midnight; cl. Sunday. A rather small restaurant with Zairean and Congolese food – *manioc, maboké*, etc. Among those who know – i.e. the Congolese – it enjoys the reputation of doing the best home-cooking in town. Book at weekends.

Chez Nacef, 26 rue de Bièvre, 5ᵉ. Above average Algerian restaurant.

Natasha, 35 rue Guersant, 17ᵉ. 45.74.23.86. Till 11; cl. Sun. A bit out of the way beyond the place des Ternes, but a number one bargain for anyone on a low budget – and an excellent meal for anyone at all. The atmosphere is simple, and youthful, though the clientele is not exclusively young. For 62F, you help yourself to hors-d'oeuvres and wine, with three other very respectable courses to follow.

L'Orient Express, 72 rue des Gravilliers, 3ᵉ. 42.72.68.21. Modest prices and a deservedly good reputation for its Cantonese and Peking dishes. Popular with the Chinese community.

Au Petit Moulin, 17 rue Tholozé, 18ᵉ. 42.52.42.16. Till midnight: cl. Wed. In a tiny picturesque corner house on the slopes of Montmartre – and not touristy. The menu is changed every day. Midday menu at 45F; *carte* at around 75F.

Le Petit Poucet, 1 bd de Levallois, Ile de la Jatte. Cl. Sun. Tables under the trees, overlooking a Seine backwater used by barge-dwellers. Good food for around 120F. A bit hard to get to, it's towards the north end of the island of Jatte. Cross either Pont de Neuilly and turn right, or Pont de Levallois and go down the steps in mid-bridge and walk along the side of the derelict industrial estate.

Au Petit Riche, 25 rue le Peletier, 9ᵉ. 47.70.68.68. Open till 12.15am; cl. Sun and second half of August. A long-established restaurant with a mirrored 1900s interior. Prompt and attentive service, good food – a menu at 110F (more like 130–140F with extras). Bit stuffy in atmosphere.

Le Petit Zinc, 25 rue de Buci, 6ᵉ. 43.54.79.34. Open till 3am. Excellent traditional food, especially seafood, in the middle of the Buci street market. Best really late at night when you won't notice that the prices are right at the top of the range.

Pizza Roma, corner of rue Rollin and rue du Cardinal-Lemoine, 5ᵉ. An excellent unpretentious Italian joint, right by the place de la Contrescarpe

Polidor, 41 rue Monsieur-le-Prince, 6ᵉ 43.26.95.34. Till 10 pm. Cl. Sun, Mon and August. A traditional cheapie, popular with artists and students. The visitor's book, they say, boasts more of history's big names than all the glittering palaces put together. Not as cheap as it was in Joyce's day but good food and great atmosphere. Midday meal at 39F, otherwise 80 – 100F.

A la Pomponnette, 42 rue Lepic, 18ᵉ. 46.06.08.36. Till 9.30; cl. Sun evening, Mon and August. An old-fashioned, smoke-stained bistro with zinc-topped bar and croaky old-timers taking a drop and swopping a tale. As near the genuine article as you can get, and the food is excellent. Prices top of this range.

Le Potiron, 16 rue du Roule, 1ᵉʳ. 42.33.35.68. Till 11; cl. Sun and Mon. Also *salon de thé*. Run by women, with changing exhibitions of women artists' work as decoration and very imaginative dishes bordering on *nouvelle cuisine*. Menu at 62F.

Pour le Plaisir, 257 rue du Faubourg-St-Antoine, 11ᵉ. Till 1am. Not the best hygienic standards, but excellent food and a piano for anyone feeling inclined to play. 70F menu, without wine or service.

Restaurant A, 5 rue de Passy, 5ᵉ. 46.33.85.54. Till 11pm; cl. Wed. '*A la Cuisine de Chine du XVIII siècle*' is the full name, and the proprietor can be a bit of a pain telling you how special the place is, but there are some good and unusual dishes. Menus at 50F and 72F, excluding service.

La Route du Château, 123 rue du Château, 14ᵉ. 43.20.09.59. Till 12.30am; cl. Sun, Mon midday and August. Linen tablecloths, a rose on your table, an unpretentious, old-fashioned bistro atmosphere. The food is good, without being exciting or unusual. The clientele is mixed, a little gayer than straight. Menu at 64F.

Bar Sassia, 12 place de la Bastille, 11ᵉ. Till 12.45am. Brilliant Moroccan *tagines*, First Empire mirrors and 20C palm trees. Friendly service.

Le Tchaïka, 9 rue de l'Eperon, 6ᵉ. Till 10.30; cl. weekends. *Tarama*, caviar, *blinis*, salmon *bortsch* and vodka – cheaper than most White Russians. Another establishment at 7 rue de Lappe, 11ᵉ.

Les Trois Claudes, 119 rue de Reuilly, 12ᵉ. Cl. Sat evening and Sun. The *trois* are the three family members running the place – is the baby responsible for the toy parrots? 45F at midday, 75F in the evening. Reasonable wine and good quality food for the price.

La Vallée des Bambous, 35 rue Gay-Lussac, 5ᵉ. 43.54.99.47. Till 10.30; cl. Tues and August. You usually have to queue for this popular Chinese. An excellent value menu at 37F all in, otherwise around 80F.

Le Vaudeville, 29 rue Vivienne, 2ᵉ. 42.33.39.31. Till 2am. A lively late-night *brasserie* – you might easily have to queue – with good food and an attractive marble and mosaic interior. Menu at 103F, without service.

Au Vieux Paris, 2 rue de l'Abbaye, 6ᵉ. 43.26.21.92. Cl. Mon evening and Tues. In a narrow mansarded beamed house close to Saint-Germain-des-

Prés. Simple food, with a Greek slant, and friendly service. Menu at 55F,
but more likely to cost you around 80F.

Village Bulgare, 8 rue de Nevers, 6ᵉ. Try the *Cirène au four* (baked
sheep's milk cheese with vegetables) and *Gamza* wine.

Zerda, corner rue Chéroy and rue des Dames, 17ᵉ. Unpretentious and
very satisfying Moroccan food.

130–200F

Aux Abeilles d'Or, 12 rue Royer-Collard, 5ᵉ. Vegetarian *nouvelle cuisine*

Antalya, rue d'Enghien, 10ᵉ. Turkish cuisine. Superb starters and sea bass.
Raki to go with it. No menus, so the bill can be tiny or rather a lot.

Baalbeck, 16 rue Mazagran, 10ᵉ. 47.70.70.02. 12 – 3, 8 – 1. Much liked
by the monied refugees, a Lebanese restaurant with dozens of starters.
For 350F you can have a representative selection for four, with *arak* to
drink. Sticky Levantine/Turkish cakes too. Very busy, so book or go
early.

Bofinger, 3–7 rue de la Bastille, 3ᵉ. 42.72.87.82. Daily to 1am. A well-
established and popular turn-of-the-century *brasserie*, serving the arche-
typal fare of *sauerkraut* and seafood. You should be able to manage on
140F.

Les Chants du Piano, 3 rue Steinlen, 18ᵉ. 46.06.37.05. Till 11; cl. Sun
and Mon, first half of February and first half of August. Really good
food and beautiful décor. The menus are 130F and 230F.

Douchka, 6 rue du Pont-aux-Choux, 3ᵉ. 42.72.17.00. Till 2am; cl. Mon
and August. Pre-revolutionary (Russian) decadence, in spite of the red
walls, with caviar, vodka, *balalaika* players and so forth. Not less than
200F.

La Fermette Marbeuf, 5 rue Marbeuf, 8ᵉ. 47.20.63.53. Daily until 11.30.
Try to eat in the tiled and domed inner room, where the original *art
nouveau* décor was recently discovered hidden by false walls and restored.
A rather well-heeled bourgeois clientele, foreign as well as French, but
not stuffy. A good inclusive menu for 123F.

Flo, 7 cours des Petites-Ecuries, 10ᵉ. 47.70.13.59. Open until 1.30am; cl.
August. A handsome old-time *brasserie*, all dark-stained wood, mirrors
and glass partitions in an attractive courtyard off rue du Faubourg-St-
Denis. You eat elbow to elbow at long tables served by waiters in ankle-
length aprons. Excellent food and thoroughly enjoyable atmosphere. If
careful you can get away with about 140F. Essential to book.

Fouquet's, 99 Champs-Elysées, 8ᵉ. 47.23.70.60. Daily to midnight. A
classic name like *Maxim's* and outrageous for the price – 200F, – but
you're paying for the past and present clientele, the *terrasse* on the
Champs-Elysées and the snobbishness of the whole affair.

Au Franc Pinot, 1 quai de Bourbon, 4ᵉ. 43.29.46.98. Mº Pont-Marie

Open to 11; cl. Sun and Mon. *Nouvelle Cuisine* and high class wines at high prices, but still a bargain for this kind of cooking and for the 17C surroundings. Book well in advance.

Jadorie, 103 rue de Tolbiac, 13ᵉ. 45.82.88.77. Mᵒ Tolbiac. Open till 10.30; cl. Mon. In the ugliest of settings – the concrete platform of tower blocks just south of rue de Tolbiac – *Jadorie* serves exquisitely designed Chinese food cooked somewhat along *nouvelle cuisine* lines. A novel experience.

Julien, 16 rue du Faubourg-St-Denis, 10ᵉ. 47.70.12.06. Till 1.30am; cl. July. Part of the same enterprise as *Flo*, with an even more splendid original décor. Same good Alsatian – vaguely Germanic – cuisine; same prices and similarly crowded.

Les Muses, 165 rue St-Honoré, 1ᵉʳ. Fine seafood, steaks and so on in old-fashioned surroundings overlooking the place du Théâtre Français. Prices in the middle of the range.

Le Paprika, 43 rue Poliveau, 5ᵉ. 43.31.65.86. Till 11; cl. Sat midday. Genuine and skillfully prepared Hungarian cuisine but far from cheap. Around 170F.

La Petite Chaumière, 41 rue des Blancs-Manteaux, 4ᵉ; open till 10; cl. Sun midday and August; 42.72.13.90. Wonderful seafood dishes and other original recipes based on classic sauces, cooked by one of the best woman chefs in Paris.

Au Pied de Cochon, 6 rue Coquillière, 1ᵉʳ. 42.36.11.75. Open 24 hours. For extravagant middle-of-the-night pork chops and oysters. At the top of the price range.

Plateau Gourmand, 18 rue du Plateau, 19ᵉ. 42.45.71.39. Cl. weekends. No long menus to dither over, just one good midday and evening option. Around 150F in the evening, 80F at noon.

Au Ras du Pavé, 15 rue du Buisson-St-Louis, 10ᵉ. 42.01.36.36. 12 – 2.30, 8 – 10.30; cl. Sun and Mon. Classic French dishes. Keep your head and you'll keep the bill under 200F.

Restaurant des Saints-Pères, 175 bd St-Germain, 6ᵉ. 45.48.56.85. No orders after 9.45pm; cl. Wed, Thurs and mid-August to mid-September. Very small, traditional, very French and very good. Around 130F.

Sud-Ouest, 40 rue de la Montagne-Sainte-Geneviève, 5ᵉ. 46.33.30.46. Till 10.30; cl. Sun and August. Specialises in *cassoulet* and other south-western regional dishes, with menus at 125F and 155F, plus the service charge.

Terminus Nord, 23 rue de Dunkerque, 10ᵉ. 42.85.05.15. Till 12.30am every day. Same as *Flo* and *Julien*, but slightly more expensive.

Le Train Bleu, 1st floor, Gare du Lyon, bd Diderot, 12ᵉ; 43.43.09.06. Open till 10. You pay not for the food but the ludicrous *fin-de-siècle* stucco and murals of favoured train destinations.

Restaurant Tyr, 3 rue de la Michodière, 2ᵉ. Probably the best Lebanese restaurant and therefore expensive, with mercenary-hirers, escort girls and ridiculously amplified music – Lebanese, albeit. Delicious food but top of the range.

And over the top . . .
If you're feeling slightly crazed – or you happen on a 500F note or winning lottery ticket – there are, of course, some really spectacular restaurants. For **Nouvelle Cuisine** at its very best *Robuchon's* (32 rue de Longchamp, 16ᵉ), *Lucas Carton* (9 place de la Madeleine, 8ᵉ) and *Taillevent* (15 rue Lamenais, 8ᵉ) are said to be the points of true experience and not just for bills that can reach 10,000F for two. *La Marée* (1 rue Daru, 8ᵉ) serves the same clientele on the **classic** recipe front, and for pride of **place** if not so much for *plats* there's *Jules Vernes* on the second floor of the Eiffel Tower. Unfortunately the moment's madness that would inspire you to eat in any of these restaurants would most likely be months too late to book.

ETHNIC

Our selection scarcely scratches the surface of what's available. **Indo-Chinese** restaurants are widely scattered throughout the city, with notable concentrations around av de la Porte-de-Choisy in the 13ᵉ and in the Belleville Chinatown. **North African** places are also widely distributed; apart from rue Xavier-Privas in the Latin Quarter, where the trade is chiefly tourists, the heaviest concentration is the 'Little Maghreb' district along bd de Belleville. The Greeks too are tightly corralled, in rue de la Huchette/ rue Xavier-Privas and along rue Mouffetard, all in the 5ᵉ – and frankly, a rip-off.

Ethnic restaurants do not have the prominence in French dining habits that they have in British, because of the strength of France's own cooking traditions. They should not be regarded as automatically cheap alternatives to the homegrown product. Usually they're not.

Central/West African
Bar des Sports (Cameroon) Around 50F. p.173.
Fouta Toro (Senegal) Around 50F. p.172
Kinkeliba (Gabon). Up to 130F. p.175
Kin Malebo (Zaire). Up to 130F. p.175
M'Zadette M'Foua (Zaire). Up to 130F. p.176
Port de Pidjiguiti (Guinea-Bissau). Around 50F. p.173

North Africa
Hassan (Moroccan). Up to 130F. p.175
El Karnak (Egyptian). Around 50F. p.172

Chez Marcel (Algerian). Around 50F. p.172
Chez Nacef (Algerian). Up to 130F. p.176
Oaj-Djerba (Tunisian). Around 50F. p.172
Bar Sassia (Moroccan). Up to 130F. p.177
Zerda (Moroccan). Up to 130F. p.178

Indo-Chinese
L'Auberge des Temples (Chinese Vietnamese/Thai/Cambodian/Japanese). Up to 130F. p.173
Aux Délices de Széchuen (Chinese) Up to 130F. p.174
Eléphant Blanc Laotian/Thai). Up to 130F. p.175
Escale de Saigon (Vietnamese). Up to 130F. p.175
Jadorie (Chinese). 130–200F. p.179
Restaurant Lyly (Vietnamese). Around 50F. p.172
Orient Express (Chinese). Up to 130F. p.176
Qhan Nho (Vietnamese) Around 50F. p.173
Restaurant A (Chinese). Up to 130F. p.177
La Vallée des Bambous (Chinese). Up to 130F. p.177
Yakitori (Japanese) Around 50F. p.173

Lebanese/Turkish
Antalya (Turkish). 130–200F. p.178
Baalbeck (Lebanese). 130–200F. p.178
Le Liban à la Mouff (Lebanese). Around 50F. p.172
Restaurant Tyr (Lebanese). 130–200F. p.179

Ile de la Réunion
Le Bernica Up to 130F. p.174
Ile de la Réunion Up to 130F. p.175
Mascareigne Up to 130F. p.176

Russian/East European
Les Balkans (Hungarian). Around 50F. p.171
La Cracovia (Polish) Up to 130F. p.174
Douchka (Russian) 130–200F. p.178
Kazatchok (Russian) Up to 130F. p.175
Paprika (Hungarian) 130–200F. p.179
Le Tchaïka (Russian) Up to 130F. p.177
Village Bulgare (Bulgarian) Up to 130F. p.178

Italian
Il Barone Up to 130F. p.173
Le Bistro Romain Up to 130F. p.174
Pizza Roma Up to 130F. p.176

Miscellaneous
Anahi (South American) Up to 130F. p.173
La Corrosol Doudou (Antillais) Up to 130F. p.174
Goldenberg (Jewish) Up to 130F. p.175
Le Golestan de Perse (Iranian) Up to 130F. p.175

VEGETARIAN

Not Paris's strongest suit – these seven are all the specifically vegetarian places we could discover. Bear in mind, though, the possibilities of vegetarian eating in some of the ethnic places (vegetable *tagine*, say, in a North African restaurant) and in ordinary French restaurants or cafés, any of which will do good-looking omelettes and salads, as well as their vegetable side dishes.

Aux Abeilles d'Or. 130–200F. p.178
Le Bol en Bois. Around 50F. p.171
Le Grenier de Notre-Dame. Around 50F. p.172
Au Grain de Folie. Up to 130F. p.175
Mary's Restaurant. Around 50F. p.172
Piccolo Teatro. Salon de thé. p.169
Restaurant Végétarien. Around 50F. p.173

Late-night openers

Cafés, bars, beer cellars and snackbars
Most Paris cafés stay open through to midnight – and those that are more bar than café some way beyond. The listings below, then, unless stated, are for all-night opening.

BARS
Brasserie de l'Etoile. p.161
Le Grand Café. p.162
Le Pigalle. p.162
Polly Magoo. p.162
Harry's New York Bar (Till 4am). p.164
Le Select (Till 3am). p.163

BEER CELLARS/PUBS
Guinness Tavern (Till 4am). p.167
Mayflower. p.167
Pub Saint-Germain. p.167

SNACKS
Drugstore Elysées/Matignon/Saint-Germain. p.169

Restaurants
9.30 or 10pm is usually about the limit for walking into a
restaurant and ordering, though once ensconced, of course, you can
often remain well into the night. The listings below are for
unusually (or specifically) late-night places; **hours** given are for
stated last orders (though to be on the safe side you'd do well to
arrive 30 minutes ahead).

AROUND 50F
Bistro de la Gare (1am). p.171
El Karnak (12.30am). p.172
Oaj-Djerba (Midnight). p.172
Le Petit Mabillon (11.30pm). p.172

UP TO 130F
Anahi (Midnight). p.173
Brasserie Les Alsaces aux Halles (All night). p.173
Brasserie Balzar (12.30am). p.173
La Coupole (1.45am). p.174
La Corrosol Doudou (7am). p.174
Hassan (Midnight). p.175
Kazatchok (2am). p.175
Lipp (12.45am). p.175
La Mascareigne (2am). p.176
Le Muniche (3am). p.176
M'Zadette M'Foua (Midnight). p.176
Au Petit Moulin (Midnight). p.176
Au Petit Riche (12.15am). p.176
Le Petit Zinc (3am). p.176
Pour le Plaisir (1am). p.177
La Route du Château (12.30am). p.177
Bar Sassia (12.45am). p.177
Le Vaudeville (2am). p.177

130–200F
Baalbeck (1am). p.178
Bofinger (1am). p.178
Douchka (2am). p.178
La Fermette Marbeuf (11.30pm). p.178

Chapter six
MUSIC AND NIGHTLIFE

French **rock** deserves its miserable reputation. Boy George is better known to French kids than any home-grown pin-up and what isn't American or British on the juke box is crooning French schmaltz that makes Abba sound ultra-radical. The Belgians have much better bands. The city's foreign populations, however, more than make up for this. West and Central African, Caribbean and Latin American music thrive with both city-based bands and groups on tour. So ignore French rock, which has always failed to take on black rhythms, and go for **salsa, calypso, reggae** and the less familiar **African sounds** from Zaire, Congo and Nigeria. The latter play mainly in the nightclubs rather than rock venues.

The only truly home-grown music is the tradition of **popular songs** epitomised by Edith Piaf, though even here the Belgians have an equal contribution in Jacques Brel, the most famous post-war singer in the French language. Two of the best contemporary *chansonniers* are Alain Souchon and Serge Lama. Despite the emphasis on poetical lyrics, French folk songs can cross frontiers, as Françoise Hardy proved in the 1960s. But English audiences, permeated by rock, are likely to find most of this form unbearably vapid and whimpish.

Jazz fans, on the other hand, are in for a treat. Paris has long been home to new styles and old-time musicians. The *New Morning* club hosts big names from all over the world and many pleasant evenings through to mornings can be had passing from one club to another in St-Germain or Les Halles. Standards are high and the line-ups well varied. The ancient cellars housing many of the clubs make for great acoustics and atmosphere. The only trouble is that, with the notable exception of *Le 28 Dunois*, entry charges and obligatory drinks limit the number of nights you can dedicate to jazz on a tight budget.

Classical music, as you might expect in this neo-classical city, is alive and well and takes up twice the space of 'jazz-pop-folk-rock' in the listings magazines. Advance booking rather than price is the major inhibiting factor (save for the concerts held in churches) and opera is as overpriced as it is everywhere. The contemporary scene of Systems composition laps up funds and pleases the minute coterie who see sense in the sounds.

Gay and lesbian clubs are featured at the end of the **Nightclubs and Discos** section. The choice of venues for women is very limited, though they are welcome in some of the predominantly male clubs. For men, not only are there numerous gay clubs but in certain areas, the Marais most of all, straight clubs are usually sympathetic. For a complete run-down, you should consult the *Gai-Pied Guide* (see Gay bookshops p.145).

The final listings give all the **large-scale stadium venues**, where you'll find anything from heavy metal to opera, as well as major sports events.

MAINLY ROCK AND LATIN

International rock stars, unsurprisingly, live in New York, not Paris. Though Mick Jagger or Bruce Springsteen are accorded all superstar status when they perform in France, rock does not come under the heading of music, but rather in a blacklist of drugs, sex, riots and disorder. There's also the chauvinism that cannot bear to recognise an art so dominated by the English language. French bands exist, but their records usually have a toy-town sound about them – annoying even on first listening – or go in for ponderous jazz-rock. Some names to look for, if you are still interested, are: the duo Rita Mitsouko, Taxi Girl, Cyclops, Wild Child, King Snakes, Marc Seberg and Etienne Daho. Charlélie Couture was a recent hopeful, with rock funk and complex lyrics, and Bernard Lavilliers introduced some politics of a sort to his songs, but neither managed to start any new trends.

Brazilian sounds dominate the popular music scene in Paris and have done for several years now. Everyone dances to salsa and the divisions between Latin rhythms, jazz and African beats are progressively harmonised in mixed bands and mixed venues.

Venues
Baiser Salé
58 rue des Lombards, 1er; 42.33.37.71; Mº Châtelet. 8.30 – 4am. A languid place, peeling at the edges though its era is only 1980s. When the music's good, – rhythm & blues, Latino-rock, reggae or Brazilian – then the cocktails and comfort are great. Otherwise it's videos in the bar and men on the pick-up.
Centre Latino-Américain
1 rue Montmartre, 1er; 45.08.48.28; Mº Châtelet. 8.30 onwards; cl. Mon and Tues. Excellent concerts from leading Brazilian and Latin groups.
Chapelle des Lombards
19 rue de Lappe, 11e; 43.57.24.24; Mº Bastille. 10.30 – dawn; bands Thurs-Sat; cl. Sun and Mon. This erstwhile *bal musette* of the rue de Lappe still plays the occasional waltz and tango but in the main the music is salsa, reggae, steel drums, gwo-kâ and the blues. The doormen are not too friendly but it's relatively cheap and once inside a good night is assured.

Le Cloître des Lombards
62 rue des Lombards, 1ᵉʳ; 42.33.54.09; Mᵒ Châtelet. 10.30 – 4 am. Not as good as the *Chapelle des Lombards* and more of a jazz club atmosphere though the music is definitely Caribbean.

Discophage
11 passage du Clos-Bruneau (off 31–33 rue des Ecoles), 5ᵉ; 43.26.31.41; Mᵒ Maubert-Mutualité. 9 – 3 am; cl. Sun and August. A packed out, tiny and under-ventilated space but all such discomforts irrelevant for the best Brazilian sounds you can hear in Paris.

L'Ecume
99 rue de l'Ouest, 14ᵉ; 45.42.71.16; Mᵒ Pernety. Till 3 am. Live music at weekends in a dark, cramped, smokey cellar – just as Paris dives are supposed to be. Upstairs people drink, play cards and chess and chat to anyone while from midnight onwards Brazilian or Caribbean sounds emanate from below.

L'Escale
15 rue Monsieur-le-Prince, 6ᵉ; 43.54.63.47; Mᵒ Odéon. 11 – 4am. More Latin American musicians must have passed through here than any other club. The dancing sounds, salsa mostly, are in the basement (disco on Wed) while on the ground floor all South American music is given an outlet – pipes from the Andes, Flamenco, Columbian drumming – accompanied sometimes by literary visitors, Gabriel Garciá Márquez amongst them.

Gibus
18 rue du Faubourg-du-Temple, 11ᵉ; 47.00.78.88; Mᵒ République. 11 – 5am; cl. Sun, Mon and weekdays in August. For twenty years English rock bands on their way up have played their first Paris gig at Gibus, the Clash and Police among them. Fourteen nights of dross will throw up one decent band a fortnight, but it's always hot, loud, energetic and crowded with young Parisians heavily committed to the rock scene. It's also one of the cheaper clubs, both for entry and drinks.

Péniche Eliane
Pont de Billancourt, Boulogne-Billancourt; Mᵒ Porte de St-Cloud and longish walk. Unfortunately no phone number and no guarantee that this disco-barge is still moored under the bridge on the right bank. If it is, then Saturday evenings are salsa nights with live bands some weekends, entry is cheap, the ambiance is wonderful and the bopping weight sends the water well above the port holes.

Phil'One
Place de la Patinoire, 3ᵉ niveau, Parvis de la Défense; 47.76.44.26; opposite CNIT building; RER La Défense. Thurs-Sat, 10 onwards. An unprepossessing entrance and long corridor leads to one of the best venues in Paris – brilliant sound system, no trendy décor, pit and gallery dance floor and tables, and quirky musical policy encompassing Antillais,

African, a bit of jazz, English and French rock, the bands a good mix of the well-established and the new.

Rex Club
3 bd Poissonnière, 2ᵉ; 42.36.83.96; Mᵒ Rue Montmartre. 8.30 – 5 am.
Rock concerts upstairs in the Rex Cinema, mainly French and US, otherwise a mixture of live music, transvestites' nights out and similar, with black bands most Friday nights.

Les Trottoirs de Buenos Aires
37 rue des Lombards, 1ᵉʳ; 42.60.44.41; Mᵒ Châtelet. 9.30 onwards; cl. Mon. Argentinian tango is the only music performed on the stage of 'the pavements of Buenos Aires'. The bands change every two months or so; the drinks are very expensive; no-one dances save professional artistes. But the world of music built around tango rhythms encompasses far more than Marlon Brando and Maria Schneider and conjures climates that never inhabit Paris. You will either be transported in an aural addiction not unallied to other luxuries from the South American continent or vow never to take these recommendations again.

See also the listings at the end of this chapter (p.197) for the **big performance venues** *where you'll catch touring British or American rock bands.*

NIGHTCLUBS AND DISCOS

Expense can be a problem with **nightclubs and discos**. Entry is usually cheaper during the week but that's when you're least likely to hear live – and particularly **African – music**, one of the more genuine reasons for visiting some of the venues below.

Clubs come and go at an exhausting rate, the business principle being to take over a place, make a major investment in the décor, and close after two years, well in pocket. As a customer, not only do you contribute on a financial level – in many places your ornamentation potential is equally important. Being sized up by a leather-clad American bouncer acting as the ultimate arbiter of style and class can be a very demeaning experience. Men generally have a harder time than women, English speakers are at an advantage, blacks not. The one place that doesn't discriminate and should be at the top of any **disco** list is *Le Palace 999*. And for a real Paris tradition, you must also try one of the **popular dance halls** of the rue de Lappe – still going strong after decades, still cheap and offering perhaps the capital's most bizarre variety of people and music.

Venues
Les Bains
7 rue du Bourg-l'Abbé, 3ᵉ; 48.87.01.80; Mᵒ Etienne-Marcel. 11.30 – 6

am. This is your ego-shooting trendies club — an old Turkish bath-house where the Stones filmed part of their *Undercover of the Night* video, now redone in the anti-perspirant, passionless style pioneered for the Café Costes. The music is limited to the most familiar international hits — sometimes live (usually dross) bands on a Wednesday. The décor features a plunging pool by the dance floor in which the punters are wont to ruin their one-off colour-run creations. It's not a place where a 500-franc note has much life expectancy. Whether you can watch this spectacle depends on the bouncers, who have their fixed ideas. If you're turned away be thankful and head down the road to *Le Tchatch au Tango* (see below).

Balajo

9 rue de Lappe, 11ᵉ; 47.00.07.79; Mᵒ Bastille. Fri, Sat and Mon 10 – 4.30 am. The old-style music hall of *gai* but straight *Paris* — extravagant 1930s décor, a balcony for the orchestra above the vast dance floor, working class Parisians in their weekend best and the music everything to move to from mazurka, tango, waltz, cha-cha, twist, and the slurpy *chansons* of between the wars. There's disco and modern hits as well, but that's Monday nights when the cool kids from across town come and all the popular nostalgia disappears replaced by fad and 'in'-ness. For afternoon sessions see p.139.

Blue Moon

160 bd St-Germain, 6ᵉ; 46.34.01.04; Mᵒ St-Germain-des-Prés. The best reggae disco.

La Boule Rouge

8 rue de Lappe, 11ᵉ; 47.00.95.32; Mᵒ Bastille. Trendies trying to take over this music hall would land heavily on the pavement outside. *La Boule Rouge* has never become fashionable like *Balajo* opposite, though it shares a similar style and musical variety. It's rowdier, stuffier, cheaper (no entry charge, just drinks) and friendly enough as long as you don't look like a foreigner or non-native of the 11ᵉ *arrondissement*.

The Cellar

54/56 rue de Ponthieu, 8ᵉ; Mᵒ Franklin-Roosevelt. Till 6 am. A recent addition to the disco scene with a different style of music every night, no entry charge but pricey drinks.

5e Avenue

2bis av Foch, 16ᵉ; 45.00.00.13; Mᵒ Charles-de-Gaulle-Etoile. 11 – dawn. Couples only allowed in here (hetero that is) and speaking nice French too. Well-bred and well-behaved, boring as hell, this *seizième* hang-out is only mentioned because the music is not at all bad.

Eméraude

52 rue des Petites-Ecuries, 10ᵉ; 48.24.96.51; Mᵒ Château-d'Eau. Fridays only, 11 – dawn. Reggae and dreadlocking rastas.

Fantasia

Palais des Congrès, 78 bd Gouvion-St-Cyr, 17ᵉ; 47.58.24.46; Mᵒ Porte

Maillot. 11 – dawn. Multi-coloured strobe, tie-dye T-shirts, platform boots, Beatnik hats and crushed velvet skirts in a ludicrously large space to be dedicated to psychedelia.

La Main Jaune
Square de L'Amérique Latine, Porte de Champerret, 17e; 47.63.26.47; Mo Porte-de-Champerret. 10 – 5 am; cl. Mon and Tues. Ice-rink disco. Skate to radio hits. See p.136.

Le Malibu
44 rue Tiquetonne, 2e; 42.36.62.70; Mo Etienne-Marcel. 8.30 – 5 am. Black music from all over West Africa and the West Indies in a crowded basement beneath a restaurant. No vetting here, blacks outnumber whites and everyone is under 30.

Mambo Club
20 rue Cujas, 5e; 43.54.89.21; Mo St-Michel/Odéon. More Afro-Cuban and Antillais music in a seedy dive with people of all ages and nationalities.

Le Martial
26 rue Fontaine, 9e; Mo Blanche/Pigalle; 42.80.04.57. A seedy strip joint turned trendy with kitsch 1950s décor; French and Latin American bands every Friday night.

Memphis
3 impasse Bonne-Nouvelle, 10e; 45.23.34.47; Mo Bonne-Nouvelle. 10.45 – 6 am. Long-established, laid-back disco done out as the 'Mississippi Queen' with video screens, large dance floors and nothing very original coming out of the speakers.

L'Opéra Night
30 rue Gramont, 2e; 42.96.62.56; Mo Richelieu-Drouot. 11 – 5am. A movie-house during the day transformed to Afro-funk bopperie every evening after the last film. Renowned for the quality of the dancing more than the music, though no one would complain of the African and Carribean funk, reggae and salsa.

O'Valère
40 rue du Colisée, 8e; 42.21.51.68; Mo St-Phillipe-du-Roule. 11 – dawn. Since much is made of where the rich hang out in Paris, and a myth perpetuated that they do set foot outside the 8e and 16e *arrondissements* not just en route for Manhattan or the Côte d'Azur, here is one of their haunts. Firmly on home ground, exceedingly difficult to get into, expensive, and a confirmation of one's hopeful suspicions that these people are too snobbish to indulge in enjoyment.

Le Palace 999
8 rue du Faubourg-Montmartre, 9e; 42.46.10.87; Mo Rue Montmartre. 11 – dawn; cl. Mon and Tues. Everyone goes to the Palace, whether they've scraped up their week's savings or they're just out to exercise the gold American Express, and they all don their best party gear. Some

nights it's thematic fancy dress, some nights the music is all African, other times the place is booked for TV dance shows. It's big, the bopping is good and the clientele are an exuberant spectacle in themselves.

La Piscine

32 rue de Tilsitt, 17e; 42.27.31.39; Mo Etoile. 10 – dawn (earlier on weekdays); cl. Tues. A converted 1930s swimming bath where you dance on the tiles or in the drained main pool. Top of the league architecturally, passable music and usually a young and enthusiastic crowd.

La Plantation

45 rue de Montpensier, 1er; 42.97.46.17; Mo Palais-Royal. Despite the reputation for entertaining dukes and dustmen, the doormen are fussy, more so if you're white. Inside, excellent Cuban, Angolan, Congolese and Antillais music awaits you.

Ruby's

38 rue Dauphine, 6e; 46.33.68.16; Mo Odéon. 11 – dawn. A place to sit and listen to African harmonies when your feet can stand no more. A black bourgeois clientele.

Stand By Club

1 rue Laplace, 5e; 46.33.96.23; Mo Maubert-Mutualité. 9.30 – dawn; cl. Sun-Tues. Pretty lousy music but a nice medieval place to stay up drinking all night and then to have breakfast in the restaurant. Live bands sometimes at weekends.

Le Tchatch au Tango

13 rue au Maire, 3e; 48.87.54.78; Mo Arts-et-Métiers. 11 – 5am; cl. Sun-Tues. The tango has been played here since the turn of the century and the décor looks as if it's retained layers from every decade since. The contrast with *Les Bains* could not be greater. No vetting here, cheap entry and cheap drinks (obligatory cloakroom fee), people in whatever clothes they happen to be in, and people dancing to abandon for themselves, not for adjudicators of style. Anyone asks anyone for a dance and this is no pick-up joint. For afternoon dancing see p.139. In the evenings the music is jazzy Latin American – salsa, calypso and reggae.

LESBIAN AND GAY CLUBS

Lesbian clubs find it hard to be exclusively female and you may find that none of the varied atmospheres are agreeable. Still, you can but try... The pleasures for **gay men** are far better catered for but the scene has changed since the start of the AIDS scare. Wicked little bars with obscure corners in the area round Les Halles have all but ceased to exist. High-tech, well-lit, sense-surround disco beat is the current style. The selection below only scratches the surface – for women it more or less covers all that's on offer.

WOMEN
Le Baby Doll
71 bd St-Germain, 5ᵉ; 43.25.19.90; Mᵒ St-Michel. 11 – dawn; cl. Mon.
A new and much-needed place for women to dance and drink together without spending a fortune. It's not entirely women only – the band is usually male, Wednesday night sees a transvestite show, and the man who runs it allows in a few well-screened members of his own sex. But the atmosphere is relaxed, feminine and sympathetic, despite the name.
Chez Moune
54 rue Pigalle, 18ᵉ; 48.74.57.26; Mᵒ Pigalle. In the red light heart of Paris, this mixed but predominantly women's cabaret and disco may shock or delight feminists. The evening includes a strip-tease (by women) without the standard audience for such shows (any man causing the slightest bother or unease is kicked out). Sunday afternoons from 4.30 – 8 are strictly women only.
Le Katmandou
21 rue du Vieux-Colombier, 6ᵉ; 45.48.12.96; Mᵒ St-Sulpice. 11 – dawn.
The best-known and most upmarket of the lesbian nightclubs. Good music of the Afro-Latino varieties but not an easy place to meet people.
Le New Monocle
60 bd Edgar-Quinet, 14ᵉ; 43.20.89.55; Mᵒ Montparnasse. 11 – dawn; cl. Mon. This used to be the popular *Lolita*. Most of the old customers have now switched to *Le Baby Doll* leaving a fairly staid bunch and a scattering of men allowed in every evening.

MEN
Le BH
7 rue du Roule, 1ᵉʳ; Mᵒ Louvre/Châtelet-Halles, 10–6. The downstairs rooms have been knocked into one sizeable and illuminated disco but it's still one of the cheapest places and exclusively male.
The Broad
3 rue de la Ferronnerie, 1ᵉʳ; 42.36.59.73; Mᵒ Châtelet-Les Halles. 10.30 – dawn; cl. Mon. Young, chic and perennially popular as is the Broad Side cocktail bar that keeps the same hours next door.
Haute Tension
87 rue St-Honoré, 1ᵉʳ; Mᵒ Châtelet. 11 – dawn. Discreet and rather subdued surroundings for a hot and sweaty bar-disco that has become a favourite with all types and all ages.
Le Manhattan
8 rue des Anglais, 5ᵉ; Mᵒ Maubert-Mutualité; 43.54.98.86. 11 – 6am.
Men only with a good funky disco.
Le Piano Zinc
49 rue des Blancs-Manteaux, 4ᵉ; 42.74.32.42; Mᵒ Rambuteau. 6 – 2 am; cl. Mon. From 10pm when the piano-playing starts, this bar becomes a

happy riot of songs, music hall acts and dance which may be hard to appreciate if you don't follow French too well. Not exclusively gay but near enough and an easy place to make contact.

Scaramouche
44 rue Vivienne, 2ᵉ; Mᵒ Montmartre; 42.33.24.89. 11 – 6am. Young, trendy, gay hang-out where women are welcome. Shows every Wed and Sun evening.

JAZZ, BLUES AND *CHANSONS*

Jazz in the city covers everything from trad, through be-bop and free jazz to current experimental. Saxophonists François Jeanneau and Didier Malherbe, violinist Didier Lockwood, guitarist John McLaughlin and pianist Joe Turner all live in the city and still play small gigs despite their international reputations. The most bizarre ensemble is a group of 30 saxophonists called Urban Sax who specialise in post-holocaust costumes and descending on their venue from different directions and considerable distances. A powerful transmitter keeps them all in time as they climb down from a roof or move towards a central space.

A **jazz festival** takes place at the end of October/beginning of November and in July contemporary music, including jazz, has a nine-day gala in the *Rencontre musique et jazz des années 80.*

Piaf and Brel songs, favourite movie theme tunes, and all sort of blues are also played and sung at various **piano bars** throughout the city, often in ordinary bars and cafés with only the late night charge on the drinks.

Venues
Le Bilboquet
13 rue St-Benoît, 6ᵉ; 45.48.81.84; Mᵒ St-Germain. 7 – 2.30am; cl. Sun. A bar/restaurant with live jazz every night, usually local musicians and not bad at all.

Les Bouchons
19 rue des Halles, 1ᵉʳ; 42.33.28.73; Mᵒ Châtelet. Till 2am. American jazz singers from 1950s trad to contemporary in a room below the *brasserie* reminiscent of a gentleman's club. But surprisingly no entry charge and reasonably priced cocktails and a good place if you want to sit and talk.

Le Calvados
40 av Pierre-Ier-de-Serbie, 8ᵉ; 47.20.21.16; Mᵒ George V. 8 – 4am. For the last 25 years, Joe Turner has sat down to the piano every night at around midnight in the downstairs bar. If you go much earlier you'll find yourself too broke to have anything to sip to his seduction of the keyboard.

Le Caveau de la Bolée
25 rue de l'Hirondelle, 6ᵉ; 43.54.62.20; Mᵒ St-Michel. 9.30 – 6.30.

An ancient ramshackle place where Parisian luminaries of the likes of Baudelaire used to go to hear their favourite singer. The music is still mainly *chansons* with occasional evenings of jazz.

Le Caveau des Oubliettes

11 rue St-Julien-le Pauvre, 5e; 45.83.41.77; M° St-Michel. 9 – 2am. French popular music of bygone times – Piaf and earlier, sung with exquisite nostalgia in the ancient prisons of Châtelet.

La Closerie des Lilas

171 bd Montparnasse, 14e; 43.26.70.50; M° Port-Royal. Till 2am. Brilliant piano the nights when Ivan Meyer is on. Having chosen your cocktail you can make your musical requests and sit back in a chair that may well have the name-plate of Trotsky, Verlaine or André Gide.

Au Duc des Lombards

42 rue des Lombards, 1er; 42.36.51.13; M° Châtelet. Till 2am. Small, unpretentious bar with jazz piano every Friday and Saturday night.

La Merle Mocqueur

11 rue des Buttes-aux-Cailles, 13e; M° Place d'Italie/Corvisart. 9 – 1am. A workers' co-op bar with jazz on Monday nights and popular French songs every Thursday.

New Morning

7–9 rue des Petites-Ecuries, 10e; 47.45.82.58; M° Château-d'Eau. 9 – 1.30am (concerts start around 10). This is the venue where the big international names in all the American jazz variants come to play. Spacious, comfortable and uncluttered by clever-conscious décor, it's a treat, though not, unfortunately, a very cheap one.

Le Petit Journal

13 rue du Commandant-Mouchotte, 14e; 43.21.56.70; M°Bienvenue. 9 – 2am; cl. Sun. After years of popularity at the small bar on boulevard St-Michel, *Le Petit Journal* has moved to larger premises under the Hôtel Montparnasse. The music policy hasn't changed – mainstream traditional jazz, mostly French but with occasional visits by the likes of Lee Konitz, Buddy Tate and Memphis Slim. There are plans for a more modern programme but the main problem is rekindling the old atmosphere gone astray in the move.

Le Petit Opportun

15 rue des Lavandières-Ste-Opportune, 1er; 42.36.01.36; M° Châtelet. 11 – 3am. It's worth arriving early to get a seat for the live music in the dungeonlike cellar where the acoustics play strange tricks and where you can't always see the musicians. Mainly traditional American and revival sounds with tapes in the bar up-stairs and a crowd of genuine connoisseurs.

Slow Club

130 rue de Rivoli, 1er; 42.33.84.30; M° Louvre/Pont-Neuf. 9.30 – 2.30 am; cl. Sun & Mon. A jazz club to be-bop the night away to the sounds

of Claude Luter's sextet and visiting New Orleans musicians.
saxophonists.
Les Trois Mailletz
56 rue Galande, 5e; 43.54.00.79; Mo St-Michel. 6 – dawn; cl. Mon and Tues. The builders responsible for Notre-Dame drank in this cellar-bar, where jazz musicians of different schools now perform. Upstairs Ahmed plays any tune with a dream of ease on the piano, joined by anyone with an instrument or a desire to sing. The people here are classic Parisians – Polish immigrés, exiles from the eastern Mediterranean, young Americans preferring the Parisian gutter to Manhattan mod-cons, a Frenchman in love with the scornful waitress, and characters unclassified.
Utopia
1 rue Niepce, 14e; 43.22.79.66; Mo Pernety. 8.30 – dawn; cl. Sun and Mon. No genius here, but good French blues singers interspersed with jazz and blues tapes, the people listening mostly young and studentish. No admission charge and cheap drinks. Generally very pleasant atmosphere.
Le 28 Dunois
28 rue Dunois, 13e; 45.84.72.00; Mo Chevaleret. Concerts Fri-Mon, 8.30 – 11.30. Modern European improvised jazz gets consistent support from this out-of-the-way warehouse venue which is large enough for very big bands. It's also very pleasant for being out of the Latin Quarter and Les Halles, cheap and entirely unsnobbish. When there aren't jazz concerts the space is used for musical theatre, video and shows for children (see p.132).

CONTEMPORARY AND CLASSICAL MUSIC

Pierre Boulez, the most famous living French composer, has, under the Beaubourg arts centre, a vast laboratory of acoustics and 'digital signal processing' with banks of top sophisticated synthesisers and computers, all at state expense. Here, he and his team of scientist/technician/musicians indulge in a 'double dialectic' and study 'psychoacoustics' towards 'global, generalised solutions'. To what problems is unanswerable. Other performer/composers have interfaced and integrated music, science and new technology, and until Boulez can rival Laurie Anderson with a number one in the British charts, he should be doing advert jingles for his money. Perhaps this is unfair. Go and hear for yourself – on tapes in the foyer of IRCAM (entrance down the stairs by the Stravinsky pool on the south side of Beaubourg) for no charge or, with real committment, attend a performance by the resident *Ensemble Inter-Contemporain* (details from Beaubourg information desk).

Though IRCAM creams off the bulk of public money for **contemporary music**, other practitioners experiment in ethereal, electronic, eastern-western sounds where elements of Stockhausen, Brian Eno and Ravi

Shankar vibrate under the direction of those trained in counterpointal harmonies of centuries past. There are regular concerts – check *Pariscope*, etc. for details – and some of the **names to look out for** are: Olivier Messiaen, the grand old man of Paris music; Jean-Claude Eloy, who exchanged serialism for oriental sounds; Pascal Dusapin who verges into jazz, and Luc Ferrarie, an electro-acoustic producer of 'anecdotal' sounds. Apart from Boulez, the main computer freaks are Tod Machover also of IRCAM, and Iannis Xenakis at CEMAMU (Research centre for mathematics and musical automation) in Issy-Les-Moulineaux. Xenakis' baby is the UPIC, a computer in which all the parameters of sound are drawn onto a graphics tablet (a kind of computerised drawing board) and then read and played by the machine.

Paris remains a treat for **classical concerts**. Many take place in the appropriate acoustical setting of churches, and are free or very cheap, and the choice every day of the week is enormous. Other concerts take place for free at *Radio France* (166 av du Président-Kennedy, 16ᵉ; 45.24.15.16; Mᵒ Passy). The top auditoriums where you may find Barenboim conducting the *Orchestre de Paris* are *Pleyel* (252 rue du Faubourg St-Honoré, 8ᵉ; 45.63.88.73; Mᵒ Place des Ternes), *Epicerie-Beaubourg* (12 rue du Renard, 4ᵉ; 42.72.23.41; Mᵒ Hôtel-de-Ville), *Gaveau* (45 rue de la Boétie, Mᵒ Miromesnil), *Théâtre des Champs-Elysées* (15 av Montaigne, 8ᵉ; 47.23.47.77; Mᵒ Alma-Marceau), and the *Théâtre Musical de Paris* (1 place du Châtelet, 1ᵉʳ; 42.33.44.44; Mᵒ Châtelet). Tickets are best bought at the box offices, though for big names you may find overnight queues, and a large number of seats are always pre-booked by subscribers. The price range is very reasonable.

Opera is performed with all due pomp at the *Opéra* (see p.51) and with marginally less superfluous carry-on at the *Epicerie-Beaubourg* (see above) and the *Opéra-Comique* (Salle Favard, 5 rue Favard, 2ᵉ; 42.96.12.20; Mᵒ Richelieu-Drouot). Both opera and recitals are also put on at the multipurpose venues (see below). Mitterand's memento to the city, like Pompidou's Beaubourg, will be the new opera house at Bastille. It's supposed to popularise the art, which it won't, but at least opera-lovers will have a better chance of a seat than at present.

Festivals are plentiful in all the diverse fields that come under the far too specific term of 'classical'. The *Festival de Musique Ancienne* takes place at the end of May, beginning of June, based round a particular civilisation or culture. The *Soirées de Saint-Aignan* at the Hôtel St-Aignan in May feature European music of the 18C and 19C. There is also a festival of sacred music most years, a Chopin festival, a Mozart festival and the *Festival de l'Orangerie de Sceaux* of chamber music all summer at the Château de Sceaux. For details of these and more, pick up the festival programme from the Tourist Offices or the Hôtel de Ville.

THE BIG PERFORMANCE VENUES

Events at any of the venues below will be well advertised, on billboards and posters throughout the city. **Tickets** can be obtained at the venues themselves, though rather easier through any of the *FNAC* shops (see p.143).

Forum des Halles
Niveau 3, Porte Rambuteau, 15 rue de l'Equerre-d'Argent, 1er; 42.03.11.11; M° Châtelet. Varied functions – theatre, performance art, rock, etc. often with foreign touring groups.

Maison des Cultures du Monde
101 bd Raspail, 6e; 45.44.72.30; M° St-Placide. All the arts from all over the world and undominated by the Anglo-Saxons.

Olympia
28 bd des Capucines, 9e; 47.42.52.86; M° Madeleine/Opéra. An old music hall hosting occasional well-known rock groups.

Palais des Congrès
Porte Maillot, 17e; 42.66.20.75; M° Porte-Maillot. Opera, ballet, orchestral music, trade fairs, and the superstars of US and British rock.

Palais des Glaces
37 rue du Faubourg du Temple, 10e; 46.07.49.93; M° République. Smallish theatre used for rock, ballet, jazz and French folk.

Palais Omnisports
rue de Bercy, 12e; info 43.42.01.23; bookings 43.46.12.21; M° Bercy. Opera, cycle racing, Bruce Springsteen, ice hockey and Citroën launches – the newest multi-purpose venue with seats to give vertigo to the most level-headed but an excellent space when used in the round.

Palais des Sports
Porte de Versailles, 15e; 48.28.40.10; M° Porte-de-Versailles. The Earl's Court equivalent for seeing your favourite rockstar in miniature half a mile away.

Rock'n'Roll Circus
6 rue Caumartin, 9e; 42.68.05.20; M° Havre-Caumartin. A smallish venue for top French rock bands.

Zenith
Parc de la Villette, av Jean-Jaurès, 20e; M° Porte-de-Pantin. Seating for six and a half thousand people in an inflatable stadium designed exclusively for rock and pop concerts. The concrete column with a descending red areoplane is the landmark to head for.

Chapter seven
FILM, THEATRE AND DANCE

There are over 350 **films** showing in Paris in any one week, which puts moving visuals on at least equal footing with the still visuals of the art museums. And they cover every place and period, new works (with the exception of British/American movies) arriving here long before London and New York.

Theatre can be less accessible to non-natives – especially the *café-théâtre* touted by 'knowing' guidewriters – but there is stimulation in the cult of the director (Peter Brook and other exiles, as well as the French) while, crossing borders, there are exciting developments in **dance** and **mime**. **Sex shows and cabarets**, covered at the end of this chapter, have long been part of the Paris myth: they have a Hollywood curiosity at the top end (Folies Bergères, CanCan), standard degeneracy lower down the scale.

Listings for all the above are detailed in *Pariscope*, etc. **Cinema tickets** rarely need buying in advance. The easiest place to get **stage tickets** is at one of the *FNAC* shops (see p.143). Prices are no worse than London, slightly cheaper if anything, and there are weekday student discounts. A theatre kiosk in place Madeleine offers a 50% reduction on tickets for that day but the numbers are limited and the queues rather long. **Booking** well in advance is essential for new productions and all shows by the superstar directors. These are sometimes a lot more expensive, often quite reasonably so when they carry on over several days.

THE SCREEN

The French have treated cinema as an art form, deserving of state subsidy, ever since its origination with the Lumière brothers in 1895. The medium has as yet never had to bow down to TV, the seat of judgment stays in Cannes, and Paris is the cinema capital of the world. But as far as making movies is concerned, the French have kept a low and very introverted profile over the last few years. Style movies like *Diva* or *Subway* touched a trend but lacked all substance. A film like Agnès Varda's *Vagabond*, while seriously treating the issue of unbridgeable cultures, could not cross frontiers and even in France failed to hit its target. Claude Zidi's *Le Cop* about police corruption in Paris is by far the most enjoyable recent offering but atypical in its quick light-heartedness. Meanwhile foreign directors such as Kurosawa and Wajda have been benefiting from public funds and the top box office films are dominated by transatlantic imports. The new private TV channels are likely to further the decline of the film industry. But for all that, Paris remains the place to see movies, from the latest blockbuster to the least-known works of the earliest directors.

Cinema-going is not exclusively an evening occupation – the *séances* (programmes) start between 1 and 3 pm at many places and continue through to the early hours. Most cinemas have lower rates on Mondays and reductions for students Mon-Thurs, all are non-smoking, and some have ushers who need to be tipped as they get no salary. Almost all of the huge selection of foreign films are shown in the original (*v.o.* in the listings as opposed to *v.f.* which means it's dubbed into French).

THE CINEMAS

Of all the capital's **cinemas**, the most beautiful is the *Pagode* (57bis rue Babylone, 7e; Mo François-Xavier), originally transplanted from Japan at the turn of the century to be a rich Parisienne's party place. The wall panels of the *Grande Salle* are embroidered in silk, golden dragons and elephants hold up the candelabra, and a battle between Japanese and Chinese warriors rages on the ceiling. If you don't fancy the films being shown you can still come here for tea and cakes (see p.168). *Kinopanarama* (60 av Motte-Piquet, 15e; Mo La Motte-Picquet) has reintroduced organ interludes for some showings and has the widest screen in Paris. Or, for large-scale kitsch, there's *Le Grand Rex* (1 bd Poissonnière, 2e; Mo Bonne-Nouvelle) with 2,800 seats, a ceiling with moving clouds and street scenery on either side of the screen; unfortunately it goes in for dubbed movies.

A cinema that combines the big screen with *v.o.*'s is *L'Escurial Panoramas* (11 bd de Port-Royal, 13e; Mo Gobelins); this is likely to be showing something along the lines of *Eraserhead* on the small screen and the latest offering from a big name director, French, Japanese or American, on the panoramic screen. *Cosmos* (76 rue de Rennes, 6e; Mo St-Sulpice) specialises in Soviet movies. Other good places include *Utopia* (9 rue Champollion, 5e; Mo Odéon); *Rialto Bananas* (7 rue de Flandre, 19e; Mo Stalingrad) with recent offbeat or radical pictures alongside Monty Python and Hollywood horror movies; and *Le Studio des Ursulines* (10 rue des Ursulines, 5e; Mo Censier-Daubenton) where *The Blue Angel* had its world première.

Unless some funding appears from nowhere, one of the best Paris movie houses is going to have to close. *L'Olympic Entrepôt* (7–9 rue Francis-de-Pressensé, 14e; Mo Pernety) has been keeping ciné-addicts happy for years with its three screens dedicated to the obscure, the subversive and the brilliant, and to showing amongst those categories many Arab and African films. A bookshop next door sells books and posters on the cinema, but the life expectancy of the whole set up is now, alas, very short.

A similar clientele is catered for at the *cinémathèques* in Beaubourg and the Palais de Chaillot. Several different films are shown daily from their archives of complete works and international classics, and tickets are cheap.

Many of the cinemas run **festivals** so that you can pass an entire day or more watching your favourite actor/actress, director, genre or period. One such is *Le Studio* 28 (10 rue de Tholozé, 18ᵉ; Mᵒ Blanche/Abbesses), which in its early days was done over by extreme right-wing catholics, who destroyed the screen and the paintings by Dali and Ernst in the foyer, after one of the first showings of Buñuel's *L'Age d'Or*. The cinema still hosts avant-garde premières, followed occasionally by discussions with the director.

An **International Festival of Women's Films** takes place every March at the *Centre d'Action Culturelle 'Les Gémeaux'* in Sceaux, just outside Paris – details from the centre (46.60.05.64), or from the *Maison des Femmes* (8 Cité Prost, 11ᵉ; 43.48.29.91). The *Ciné-club des Filministes* shows feminist films at the *Maison des Femmes* and a similar club operates at *Femin'Autres* (40 rue Amelot, 11ᵉ; 47.70.09.65).

THE LARGEST SCREEN

There is one cinematic experience that has to be recommended however trite and vainglorious the film and however laughable the high-technical hitches. The venue in question is **La Géode,** the mirrored globe bounced off the science museum of La Villette. The 180° projection system is called Omnimax and works with a special camera and a 70mm horizontally progressing film. There are less than a dozen of these things in existence, and their owners are not the sort to produce brilliant films. What you get is a Readers' Digest view of outer space, great cities of the world, monumental landscapes or whatever, on a screen wider than your range of vision into which you feel you might fall at any moment. Low flying shots or shots from the front of moving trains or cars are rather sensational. But whatever the scene, a colony of large black snakes and blotches permanently hover – their source dirt on the lens. To be fair to the technicians, a space-age duster may now have been installed. And the two lasers may be in operation to give added flair to the trivia. There are several screenings a day (Monday excepted – for details see *Pariscope*, etc. under the 19ᵉ *arrondissement*). The film is the same for months at a time and not understanding French is a positive advantage.

TV

At the other end of the scale, that of a screen less than a metre wide, the

Cinéma de Minuit on the third television channel puts on old movies, in the original version, often Hollywood classics, every Sunday night at 8.30.

THE STAGE

DRAMA

Bourgeois farces, post-war classics, Shakespeare, Racine – all these are staged with the same range of talent or lack of it that you'd find in London. What you'll rarely find are the home-grown, socially concerned and realist dramas of the sort that keep theatre alive in Britain. An Edward Bond or David Edgar play crops up in translation often enough – the French equivalent hardly exists.

Though Samuel Beckett still lives in Paris somewhere, his generation of great playwrights – Anouilh, Genet, Camus, Sartre, Adamov, Ionesco, Cocteau – have gone. Their plays are still frequently performed. The *Huchette* has been playing Ionesco's *La Cantatrice Chauve* every night for 25 years, and Genet's *Les Paravents*, that set off riots on its opening night, can now be included alongside Corneille and Shakespeare in the programme of the *Comédie Française* (the national theatre for the classics).

And Paris theatre still has little xenophobia – foreign artists are as welcome as they've always been. In any month there might be an Italian, Mexican, German or Brazilian production playing in the original language, or offerings by revolutionary groups from Turkey, Chile, Iraq or wherever, who have no possibilities of a home venue.

But in the best contemporary work emanating from the city it is **directors**, not writers who shine. This superstar breed treats playwrights as anachronisms and classic texts as packs of cards to be shuffled into theatrical moments where spectacular and dazzling sensation take precedence over speech. These are the shows to go to see – huge casts, extraordinary sets, overwhelming sound and light effects, an experience even if you haven't understood a word.

One such director is Peter Brook, based permanently in Paris, who produces such events as a 9–hour show of the Indian epic *Mahabharata*. The Russian-born Ariane Mnouchkine went to similar lengths over Cixous' history of Cambodia. Her workers' co-op company is based at the *Théâtre du Soleil* (La Cartoucherie, rte de la Pyramide, 12ᵉ; Mᵒ Château-de-Vincennes; 43.74.24.08). Peter Brooks's theatre is the *Bouffes du Nord* (37bis bd de la Chapelle, 10ᵉ; Mᵒ Chapelle;

42.39.34.50). Other names from whom to expect the grand and avant-garde spectacle include Antoine Vitez at the *Théâtre National de Chaillot* (Palais de Chaillot, pl du Trocadéro, 16ᵉ; Mᵒ Trocadéro; 47.27.81.15) and Patrice Chéreau at the *Théâtre des Amandiers* in Nanterre (7 av Pablo Picasso, 92; RER Nanterre-Université and theatre bus; 47.21.18.81).

In similar style, Roger Planchon's Lyon-based *Théâtre National Populaire* performs in Paris at the *Odéon* (pl Paul-Claudel, 6ᵉ; Mᵒ Odéon; 43.25.70.32). In May 1968 this theatre was occupied and became an open parliament with the backing of its directors, Jean-Louis Barrault (of Baptiste fame in *Les Enfants du Paradis*) and Madeleine Renaud, one of the great French stage actresses. Promptly sacked by de Gaulle's Minister for Culture, they formed a new company and moved to the disused Gare d'Orsay until President Giscard's museum plans sent them packing. The Renaud-Barrault troupe are now based at the *Théâtre du Rond-Point* (av Franklin-Roosevelt, 16ᵉ; Mᵒ Franklin-Roosevelt; 45.56.70.80), where their performances of Beckett are brilliant.

Other theatres whose repertoires include epic directors' works and less well-established innovators are: the *Théâtre de l'Est Parisien* (15 rue Malte-Brun, 20ᵉ; Mᵒ Gambetta; 47.97.96.06); the *Théâtre de la Commune* in Aubervilliers (2 rue Edouard-Poisson; 48.34.67.67) and the *Maison des Arts de Créteil* (pl Salvador Allende, Créteil; Mᵒ Créteil-Préfecture; 48.99.18.88). The *Escalier d'Or* theatre (18 rue d'Enghien, 10ᵉ; Mᵒ Strasbourg-St-Denis; 45.23.15.10) often hosts political shows from abroad as well as radical French plays by young or little-known writers. Probably the best place for new work and fringe productions is the *Théâtre de la Bastille* (76 rue de la Roquette, 11ᵉ; Mᵒ Bastille; 43.57.42.14).

If your French is good enough for the **modern classics** the most likely venues are the *Lucenaire* (53 rue Notre-Dame-des-Champs, 6ᵉ; Mᵒ Vavin/Notre-Dame-des-Champs; 45.44.57.34) combining two theatres, a cinema, restaurant and art gallery; the *Petit Odéon* (alongside the *Odéon*) which occasionally has English theatre; the *Rond-Point;* and the *Théâtre de Paris* (15 rue Blanche, 9ᵉ; Mᵒ Trinité; 42.80.02.30).

Galerie 55 – The English Theatre of Paris (55 rue de Seine, 6ᵉ; Mᵒ Odéon/St-Germain-des-Prés; 43.74.24.08) only puts on **shows in English**, and tends towards a middle ground between the tastes of its student, diplomatic and business audiences. The theatre is small, so you need to book well in advance.

To escape the language problem all together go for the silent performing arts that are flourishing in and around the city.

DANCE AND MIME

In the 1970s all the dancers left Paris for New York and only mime remained the great performing art of the French, thanks to the Lecoq school of Mime and Improvisation, and the famous practitioner Marcel Marceau (who still performs). But in this decade contemporary dance has found its feet again in Paris. A brilliant variety of forms and styles has developed in which theatre, mime and movement leave classical ballet in a world apart. Humour, everyday actions and obsessions, social problems and the darker shades of life find expression in **new dance** works by Maguy Marin, Régine Chopinot, Karine Saporta and François Verret. The new forms share many traits with the modern epic theatre and those engaged in them are as often Japanese or American as French. Jacques Garnier's *GRCOP*, the experimental dance group at the Paris Opéra, plays an important role in bringing the current experiments in the art to a wider audience.

Some of the best performances of the new dance styles take place in the 11e *arrondissement*, notably at the *Théâtre de la Bastille* and the rehearsal space *Ménagerie de Verre* (12 rue Léchevin; 43.38.33.44; Mo Parmentier. The *Café de la Danse* (5 passage Louis-Philippe; 43.57.05.35; Mo Bastille) and the studio *La Forge* (18 rue de la Forge Royale; 43.71.71.89; Mo Ledru-Rollin) are two more. The *Théâtre de la Ville* offer early evening showings of new work with better-known and more traditional fare to follow. Other major venues that include contemporary dance in their programmes are the *Théâtre de Paris, Beaubourg* and the *American Centre* (261 bd Raspail, 14e; Mo Notre-Dames-des-Champs; 43.21.42.20).

Given the premium on space, a lot also goes on in the suburbs – Marin's company is based at the *Maison des Arts de Créteil; Les Gémeaux* at Sceaux (see p.200) hosts experimental shows, and Verret works at the Seine-St Denis *Maison de la Culture* (1 bd Lénine, Bobigny; 48.31.11.45; Mo Pablo-Picasso) where the prestigious competition for young choreographers is held every March. *Le Campagnol* company of dance and improvisation that featured in Ettore Scola's film *Le Bal* have their own theatre in the suburbs, *La Piscine* (254 av de la Division-Leclerc, Châtenay-Malabry; 46.61.14.27; RER Robinson + bus 194).

On the **mime and clown** front, the best-known and loved French clown, Coluche, died in a motorcycle accident in 1986. Most of his acts were incomprehensible to foreigners, save jests such as starting a campaign for the presidency, for which he posed nude with a feather up his bum. A troupe of mimes and clowns who debunk the serious in literature rather than politics, are *La Clown Kompanie*, famous for their Shakespearian tradegies turned into farce. Joëlle Bouvier and Régis Obadia trained both at dance school and at Lecoq's – their company *L'Equisse* combines both disciplines, takes inspiration from paintings, and portrays a dark, hallucinatory world.

The venues are much the same as those for contemporary dance – the *Théâtre de la Bastille, Le Déjazet* (41 bd du Temple, 3e; 48.87.97.34; Mo République) and the arts centres outside the city.

Plenty of space and critical attention is also given to **tap, tango and jazz dancing,** and visiting traditional dance troupes from all over the world. There are a dozen or so black African companies in Paris, but predictably they find it hard to compete with Europeans (and the fashionable Japanese) for venues. The 11ᵉ addresses are where you're most likely to find them. There are also Indian dance troupes, the *Ballet Classique Khmer* and many more from exiled cultures.

For **ballet** the highlight of the year is the *Festival International de Danse de Paris* in October and November which involves contemporary, classical and different national traditions. And all year Paris has high-quality stuff with regular visits by international star dancers and companies. Nureyev directs the French national ballet at the Opéra, whilst Maurice Béjart's *Ballet du XXe Siècle* produces new generations of French classical dancers, most often at the Palais des Congrès (see p.197).

The Opéra is where people go for *Swan Lake* and *Giselle,* though GRCOP also perform there and there are occasional indulgences to other experimental troupes. The other main venues for classical ballet are the *Théâtre Musical de Paris,* where in 1910 Diaghilev put on the first season of Russian ballet assisted by Cocteau, Rodin, Proust and others, and the *Théâtre des Champs-Elysées* (15 av Montaigne, 8ᵉ; 47.23.47.77; Mᵒ Alma-Marceau) which attempts to be even grander and more expensive than the Opéra.

Festivals combining theatre, dance, mime, classical music and its descendants, include the *Festival du Marais* in June, the *Festival 'Foire Saint-Germain'* in June and July and the *Festival d'Automne* from mid-September to mid-December.

CAFE-THEATRE

Literally a revue, monologue or mini-play performed in a place where you can drink, and sometimes eat, **café-théâtre** is probably less accessible than a Racine tragedy at the *Comédie-Française.* The humour or puerile dirty jokes, word-play and allusions to current fads, phobias and politicians can leave even a fluent French-speaker in the dark. If you want to give it a try, the *Café de la Gare* (41 rue du Temple, 4ᵉ; Mᵒ Hôtel-de-Ville/Rambuteau; 42.78.52.51), though no longer operating its turn-of-the-wheel admission price, has retained its reputation for novelty. Also in the Marais are *Blancs-Manteaux* (15 rue des Blancs-Manteaux, 4ᵉ; Mᵒ Hôtel-de-Ville/Rambuteau; 48.87.15.84) and *Point Vergule* (7 rue Ste-Croix-de-la-Bretonnerie, 4ᵉ; Mᵒ Hôtel-de-Ville/St-Paul; 42.78.67.03). Tickets are slightly cheaper than for ordinary theatre. It's still best to book in advance though you have a good chance of getting in on the night during the week.

Chapter eight
OUT FROM THE CITY

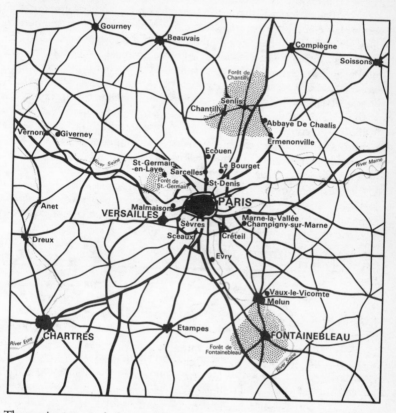

The region around the capital – known as the **Ile de France** – and the borders of the neighbouring provinces are studded with large-scale **châteaux**. Many were royal or noble retreats for hunting and other leis-ured pursuits, some like Versailles were for more serious state show. The actual mansions and palaces – and **Versailles** above all – can be tedious in the extreme. But **Vaux-le-Vicomte**, at least, is magnificent; **Fontaine-bleau** is pleasantly Italian; and at any you can get a taste of country air in the forests and parks around and get back to Paris comfortably in a day.

If you've limited time, though, and even a slight curiosity about church buildings, forget the châteaux and make for the **cathedral of Chartres** – all it is cracked up to be. Also, much closer in, on the edge of the city itself, **St-Denis** boasts a **cathedral** that is second only to Notre-Dame among Paris churches. And a visit to it could be combined with an unusual approach to the city – a walk back along the banks of the St-Denis **canal**.

Whether the various suburban **museums** deserve your attention will depend on your degree of interest in the subjects they represent. Several, however, have authoritative collections: on **china** at Sèvres, **early French history** at St-Germain-en-Laye, **Napoléon** at Malmaison, and the **Ile de France** at Sceaux. The latter, together with the **Air museum** at Le Bourget, should give kids a good deal of pleasure, while, further out, there's the **horse museum** at Chantilly.

Rustic riverside junketing as depicted in so many Impressionist canvasses is unfortunately not really on any more. If you are nostalgic for those apparently carefree scenes, you could recapture just a whiff of the atmosphere on the Marne at Joinville or Champigny or perhaps the Seine island of Chatou. But the most satisfying experience is undoubtedly **Monet's** marvellous garden at **Giverney** – inspiration for all his waterlily canvases in the Marmottan and Musée d'Orsay.

If your interest is in contemporary architecture, one of the most outrageous and startling housing experiments in Europe can be seen at the new town of **Marne-la-Vallée**.

THE TRUTH ABOUT VERSAILLES

The **Palace of VERSAILLES** is foul from every aspect, a mutated building gene allowed to run like a pounding fist for lengths no feet or eyes were made for, its décor a grotesque homage to two of the greatest of all self-propagandists – Louis XIV and Napoléon. The mirrors, in the famous Hall of, are smeared, scratched and not the originals – for these a Breton boy is currently serving fifteen years for breaking glass with explosives. In the park, a mere two and a half square miles, the fountains only gush on selected days. The rest of the time the statues on the empty pools look as bad as gargoyles taken down from cathedral walls.

It's hard to know why so many tourists come out here – in preference to all except the most obvious sights of Paris. Yet they do, and the château (9.45–5/6, except Mon) is always a crush of bodies. If you are curious, you have a choice of itineraries and whether to be guided or not, but either way you won't have much room to take your time. If you just feel like taking a look, and a walk, **the park** (open dawn to dusk) is free and the scenery better the further you go from the palace – there are even informal groups of trees near the lesser outcrops of royal mania, the Grand and Petit Trianons. There is, too, a wonderfully snobbish place to have **tea** – the *Hôtel Palais Trianon* (near the park entrance at the end of bd de la Reine), much more worthwhile than shelling out for château admission, with trayfuls of *pâtisseries* to the limits of your desire for about 50F.

The style of the *Hôtel Palais Trianon* is very much that of **the town** in general. The dominant population is aristocratic with the pre-revolutionary titles disdainful of those dating merely from Napoléon. On Bastille day both lots show their colours with black ribbons and ties.

MEUDON, SEVRES, ST-CLOUD, BIEVRES, SCEAUX

Once outlying villages in the south-west corner of the city, these places have expanded into each other, spreading right across the steep slopes of the hills above the Seine. The heights tend to be dominated by luxury apartments with expensive views. But there are still numerous desirable residences in private gardens, rural lanes and cottage corners, especially towards Clamart. It is not easy to find your way about without a car.

One accessible bit which is worth a wander is **MEUDON-VAL-FLEURY**, on the C5/C7 RER lines. And to give your walk some purpose there is a small **Rodin museum** in the house where he spent his last years, at 19 av Rodin, off rue de la Belgique. From the station you make your way up the east flank of the *val* – valley – through the twisty **rue des Vignes**. You can either go up rue de la Belgique until you reach av Rodin on the left towards the top, or turn down it to the railway embankment, go through the tunnel and take the footpath on the right, which brings you out by the house. It stands in a big picnickable garden on the very edge of the hill looking down on the Renault works in Boulogne-Billancourt. The museum has only recently been re-opened, so check the listings magazines for hours.

Right at the top of Meudon there is another **terrace with view** and an important **observatory**, but, again, too much trouble without a vehicle.

No difficulties, however, about getting to the **Musée National de Céramique** in **SEVRES**. The métro goes to Pont de Sèvres and the museum (10–12, 1.30–5.15; cl. Tues) is just to the right of the main road, close to the river bank. An acquired taste, maybe, but if you do have it, there is much to be savoured, not just French pottery and china, but Islamic, Chinese, Italian, German, Dutch, English etc, plus, inevitably, a comprehensive collection of Sèvres ware, as the stuff is made right here.

Close by, overlooking the river, the **Parc de St-Cloud** is good for some fresh air and the visual order through pools and fountains down to the river and across to the city (M° Pont-de-Sèvres, Boulogne-Pont-de-St-Cloud, then walk across the river: or, take a train from St-Lazare to St-Cloud and head south).

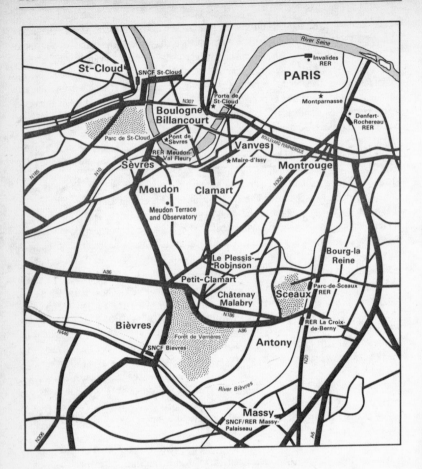

The French Photography Museum at Bièvres

What should be (and could be) one of the best museums in or around
Paris is a real let-down as well as being fiendish to get to. The **Musée
Français de la Photographie** has been lobbying for a new building (though
not a new site) for several years. Their collection that covers the entire
period, of cameras, enlargers and all the technical bits and pieces, documents and magazines, rare daguerreotypes and thousands of photographs,
is crammed into glass cases stacked in tiny rooms, or, as in the case of
most of the pictures, hidden away. Unless you're a fanatic it's not worth
the effort of a 20 min walk from the bus-stop at PETIT-CLAMART
(190A from M° Mairie d'Issy) or BIEVRES train station (RER line 8 to
Massy-Palaiseau, then SNCF direction Versailles). If you are, there's a

marker near the bus stop where Nadar ascended in a balloon to take the first ever aerial photo in 1858 (of which neither print nor negative remains).

More interesting perhaps are the **summer fêtes**, when famous living photographers, as well as amateurs and admirers of the art, congregate in Bièvres on the first weekend in June for the **Fête des Photographes** and the **Foire à la Photo**, both organised by the museum. The *Fête*, on the Saturday, consists of talks and workshops run by professionals in studios fixed up in the rickety outbuildings. On the Sunday everyone exhibits their work and trades equipment. Thousands of people make the journey and everyone is welcome. The address of the museum is 78 rue de Paris, Bièvres and it's open everyday from 9–12.30 and 1.30–6.

The Musée de l'Ile-de-France at Sceaux

The **Ile-de-France museum** is housed in the **château of SCEAUX** a 19C replacement for the original (demolished post-Revolution), which matched the now-restored Le Nôtre grounds. As a park it's the usual classical geometry of terraces, water and woods, but if you fancy a walk you can get off the RER at LA-CROIX-DE-BERNY at the southern end. Otherwise it's a 5 to 10 minute walk from PARC DE SCEAUX station (15 mins from Denfert-Rochereau): turn left then right into av R-de-Launay and right again on av Le Nôtre and you'll find the château gates on your left.

The **museum** evokes the Paris countryside; of the *ancien régime* with its aristocratic and royal domains; of the 19C, with its riverside scenes and eating and dancing places, the *guinguettes*, that inspired so many artists; and of the new towns and transport of the current age. There are models, pictures and diverse objects: a back-pack hot chocolate dispenser with a choice of two brews; 1940s métro seats; a painting of river laundering at Cergy-Pontoise alongside photos of the new town high-rise; early bicycles and a series of plates and figurines inspired by the arrival of the first giraffe in France in the 1830s. Though some of the rooms hold little excitement, most people, kids included, should find enough to make the visit worth it. Hours are 10–12;2–5/6; Mon & Fri pm only; closed Tues. Entry is cheap, and free for children of school age.

Temporary exhibitions and a summer festival of classical chamber music are held in the Orangerie which, along with the Pavillon de l'Aurore (in the north-east corner of the park), survives from the original residence. The concerts take place at weekends, from July to October – details from the museum, tel 46.61.06.71, or from the *Direction des Musées de France*, Palais du Louvre, Cours Visconti, 34 quai du Louvre, Paris 1er.

MALMAISON, CHATOU, ST-GERMAIN-EN-LAYE

Josephine Bonaparte's country house, an island in the Seine once frequented by the stars of Impressionism, and a museum of prehistoric, Celtic and Roman France – all three places lie to the west of Paris on the RER A1 line. As Saint-Germain, the furthest, is only 20 minutes away, half a day is enough to visit any of them.

Malmaison

The **Château of MALMAISON** was the home of the Empress Josephine. During the 1800–1804 Consulate Napoléon himself would drive out at weekends, though by all accounts his presence was hardly guaranteed to make the party go with a bang. Twenty minutes was all the time allowed for meals, and when called upon to sing in party games, the great man always gave a rendition of *Malbrouck s'en va-t'en guerre*, out of tune. A slightly odd choice too, when you remember that it was Malbrouck, i.e. the Duke of Marlborough, who had given the French armies a couple of drubbings 100 years earlier. Yet according to his secretary, Malmaison was 'the only place next to the battlefield where he was truly himself'. After their divorce, Josephine stayed on here, occasionally receiving visits from the Emperor, until her death in 1814.

The **château** (10–12, 1.30–4.30; cl. Tues; guided tours only) is set in the beautiful grounds of the **Bois-Préau**. It's relatively small and surprisingly enjoyable. The visit includes private and official apartments, in part with

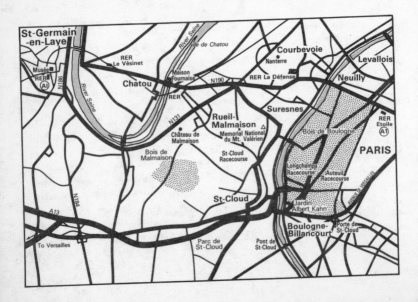

original furnishings, though complemented with pieces imported from other imperial residences. During the Nazi Occupation, the imperial chair – in the library – was rudely violated by the fat buttocks of Reichsmarschall Goering, dreaming perhaps of promotion or the conquest of Egypt. There are other Napoleonic bits in the **Bois-Préau museum** (same hours as above).

The RER goes direct to RUEIL-MALMAISON, whence you have to walk. An alternative which involves less walking would be to get off the RER at LA DÉFENSE and take bus 158A to Malmaison-Château. If you wanted to make a feature of the walk, you could go to Rueil-Malmaison and follow the GR11 from the Pont de Chatou along the left bank of the Seine and into the château park.

On a high bump of ground behind the château, and not easy to get to without a car, is the 1830s fort of **Mont Valérien**. Once a place of pilgrimage, the Germans killed four and a half thousand hostages and Resistance people there during the war. It is again a national shrine, though the memorial itself is not much to look at.

Ile de Chatou

A long narrow island in the Seine, the **ILE DE CHATOU** was once a rustic spot where Parisians came on the newly opened railway to row and dine and flirt at the riverside *guinguettes* (eating and dancing establishments). One of these survives, forlorn and derelict, just below the Pont de Chatou road bridge. It is the **Maison Fournaise**, a favourite haunt of Renoir, Monet, Manet, Van Gogh, Seurat, Sisley, Courbet . . . half of them in love with the proprietor's daughter, Alphonsine. One of Renoir's best-known canvases, *Le Dejeuner des Canotiers*, shows his friends lunching on the balcony.

Vlaminck and his fellow-Fauves, Derain and Matisse, were also habitués. In fact, it was from here that Vlaminck set off for the 1905 *Salon des Indépendants* with the truckload of paintings that caused the critics to coin the term Fauvism.

Even now the buildings are not completely untenanted, for an elderly Algerian lives in the tumbledown outhouses at one end. But at last Chatou council is taking an interest. The elegant ironwork of the balcony has been renewed, with the help of a donation from the American Friends of the Maison Fournaise. The plan is to turn it into a restaurant once again. And it's certainly a great site, with a huge plane tree shading the riverbank and a view of the barges racing downstream on the current.

The downstream end of the island has been newly made into a **park**, which tapers away into a treelined tail hardly wider than the path. The upstream end is spooky in the extreme. A track, black with oil and ooze and littered with assorted junk, bumps along past yellowed grass and bald poplar trees to a group of ruined houses stacked with beat-up cars.

Beyond the railway bridge a louche-looking chalet, guarded by Alsatians, stands beside the track. A concrete block saying No Entry in homemade lettering bars the way. If you're bold enough to ignore it, there's a view from the head of the island of the old market gardens on the right bank and the decaying industrial landscape of Nanterre on the left.

Access to the island is from the Rueil-Malmaison RER stop. Just walk straight ahead on to the Pont de Chatou. Bizarrely, there's a twice-yearly ham and antique fair on the island, which could be fun to check out (March and September).

St-Germain-en-Laye

ST-GERMAIN is not specially interesting as a town, but if you've been to the prehistoric caves of the Dordogne or plan to go, you'll get a lot from the **Musée des Antiquités Nationales** (9.45–12, 1.30–5.15; cl. Tues). It is in the unattractively renovated château (opposite the RER station), which was one of the main residences of the French court before Versailles was built.

The presentation and lighting make the visit a real pleasure. The extensive Stone Age section includes a mock-up of the Lascaux caves and a profile of Abbé Breuil, the priest who made prehistoric art respectable, as well as a beautiful collection of decorative objects, tools and so forth. All ages of prehistory are covered, right on down into historical times with Celts, Romans and Franks: abundant evidence that the French have been a talented arty lot for a very long time. The end piece is a room of comparative archaeology, with objects from cultures across the globe.

From right outside the château, a **terrace** – Le Nôtre arranging the landscape again – stretches for more than 2km above the Seine with a view over the whole of Paris. All behind it is the **forest of St-Germain**, a sizeable expanse of woodland, but crisscrossed by too many roads to be convincing as wilderness.

ST-DENIS AND LE BOURGET

Amid the amorphous sprawl of suburbs north-east of the city, the names of St-Denis and Le Bourget appear no more distinguished than a host of others. Yet you would be missing something if you ignored them, for both have more claims on the attention than you would expect, especially St-Denis.

St-Denis

30,000-strong in 1870, 100,000-strong today, the people of **ST-DENIS** have seen their town grow into the most heavily industrialised community in France, bastion of the Red suburbs, stronghold of the Communist Party, with nearly all the principal streets bearing some notable leftwing name. Today, though, recession and the West Pacific have taken a heavy toll in closed factories and unemployment.

Never a beauty, the centre of St-Denis still retains traces of its small-town origins, while all around the tower cranes swing hoppers of ready-mixed concrete over the rising shells of cheap-jack workers' flats. The thrice-weekly **market** still takes place in the square by the Hôtel de Ville and the covered *halles* nearby. It is a multi-ethnic affair these days, and the quantity of offal on the butchers' stalls – ears, feet, tails and bladders – shows it is no rich man's territory.

The town's chief claim to fame in conventional tourist terms is a magnificent **Cathedral**, close to the exit from the métro station, St-Denis Basilique – much the simplest way of getting to St-Denis.

Begun by Abbot Suger, friend and adviser to kings, in the first half of the 12C, it is generally regarded as the birthplace of the Gothic style in

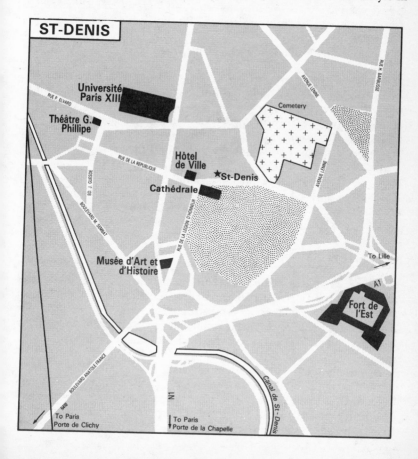

European architecture. Though its west front was the first ever to have a rose window, it is in the **choir** that you see the clear emergence of the new style: the slimness and lightness that comes with the use of the pointed arch, the ribbed vault and the long shafts of half-column rising from pillar to roof. It is a remarkably well-lit church too, thanks to the clerestory being almost 100 per cent glass – another first for St-Denis, – and the transept windows so big they occupy their entire end walls.

Once the place where the kings of France were crowned, since AD1000 the cathedral has been the burial place of all but three. Their very fine **tombs and effigies** are deployed about the transepts and ambulatory – though there is a shocking charge for entry to this part of the church (open 10–6 daily). Among the most interesting is the enormous Renaissance memorial to François 1er on the right just beyond the entrance, in the form of a triumphal arch with the royal family perched on top and battle scenes depicted below. Close to the altar steps on the left, Philippe the Bold's is one of the earliest look-alike portrait statues. To the right of the ambulatory steps you can see the stocky little general, Bertrand du Guesclin, who gave the English a run-around after the death of the Black Prince, and on the level above him, invariably graced by bouquets of flowers from the lunatic royalist fringe, the undistinguished statues of Louis XVI and Marie-Antoinette. And round the corner on the far side of the ambulatory is Clovis himself, king of the Franks way back in 500, a canny little German who wiped out Roman Gaul and turned it into France with Paris for a capital.

Not many minutes' walk away on rue Gabriel-Péri is the **Musée d'Art et d'Histoire de la Ville de St-Denis** (10–5.30, Sun 2-6.30; cl. Tues & Sun am; free Sun). The quickest route is along rue de la Légion d'Honneur, then take the third right. It's new, housed in a carefully restored former Carmelite convent, rescued from the clutches of the developers. The exhibits on display at present – the museum will grow – are not of enormous interest, though the presentation is excellent – so good, in fact, that the museum won the European Museum of the Year award. The **local archaeology** collection is particularly good and there are some interesting paintings of 19C and 20C industrial landscapes, including the St-Denis canal. The one unique collection is of documents relating to **the Commune**: posters, cartoons, broadsheets, paintings, plus an audio-visual presentation. Daumier engravings, modern painters (including Bonnard, Picasso and Léger), and an exhibition of manuscripts and rare editions of the Communist poet, Paul Eluard, native son of St-Denis, are to follow as the museum expands.

The Canal St-Denis

To get to the canal you follow rue de la République from the Hôtel de Ville to its end by a church, then go down the left side of the church until you reach the canal bridge. If you turn left, you can walk all the way back **to Paris** along the towpath – about 1½ hours to Porte de la Villette. There are stretches where it looks as if you're probably not supposed to be there. Just pay no attention and keep going.

Not far from the start of the walk, past some peeling villas with lilac and cherry blossom in their unkempt gardens, you come to a cobbled ramp on the left with a cheap friendly restaurant, *La Péniche* (The Barge, needless to say). Rue Raspail leads thence to a dusty square where the town council has named a side street for Bobby Sands. Nearby a forlorn Yugoslav runs a shop nostalgically called *Makedonia*. The whole neighbourhood is calm, poor and forgotten.

Continuing along the canal, you can't get lost. The Sacré-Coeur is visible up ahead all the way, your guiding landmark, as you pass country cottages with sunny yards open on the water, patches of greenery, sand and gravel docks, waste ground where larks rise singing above rusting bedsteads and doorless fridges, lock-keepers' cottages with roses and vegetable gardens, decaying tenements and improvised shacks as brightly painted as a Greek island house, derelict factories and huge sheds where trundling gantries load bundles of steel rods on to Belgian barges. Barge traffic is regular and the life appears attractive – to the outsider, at least. The old steel hulks slide by, gunwhales down, a dog at the prow, lace curtains at the window, a potted plant, bike propped against the cabin side, a couple of kids . . .

But the keynote is decay. This is ground for the industrial archaeologist, not your go-getters of the electronic age.

Le Bourget

The French were always adventurous, pioneering aviators and the name of **LE BOURGET** is intimately connected with their earliest exploits. Lindbergh landed here after his epic trans-Atlantic flight – the first ever. From the First War to the development of Orly in the 1950s it was Paris's principal airport. Today it is used only for internal flights, though some of the older buildings have been turned into a fascinating **museum of flying machines**. Luckily for Le Bourget, because nothing else would bring you here.

To get there you can take the RER from Gare du Nord to DRANCY, where the Germans had a concentration camp for Jews en route to Auschwitz and where, among others, the poet Max Jacob died. Be sure to get a train that stops at Drancy. From the station follow av Francis de Pressensé as far as the main road. Turn left and, by a *tabac* on the left at the first crossroads, get bus 152 to LE BOURGET/MUSÉE DE L'AIR. Alternatively, bus 350 from Gare du Nord, Gare de l'Est, Porte de la Chapelle or 152 from Porte de la Villette.

The **Musée de l'Air et de l'Espace** (open 10–6 May 1–Oct 30, 10–5 1 Nov–30 Apr; cl. Mon, 25 Dec & 1 Jan) occupies the old airport buildings.

It consists of five adjacent hangars, the first devoted to **space**, with rockets, satellites, space capsules, etc. Some are mock-ups, some the real thing. Among the latter are a Lunar Roving Vehicle, the Apollo XIII command module in which James Lovell and his fellow-astronauts nearly came to grief, the Soyuz craft in which a French astronaut flew, and France's own first successful space rocket. Everything is accompanied by extremely good explanatory panels – in French only.

The remainder of the exhibition is arranged in chronological order, starting with hangar A (the furthest away from the entrance), which covers the **period 1919–39**. Several record-breakers here, including the Bréguet XIX which made the first-ever crossing of the South Atlantic in 1927. Also, the corrugated iron job that featured so long on US postage stamps: a Junkers F13, which the Germans were forbidden to produce after the First World War and which was taken over instead by the US mail.

Hangar B shows a big collection of **Second World War planes**, including a V1 flying bomb and the Nazis' last jet fighter, the largely wooden Heinkel 162A. Incredibly, the plans were completed on 24 Sept 1944 and it flew on 6 Dec. There are photographic displays and some revealing statistics on war damage in France that sneering Brits might take note of. Destroyed: two-thirds of railway wagons, four-fifths of barges, 115 large railway stations, 9,000 bridges, 80 wharves, 1 house in 22 (plus 1 in 6 partially destroyed).

C and D cover the years **1945 to the present day**, during which the French aviation industry, having lost 80 per cent of its capacity in 1945, has recovered to a preeminent position in the world. Its high-tech achievement is represented here by the super-sophisticated best-selling Mirage fighters, the first Concorde prototype and – symbol of national vigour and virility – the Ariane space-launcher (the two latter parked on the tarmac outside). No warheads on site, as far as we know . . . Hangar E is light and sporty aircraft.

HORSES FOR COURSES: CHANTILLY, SENLIS, ECOUEN

CHANTILLY is the kind of place you go when you think it's time you did something at the weekend, like get out and get some culture and fresh air. Château, park, museum . . . Two, in fact. One with a difference: it's devoted to live horses. For Chantilly is a racing man's Mecca. Some 3,000 thoroughbreds prance the forest rides of a morning, and two of the season's classiest flat races are held here. 40km north of Paris the town is accessible **by train** from the Gare du Nord. The footpaths **GR11 and 12** pass through the park and forest, for a more peaceful and leisurely way of exploring this bit of country.

The Chantilly estate used to belong to two of the most powerful clans in France, the Montmorencys, then through marriage to the Condés. The present **Château** (10–5, cl. Tues) was put up in the late 19C. It replaced a palace, destroyed in the Revolution, which had been built for the Grand Condé, who smashed Spanish military power for Louis XIV in 1643. It's an imposing rather than beautiful structure, too heavy for grace, but it stands well, surrounded by water and looking out in haughty manner over a formal arrangement of pools and pathways designed by the busy Le Nôtre.

The story always told about it is the suicide of Vatel, temperamental majordomo to the mighty and orchestrator of financier Fouquet's fateful supper party ten years earlier in 1661 (see p.221). Wandering the corridors in the small hours, distraught because two tables had gone meatless at the royal dinner – Louis XIV was staying, – Vatel bumped into a kitchen boy carrying some fish for the morrow. 'Is that all there is?' 'Yes,' says the boy, whereupon Vatel, dishonoured, played the Roman and ran upon his sword.

The entrance to the château is across a moat past two realistic bronzes of hunting hounds. The visitable parts are all **museum** (same hours as the château): mainly, an enormous collection of paintings and drawings. They are not well displayed and you quickly get visual indigestion from the massed ranks of good, bad and indifferent, deployed as if of equal value. Some highlights, however, are a collection of portraits of 16C and 17C French monarchs and princes in the Galerie de Logis; interesting Greek and Roman bits in the tower room called the Rotonde de la Minerve; a big series of sepia stained glass illustrating Apuleius's *Golden Ass* in the Galerie de Psyche, together with some very lively portrait drawings; and, in the so-called Santuario, some Raphaels, a Filippino Lippi and 40 miniatures from a 15C *Book of Hours* attributed to the French artist Jean Fouquet.

The museum's single greatest treasure is in the library, the Cabinet des Livres, entered only in the presence of the guide. It is **Les Très Riches Heures du Duc de Berry,** the most celebrated of all Books of Hours. The illuminated pages illustrating the months of the year with representative scenes from contemporary (early 1400s) rural life – like harvesting and ploughing, sheepshearing and pruning: all drawn from life – are richly coloured and drawn with a delicate naturalism, as well as being sociologically interesting. Unfortunately, and understandably, only facsimiles are on display, but they give an excellent idea of the original. Sets of postcards, of middling fidelity, are on sale in the entrance. There are thousands of other fine books as well.

Five minutes' walk along the château drive the colossal stable block has been transformed into a museum of the horse, the **Musée Vivant du Cheval.** The building was erected at the beginning of the 18C by the incumbent Condé prince, who believed he would be reincarnated as a horse and wished to provide fitting accommodation for 240 of his future relatives.

In the main hall horses of different breeds from around the world are stalled, with a ring for demonstrations, followed by a series of life-size models illustrating the various activities horses are used for. In the rooms off are collections of paintings, horseshoes, veterinary equipment, bridles and saddles, a mock-up of a blacksmith's, children's horse toys, including a chaindriven number with handles in its ears that belonged to Napoléon III, and a fanciful Sicilian cart painted with scenes of Crusader battles.

Opening hours are complicated: 10.30–6 1 Apr–31 Oct, with demonstrations at 11.45, 3.15 & 5.15; 1–5 weekdays 1 Nov–31 Mar, with demonstrations at 3 & 5; 10.30–5.30 Sat, Sun & hols throughout the year, with demonstrations at 11.45, 3 & 5. Admission is pricey, though there is a slight reduction for children. And visitors with more princely ambitions might care to know that the authorities can arrange a *spectâcle* plus dinner party for up to 500 guests or cocktails for 1000.

Senlis, Ermenonville and Ecouen

An attractive old town 10km east of Chantilly, **SENLIS** (trains from Gare du Nord) has a cathedral contemporary with Notre-Dame and all the trappings of medieval ramparts, Roman towers and royal palace remnants to entice hordes of daytrippers and weekenders from the capital. Blood sports enthusiasts can see how the French do it at the **Musée de la Vénerie** (10–12, 2–5/6 in summer; cl. Tues & Wed am). Another dozen kilometres away is the 18C château and park of **ERMENONVILLE**, where **Rousseau** died and was buried on an island in the lake; shortly afterwards the Revolution moved him to the Panthéon.

ECOUEN lies to the south on the N16, the Chantilly-Paris road, just before the monstrous high-rise suburb of Sarcelles. Its **Renaissance château**, that belonged like Chantilly first to the Montmorencys, then to the Condés, has been converted into the **Musée National de la Renaissance** (10–5; cl. Tues). In addition to some of the original interior decoration, including frescoes and magnificent carved fireplaces, the rooms display a choice and manageable selection of Renaissance furniture, tapestries, woodcarvings, jewellery and so forth. But you need to know you have a definite interest in the period to make it worth the effort of getting there.

IN THE LOOPS OF THE MARNE

In the good old days of the 19C, people with time, spirit, and a few *sous* would leave the city of an evening for a meal and a dance at their favourite *guinguette*. These mini-music halls-cum-restaurants were to be found on the banks of the Seine, the Marne, the Bièvre, – some of them feature in the Gare d'Orsay Impressionist collection. One of the most beloved by Bohemians was the tree-house at ROBINSON-PLESSY, of which there's a painting at the Musée de l'Ile-de-France (see p.209). It has disappeared, as have most of them, along with their surroundings of meadows, poplar-lined paths and peasant villages. But the same combination of open-air eating, riverside views and live music can still be had in a *guinguette* established in the 1900s: *Chez Gégène*, 162bis quai de Polangis, JOINVILLE-LE-PONT, open from March to October.

JOINVILLE-LE-PONT is east of Paris, just across the Marne from the Bois de Vincennes (RER line A2, then buses 106 & 108 from rue J.Mermoz or walk to cross the river). Quai de Polangis runs upstream (northwards at this point). There are several places where you can hire canoes or pedalos – for much better **boating** than on the Vincennes lakes.

Downstream (or three stops on the RER, then buses 208/116 or bus 108A from Joinville) is CHAMPIGNY-SUR-MARNE, one of the few *banlieue* addresses which feels like a place in its own right. There are tiny terraced flats with wooden stairs and balconies beside the bridge; a gracefully sweet and ancient church, St-Saturnin, nestling on a cobbled square a block away from place Lénine and the central crossroads. Old

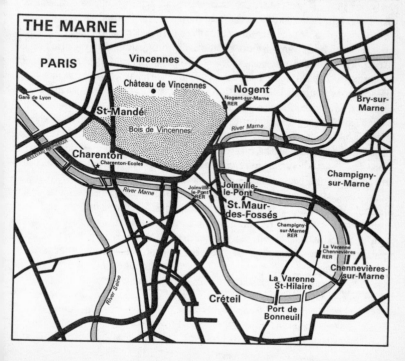

and new co-exist and most of the streets bear revolutionary or Resistance names. A monument up on a hill to the east (on rue du Monument) commemorates a miserable and bloody defeat during the Siege of Paris when the Parisians, led by the incompetent Ducroz, failed to break through the Prussian lines in the first sortie for several weeks.

Another period of defeat, 70 years later, is the subject of the **Musée de la Résistance Nationale** at 88 av Marx Dormoy (bus 208 from the station or the centre; stop Musée de la Résistance). Only recently opened and exemplary in its high tech design and its facilities – projection room for films and archive material, press button audio-visuals in the galleries, library with special sections for children – it nevertheless lacks a clearly defined purpose. Since the 40th anniversary of the liberation of France, Resistance museums are back in vogue. This one, to its credit, includes the immediate pre-war period and the *Front Populaire*, acknowledges the major role of the Communists in the Resistance and covers the Socialist reforms after the liberation. But it can't escape the need to recuperate French glory nor can it relate the dignity it accords to this resistance with other clandestine revolts whether in the past or the present. The museum is open 10–5; Sun pm only; Fri closed 12–2; closed all day Tues.

You can hire boats from the *Centre Nautique* in Champigny (near the railway bridge ¾km upstream from the road bridge) or you can wander down the quayside path on the left bank to the **Pont de Chennevières**. There are some good **riverside restaurants** too such as *L'Ecu de France*, 31 rue de Champigny before you reach the Chennevières bridge; *Le Pavillon Bleu*, a genuine *guinguette* at 66 promenade des Anglais, further on towards the Pont de Bonneuil on the right bank; and *La Bréteche*, 171 quai de Bonneuil, on the same side, past the Bonneuil bridge. The nearest RER station is La Varenne-Chennevières.

One other possible stop on these meanders of the Marne is **NOGENT-SUR-MARNE**, back by the Bois de Vincennes north of Joinville. The one remaining pavillion of the **old market at Les Halles** has been resurrected there in a bizarre setting of ocean liner appartment blocks on one side and mismatched pre-war houses on the other. Baltard's construction, all gleaming glass and paint above the diamond patterned brickwork, is a pleasure to behold. In front of the entrance is a '**square of bygone Paris**', replete with Wallace fountain, theatre ticket kiosk, cobbles and twirly lamp post. But that is all there is to see since the hall is given over to private functions for most of the year – fashion shows, International Police Association balls, weapon fairs and the like. There are cultural events open to all but disseminating the programme is not a high priority. From Nogent-sur-Marne RER you exit onto av de Joinville, cross over and turn left past the SI (who can tell you if there is anything interesting on) and then first left into av Victor Hugo, which brings you to the unmistakable building.

Further downstream from all these places, where the Marne meets the Seine just outside the city, is **Charenton** where millions upon millions of bottles of wine are stored before reaching the Parisian throat. But the **museum** to see here is dedicated to the other vital substance – bread. Gathered together in a smallish attic room, this fussy but comprehensive collection has songs, pictures, bread tax decrees of the *ancien régime*, old *boulangerie* signs, baking trays, baskets and cupboards for bread, pieces sculpted out of dough and the thing itself – over 4,000 years old in one instance. If you're fond of museums you'll like this one. Otherwise don't bother and don't take kids along. Situated above the flour milling firm *S.A.M.* at 2bis rue Victor Hugo, the **Musée Français du Pain** is open only on Tues and Thurs, 2–4.30. From Paris take the Créteil-Préfecture métro to Charenton-Ecoles, exit place des Ecoles and rue Victor Hugo goes down to the right of the *Monoprix* supermarket in front of you. From the Bois de Vincennes, av Cholet runs to place des Ecoles from av de Grevelle on the edge of the wood, due south of Lac Daumesnil.

VAUX-LE-VICOMTE AND FONTAINEBLEAU

VAUX-LE-VICOMTE, 46km south-east of Paris, is one of the great classical châteaux. Louis XIV's finance superintendent, Nicholas Fouquet, had it built at colossal expense using the top designers of the day – the royal architect Le Vau, the painter Le Brun and Le Nôtre, the landscape gardener. The result was magnificence and precision in perfect proportion and a bill that could only be paid by someone who occasionally confused the state's account with his own. The housewarming party to which the king was invited was more extravagant than any royal event – a comparison that other finance ministers ensured that Louis took to heart. Within three weeks Fouquet was jailed for life on trumped-up charges and Louis carted Le Vau, Le Brun and Le Nôtre off to Versailles to work on a gaudy and gross piece of one-upmanship. The château is **open** April-October 10–6 (winter: weekend afternoons only; and cl. Jan); **trains** from the Gare de Lyon leave for MELUN (25 mins) and there are direct **buses** from Melun SNCF to the château.

Energetically, you could spend the morning at Vaux-le-Vicomte and continue by train from MELUN to **FONTAINEBLEAU** – an instructive and remarkably pleasant exercise in rapid châteaux touring. A hunting lodge from as early as the 12C, the château here began its transformation into a palace under the 16C François I. A vast, rambling place, unpretentious despite its size, it owes its distinction to a colony of Italian artists imported for the decoration – above all Rosso Il Fiorentino, who completed the celebrated **Galerie François I**, vital to the evolution of French aristocratic art and design. The gardens are equally luscious but if you want to escape to the wilds, the surrounding **forest of Fontainebleau** is full of walking and cycling trails and its rocks are a favourite training-ground for French climbers. Paths and tracks are all marked on Michelin map 196 (*Environs de Paris*).

The château, rarely overcrowded, is **open** 10–12.30 & 2–6 (cl. Tues). **Trains** take around 45 mins from Gare de Lyon (25 mins from Melun) and there's a local bus to the gates from the SNCF.

CHARTRES

The mysticisms of medieval thought on life, death and deity, expressed in material form by the masonry of **CHARTRES Cathedral**, should best be experienced on a cloudfree winter's day. The low sun transmits the

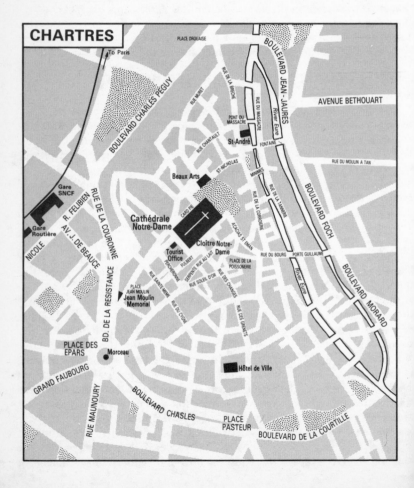

stained glass colours to the interior stone, the quiet scattering of people leaves the acoustics unconfused, and the exterior is unmasked for miles around. The masterwork is flawed only by changes in Roman Catholic worship. The immense distance from the door to the altar which, through mists of incense and drawn-out harmonies, emphasised the distance between worshippers and worshipped, with priests as sole mediators, has been abandoned. The central altar (from a secular point of view) undermines the theatrical dogma of the building and puts cloth and boards where the coloured lights should play.

A less recent change, of allowing the congregation chairs, covers up the **labyrinth** on the floor of the nave – an original 13C arrangement and a great rarity, since the authorities at other cathedrals had them pulled up as distracting frivolities. The Chartres labyrinth traces a path over 200m long enclosed within a diameter of 13m, the same size as the rose window above the main doors. The centre used to have a bronze relief of Theseus and the Minotaur and the pattern of the maze was copied from classical texts, the idea of the path of life to eternity being fairly similar in Greek myth and medieval Catholicism. During pilgrimages, the chairs are removed so you may be lucky and see the full pattern.

A life of 750 years may have taken its toll, but the geometry of the building, the details of the stonework – above all the Renaissance choir screen and hosts of sculpted figures above each door – and the shining circular symmetries of the transept windows, are wonders enough to enthrall. Among paying extras, the **crypt** and **treasures** can wait for another time but, crowds permitting, it's worth climbing the **north tower**. Admission hours for the main building are 7.30–7.30/7. There are gardens at the back from where you can contemplate at ease the complexity of stress factors balanced by the flying buttresses.

The town

Though the cathedral is why you come here, **Chartres town** is not without appeal. The **Beaux Arts museum** in the former episcopal palace just north of the cathedral has some beautiful tapestries, a room full of Vlaminck and Zurbaran's *Ste Lucie*, as well as good temporary exhibitions 10–12 & 2–5; cl. Tues). Behind it, rue Chantault leads past old town houses to the **River Eure** and Pont des Massacres. You can follow this reedy river lined with ancient wash-houses upstream via rue des Massacres on the right bank. The cathedral appears from time to time through the trees and, closer at hand, on the left bank is the Romanesque church of **St-André** now used for art exhibitions, jazz concerts, etc. Crossing back over at the end of rue de la Tannerie into rue du Bourg takes you back to the cathedral through the medieval town, decorated with details such as the carved salmon on a house on place de la Poissonerie. Further south, around **rue du Cygne** is the place to look for bars and restaurants.

The **SI** is on the cathedral *parvis*, at 7 Cloître Notre-Dame, and ca
supply **free maps** and help with **rooms** if you want to stay.

Arriving at the **Gare SNCF** (frequent trains from Paris-Montparnass
in 50–65 mins), av J-de-Beauce leads straight up to place Châtelet. Pa
all the coaches on the other side of the *place*, rue Ste-Même crosses plac
Jean Moulin – the cathedral is down to the left. Rue d'Harleville goes t
the right to bd de la Résistance, a section of the main ring road aroun
the old town. The memorial on the corner of the street and the boulevar
is to **Jean Moulin,** Prefect of Chartres until he was sacked by the Vich
government in 1942. When the Germans occupied Chartres in 1940, h
had refused under torture to sign a document to the effect that blac
soldiers in the French army were responsible for Nazi atrocities. He late
became de Gaulle's number one man on the ground, coordinating th
driving towards western Normandy from Paris – or towards Rouen fror
Chartres.

GIVERNEY AND ANET

Two excursions some way out of Paris to the west. **Monet's garden** a
Giverney is really special: worth all the effort of a train ride out fro
Paris and then further 6km by taxi, foot or thumb. The château at **Ane**
20km or so north of DREUX, is a stop worth considering if you'
driving towards Western Normandy from Paris – or towards Rouen fror
Chartres.

Giverney
Giverney overlooks the Seine halfway between Paris and Rouen. Mone
lived here from 1883 till his death in 1926 and the gardens that he lai
out were considered by many of his friends his masterpiece. Each mont
is reflected in a dominant colour, as are each of the rooms, hung as h
left them with his Japanese print collection. May and June, when th
rhododendrons flower round the lily pond and the wistaria winds ov
the Japanese bridge, are the best of all times to visit. But any mont
from spring to autumn, is overwhelming in the beauty of this arrangeme
of living shades and shapes. You'll have to contend with crowds and litt
black boxes snapping up images of the waterlilies far removed fror
Monet's rendering – and admission is expensive – but there's no plac
like it. The gardens are open 10–6; the house 10–12 & 2–6, April-O
only.

Without a car, the easiest **approach to Giverney** is by train to VERNO
from Paris-St-Lazare (35–60 mins, hourly). There's no bus connection
Giverney, so you have to take a taxi, hitch or walk the remaining 6kn
For the latter, cross the river and turn right on the D5. Be careful as yc
enter Giverney to take the left fork, otherwise you'll find yourself makir
a long detour to reach the garden entrance.

Anet

Diane de Poitiers, respected widow in the court of François Ier and powerful lover of the king's son Henri, decided that her marital home at **ANET** needed to be bigger and more comfortable. Work started with Philippe de l'Orme as the architect in charge and the designs as delicate and polished as the Renaissance could produce. Within a year Henri inherited the throne and immediately gave Diane the château of Chenonceau. But the Anet project continued, luckily for Diane, since Henri's reign was brought to an untimely end and his wife demanded Chenonceau back. Diane retired to Anet where she died. Her grandson built a chapel for her tomb alongside the château which has remained intact. The château would have been completely destroyed by the first owner after the Revolution had it not been for a protest riot by the townspeople that sent him packing. As it is, only the front entrance, one wing and the château chapel remain, now restored to its former glorification of hunting and feminine eroticism with the swirling floor and domed ceiling of the chapel its climax. The château is open March–Nov 2.30–6.30 except Tues; Sun all year 10–11.30 & 2–6.30/5.

THE NEW TOWNS AND *GRANDS ENSEMBLES*

Investigating life in the **suburbs** is never a high priority when visiting famous, or indeed any, cities. Whether Milan, Cardiff or Warsaw, they're usually pretty similar, and Paris doesn't boast much that's exceptional. So this section is strictly for those interested in the problems of living space and community, and with the arrogance of architects and their bureacratic backers, the urban planners.

Wealthy Parisians who have moved out from the *Beaux Quartiers* have their flats or houses south-west of the city, in the garden suburbs with tennis courts and swimming pools, that stretch out to Versailles. In all the towns round the city, now inseparable in the urban sprawl, there are neat, individualised detached houses known as *pavillons*, built in the 1920s and 1930s. Some might still lack certain sanitary amenities, but everyone would like to own one or build a new one. That, of course, has never been made possible, and when the city housing problem caused by the slum clearance and population growth in the 1950s could no longer be ignored, high-rise density in 'Greater Paris' was the answer. These giant concrete camps came to be known as *Grands Ensembles*.

SARCELLES, 12km to the north, is the most notorious of the *Grands Ensembles*. It gave a new word to the French language, sarcellitis, the social disease of delinquency and despair spread by the horizons of interminable, identical, high-rise hutches. It's not worth a visit but it did teach the planners a few lessons. A few years after Sarcelles' creation, at the end of the 1960s, the architect Emile Aillaud tried a very different approach in the *Grand Ensemble* called **LA GRANDE BORNE**. 25km south of Paris and directly overlooking the Autoroute du Sud which cuts it off from the town centre and nearest rail connection of GRIGNY, it was hardly a promising site. But for once a scale was used that didn't belittle the inhabitants and the buildings were shaped by curves instead of corners. The façades are coloured by tiny glass and ceramic tiles, there are inbuilt artworks – landscapes, animals, including two giant sculpted pigeons, and portraits of Rimbaud and Kafka – and the whole ensemble is pedestrians only. To get there by public transport can be quite a drag – train from the Gare de Lyon, direction Corbeil-Essonnes, to Grigny-Centre then bus or walk – but with wheels it's a quick flit down the A6 from Porte d'Orléans; turn off it to the right on the D13 and both the first and second right will take you into the estate.

Having come out this way, you could also take a look at **EVRY**, one of the five new towns in the Paris region (Evry-Courcouronnes SNCF two stops on from Grigny). The *Villes Nouvelles* became the mode in the late 1960s when it had begun to sink in that throwing up housing estates all over the place left a lot to be desired. Unlike their English equivalents, they were grafted on to existing towns but conceived as satellites to the capital rather than separate places in their own right. Streets of tiny *pavillons* with old-time residents cower beneath buildings from another world, unfortunately the present one. As with any new town there's the unsettling reversal that the people are there because of the town and not vice versa, and the towns seem to be there only because of the rail and RER lines.

But as tourists, with limited access to life, it's the architects we come to pay court to. So follow the signs from Evry station to the *centre commercial* and keep going through it till you surface on a walkway that bridges bd de l'Europe. This leads you into **Evry 1 housing estate**, a multi-matt-coloured ensemble resembling a group of ransacked wardrobes and chests-of-drawers. The architects call it pyramidal and blather on about how the buildings and the urban landscape articulate each other. But it's quite fun really even if the 'articulating' motifs on the façade overlooking the park are more like fossils than plants.

The New Town with the most to shock or amuse, or even please, is undoubtedly **MARNE-LA-VALLEE**, where Terry Gilliam's totalitarian fantasy *Brazil* was filmed and where the real-life European Disneyland is going to be. It starts 10km east of Paris and hops for 20km from one new outburst to the next with odd bits of wood and water between. The RER stops from Bry-sur-Marne to the Torcy terminus are all in Marne-la-Vallée, but if your journey's not on that straight line, it's tough and buses aren't much help.

You can, however, sample the extreme without too much legwork if you get off at **NOISY-LE-GRAND**, or MONT D'EST as the planners

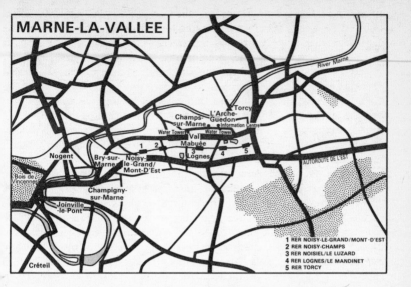

call it. You surface on the Arcades, a stony substitute for a town square and there you have the poetic panorama of a controlled community environment. Bright blue tubing and light blue tiling on split level walkways and spaceless concrete fencing; powder blue boxes growing plants on buildings beside grey blue roofs of multi-angled leanings; walls of blue, walls of white, deep blue frames and tinted glass reflecting the water of a chopped-up lake; islands linked by bridges with more blue railings . . . The two acclaimed architectural pieces in this monolith have only one thing in their favour – neither is blue in any bit. They are both low-cost housing units, they are both gigantic, quite unlike anything you're likely to have seen before and both are unmitigatedly horrible. The **Arènes de Picasso** is in the group of buildings to the right of the RER line as you look at the lakes from the Arcades, about ½km away. It's soon visible as you approach: two enormous circles like loud speakers facing each other across a space that would do nicely for a Roman stadium. Prepare to feel as if the lions are waiting. At the other end of Mont d'Est, facing the capital, is the extraordinary semi-circle, arch and half square of *Le Théâtre et Palacio d'Abraxas*, creation of Ricardo Boffil. Ghosts of ancient Greek designs haunt the façades but proportion there is none, whether classical or any other.

For those with wheels, further delights of Marne-la-Vallée include the mosaiced 'Totem' water tower with clown and robot faces in the woods by **LE LUZARD**; another water tower, with plants growing through its grill cladding, at the head of bd Salvador Allende at **NOISIEL MAIRIE**;

sympathetic small-scale housing in **LE VAL MAUBOUÉ** and, with easy access, an **RER station on a lake, LOGNES-LE MANDINET.**

Maps and information for Marne-la-Vallée as well as models and photos on view can be had from the CIVN, 2 place de l'Arche-Guédon, Torcy; bus 220 from Noisiel RER, direction Torcy, stop L'Arche-Guédon.

Part three
CONTEXTS

THE CITY IN HISTORY

2000 years of compressed history — featuring riots and revolutions, shanty-towns, palaces, new street plans, sanitation and the Parisian people.

Beginnings

Rome put Paris on the map, as it did the rest of western Europe. When Julius Caesar's armies arrived in 52BC, they found a **Celtic** settlement confined to the island in the Seine — the Ile de la Cité. It must already have been fairly populous as it had sent a contingent of 8000 men to stiffen the Gallic chieftain Vercingetorix's doomed resistance to the invaders. Under the name of *Lutetia*, it remained a **Roman colony** for the next 300 years, prosperous commercially because of its commanding position on the Seine trade-route, but insignificant politically. The Romans established their administrative centre on the Ile de la Cité and their town on the Left Bank on the slopes of the Montagne Sainte-Geneviève. Though no monuments of their presence remain except the baths by the Hôtel de Cluny and the amphitheatre in rue Monge, their **street plan**, still visible in the north-south axis of rue St-Martin and rue St-Jacques, determined the future growth of the city.

When Roman rule disintegrated under the impact of **Germanic invasions** around 275, Paris held out until it fell to **Clovis the Frank** in 486. In 511 Clovis's son commissioned the **cathedral of St-Etienne**, whose foundations can be seen in the *crypte archéologique* under the square in front of Notre-Dame. Clovis's own conversion to Christianity hastened the Christianisation of the whole country, and under his successors Paris saw the foundation of several rich and influential monasteries, especially on the Left Bank.

With the election of **Hugues Capet, Comte de Paris**, as king in 987, the fate of the city was inextricably identified with that of the **monarchy**. The presence of the kings, however, prevented the development of the middle class, republican institutions that the rich merchants of Flanders and Italy were able to obtain for their cities. The result was recurrent political tension, which led to open **rebellion**, for instance, in 1356 when **Etienne Marcel**, a wealthy cloth merchant,

demanded greater autonomy for the city. Further rebellions, fuelled by the hopeless poverty of the lower classes, led to the king and court abandoning the capital in 1418, not to return for more than a hundred years.

The Right Bank, Latin Quarter and Louvre

As the city's livelihood depended from the first on its river-borne trade, commercial activity naturally centred round the place where the goods were landed. This was the **place de Grève** on the **Right Bank**, where the Hôtel de Ville now stands. Marshy ground originally, it was gradually drained to accommodate the business quarter. Whence the continuing association of the Right Bank with commerce and banking today.

The **Left Bank**'s intellectual associations are similarly ancient, dating from the growth of schools and student accommodation round the two great **monasteries of Ste-Geneviève and St-Germain-des-Prés**. The first, dedicated to the city's patron saint who had saved it from destruction by Attila's raiders, occupied the site of the present Lycée Henri IV on top of the hill behind the Panthéon. In 1215 a papal licence allowed the formation of what gradually became the renowned **University of Paris**, eventually to be known as the **Sorbonne**, after Robert de Sorbon, founder of a college for poor scholars. It was the fact that Latin was the language of the schools both inside and outside the classroom that gave the district its name of **Latin Quarter**.

To protect this burgeoning city **Philippe Auguste** (king from 1180–1223) built the **Louvre fortress** (remains of which are now on display in the newly excavated Cour Carrée in the Louvre museum) and a **wall**, which swung south to enclose the Montagne Sainte Geneviève and north and east to encompass the Marais. The administration of the city remained in the hands of the king until 1260, when Saint Louis ceded a measure of responsibility to the leaders of the Paris watermen's guild, whose power was based on their monopoly control of all river traffic and taxes thereon. The **city's government**, when it has been allowed one, has been conducted ever since from the **place de Grève/place de l'Hôtel de Ville**.

Civil wars, foreign occupation, massacres and muck

From the mid–13 to mid–14C Paris shared the same unhappy fate as the rest of France, embroiled in the long and destructive **Hundred Years War** with the English. Etienne Marcel let the enemy into the city in 1357, the Burgundians did the same in 1422, when the Duke of Bedford set up his government of northern France here. **Joan of Arc** made an unsuccessful attempt to drive them out in 1429 and was wounded in the process at the Porte St-Honoré. The following year the English king, **Henry VI**, had the cheek to have himself crowned king of France in Notre-Dame.

It was only when the English were expelled – from Paris in 1437 and from France in 1453 – that the economy had the chance to recover from so many decades of devastation. It received a further boost when **François Ier** decided to re-establish the royal court in Paris in 1528. Work began on **reconstructing the Louvre** and building the **Tuileries palace** for **Cathérine de Médicis**, and on transforming **Fontainebleau** and other country residences into sumptuous Renaissance palaces.

But before these projects reached completion, war again intervened, this time **civil war** between Catholics and Protestants, in the course of which Paris witnessed one of the worst atrocities ever committed against French Protestants. Some 3000 of them were gathered in Paris for the wedding of Henri III's daughter Marguerite to Henri, the Protestant king of Navarre. On August 25th 1572, St Bartholomew's Day, they were massacred at the instigation of the Catholic Guise family. When, through this marriage, Henri of Navarre became heir to the French throne in 1584, the Guises drove his father-in-law, Henri III, out of Paris. Forced into alliance, the two Henris laid **siege** to the city. Five years later, Henri III having been assassinated in the meantime, Henri of Navarre entered as king **Henri IV**. 'Paris is worth a Mass,' he is reputed to have said to justify renouncing his Protestantism in order to smooth Catholic susceptibilities.

The Paris he inherited was not a very salubrious place. It was overcrowded. No domestic building had been permitted beyond the limits of Philippe Auguste's 12C walls because of the guilds' resentment of the unfair advantage enjoyed by craftsmen living outside the jurisdiction of the city's tax regulations. The population had doubled to around 400,000, causing acute **housing shortage** and a terrible strain on the elementary **water supply** and **drainage system**. It is said that the first workmen who went to clean out the city's cesspools in 1633 fell dead from the fumes. It took seven months to clean out 6,420 cartloads of filth that had been accumulating for two centuries. The overflow ran into the Seine, where Parisians got their drinking water.

Planning and Expansion, absolute monarchy style

The first **systematic attempts at planning** were introduced by **Henri IV** at the beginning of the 17C: regulating street lines and uniformity of facade, and laying out the first geometric squares. The **place des Vosges** dates from this period and the **Pont Neuf**, the first of the Paris bridges not to be cluttered with medieval houses. He thus inaugurated a tradition of grandiose public building, that was to continue to the Revolution and beyond, that perfectly symbolised the bureaucratic, centralised power of the newly self-confident state concentrated in the person of its absolute monarch.

The process reached its apogee under **Louis XIV** with the construction of the **boulevards** from the Madeleine to the Bastille, the **places Vendôme and Victoire**, the **Porte Saint-Martin** and **Saint-Denis** gateways, the **Invalides**, **Observatoire** and the **Cour Carrée** of the Louvre – not to mention the vast palace at **Versailles** whither he repaired with the court in 1671. The aristocratic **hôtels** or mansions of the **Marais** were also erected during this period, to be superseded early in the 18C by the **faubourg St-Germain** as the fashionable quarter of the rich and powerful.

The underside of all this bricks and mortar self-aggrandisement was the general neglect of the living conditions of the ordinary citizenry of Paris. The **centre of the city** remained a densely packed and insanitary warren of medieval lanes and tenements. And it was only in the years immediately **preceding the 1789 revolution** that any attempt was made to clean it up. The buildings crowding the bridges were dismantled as late as 1786. Pavements were introduced for the first time and attempts were made to improve the drainage. A further source of pestilential infection was removed with the emptying of the overcrowded cemeteries into the **catacombs**. One gravedigger alone claimed to have buried more than 90,000 people in thirty years, stacked 'like slices of bacon' in the charnel-house of the Innocents, which had been receiving the dead of twenty-two parishes for 800 years.

In 1786 Paris also received its second from last ring of fortifications, the so-called **wall of the Fermiers Généraux**, with 57 *barrières* or toll gates (one of which survives in the middle of place Stalingrad by the international coach station), where a tax was levied on all goods entering the city.

The 1789 Revolution

The immediate cause of the revolution of 1789 was a campaign by the privileged classes of the clergy and nobility to protect their status, especially exemption from taxation, against erosion by the royal government. The **revolutionary movement**, however, was quickly taken over by the middle classes, relatively well off but politically underprivileged. In the initial phases this meant essentially the **provincial bourgeoisie**. It was they who comprised the majority of the representatives of the **Third Estate**, the 'order' that encompassed the whole of French society after the clergy, who formed the first Estate, and the nobility who formed the second. It was they who took the initiative in setting up the **National Assembly** on June 17th 1789. The majority of them would probably have been content with constitutional reforms that checked monarchical power on the English model. But their power depended largely on their ability to wield the threat of a **Parisian popular explosion**.

Although the effects of the revolution were felt all over France and indeed Europe, it was in Paris that the most profound changes took place. Being as it were on the spot, the people of Paris discovered themselves in **the revolution**. They formed the revolutionary shock troops, the driving force at the crucial stages of the Revolution. They

marched on Versailles and forced the king to return to Paris with them. They stormed and destroyed the **Bastille** on July 14th 1789. They occupied the Hôtel de Ville, set up an insurrectionary Commune and captured the Tuileries palace on August 10th 1792. They invaded the Convention in May 1793 and secured the arrest of the more conservative Girondin faction of deputies.

Where the bourgeois deputies of the Convention were concerned principally with political reform, the **sans culottes** – literally, the people without breeches – expressed their **demands** in economic terms: price controls, regulation of the city's food supplies and so on. In so doing they foreshadowed the rise of the working class and socialist movements of the 19C. They also established by their practice of taking to the streets and occupying the Hôtel de Ville a **tradition of revolutionary action** that continued through to the 1871 Commune.

Napoleon's Paris and the Barricades of 1830 and 1848

Apart from some spectacular blood-letting, and yet another occupation of the city by foreign powers (in 1814) Napoléon's chief legacy to France was a very centralised, authoritarian and efficient **bureaucracy** that put Paris in firm control of the rest of the country. In Paris itself, he left his share of pompous architecture – in the **Arcs de Triomphe** and **Carrousel, rue de Rivoli** and **rue de la Paix**, the **Madeleine** and facade of the **Palais-Bourbon** plus a further extension for the Louvre and a revived tradition of court flummery and extravagant living among the well-to-do. For the rest of the 19C after his demise, France was left to fight out the contradictions and unfinished business left behind by the revolution of '89. And the arena in which these conflicts were resolved was, literally, the streets of the capital.

On the one hand, there was a tussle between the class that had risen to wealth and power as a direct result of the destruction of the monarchy and the old order, and the survivors of the old order, who sought to make a comeback in the 1820s under the restored monarchy of **Louis XVIII** and **Charles X**. This conflict was finally resolved in favour of the **new bourgeoisie**. When Charles X refused to accept the result of the 1830 National Assembly elections,

Adolphe Thiers – the veteran conservative politician of the 19C – led the opposition in revolt. Barricades were erected in Paris and there followed three days of bitter street fighting, known as **les trois glorieuses**, in which 1800 people were killed (they are commemorated by the column on place de la Bastille). The outcome was the election of **Louis-Philippe** as constitutional monarch, and the introduction of a few liberalising reforms, most either cosmetic or serving merely to consolidate the power of the wealthiest stratum of the population. Radical republican and working class interests remained completely unrepresented.

The other, and more important, major political conflict was the extended struggle between this **enfranchised and privileged bourgeoisie** and the **heirs of the 1789 sans-culottes**, whose political consciousness had been awakened by the revolution but whose demands remained unsatisfied. These were the people who died on the barricades of July to hoist the bourgeoisie firmly into the saddle.

As their demands continued to go unheeded, so their radicalism increased, exacerbated by deteriorating **living and working conditions** in the large towns, especially Paris, as the **industrial revolution** got under way. There were, for example, 20,000 deaths from cholera in Paris in 1832, and in 1848 65% of the population were too poor to be liable for tax. Eruptions of discontent invariably occurred in the capital, with insurrections in 1832 and 1834. In the absence of organised parties, opposition centred on newspapers and clandestine or informal **political clubs** in the tradition of '89. The most notable – and the only one dedicated to the violent overthrow of the regime – was Auguste Blanqui's *Société Républicaine*.

In the 1840s the publication of the **first Socialist works** like Louis Blanc's *Organisation of Labour* and Proudhon's *What is Property?* gave an additional spur to the impatience of the opposition. When the lid blew off the pot in **1848** and the **Second Republic was proclaimed** in Paris, it looked for a time as if working class demands might be at least partly met. The provisional government included Louis Blanc and a Parisian manual worker. But in the face of demands for the control of industry, the setting up of co-operatives and so on, backed by agitation in the streets and the proposed inclusion of men like Blanqui and Barbès in the government, the more conservative Republicans lost their nerve. The nation returned a spanking reactionary majority in the April elections. Revolution began to appear the only possible defence for the radical left. On June 23rd, **working class Paris** – Poissonière, Temple, Saint-Antoine, the Marais, Quartier latin, Montmartre – rose in **revolt**. Men, women and children fought side by side against 50,000 troops. In three days of fighting, 900 soldiers were killed. No one knows how may of the **insurgés** died. 15,000 people were arrested and 4,000 sentenced to prison terms.

Despite the shock and devastation of civil war in the streets of the capital, the ruling classes failed to heed the warning in the events of June 1848. Far from redressing the injustices which had provoked them, they proceeded to exacerbate them – by, for example, reducing the representation of what Adolphe Thiers called 'the vile multitude'. The Republic was brought to an end in a coup d'état by **Louis Napoléon**, who within 12 months had himself crowned Emperor Napoléon III.

The rewards of colonialism and laissez-faire capitalism

There followed a period of **foreign acquisitions** on every continent and of **laissez-faire capitalism** at home – both of which greatly increased the economic wealth of France – then lagging far behind Britain in the **industrialisation** stakes. Foreign trade trebled, a huge expansion of the railway network was carried out, investment banks were set-up and so forth. The rewards, however, were very unevenly distributed, and the regime relied unashamedly on repressive measures – press censorship, police harassment and the forcible suppression of strikes – to hold the underdogs in check.

The response was entirely predictable. **Opposition** became steadily more organised and determined. In 1864, under the influence of Karl Marx in London, a French branch of **the International** was established in Paris and the youthful **trade union movement** gathered its forces in a federation. In

1869 the far from socialist Gambetta, briefly deputy for Belleville, declared: 'Our generation's mission is to complete the French Revolution.'

During these nearly twenty years of the Second Empire, while conditions were ripening for the most terrible of all Parisian revolutions, the 1871 Commune, the city itself suffered the greatest ever shock to its system. **Baron Haussmann**, appointed Prefect of the Seine department by Napoléon III with responsibility for Paris, undertook the total **transformation of the city**. In love with the straight line and grand vista, he drove 85 miles of broad **new streets** through the cramped quarters of the medieval city, linking the interior and exterior boulevards, and creating north-south, east-west cross-routes. His taste dictated the **uniform grey stone facades**, mansard roofs and six to seven storeys that are the still the architectural hallmark of the Paris street today. In fact, such was the logic of his planning that construction of his projected streets continued long after his death, bd Haussmann itself being completed only in 1927.

While it is difficult to imagine how Paris could have survived without some Haussmann-like intervention, the scale of demolitions entailed by such massive redevelopment brought the direst **social consequences**. The city boundaries were extended to the 1840 fortifications where the *boulevard périphérique* now runs. The prosperous classes moved into the new western *arrondissements*, leaving the decaying older properties to the poor. These were divided and subdivided into ever smaller units as landlords sought to maximise their rents. **Sanitation** was non-existent. Water stand-pipes were available only in the street. **Migrant workers** from the provinces, sucked into the city to supply capitalists' vast labour requirements, crammed into the old villages of Belleville and Ménilmontant. Many, too poor to buy furniture, lived in barely furnished digs or *demi-lits*, where the same bed was shared by several tenants on a shift basis. **Cholera and TB** were rife. Attempts to impose sanitary regulations were resisted by landlords as covert socialism. Many considered even connection to Haussmann's water mains an unnecessary luxury. Until 1870 refuse was thrown into the streets at night to be collected the following morning. When, in 1884, the Prefect of the day required landlords to provide proper containers, they retorted by calling the containers by his name, *poubelle* – and the name has stuck as the French word for dustbin.

Far from being concerned with Parisians' welfare, Haussmann's scheme was at least in part designed to keep the workers under control. **Barracks** were located at strategic points like the place du Château d'Eau, now République, controlling the turbulent eastern districts, and the broad **boulevards** were intended to facilitate troop movements and artillery fire.

The Siege of Paris and the Commune, 1870–71

In September 1870, Napoléon III surrendered to Bismark at the border town of Sedan, less than two months after France had declared war on the well-prepared and superior forces of the Prussian state. The humiliation was enough for a Republican Government to be instantly proclaimed in Paris. The **Prussians** advanced and by the 19th September were laying **siege** to the capital. Gambetta was flown out by hot air balloon to rally the provincial troops but the country was defeated and liaison with Paris almost impossible. Further balloon messengers ended up in Norway or the Atlantic; the few attempts at military sorties from Paris turned into yet more blundering failures. Meanwhile the city's restaurants were forced to change menus to fried dog, roast rat or peculiar delicacies from the zoos. For those without savings, death from disease or starvation became an ever more common though hardly novel fate. At the same time the peculiar conditions of a city besieged gave a greater freedom to collective discussion and dissent.

The government's half-hearted defence of the city – more afraid of revolution than of the Prussians – angered the Parisians, who clamoured for the creation of an '89–style Commune. The Prussians meanwhile were demanding a proper government to negotiate with. In January 1871 those in power agreed to hold **elections** for a new national assembly with the authority to surrender officially to the Prussians. A large **monarchist** majority, with Thiers at its head, was returned, again demonstrating the isolation from the countryside of the Parisian leftists, among whom many prominent old-timers, veterans of '48 and the empire's jails, like Blanqui and Delescluze were still active.

On March 1st Prussian troops marched down the Champs-Elysées and garrisoned the city for three days while the populace remained behind closed doors in silent protest. On March 18th, amid growing resentment from all classes of Parisians, Thiers' attempt to take possession of the National Guards' artillery in Montmartre (see p.88) set the barrel alight. **The Commune** was proclaimed from the Hôtel de Ville and Paris was promptly subjected to a **second siege**, by Thiers' government which had fled to Versailles, followed by all the remaining Parisian bourgeoisie.

The Commune lasted 72 days – a festival of the oppressed, Lenin called it. Socialist through and through, it had no time to implement lasting reforms. Wholly occupied with defence against Thiers it succumbed finally on May 28th 1871, after a week of **street by street warfare**, in which 3000 Parisians died on the barricades and another 20–25,000 men, women and children were killed in random revenge shootings by government troops. Thiers could declare with satisfaction – or so he thought: 'Socialism is finished for a long time.'

Among the non-human **casualties** were several of the city's landmark buildings, including the **Tuileries palace**, **Hôtel de Ville**, **Cours des Comptes** (where the Musée d'Orsay now stands) and a large chunk of the **rue Royale**.

The *Belle Epoque*

Physical recovery was remarkably quick. Within six or seven years few signs of the fighting remained. Visitors remarked admiringly on the teeming streets, the expensive shops and energetic night life. Charles Garnier's **Opéra** was opened in 1875. Aptly described as the 'triumph of moulded pastry', it was a suitable image of the frivolity and materialism of the so-called **naughty 80s and 90s.** In 1889 the **Eiffel Tower** stole the show at the great Exposition. For the 1900 repeat, the **Métropolitain** (métro) – or *Nécropolitain*, as it was dubbed by one wit – was unveiled.

The lasting social consequence of the Commune was the confirmation of the

them and us divide between bourgeoisie and working class. Any stance other than a revolutionary one after the Commune appeared not only feeble, but also a betrayal of the dead. None of the contradictions had been resolved. The years up to the First World War were marked by the increasing **organisation of the left** in response to the unstable, but thoroughly conservative governments of the Third Republic. The trade union movement unified in 1895 to form the **Confédération Générale du Travail** (CGT) and in 1905 Jean Jaurès and Jules Guesde founded the **Parti Socialiste** (also known as the SFIO). On the extreme right, **Fascism** began to make its ugly appearance with Maurras' proto-Brownshirt organisation, the *Camelots du Roi* – inaugurating another French tradition, of violence and thuggery on the far right.

Yet despite – or maybe in some way because of – these tensions and contradictions, Paris provided the supremely inspiring environment for a concentration of **artists and writers** – the so called **Bohemians**, both French and foreign – such as western culture has rarely seen. *Impressionism*, *Fauvism* and *Cubism* were all born in Paris in this period, while French poets like Apollinaire, Laforgue, Max Jacob, Blaise Cendrars and Breton were preparing the way for Surrealism, concrete poetry and symbolism. Film too saw its first developments. After the First World War, Paris remained the world's art centre, with an injection of foreign blood and a shift of venue from Montmartre to Montparnasse.

In the **post-war struggle for recovery** the interests of the urban working class were again passed over, with the exception of Clemenceau's 8–hour day legislation in 1919. An attempted general strike in 1920 came to nothing, and workers' strength was again weakened by the irredeemable split in the Socialist Party at the 1920 Congress of Tours. The pro-Lenin majority formed the **French Communist Party**, while the minority faction, under the leadership of Léon Blum, retained the old SFIO title.

As **Depression** deepened in the 1930s and Nazi power across the Rhine became more menacing, fascist thuggery and anti-parliamentary activity increased in France, culminating in a pitched battle outside the Chamber of

Deputies in February 1934. (Léon Blum was only saved from being lynched by a funeral cortege through the intervention of some building workers who happened to notice what was going on in the street below.) The effect of this fascist activism was to unite the Left, including the Communists led by the Stalinist Maurice Thorez, in the **Popular Front**. When they won the 1936 elections with a handsome majority in the Chamber, there followed a wave of strikes and factory sit-ins – a spontaneous expression of working-class determination to get their just desserts after a century and a half of frustration. Frightened by the apparently revolutionary situation, the major employers signed the Matignon Agreement with Blum, which provided for wage increases, nationalisation of the armaments industry and partial nationalisation of the Bank of France, a 40–hour week, paid annual leave and collective bargaining on wages. These **reforms** were pushed through parliament, but when Blum tried to introduce exchange controls to check the flight of capital, the Senate threw the proposal out and he resigned. The Left returned to Opposition, where it remained with the exception of coalition governments until 1981. Most of the Popular Fronts reforms were promptly undone.

WW2: The German occupation

During the **occupation of Paris** in the Second World War, the Germans found some sections of Parisian society only too happy to hobnob with them. For four years the city suffered fascist rule with curfews, German garrisons and a Gestapo HQ. Parisian Jews were forced to wear the star of David and in 1942 were rounded up – by other Frenchmen -- and shipped off to Auschwitz (see p.80).

The **Resistance** was very active in the city, gathering people of all political persuasions into its ranks, but with Communists and Socialists well to the fore. The job of torturing them when they fell into Nazi hands – often as a result of betrayals – was left to their fellow-citizens in the fascist militia. Those who were condemned to death – rather than the concentration camps – were shot against the wall below the old fort of Mont Valérien above St-Cloud.

As Allied forces drew near to the city in 1944, the **FFI** (armed Resistance units), determined to play their part in driving the Germans out, called their troops onto the streets – some said, in a leftist attempt to seize political power. To their credit the Paris police also joined in, holding their Ile de la Cité HQ for three days against German attacks. Liberation finally came on August 25th 1944.

One more try at revolution

Post-war Paris has remained no stranger to **political battles** in its streets. Violent demonstrations accompanied the Communist withdrawal from the coalition government in 1947. In the 50s the left took to the streets again in protest against the colonial wars in Indochina and Algeria.

In **May '68** a radical, leftist movement spread from the Paris universities to a general strike lasting several weeks by 9 million workers in the biggest confrontation that any contemporary Western state has had to deal with. The old-fashioned and reactionary university structures that set off the revolt found reflection in the hierarchical and rigid organisations in every other institution. The position of women, of youth, of culture and modes of behaviour were suddenly highlighted in the general dissatisfaction with a society in which big business ran the state. This was no revolutionary situation on the 1917, or even 1848, model. The vicious street battles with the police instilled fear not inspiration in the peasants and bourgeois outside Paris – as the government cynically exploiting the scenes for TV knew full well. And there was certainly no shared economic or political aim in the ranks of the opposition. The French Communist Party was still stuck with Stalinism and the Socialists were determined at all costs to keep them out of government. With no common programme on the Left, with right-wing demonstrations orchestrated by de Gaulle at the end of May and public opinion craving stability and peace, with a great many workers satisfied with a new system for wage agreements, the **elections** called in June **returned the Right** to power. The occupied buildings emptied and the barricades in the Latin Quarter came down. For those who thought they were experiencing The Revolution, the defeat was catastrophic.

But French institutions and French

society did change, shaken and loosened by the events of May '68. And most importantly for revolutionaries, it opened up the debate of a new road to Socialism, one in which no old models would give all the answers. The experiment of the Left in power has now been witnessed; Paris has gone 20 years without a barricade and maybe will never lead the country when it comes to revolution, but the debate goes on.

The contemporary city

Up to the Second World War, Paris remained pretty much as Haussmann had left it. Housing conditions showed little sign of improvement. There was even an outbreak of bubonic plague in Clignancourt in 1921. In 1925 a third of the houses still had no sewage connection. Of the seventeen worst blocks of **slums** designated for clearance, most were still intact in the 1950s, and even today they have some close rivals in parts of Belleville and elsewhere.

Migration to the suburbs continued, with the creation of **shanty-towns** to supplement the hopelessly inadequate housing stock. Post-Second World War, these became the exclusive territory of **Algerian** and other **North African immigrants**. In 1966 there were eighty-nine of them, housing 40,000 immigrant workers and their families.

It is only in the last thirty years that the authorities have begun to grapple with the housing problem, not by expanding possibilities within Paris, but by siphoning huge numbers of people into the ring of **satellite towns** that have been constructed throughout the greater Paris region.

In **Paris proper**, this same period has seen the final breaking of the mould of Haussmann's influence. Intervening architectural fashions, like Art Nouveau, Le Corbusier's International style and the neo-classicism of the 30s, had little more than localised cosmetic effects. It was devotion to the needs of the motorist – a cause unhesitatingly espoused by Pompidou – and the development of the high-rise tower that finally did the trick, starting with the **Tour Maine-Montparnasse, La Défense**, the redevelopment of **the 13e**, and, in the **70s**, projects like Beaubourg the **Front de Seine**, **Les Halles** and, most recently, the **Parc de la Villette**.

When the Les Halles flower and veg market was dismantled, however, it was not just the 19C architecture that was mourned. The city's **social mix** has changed more in the last 20 years than in the previous hundred. **Gentrification** of the remaining working-class districts is well advanced. The population has become essentially middle class and white-collar. As a sign posted during the Les Halles redevelopment lamented: 'The centre of Paris will be beautiful. Luxury will be king. But we will not be here'. And now it is not just the centre of the city. If those 'we' come into Paris at all any more, it is as commuting service workers or week-end shoppers. 'Renovation is not for us'.

THE POLITICAL PRESENT

In May 1981, people danced in the streets of Paris to celebrate the end of 23 years of right wing rule – and the victory of François Mitterand's Socialist Party. The experiment, however, lasted for just five years. The **1986 election** saw the Socialists conclusively lose their majority in the *Assemblée Nationale* (parliament), whilst the Communists, their coalition partners in the first two years of government, suffered even heavier defeats, the **Centre-Right** even managing to break through the traditional 'red belt' around the capital. The new Prime Minister after this realignment – ominously, for anyone who had witnessed his autocratic methods and law and order campaigns on the domestic front – was the Paris mayor, **Jacques Chirac***.

The Socialist government had certainly recognised the omens, and the dramatic change that was in store, fighting their election campaign under the slogan, 'Help – the Right is coming back!', a slogan they defended as showing their sense of humour. For the unemployed and the low paid, for immigrants and their families, for women wanting the choice of whether to have children, for the young, the old and all those attached to certain civil liberties, the return of the Right was no laughing matter.

But with sporadic credits – in labour laws and women's rights, notably – nor were the **Socialists' years in power**. Cover-ups, corruption, and ultimately murder had stained the hands of the government. The fate of the Greenpeace photographer bombed by French military agents on the Rainbow Warrior in New Zealand, and, a year later, the revelation of a massive misappropriation of public funds destined for development in Africa, implicated ministers as well as the DGSE (the MI5 or CIA equivalent) from whom, after all, all secrecy and no morality is expected. The French greatly enjoy their political scandals and they don't go in for the minor pruderies of the British. Their shock horrors are always very serious, always revealed by the one and only investigative paper, *Le Canard Enchaîné*, and usually amuse rather than provoke public opinion. Though the minister for foreign affairs had to resign over the Rainbow Warrier affair, no-one protested on the streets that a man had been murdered.

France is a highly secretive state. More so, if anything, than Britain (whose hard-hitting TV documentaries would not find airtime across the Channel) or the US, with its freedom of information statutes. And as in Britain, the truth about such things as nuclear accidents and agreements with foreign powers simply is not told by the government. That the radioactive cloud from Chernobyl passed over areas of France was admitted very very belatedly (and no advice given) when too many people had sussed the implausibility of the cloud being deflected by the French-German frontier. As regards their own **nuclear industry**, the biggest in the world in proportion to its energy needs, almost every French citizen believes that there has never been an accident. A halt to nuclear plant construction and increased investment in renewable sources promised by the Socialists in 1981 was immediately dropped. Like Britain, France has a nuclear reprocessing plant – on the Cotentin peninsular in Normandy – that discharges its waste into the sea. Cotentin also provided some air space for the American bombing raid on Libya in 1986 despite smug protestations that overfly had been denied.

In all these things it makes scant difference whether power resides with the right or the so-called left, save in the **relations to the superpowers**. Contrary to what you might expect, negotiation and trade with the Soviet Union always benefits by a Gaullist government, while Mitterand is as beloved of Reagan as Thatcher is. The taste for truculence on the right towards American desires goes back to de Gaulle and represents not anti-Americanism but pro-Frenchness.

*Because of the different terms of tenure, **Mitterand**, leader of the Socialist Party, remains president through to 1988, even though the government (which he technically controls) has been superseded by the right-wing Gaullist-Giscardian coalition headed by **Jacques Chirac**.

The independent nuclear arsenal and non-membership of NATO (for which there is total cross-party consensus) is one of the major sources of French pride, French glory and French chauvinism.

When it comes to **France's overseas territories**, there is similar consensus on 'No' to independence claims, with slight cosmetic differences. When the Kanaks of Nouvelle Calédonie (an island near New Zealand) began to rebel against the direct, unelected rule by Paris, Mitterand granted them compensation for their appropriated lands. Chirac reversed this. Mitterand's 'autonomy' measures for the island were not a problem since they kept defence, foreign affairs, control of the television, law and order and education firmly in the French governor's hands. A massacre of indigenous tribesmen in October 1986 by white settlers was deemed 'self defence' and appeals against the judgement prohibited by Paris. Both the New Zealand and Australian governments have been warned by Chirac to desist from their support for the islands' independence – to stop meddling in French internal affairs as Paris sees it. Both countries take strong stands against the nuclear tests at Muroroa (with the concomitant suppression of information and heavy arm tactics against protestors) – all sacrosanct to both sides of the political French fence. And the subjugation of the Polynesian people to French interests, so that slum dwellers survive on subsistence and imported French food in these paradise islands, is of no concern to anybody.

On the **law and order** front, opinion polls suggest that Chirac hit a chord in most Frenchmen and Frenchwomen's hearts even before the Lebanese-inspired bombing campaign in the capital. The death sentence has not been re-introduced – the message seems to have got through that 'civilised' European nations don't do that sort of thing. But maximum penalties of thirty years' imprisonment without parole are now on the statute books along with no juries for terrorist offences, a supergrass system, detention without charge increased to a maximum of four days and police powers of arrest extended. While French jails have become absurdly overcrowded, the response to 'state-terrorism' is always to wheel and deal. Understandably, the Parisian population reacts to a spate of random and density-targeted bombing campaigns with heightened paranoia. After each attack the normal lingering street-life vanishes, leaving the city as if it was at war. But people retreat to their homes and personal security rather than putting pressure on the government.

The practise of **demanding ID papers** more or less randomly (e.g. from people who are young, black, not wearing suits, etc) was enshrined in law soon after the Right's return to power. If a policeman doesn't like the look of your passport or ID card, they can take you off to the station, photograph and finger-print you, refuse you access to a lawyer and charge you with non-cooperation if you get bolshy. There has been some bad publicity on this in Paris, with children as young as 13 and foreign tourists getting the treatment, but on the whole the government has been as successful as the British Tories in stuffing crime statistics and images of riotous blacks and youth down the throats of the populace.

The record of the **police** when it comes to '*bavures*' ('blunders' literally, usually resulting in the death or injury of an innocent person) is becoming alarming to say the least. After one such incident, which followed a week on from the shooting of a policeman in the south, the Interior Minister made clear his view (shared by the police federation) that the one exempted the other, and in no event was an individual policeman to blame. The atmosphere in Paris has noticeably changed, with agents of the law arrogantly acting out their fantasies of power.

Unemployment still has a way to go before it becomes a key issue (Britons may recall, no-one was that bothered during Thatcher's first term). When Chirac came to power in 1986 the official figures stood at 2.4 million. During the election, the comedian Coluche set up thousands of '*restaurants du coeur*' (restaurants of the heart) to hand out soup and food parcels to those living below the poverty line, many of them the long term unemployed. The money was raised through TV appeals. But if Coluche hoped to bring a point home rather than simply mock the politicians, he failed. Falling outside the riddled net of the social security system is only too easy, and luxuries like rents are certainly not paid. What this means can be seen at a glance in the Paris métro. The numbers and the age of people begging has drastically changed: The notices they hold almost all say '*Je suis chomeur/se*' ('I'm unemployed'). Chirac has mouthed concern for youth unemployment and money is forthcoming to businesses to take youngsters on. But jobs continue to go in the mines, shipyards, transport and in the denationalised industries.

Though the Socialist Party has become Social-Democratic in all but name – the left-wing faction within it, CERES, has disbanded itself and repudiated Marxism – it does make a difference on the home front that they are no longer in power. Law and Order, immigration, state ownership of industries, taxation, employment and housing are all now being organised along lines only too familiar to Britons. And the cast of characters in this are considerably more vicious. The Minister for the Interior, **Charles Pasqua**, once headed a gaullist vigilante group that was outlawed by de Gaulle. Together with Jacques Chirac he promulgates a high-handed thug approach very different from the subtle sophistication of the last right-wing government of Giscard d'Estaing.

It used to be classic electoral practice to offer an amnesty for parking tickets (this is not quite as silly as it sounds – the French take car matters very seriously). However, this government privatised the clamping of parked cars and its **gift amnesty** was much more serious. Currency smuggling, which boomed immediately after the Socialists won in 1981, was retrospectively decriminalised in the hope that everyone would transfer their accounts back out of Switzerland. Anonymity in gold dealing has been brought back. Tax inspectors' time limits on examining accounts have been severely reduced, Mitterand's wealth tax has been abolished, corporation tax lowered, etc., etc. All very predictable aids to the rich to get richer. And for balance at the other end, rent controls and tenants' rights have been shifted and small employers can sack workers at their discretion. University fees have been increased by 30% and in a petty measure to aggravate the young, the fee for driving tests has been doubled.

The **privatisation programme** has gone much further than reversing the preceding Socialists' nationalisations – banks that de Gaulle took into the public sector after 1945 have been sold off along with Dassault the aircraft manufacturer and Elf-Aquitaine, the biggest French oil company. As in Britain monopoly capitalism is having a field day with mergers and takeovers ever decreasing the number of independent businesses. The contradiction for French national consciousness is that this process opens up French firms to Italian, German, British or other EEC ownership. That the Americans are kept at bay makes little difference to Gallic pride.

The **trade unions** have inevitably been weakened by falling numbers and the fear of lay-offs – they remain more or less silent on the new sacking rights of small employers. The unions are organised along political lines rather than by industry (save for farmers and teachers) and with the current divisions between the socialist CFDT and the Communist CGT, industrial action has not been forthcoming and the government has not had to restrict union power. The right to strike is written into the constitution, but closed shops have long been illegal (with exceptions for docks and newspapers), and secondary action is rare.

Chirac replaced the most popular of the socialist ministers, Jack Lang, with **François Léotard** under the new title of **Minister for Culture and Communication**. The appointment of this American-style conservative had nothing to do with his commitment to or interest in the arts. Léotard is secretary-general of the Parti Républicain – Giscard's party – and has his eye on the UDF presidential nomination along with Barre and Giscard for 1988. Chirac, by promoting Léotard and giving no position to Giscard, is concerned soley with his own path to the Elysée. As the *Nouvel Observateur* wrote, 'All living culture is threatened by this game of dupes.' The direction of the new ministry has been predictable: encouraging the traditional and ignoring or suppressing ventures tainted by feminism, gay rights, atheism, socialism, etc. Luckily Lang's work in Paris was so popular even with conservative museum curators and the like, that it can't be dismantled at a stroke.

In the culture and politics of the oppressed, **feminism and anti-racism** have begun to take issue together. The racism of the French establishment – scarcely less apparent even with the Communists (who have enlisted racist attitudes to win working-class support away from the far right) – is now trumpeting under the Gaullists. Natality measures and the position of immigrants' wives and daughters have brought French feminists into the battle. It is the existence of thirty-five **Front National** (National Front) *députés* in parliament, however, under the socialists' Proportional Representation election system, that has had most effect – shocking a broad range of French into recognising the urgency to take on and defeat racism. The pedigrees of the Front National deputies are almost ludicrously extreme. They include members of the Moonies, publishers of Hitler's speeches, a defector from the Gaullists for being too soft in the Rainbow Warrior affair, an 86–year-old who as a Paris councillor in 1943 voted for full powers to Marshall Pétain's Vichy regime, and the party leader, **Jean-Marie Le Pen** himself, elected, disturbingly, by the people of Paris.

The history of **immigrants** in France is a familiar one. From the mid-l950s to the mid–1970s a labour shortage led to massive recruitment campaigns in North Africa, Portugal, Spain, Italy and Greece. People were promised housing, free medical care, trips home and well-paid jobs. When they arrived in France they found themselves paid half of what their French workmates earned, accommodated in prison-style hostels, and sometimes poorer than they were at home. They had no vote, no automatic permit renewal, were threatened with deportation at the slightest provocation, were subject to constant racial abuse and assault and, until 1981, were forbidden to form their own associations. The Socialist government lifted this ban, gave a ten year automatic renewal for permits, and even spoke about voting rights. Able to organise for the first time, immigrant workers immediately took on their employers at several car factories on the issue of racism in the selection of workers being laid-off. Meanwhile in Paris, Chirac, as mayor of the city, was increasing maternity leave for French women to have their third child, while

ensuring that no foreigner received the benefit. His line on population growth (a French obsession since 1945 with no basis whatsover in the new technology age) was that unless French women were encouraged to reproduce, nothing would stop the hordes south of the Mediterranean from taking over the north. In the context of newly won abortion rights, many women, whether they were concerned with racism or not, began to worry.

Chirac's **anti-terrorism and immigration laws** have provoked unprecedented alliances. The Archbishop of Lyon and the head of the Muslim institute in Paris together condemned the injustice of their introduction, with the Catholic leader giving his blessing to a hunger-strike protest. Human rights groups, churches, and trade unions joined immigrants' groups in saying France was on its way to becoming a **police state**. No idle rhetoric, the measures included the right of the police to expel immigrants without the interference of any courts or any other ministry save their own, Mr Pasqua's; the annulment of automatic citizenship to people born in France; the re-introduction of visas for visitors from North Africa, Turkey and the Middle East, and immediate deportation for any criminal offence. Since the 1986 bomb attacks visa requirements have also been in force for all non-EEC nationals – prompting outraged demands for exemption from Austria, Switzerland and Sweden.

Luckily for Chirac, the **constitution** makes it easy for bills to be steam-rollered through parliament even in the present unique situation of president and prime minister being on opposite sides. Laws can be made by decree needing only the presidential signature. Mitterand voices his dislike of this method, but goes along with it most of the time, for his own future is dependent on things running smoothly. The success of 'cohabitation' between the Gaullist prime minister and Socialist president has surprised people and done wonders for Mitterand's popularity. The odds are still on Chirac for the **1988 Presidential election**, but Mitterand may yet run him close for a second term.

BOOKS

History
Barbara Tuchman, *Distant Mirror* (Penguin, 1980). Tells the history of the 14C – plagues, wars, peasant uprisings and crusades – by following the life of a sympathetic French nobleman. Deals only obliquely with Paris itself, though there's a description of Etienne Marcel's revolt.
J.W. Huizinga, *The Waning of the Middle Ages* (1924 Pelican, 1985). Primarily a study of the Burgundian and French courts – but a masterpiece that goes far beyond this, building up meticulous detail to recreate the whole life and mentality of the 14C and 15C.
Alfred Cobban, *A History of Modern France* (3 vols: 1715–99, 1799–1871 and 1871–1962; Penguin, 1961–2). Complete and very readable account of the main political, social and economic strands in French – and inevitably Parisian – history.
Christopher Hibbert, *The French Revolution* (Penguin, 1982). Good concise popular history of the period and events.
Norman Hampson, *A Social History of the French Revolution* (Routledge & Kegan Paul, 1986). An analysis that concentrates on the personalities involved, their backgrounds and inter-relations. Its particular interest lies in the attention it gives to the *sans culottes*, the ordinary poor of Paris.
Karl Marx, *Surveys from Exile* Penguin,1984). *On the Paris Commune* (Lawrence & Wishart,1984). 'Surveys' includes Marx's speeches and articles at the time of the 1848 revolution and after, including an analysis, riddled with jokes, of Napoléon III's rise to power. 'Paris Commune', more rousing prose, has a history of the Commune by Engels.
Theodore Zeldin, *France, 1845–1945* (OUP, 5 paperback volumes, 1983–5). Series of thematic volumes on all matters French – all good reads.
Ronald Hamilton *A Holiday History of France* (Hogarth Press, 1985). Convenient pocket reference book: who's who and what's what.

Society and politics
John Ardagh, *France in the 1980s* (Penguin, 1983). Comprehensive overview up to 1982 – covering food, film, education and holidays as well as politics and education – from a social democrat and journalist position. Good on detail for the urban suburbs (and the shift there from the centre) of Paris.
Theodore Zeldin, *The French* (Fontana, 1985). A coffee table book without the pictures, based on the author's conversations with an extremely wide range of people, about money, sex, phobias, parents and everything else.
D. L. Hanley, A. P. Kerr and N. H. Waites, *Contemporary France* (Routledge and Kegan Paul, 1984). Well written and academic textbook if you want to fathom the practicalities of power in France – the constitution, parties, trade unions, etc. Includes an excellent opening chapter on the period since the war.
Claire Duchen, *Feminism in France: From May '68 to Mitterand* (Routledge & Kegan Paul, 1985). Charts the evolution of the women's movement through to its present crisis, clarifying the divergent political stances and feminist theory which informs the various groups.
Simone de Beauvoir, *The Second Sex* (Penguin, 1983); One of the prime texts of western feminism, written in 1949, covering women's inferior status in history, literature, mythology, psychoanalysis, philosophy and everyday life. The style is dry and intellectual but the subject matter easily compensates.
Jolyon Howorth, *The Politics of Peace* (END/Merlin Press, 1985). Short, to the point, and utterly readable analysis of why the French peace movement is so behind its European neighbours.
Roland Barthes *Mythologies* (1957, Paladin 1976). *Selected Writings* (Fontana, 1982). The first – though dated – is the classic: a brilliant description of how the ideas, prejudices and contradictions of French thought and behaviour manifest themselves, in food, wine, cars, travel guides and other cultural offerings. Barthes' piece on the Eiffel Tower doesn't appear – but it's included in the *Selected Writings* (edited by Susan Sontag).

Art, architecture and photographs
Norma Evenson, *Paris: A Century of Change, 1878–1978* (Yale, 1979). A

large illustrated volume which makes the development of urban planning and the fabric of Paris an enthralling subject – mainly because the author's concern is always with people not panoramas.

William Mahder, ed., *Paris Arts: The '80s Renaissance* (Autrement, 1984). Illustrated, magazine-style survey of French arts now. The design and photos are reason enough in themselves to look it up – fortunately, for the English edition now seems to be out of print; the French, *Paris Creation: Une Renaissance*, isn't.

Brassaï, *Le Paris Secret des Années 30* (Gallimard, Paris 1976). Extraordinary photos of the capital's nightlife in the 1930s – brothels, music halls, street cleaners, transvestites and the underworld – each one a work of art and a familiar world (now long since gone) to Brassaï and his mate Henry Miller who accompanied him on his night-time expeditions.

Edward Lucie-Smith, *Concise History of French Painting* (Thames & Hudson, 1971); If you're after an art reference book then this will do as well as any . . . though there are of course dozens of other books available on particular French artists and art movements.

John James, *Chartres* (Routledge & Kegan Paul, 1982). The story of Chartres Cathedral – with insights into the medieval context – the character and attitudes of the masons, the symbolism and the advanced mathematics of the building's geometry.

Paris in fiction
BRITISH/AMERICAN

Charles Dickens, *A Tale of Two Cities* (1849, Penguin 1986). Paris and London during the '89 revolution and before. The plot's pure Hollywood but the streets and at least some of the social backdrop are for real.

George Orwell, *Down and Out in Paris and London* (1933 Penguin 1986). Breadline living in the 1930s – Orwell at his best.

Ernest Hemingway, *A Moveable Feast* (1960, Bantam 1985). Hemingway's American-in-Paris account of life in the '30s with F. Scott Fitzgerald, Gertrude Stein, Ezra Pound, etc. Dull, pedestrian stuff despite the classic – and best seller – status.

Henry Miller, *Tropic of Cancer* (1934, Grafton 1985). *Quiet Days in Clichy* (1955, out of print). Again 1930s Paris

though from a more focused angle – sex, essentially. Erratic, wild, self-obsessed writing, but with definite flights of genius.

Anaïs Nin, *The Journals 1931–1974* (7 vols, Quartet 1973–1982). Miller's best Parisian mate. Not fiction but a detailed literary narrative of French and US artists and fiction makers from the first half of this century – not least Nin herself – in Paris and elsewhere. The more famous *Erotica* (Quartet) was also of course written in Paris – for a Parisian porno connoisseur. And if this is all you've read, get hold of *A Spy in the House of Love* (Penguin), finest of her novels.

Jack Kerouac, *Sartori in Paris* (1966 Quartet 1973). . . . and in Brittany, too. Uniquely inconsequential Kerouac experiences. Recommended.

Brion Gysin, *The Last Museum* (Faber & Faber, 1986). Setting is the Hotel Bardo – the Beat Hotel, co-residents Kerouac, Ginsberg and Burroughs. Published posthumously, this is 60s Paris in its most manic, fantasised mode.

FRENCH (IN TRANSLATION)

Gustave Flaubert, *Sentimental Education* (1869 Penguin Classics 1986). A lively, detailed reconstruction of the life, manners, characters and politics of Parisians in the 1840s – including the 1848 revolution.

Victor Hugo, *Les Misérables* (1862 Penguin Classics 1984). A racy, eminently readable novel by the French equivalent of Dickens, about the Parisian poor and low-life in the first half of the 19C. Book Four contains an account of the barricade fighting during the 1832 insurrection.

Emile Zola, *Nana* (1880 Penguin Classics 1986). The rise and fall of a courtesan in the decadent times of the Second Empire. Not bad on sex but confused on sexual politics. A great story nevertheless, which brings mid 19C Paris alive, direct to present-day senses. Paris is also the setting for Zola's *L'Assommoir* (1877 Penguin Classics 1985), *L'Argent* (1891 Penguin Classics 1984) and *Thérèse Raquin* (1867 Penguin Classics, 1985).

Alexandre Dumas, *The Count of Monte Cristo* (1884). One hell of a good yarn, with Paris and Marseilles locations.

Marcel Proust, *Remembrance of Things Past* (1913–27 Penguin Classics – 3 volumes). Written in and of Paris – absurd but bizarrely addictive.

Georges Simenon, *Maigret at the*

Crossroads (1955 Penguin Omnibus 1986), or any other of the *Maigret* novels. Ostensibly crime thrillers but, of course, Real Literature too. The Montmartre and seedy criminal locations are unbeatable.

André Breton, *Nadja* (1930 out of print but in most libraries). A surrealist evocation of Paris. Fun.

Jean-Paul Sartre, *Roads to Freedom Trilogy* (1945–49 Penguin). Metaphysics and gloom, despite the title.

LANGUAGE

French is a far from easy language, despite the number of shared words with English but the bare essentials are not difficult and make all the difference. Even just saying *'Bonjour Madame/Monsieur'* when you go in a shop and then pointing will usually get you a smile and helpful service. People working in hotels, restaurants, etc. almost always speak English and tend to use it even if you're trying in French – be grateful not insulted.

Differentiating words is the initial problem in **understanding spoken French** – it's very hard to get people to slow down. In the last resort of getting them to write it down you'll probably find you know half the words anyway.

Pronunciation

One easy rule to remember is that consonants at the ends of words are usually silent. *Pas plus tard* (not later), for example, is pronounced pa plu tarr. But when the following word begins with a vowel, you run the two together, thus: *pas après* (not after) becomes pazapre.

Vowels are the hardest sounds to get right. Roughly:

a	as in **hat**
e	as in **get**
é	between **get** and **gate**
è	between **get** and **gut**
eu	like the u in **hurt**
i	as in mach**i**ne
o	as in h**o**t
ô, au	as in **o**ver
ou	as in f**oo**d
u	as in a pursed-lip version of **u**se

More awkward are the combinations in/im, en/em, an/am, on/om, un/um at the ends of words or followed by consonants other than n or m. Again, roughly:

in/im	like the **an** in **an**xious
an/am, en/em	like the **don** in **Don**caster when said by a Brummie or someone with a nasal accent
on/om	like the **don** in **Don**caster said by someone with a heavy cold or thirty years of good port and cigars under the belt
un/um	like the **u** in understand

Consonants are much as in English, except that: ch is always sh, ç is s, h is silent, th is the same as t, ll is like the y in yes, w is v and r is growled.

Questions and requests

The simplest way of asking a question is to start with *s'il vous plaît* (please), then name the thing you want in an interrogative tone of voice. For example:

Where is there a bakery?	*S'il vous plaît, la boulangerie?*
Can you show me the road to Lyon?	*S'il vous plaît, la route pour Lyon?*

Similarly with requests

We'd like a room for two	*S'il vous plaît, une chambre pour deux.*
Can I have a kilo of oranges?	*S'il vous plaît, un kilo d'oranges.*

Question words

where	*où*
how	*comment*
how many	*combien*
how much	
when	*quand*
why	*pourquoi*
at what time	*à quelle heure*
what is/which is	*quel est*

Some basic words and phrases

French nouns are divided into masculine and feminine. This causes difficulties with adjectives, whose endings have to change to suit the gender of the nouns they are attached to. If you know some grammar, you will know what to do. If not, stick to the masculine form, which is the simplest – it's what we have done in this glossary.

yes	*oui*
no	*non*
today	*aujourd'hui*
yesterday	*hier*
tomorrow	*demain*
in the morning	*le matin*
in the afternoon	*l'après-midi*
in the evening	*le soir*
now	*maintenant*
later	*plus tard*
at one o'clock	*à une heure*
at three o'clock	*à trois heures*
at ten-thirty	*à dix heures et demie*

at midday	*à midi*
man	*un homme*
woman	*une femme*
here	*ici*
there	*là*
this one	*ceci*
that one	*celà*
open	*ouvert*
closed	*fermé*
big	*grand*
small	*petit*
more	*plus*
less	*moins*
a little	*un peu*
a lot	*beaucoup*
cheap	*bon marché*
expensive	*cher*
good	*bon*
bad	*mauvais*
hot	*chaud*
cold	*froid*
with	*avec*
without	*sans*
day	*jour*
week	*semaine*
month	*mois*

Talking to people

When addressing people you always use *Monsieur* for a man, *Madame* for a woman, *Mademoiselle* for a girl. Plain *bonjour* by itself is not enough. This isn't as formal as it seems, and you'll find it has its uses when you've forgotten someone's name or want to attract someone's attention.

Excuse me, do you speak English?	*Pardon, Madame, vous parlez anglais?*
How do you say it in French?	*Comment ça se dit en français?*
What's your name?	*Comment vous appelez-vous?*
My name is . . .	*je m'appelle*
I'm English/ Irish/ Scottish/ Welsh/ American/ Australian/ Canadian/ a New Zealander	*Je suis anglais(e)/ irlandais(e)/ écossais(e)/ gallois(e)/ américain(e)/ australien(ne)/ canadien(ne)/ néo-zélandais(e)*
Dutch	*hollandais(e)*
I understand	*Je comprends*
I don't understand	*Je ne comprends pas*
Can you speak slower, please?	*S'il vous plaît, parlez moins vite*

OK/agreed	*d'accord*
please	*s'il vous plaît*
thank you	*merci*
hello	*bonjour*
goodbye	*au revoir*
good morning/ afternoon	*bonjour*
good evening	*bonsoir*
good night	*bonne nuit*
How are you?	*Comment allez-vous?/Ça va?*
Fine, thanks	*Très bien, merci*
I don't know	*Je ne sais pas*
Let's go	*Allons-y*
See you tomorrow	*A demain*
See you soon	*A bientôt*
Sorry/Excuse me	*Pardon/Je m'excuse*
Leave me alone (aggressive)	*Fichez-moi la paix!*
Please help me	*Aidez-moi, s'il vous plaît*

Accommodation

a room for one/two/three people	*une chambre pour une/deux/trois personnes*
a double bed	*un lit double*
a room with a shower	*une chambre avec douche*
a room with a bath	*une chambre avec salle de bain*
Can I see it?	*Je peux la voir?*
for one/two, three/nights	*pour une/deux/trois nuits*
hot water	*eau chaude*
cold water	*eau froide*
youth hostel	*auberge de jeunesse*
1/HA Card	*la carte internationale*
breakfast	*petit déjeuner*
Is breakfast included?	*est-ce que le petit déjeuner est compris?*
I would like breakfast	*je voudrais prendre le petit déjeuner*
I don't want breakfast	*je ne veux pas de petit déjeuner*
a room on the courtyard	*une chambre sur la cour*
a room on the street side	*une chambre sur la rue*
first floor	*premier étage*
second floor	*deuxième étage*
with a view	*avec vue*
key	*clef*
to iron	*repasser*
do laundry	*faire la lessive*
sheets	*draps*
blankets	*couvertures*

quiet	*calme*
noisy	*bruyant*

Finding the way

bus/ car/train/ taxi/ferry	*autobus, bus, car/ voiture/train/ taxi/ferry*
boat/plane	*bateau/avion*
bus station	*gare routière*
bus stop	*arrêt*
railway station	*gare*
platform	*quai*
What time does it leave?	*Il part à quelle heure?*
What time does it arrive?	*Il arrive à quelle heure?*
hitch-hiking	*autostop*
on foot	*à pied*
how many km?	*combien de kilometres?*
how many hours?	*combien d'heures?*
Where are you going?	*Vous allez ou?*
I'm going to . . .	*Je vais à*
I want to get off at . . .	*Je voudrais descendre à . . .*
the road to	*la route pour*
near	*près/pas loin*
far	*loin*
a ticket to . . .	*un billet pour . . .*
single ticket	*aller simple*
return ticket	*aller retour*
validate your ticket	*composter votre billet*
ticket office	*vente de billets*
a book of bus/métro tickets	*un carnet*
bus/métro pass	*carte orange*
weekly	*hebdomadaire*
monthly	*mensuel*
valid for	*valable pour*
street	*rue*
first street on the left	*premiere rue à gauche*
first street on the left	*premiere rue à gauche*
first street on the right	*première rue à droite*
traffic lights	*feux*
red light	*feu rouge*
green light	*feu vert*
on the corner of	*à l'angle de*
next to	*à côté de*
behind	*derrière*
in front of	*devant*
before	*avant*
after	*après*
under	*sous*

bridge	*pont*
to cross	*traverser*
on the other side of	*de l'autre côté de*
straight on	*tout droit*

Cars

garage	*garage*
service	*service*
to park the car	*garer la voiture*
car park	*un parking*
parking prohibited	*défense de stationner/ stationnement interdit*
petrol station	*poste d'essence*
petrol	*essence*
fill up with petrol	*faire le plein*
oil	*huile*
air line	*ligne à air*
blow up the tyres	*gonfler les pneus*
battery	*batterie*
the battery is dead	*la batterie est morte*
plugs	*bougies*
to breakdown	*tomber en panne*
petrol can	*bidon*
insurance	*assurance*
green card	*carte verte*
log book	*carte grise*

Health matters

doctor	*médecin*
I don't feel well	*je ne me sens pas bien*
medicines	*médicaments*
prescription	*ordonnance*
I feel sick	*j'ai mal au coeur*
headache	*mal à tête*
stomach ache	*mal à l'estomac*
period	*règles*
pains	*douleurs*
it hurts	*ça fait mal*
aspirin	*aspirine*
chemist's	*pharmacie*
hospital	*hôpital*

Money matters

bank	*banque*
a one franc/five franc coin	*une pièce/d'un franc/de cinq francs*
exchange	*bureau de change*
a 100F note	*un billet de cent francs*
exchange rate	*cours de change*
travellers cheques	*chéques de voyage*
credit card	*carte de crédit*
money	*argent*
change	*la monnaie*
cashier	*caisse*

Other needs

bakery	*boulangerie*
food shop	*alimentation*
supermarket	*supermarché*
to eat	*manger*
to drink	*boire*
tobacconist	*tabac*
Post Office	*la Poste/bureau de poste*
stamps	*timbres*
toilet	*toilettes*
police	*police*
telephone	*téléphone*
cinema	*cinéma*
theatre	*théâtre*
club/music	*une boîte/un club*
hairdresser	*coiffeur*
museum	*musée*
to reserve/book	*réserver*

Numbers and days

1	*un*	21	*vingt-et-un*
2	*deux*	22	*vingt-deux*
3	*trois*	30	*trente*
4	*quatre*	40	*quarante*
5	*cinq*	50	*cinquante*
6	*six*	60	*soixante*
7	*sept*	70	*soixante-dix*
8	*huit*	75	*soixante-quinze*
9	*neuf*	80	*quatre-vingts*
10	*dix*	90	*quatre-vingt-dix*
11	*onze*	95	*quatre-vingt-quinze*
12	*douze*	100	*cent*
13	*treize*	101	*cent-et-un*
14	*quatorze*	200	*deux cents*
15	*quinze*	300	*trois cents*
16	*seize*	500	*cinq cents*
17	*dix-sept*	1,000	*mille*
18	*dix-huit*	2,000	*deux milles*
19	*dix-neuf*	1,000,000	*un million*
20	*vingt*	1986	*dix-neuf cent-quatre-vingt-sept*

Days of the week and dates

Sunday	*dimanche*
Monday	*lundi*
Tuesday	*mardi*
Wednesday	*mercredi*
Thursday	*jeudi*
Friday	*vendredi*
Saturday	*samedi*
first	*premier*
second	*deuxième*
third	*troisième*
fourth	*quatrième*
fifth	*cinquième*
sixth	*sixième*
seventh	*septième*
eighth	*huitième*
ninth	*neuvième*
tenth	*dixième*
September 1st	*le premier septembre*
March 2nd	*le deux mars*
July 14th	*le quatorze juillet*

Phrasebooks and dictionaries

There are any number of French **phrasebooks** around, most of them adequate: *French Travelmate* (Drew, £1.25) is particularly well put together and easy to refer to. So too – and more complete, with English/French and French/English sections – is *French at your Fingertips* (RKP, £3.95).

Among **dictionaries**, Harraps is the standard school dictionary; otherwise pick according to size and price. The *Dictionary of Modern Colloquial French* by Hèrail and Lovatt (RKP, £5.95) makes great reading – as much for the English expressions as the French. It's French to English only and includes the language of sex, crime, drugs – indeed all the words you ever wanted to understand.

INDEX